D1002333

The
Millennials

AMERICANS
BORN 1977 to 1994

4th EDITION

The Millennials

AMERICANS BORN 1977 to 1994

4th EDITION

The American
Generations Series

BY THE NEW STRATEGIST EDITORS

New Strategist Publications, Inc.
Ithaca, New York

New Strategist Publications, Inc.
P.O. Box 242, Ithaca, New York 14851
800/848-0842; 607/273-0913
www.newstrategist.com

Copyright 2009. NEW STRATEGIST PUBLICATIONS, INC.

All rights reserved.

No part of this book may be reproduced, stored in a retrieval system, or transmitted in any form or by any means, electronic, mechanical, photocopying, microfilming, recording, or otherwise without written permission from the Publisher.

ISBN 978-1-935114-15-4

Printed in the United States of America

Table of Contents

Chapter 4. Housing

Chapter 5. Income

Chapter 6. Labor Force

Chapter 7. Living Arrangements

Chapter 8. Population

Tables

Chapter 11. Wealth

Part Two: The iGeneration

Chapter 12. Education

Chapter 13. Health

Chapter 14. Housing

Chapter 15. Income

Chapter 16. Labor Force

Chapter 17. Living Arrangements

Chapter 18. Population

Chapter 19. Spending

Chapter 20. Time Use

Illustrations

Part Two: The iGeneration

Introduction

The Millennial generation—America's teens and young adults—was once the new kid in town. No longer. Although the youngest Millennials are still in their teens, the oldest are in their thirties. This fourth edition of *The Millennials: Americans Born 1977 to 1994* provides a demographic and socio-economic profile of the generation now that its characteristics have fully emerged.

Millennials ranged in age from 15 to 32 in 2009. They numbered 76 million and accounted for 24.9 percent of the total population—almost equal to the Baby Boom's 25.1 percent share. A special supplement, included in this book for the first time, profiles the generation that follows Millennials—a group we call the iGeneration—born in 1995 or later (the oldest turned 14 in 2009) and now comprising the nation's children. Today, the iGeneration numbers 57 million and accounts for 19 percent of the population, a larger share than Generation X.

The Millennial generation's beginning marked the end of the small Generation X, once known as the baby-bust generation. The oldest Millennials were born in 1977, when the long-anticipated echo boom of births began. In that year, the number of births ticked up to 3.3 million. This followed a 12-year lull in births that is called Generation X. By 1980, annual births had risen to 3.6 million. By 1990, they topped 4 million. Altogether, 68 million babies were born between 1977 and 1994. Since then, the number of Millennials has grown to 76 million because of immigration.

As is true with Boomers, the Millennial generation is defined by its numbers. When Millennials moved through the educational system, schools were strained by rising enrollments. Colleges and universities that had been competing for scarce Gen Xers could pick and choose from among the best as applications soared. Millennials have also made their mark in the housing market, with homeownership rates rising among young adults. Fortunately, few Millennials bought houses during the housing bubble, avoiding the nation's overpriced real estate. Now they are well positioned to buy homes at much lower prices, which should boost their net worth in the years ahead.

Every generation of Americans is unique, shaped not only by its numbers but also by the historical moment. Millennials are no exception. Three characteristics have emerged to define the generation. One, Millennials are racially and ethnically diverse—so diverse, in fact, that in many parts of the country the term "minority" no longer has meaning for their peer group. Two, they are fiercely independent thanks to divorce, day care, single parents, latchkey lifestyles, and the technological revolution that has made communication with family and friends instantaneous and continuous. Three, Millennials feel powerful—even in the midst of the economic downturn. Raised by indulgent parents, they have a sense of well-being not shared by Gen Xers. Optimistic about the future, Millennials see opportunity where others see problems.

The Millennials: Americans Born 1977 to 1994 examines the teen and young-adult generation as they become workers, householders, parents, and consumers struggling to gain a foothold in the nation's increasingly fragile middle class. The special supplement on the iGeneration examines the socioeconomic status of the nation's children—looking at the labor force participation of mothers, the daycare arrangements of preschoolers, and the spending of married couples with children, for example. Together, the two perspectives provide a comprehensive picture of Americans under the age of 30.

How to use this book

The Millennials: Americans Born 1977 to 1994 is designed for easy use. It is divided into 11 chapters, organized alphabetically: Attitudes, Education, Health, Housing, Income, Labor Force, Living Arrangements, Population, Time Use, Spending, and Wealth. The special supplement on the iGeneration is divided into nine chapters that examine the characteristics of families with children: Education, Health, Housing, Income, Labor Force, Living Arrangements, Population, Time Use, and Spending,

The fourth edition of *The Millennials* includes the latest data on the changing demographics of homeownership, based on the Census Bureau's 2008 Housing Vacancies and Homeownership Survey. In the Health chapter, you will find up-to-date statistics on health insurance coverage, as well as new data on the use of alternative medicine. The Income chapter, with statistics from the 2008 Current Population Survey, reveals the struggle of so many Americans to stay afloat. *The Millennials* presents labor force data for 2008, including the government's updated labor force projections, which show falling labor force participation rates among teens and young adults as the recession took root. This book contains new data on the health of the population, including updated estimates of the overweight. The Census Bureau's latest population estimates are also included in the book, showing the enormous diversity of Millennials and the even greater diversity of the iGeneration. *The Millennials* also presents estimates of the wealth of householders under age 35 from the Federal Reserve Board's 2007 Survey of Consumer Finances, which reveals their financial status just as the housing bubble burst and the recession began. New to this edition is an Attitudes chapter with data from the 2008 General Social Survey that compares the perspectives of the generations.

Most of the tables in *The Millennials* are based on data collected by the federal government, in particular the Census Bureau, the Bureau of Labor Statistics, the National Center for Education Statistics, the National Center for Health Statistics, and the Federal Reserve Board. The federal government is the best source of up-to-date, reliable information on the changing characteristics of Americans. By having *The Millennials* on your bookshelf, you can get the answers to your questions faster than you can online. Even better, visit www.newstrategist.com and download the PDF version of *The Millennials*, which includes links to an Excel version of every table in the book, which will enable you to do your own analyses, put together a PowerPoint presentation, etc.

Each chapter of *The Millennials* includes the demographic and lifestyle data most important to researchers. Within each chapter, most of the tables are based on data collected by the federal government, but they are not simply reproductions of government spreadsheets—as is the case in many reference books. Instead, each table is individually compiled and created by New Strategist's editors, with calculations designed to reveal the trends. The task of extracting and processing raw data from the government's web sites to create a single table can require hours of effort. New Strategist has done the work for you, with each table telling a story about Millennials—a story explained by the accompanying text and chart, which analyze the data and highlight future trends. If you need more information than the tables and text provide, you can plumb the original source listed at the bottom of each table.

The book contains a comprehensive list of tables to help you locate the information you need. For a more detailed search, see the index at the back of the book. Also at the back of the book is the glossary, which defines the terms and describes the many surveys referenced in the tables and text.

Each generation of Americans is unique and surprising in its own way. With *The Millennials: Americans Born 1977 to 1994* on your bookshelf, you will be ready to serve the nation's young adults and prepared for the generation that follows, still living at home, but soon to add its own flavor to the dynamic American culture.

CHAPTER 1

Attitudes

■ Older Americans are the most trusting. Forty-one percent of older Americans say most people can be trusted. In contrast, only 24 percent of Millennials say others can be trusted.

■ Generation Xers are least satisfied with their finances, with 36 percent saying they are not at all satisfied.

■ Boomers are most likely to say that their pay has not kept pace with inflation. Forty-five percent of Boomers feel like they are falling behind.

■ Older Americans are by far most likely to think they are much better off than their parents were at the same age (45 percent). Generation Xers are least likely to agree (24 percent).

■ The percentage of people who think two children is ideal ranges from a high of 55 percent among Baby Boomers to a low of 41 percent among Millennials. A larger 44 percent of Millennials think three or more children is ideal.

■ While only 40 percent of older Americans believe in evolution, the share climbs to 48 percent among Boomers, to 52 percent among Gen Xers, and to 62 percent among Millennials.

■ The 52 percent majority of Millennials sees nothing wrong with sexual relations between adults of the same sex. Support shrinks to 45 percent among Gen Xers, 34 percent among Boomers, and to a mere 19 percent among older Americans.

Older Americans Are the Happiest

Most of the married are very happily married.

When asked how happy they are, only about one in three Americans say they are very happy. The 54 percent majority reports feeling only pretty happy. Older people are happier than middle-aged or younger adults. Forty percent of older Americans say they are very happy compared with 31 percent of Baby Boomers and Generation Xers and just 27 percent of Millennials.

The 62 percent majority of married Americans say they are very happily married. Here, too, older Americans are the happiest group, with 67 of them saying they are very happily married. Only 60 percent of Boomers say the same.

Americans are almost evenly split on whether life is exciting (47 percent) or pretty routine (48 percent). Variations by generation are small, but Generation X is slightly more likely than others to find life exciting.

Few believe most people can be trusted. Only 32 percent of the public says that most people can be trusted, down from 37 percent who felt that way 10 years earlier. Younger generations are far less trusting than older Americans, as only 24 percent of Millennials believe most people can be trusted compared with 41 percent of people aged 63 or older.

■ Younger generations of Americans are struggling with a deteriorating economy, which reduces their happiness and increases their distrust.

Few Millennials trust others

(percent of people aged 18 or older who think most people can be trusted, by generation, 2008)

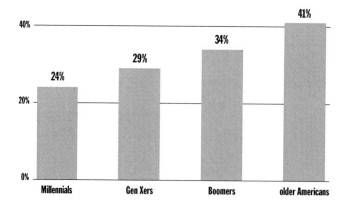

Table 1.1 General Happiness, 2008

"Taken all together, how would you say things are these days—would you say that you are very happy, pretty happy, or not too happy?"

(percent of people aged 18 or older responding by generation, 2008)

	very happy	pretty happy	not too happy
Total people	**31.7%**	**54.4%**	**13.9%**
Millennial generation (aged 18 to 31)	27.4	55.8	16.8
Generation X (aged 32 to 43)	31.0	57.0	12.0
Baby Boom (aged 44 to 62)	30.8	55.6	13.6
Older Americans (aged 63 or older)	39.7	47.2	13.1

Source: Survey Documentation and Analysis, Computer-assisted Survey Methods Program, University of California, Berkeley, General Social Surveys, 1972-2008 Cumulative Data Files, Internet site http://sda.berkeley.edu/cgi-bin32/hsda?harcsda+gss08; calculations by New Strategist

Table 1.2 Happiness of Marriage, 2008

"Taking all things together, how would you describe your marriage?"

(percent of currently married people aged 18 or older responding by generation, 2008)

	very happy	pretty happy	not too happy
Total married people	**62.1%**	**35.3%**	**2.6%**
Millennial generation (aged 18 to 31)	63.7	35.1	1.1
Generation X (aged 32 to 43)	61.5	35.7	2.7
Baby Boom (aged 44 to 62)	60.0	36.7	3.3
Older Americans (aged 63 or older)	66.6	31.7	1.7

Source: Survey Documentation and Analysis, Computer-assisted Survey Methods Program, University of California, Berkeley, General Social Surveys, 1972-2008 Cumulative Data Files, Internet site http://sda.berkeley.edu/cgi-bin32/hsda?harcsda+gss08; calculations by New Strategist

Table 1.3 Is Life Exciting, Routine, or Dull, 2008

"In general, do you find life exciting, pretty routine, or dull?"

(percent of people aged 18 or older responding by generation, 2008)

	exciting	pretty routine	dull
Total people	**47.2%**	**48.1%**	**3.8%**
Millennial generation (aged 18 to 31)	47.4	48.5	3.8
Generation X (aged 32 to 43)	48.6	46.5	3.1
Baby Boom (aged 44 to 62)	46.7	49.0	3.9
Older Americans (aged 63 or older)	46.4	47.7	4.4

Note: Numbers will not sum to total because "don't know" is not shown.
Source: Survey Documentation and Analysis, Computer-assisted Survey Methods Program, University of California, Berkeley, General Social Surveys, 1972-2008 Cumulative Data Files, Internet site http://sda.berkeley.edu/cgi-bin32/hsda?harcsda+gss08; calculations by New Strategist

Table 1.4 Trust in Others, 2008

"Generally speaking, would you say that most people can be trusted or that you can't be too careful in life?"

(percent of people aged 18 or older responding by generation, 2008)

	can trust	cannot trust	depends
Total people	**31.9%**	**63.9%**	**4.3%**
Millennial generation (aged 18 to 31)	24.5	71.1	4.4
Generation X (aged 32 to 43)	29.3	66.7	4.1
Baby Boom (aged 44 to 62)	34.3	61.5	4.2
Older Americans (aged 63 or older)	40.5	55.4	4.1

Source: Survey Documentation and Analysis, Computer-assisted Survey Methods Program, University of California, Berkeley, General Social Surveys, 1972-2008 Cumulative Data Files, Internet site http://sda.berkeley.edu/cgi-bin32/hsda?harcsda+gss08; calculations by New Strategist

Belief in Hard Work Is Strong among Younger Generations

Generation Xers are most likely to own a business.

How do people get ahead? Two-thirds of Americans say it is by hard work. Only 12 percent believe luck alone gets people ahead. Generation Xers (71 percent) and Millennials (70 percent) believe most strongly in hard work to get ahead, whereas Boomers (63 percent) give the least credence to hard work.

Millennials are most likely to live in the same city as they did when they were 16 years old, in part because they have had less time to move than older generations. Boomers are less likely than Gen Xers or older Americans to live in a different state than they did at age 16.

The likelihood of owning a business is greatest among Generation Xers (18 percent) and Boomers (15 percent). Only 8 percent of Millennials own a business, and the share among older Americans is an even smaller 6 percent.

■ The belief in luck as the most important way to get ahead is strongest among older Americans.

Business ownership peaks in middle age

(percent of people aged 18 or older who currently own and help manage a business, by generation, 2008)

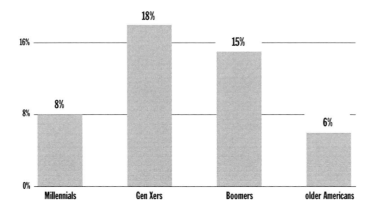

Table 1.5 How People Get Ahead, 2008

"Some people say that people get ahead by their own hard work;
others say that lucky breaks or help from other people are more important.
Which do you think is most important?"

(percent of people aged 18 or older responding by generation, 2008)

	hard work	both equally	luck
Total people	**67.1%**	**20.8%**	**12.1%**
Millennial generation (aged 18 to 31)	70.2	18.0	11.8
Generation X (aged 32 to 43)	70.7	20.5	8.9
Baby Boom (aged 44 to 62)	63.4	23.7	12.9
Older Americans (aged 63 or older)	66.2	19.2	14.7

Source: Survey Documentation and Analysis, Computer-assisted Survey Methods Program, University of California, Berkeley, General Social Surveys, 1972-2008 Cumulative Data Files, Internet site http://sda.berkeley.edu/cgi-bin32/hsda?harcsda+gss08; calculations by New Strategist

Table 1.6 Geographic Mobility Since Age 16, 2008

"When you were 16 years old, were you living in this same (city/town/county)?"

(percent of people aged 18 or older responding by generation, 2008)

	same city	same state different city	different state
Total people	**40.0%**	**23.2%**	**36.8%**
Millennial generation (aged 18 to 31)	55.4	16.6	28.0
Generation X (aged 32 to 43)	34.1	22.9	43.0
Baby Boom (aged 44 to 62)	37.0	27.1	35.9
Older Americans (aged 63 or older)	32.9	24.5	42.6

Source: Survey Documentation and Analysis, Computer-assisted Survey Methods Program, University of California, Berkeley, General Social Surveys, 1972-2008 Cumulative Data Files, Internet site http://sda.berkeley.edu/cgi-bin32/hsda?harcsda+gss08; calculations by New Strategist

Table 1.7 Business Ownership, 2008

"Are you, alone or with others, currently the owner of a business you help manage, including self-employment or selling any goods or services to others?"

(percent of people aged 18 or older responding by generation, 2008)

	yes	no
Total people	**12.6%**	**87.4%**
Millennial generation (aged 18 to 31)	8.4	91.6
Generation X (aged 32 to 43)	18.1	81.9
Baby Boom (aged 44 to 62)	15.4	84.6
Older Americans (aged 63 or older)	5.8	94.2

Source: Survey Documentation and Analysis, Computer-assisted Survey Methods Program, University of California, Berkeley, General Social Surveys, 1972-2008 Cumulative Data Files, Internet site http://sda.berkeley.edu/cgi-bin32/hsda?harcsda+gss08; calculations by New Strategist

More than One-Third of Gen Xers Are Dissatisfied with Their Finances

Many say that their pay has not kept up with the cost of living.

Few Americans identify with the lower class, but even fewer think they are in the upper class. The 89 percent majority of every generation sees itself as either working class or middle class, but the distribution varies greatly. Whereas Millennials, Xers, and Boomers are more likely to call themselves working class than middle class, the opposite is true for older Americans. The highest share of self-identified lower-class people occurs among Millennials (8 percent). Older Americans are most likely to describe themselves as upper class (5 percent).

A 47 percent plurality of Americans believes their family income is average, while not quite one-third says they make less than average. Baby Boomers are most likely to say they have above average incomes, and they may well be right since they are in their peak earning years.

The share of people who are satisfied with their financial situation stood at 29 percent in 2008, down slightly from the 31 percent of 1998. In parallel, those more or less satisfied with their finances have declined from 44 to 42 percent. Satisfaction with personal finances is greatest among older Americans, only 20 percent of whom are not at all satisfied. The dissatisfied share peaks among Generation Xers at 36 percent, as they juggle college loans, mortgages, and the expenses of growing families.

When asked whether the pay at their current job has kept pace with the cost of living, Boomers are by far most likely to say it has not. The Millennial generation has the largest share of people who say their pay has just about kept pace with inflation. In each generation about one in four say their pay has risen faster than the cost of living.

■ Financial backsliding was common among working Americans even before the current economic disruptions.

Many Boomers and younger adults are dissatisfied with their financial situation

(percent of people aged 18 or older who say they are not at all satisfied with their financial situation, by generation, 2008)

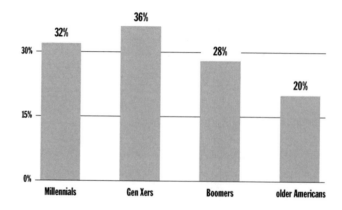

Table 1.8 Social Class Membership, 2008

"If you were asked to use one of four names for your social class, which would you say you belong in: the lower class, the working class, the middle class, or the upper class?"

(percent of people aged 18 or older responding by generation, 2008)

	lower	working	middle	upper
Total people	**7.3%**	**45.7%**	**43.4%**	**3.6%**
Millennial generation (aged 18 to 31)	8.1	49.4	40.1	2.5
Generation X (aged 32 to 43)	6.7	50.5	38.6	4.2
Baby Boom (aged 44 to 62)	7.3	45.5	43.7	3.5
Older Americans (aged 63 or older)	6.6	35.3	53.2	4.8

Source: Survey Documentation and Analysis, Computer-assisted Survey Methods Program, University of California, Berkeley, General Social Surveys, 1972-2008 Cumulative Data Files, Internet site http://sda.berkeley.edu/cgi-bin32/hsda?harcsda+gss08; calculations by New Strategist

Table 1.9 Family Income Relative to Others, 2008

"Compared with American families in general, would you say your family income is far below average, below average, average, above average, or far above average?"

(percent of people aged 18 or older responding by generation, 2008)

	far below average	below average	average	above average	far above average
Total people	**6.3%**	**25.2%**	**46.7%**	**19.8%**	**2.0%**
Millennial generation (aged 18 to 31)	6.6	26.8	49.4	16.5	0.7
Generation X (aged 32 to 43)	7.8	25.5	43.9	20.7	2.2
Baby Boom (aged 44 to 62)	5.6	22.8	46.2	22.4	3.1
Older Americans (aged 63 or older)	5.0	27.8	47.9	17.9	1.4

Source: Survey Documentation and Analysis, Computer-assisted Survey Methods Program, University of California, Berkeley, General Social Surveys, 1972-2008 Cumulative Data Files, Internet site http://sda.berkeley.edu/cgi-bin32/hsda?harcsda+gss08; calculations by New Strategist

Table 1.10 Satisfaction with Financial Situation, 2008

"So far as you and your family are concerned, would you say that you are pretty well satisfied with your present financial situation, more or less satisfied, or not satisfied at all?"

(percent of people aged 18 or older responding by generation, 2008)

	satisfied	more or less satisfied	not at all sarisfied
Total people	**28.9%**	**41.7%**	**29.4%**
Millennial generation (aged 18 to 31)	24.8	43.7	31.5
Generation X (aged 32 to 43)	20.5	43.7	35.7
Baby Boom (aged 44 to 62)	27.3	44.2	28.4
Older Americans (aged 63 or older)	48.0	31.6	20.4

Source: Survey Documentation and Analysis, Computer-assisted Survey Methods Program, University of California, Berkeley, General Social Surveys, 1972-2008 Cumulative Data Files, Internet site http://sda.berkeley.edu/cgi-bin32/hsda?harcsda+gss08; calculations by New Strategist

Table 1.11 How Has Pay Changed, 2008

"Thinking about your current employer, how much has your pay changed on your current job since you began? Would you say . . . "

(percent of employed people aged 18 to 62 responding by generation, 2008)

	my pay has gone up more than the cost of living	my pay has stayed about the same as the cost of living	my pay has not kept up with the cost of living
Total people	**23.5%**	**35.6%**	**40.9%**
Millennial generation (aged 18 to 31)	22.7	41.9	35.3
Generation X (aged 32 to 43)	24.9	37.7	37.4
Baby Boom (aged 44 to 62)	22.9	32.3	44.8

Source: Survey Documentation and Analysis, Computer-assisted Survey Methods Program, University of California, Berkeley, General Social Surveys, 1972-2008 Cumulative Data Files, Internet site http://sda.berkeley.edu/cgi-bin32/hsda?harcsda+gss08; calculations by New Strategist

The American Standard of Living May Be Falling

Fewer Americans believe they are better off than their parents.

When comparing their own standard of living now with that of their parents when they were the same age, 63 percent of respondents say they are better off. The figure was 66 percent 10 years earlier. Older Americans are by far most likely to think they are much better off than their parents were at the same age (45 percent). Generation Xers are least likely to agree (24 percent).

When asked whether they think they have a good chance to improve their standard of living, 59 percent of Americans agree. This is down sharply from the 74 percent of a decade earlier. Not surprisingly, younger people—with most of their life ahead of them—are more hopeful than older Americans. Seventy-two percent of Millennials, but only 47 percent of older Americans, believe that their standard of living will improve.

Sixty percent of respondents believe their children will have a better standard of living when they reach the respondent's present age. The share is 67 percent among Millennials, 61 percent among Xers, 57 percent among Boomers, and 53 percent among older Americans. One in four Boomers and older Americans predict their children will be worse off, but fewer Xers (16 percent) and Millennials (13 percent) agree.

■ The Americans who now have the least are most likely to believe things will be better in the future.

Most still believe children will be better off

(percent of people aged 18 or older with children who think their children's standard of living will be somewhat or much better than theirs is now, by generation, 2008)

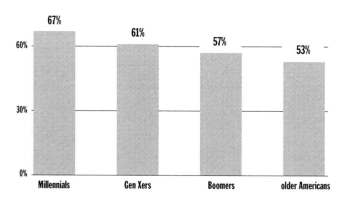

Table 1.12 Parents' Standard of Living, 2008

"Compared to your parents when they were the age you are now, do you think your own standard of living now is much better, somewhat better, about the same, somewhat worse, or much worse than theirs was?"

(percent of people aged 18 or older responding by generation, 2008)

	much better	somewhat better	about the same	somewhat worse	much worse
Total people	**31.6%**	**31.1%**	**21.1%**	**11.5%**	**4.6%**
Millennial generation (aged 18 to 31)	32.9	32.6	20.3	10.5	3.7
Generation X (aged 32 to 43)	24.1	31.6	22.0	16.3	6.1
Baby Boom (aged 44 to 62)	28.9	31.4	22.3	12.4	5.1
Older Americans (aged 63 or older)	45.1	27.9	19.1	5.2	2.7

Source: Survey Documentation and Analysis, Computer-assisted Survey Methods Program, University of California, Berkeley, General Social Surveys, 1972-2008 Cumulative Data Files, Internet site http://sda.berkeley.edu/cgi-bin32/hsda?harcsda+gss08; calculations by New Strategist

Table 1.13 Standard of Living Will Improve, 2008

"The way things are in America, people like me and my family have a good chance of improving our standard of living. Do you agree or disagree?"

(percent of people aged 18 or older responding by generation, 2008)

	strongly agree	agree	neither	disagree	strongly disagree
Total people	**14.7%**	**44.7%**	**13.9%**	**22.9%**	**3.8%**
Millennial generation (aged 18 to 31)	19.6	52.2	11.3	14.0	2.9
Generation X (aged 32 to 43)	15.2	44.7	13.7	21.7	4.6
Baby Boom (aged 44 to 62)	12.0	44.9	11.8	27.9	3.4
Older Americans (aged 63 or older)	13.2	33.6	22.3	26.0	4.9

Source: Survey Documentation and Analysis, Computer-assisted Survey Methods Program, University of California, Berkeley, General Social Surveys, 1972-2008 Cumulative Data Files, Internet site http://sda.berkeley.edu/cgi-bin32/hsda?harcsda+gss08; calculations by New Strategist

Table 1.14 Children's Standard of Living, 2008

"When your children are at the age you are now, do you think their standard of living will be much better, somewhat better, about the same, somewhat worse, or much worse than yours is now?"

(percent of people aged 18 or older with children responding by generation, 2008)

	much better	somewhat better	about the same	somewhat worse	much worse
Total people with children	**30.7%**	**29.2%**	**20.0%**	**14.3%**	**5.8%**
Millennial generation (aged 18 to 31)	40.1	27.0	19.3	8.0	5.5
Generation X (aged 32 to 43)	25.5	36.0	22.9	12.4	3.6
Baby Boom (aged 44 to 62)	27.7	29.5	18.4	17.7	6.5
Older Americans (aged 63 or older)	30.3	23.2	21.3	17.5	7.6

Source: Survey Documentation and Analysis, Computer-assisted Survey Methods Program, University of California, Berkeley, General Social Surveys, 1972-2008 Cumulative Data Files, Internet site http://sda.berkeley.edu/cgi-bin32/hsda?harcsda+gss08; calculations by New Strategist

Two Children Are Most Popular

Many Millennials think three children is the ideal number, however.

Across generations a plurality of Americans thinks that two is the ideal number of children. Boomers, who are finished with their childbearing, are most enthusiastic about two—55 percent say two children is ideal and only 29 percent think three or more is best. In contrast, only 41 percent of Millennials think two is ideal and a larger 44 percent say three or more is best. Millennials are more likely than the oldest Americans—who gave birth to the Baby Boom generation—to think three or more children is ideal.

Regardless of their number, most children are subject to a good, hard spanking when they misbehave. Seventy-one percent of Americans believe children sometimes must be spanked, with little difference by generation.

The 52 percent majority of older Americans believes it is better for everyone involved if the man is the achiever outside the home and the woman takes care of the home and family. Only about one-third of the younger generations agree. A similar gap exists with regard to working mothers. Among Boomers and younger generations, about three out of four think a working mother can have just as warm and secure a relationship with her children as a mother who does not work. Only 62 percent of older Americans agree.

Support for the view that government should help people who are sick and in need is strongest among Millennials and declines with age. Twenty-one percent of older Americans—the only age group that is covered by government-provided health insurance—believe people should help themselves. Only 12 percent of Millennials agree.

■ The generation gap in attitudes between Boomers and their parents is greater than the gap between Boomers and their children.

Few among the younger generations think traditional sex roles are best

(percent of people aged 18 or older who think traditional sex roles are best, by generation, 2008)

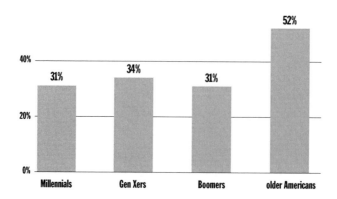

Table 1.15 Ideal Number of Children, 2008

"What do you think is the ideal number of children for a family to have?"

(percent of people aged 18 or older responding by generation, 2008)

	none	one	two	three	four or more	as many as want
Total people	**1.0%**	**2.5%**	**47.7%**	**26.6%**	**10.1%**	**12.1%**
Millennial generation (aged 18 to 31)	0.7	3.9	40.6	34.3	10.1	10.4
Generation X (aged 32 to 43)	0.0	2.5	44.4	29.3	12.0	11.9
Baby Boom (aged 44 to 62)	1.5	1.6	55.2	19.2	9.4	13.2
Older Americans (aged 63 or older)	1.4	2.5	45.5	28.3	9.6	12.6

Source: Survey Documentation and Analysis, Computer-assisted Survey Methods Program, University of California, Berkeley, General Social Surveys, 1972-2008 Cumulative Data Files, Internet site http://sda.berkeley.edu/cgi-bin32/hsda?harcsda+gss08; calculations by New Strategist

Table 1.16 Spanking Children, 2008

"Do you strongly agree, agree, disagree, or strongly disagree that it is sometimes necessary to discipline a child with a good, hard, spanking?"

(percent of people aged 18 or older responding by generation, 2008)

	strongly agree	agree	disagree	strongly disagree
Total people	**24.7%**	**46.2%**	**23.1%**	**6.0%**
Millennial generation (aged 18 to 31)	29.8	41.0	23.0	6.2
Generation X (aged 32 to 43)	19.9	52.3	22.6	5.2
Baby Boom (aged 44 to 62)	24.7	46.1	22.7	6.5
Older Americans (aged 63 or older)	22.9	46.1	25.2	5.7

Source: Survey Documentation and Analysis, Computer-assisted Survey Methods Program, University of California, Berkeley, General Social Surveys, 1972-2008 Cumulative Data Files, Internet site http://sda.berkeley.edu/cgi-bin32/hsda?harcsda+gss08; calculations by New Strategist

Table 1.17 Better for Man to Work, Woman to Tend Home, 2008

"It is much better for everyone involved if the man is the achiever outside
the home and the woman takes care of the home and family."

(percent of people aged 18 or older responding by generation, 2008)

	strongly agree	agree	disagree	strongly disagree
Total people	**8.2%**	**27.0%**	**47.2%**	**17.5%**
Millennial generation (aged 18 to 31)	7.3	24.0	44.5	24.2
Generation X (aged 32 to 43)	8.4	25.2	47.8	18.6
Baby Boom (aged 44 to 62)	7.5	24.0	50.7	17.8
Older Americans (aged 63 or older)	11.3	40.5	42.6	5.5

Source: Survey Documentation and Analysis, Computer-assisted Survey Methods Program, University of California, Berkeley, General Social Surveys, 1972-2008 Cumulative Data Files, Internet site http://sda.berkeley.edu/cgi-bin32/hsda?harcsda+gss08; calculations by New Strategist

Table 1.18 Working Mother's Relationship with Children, 2008

"Do you strongly agree, agree, disagree, or strongly disagree with
the statement: A working mother can establish just as warm and secure
a relationship with her children as a mother who does not work."

(percent of people aged 18 or older responding by generation, 2008)

	strongly agree	agree	disagree	strongly disagree
Total people	**26.3%**	**46.0%**	**22.2%**	**5.4%**
Millennial generation (aged 18 to 31)	26.0	46.1	22.5	5.4
Generation X (aged 32 to 43)	31.4	44.5	20.9	3.2
Baby Boom (aged 44 to 62)	26.3	49.0	19.0	5.6
Older Americans (aged 63 or older)	20.7	41.4	29.9	7.9

Source: Survey Documentation and Analysis, Computer-assisted Survey Methods Program, University of California, Berkeley, General Social Surveys, 1972-2008 Cumulative Data Files, Internet site http://sda.berkeley.edu/cgi-bin32/hsda?harcsda+gss08; calculations by New Strategist

Table 1.19 Should Government Help the Sick, 2008

"Some people think that it is the responsibility of the government in Washington to see to it that people have help in paying for doctors and hospital bills; they are at point 1. Others think that these matters are not the responsibility of the federal government and that people should take care of these things themselves; they are at point 5. Where would you place yourself on this scale?"

(percent of people aged 18 or older responding by generation, 2008)

	1 government should help	2	3 agree with both	4	5 people should help themselves
Total people	**34.9%**	**18.7%**	**30.0%**	**9.3%**	**7.1%**
Millennial generation (aged 18 to 31)	39.0	23.1	25.9	5.2	6.8
Generation X (aged 32 to 43)	35.0	19.8	30.7	9.4	5.1
Baby Boom (aged 44 to 62)	35.2	18.5	28.0	11.4	7.0
Older Americans (aged 63 or older)	28.7	11.2	39.1	10.0	11.0

Source: Survey Documentation and Analysis, Computer-assisted Survey Methods Program, University of California, Berkeley, General Social Surveys, 1972-2008 Cumulative Data Files, Internet site http://sda.berkeley.edu/cgi-bin32/hsda?harcsda+gss08; calculations by New Strategist

Religious Diversity Is on the Rise

Share of Protestants dwindles with each successive generation.

Asked whether science makes our way of life change too fast, the 52 percent majority of Americans disagrees with the statement. Each successive generation is a little surer than the previous one. While 51 percent of older Americans think things change too fast, only 45 percent of Millennials hold that opinion.

Americans are almost equally divided between those who believe in evolution (51 percent) and those who do not (49 percent), but there are large differences by generation. While only 40 percent of older Americans believe in evolution, the share climbs to 48 percent among Boomers, to 52 percent among Gen Xers, and to 62 percent among Millennials.

Among older Americans, 60 percent are Protestants. Among Baby Boomers, the figure is 58 percent. Yet only 39 percent of Generation Xers and Millennials call themselves Protestant. Conversely, the share of people with no religious preference climbs from a mere 7 percent among older Americans to a substantial 27 percent among Millennials. Older Americans are twice as likely as members of younger generations to describe themselves as very religious and they are more likely to see the Bible as the word of God.

The majority of Americans disapproves of the Supreme Court decision barring local governments from requiring religious readings in public schools. While the slight majority of Millennials and nearly half the Generation Xers support the decision, only 36 percent of Baby Boomers and just 31 percent of older Americans back the Supreme Court's decision.

■ Along with the growing racial and ethnic diversity of the American, religious preferences are also growing more diverse.

Younger generations are less Protestant

(percent of people aged 18 or older whose religious preference is Protestant, by generation, 2008)

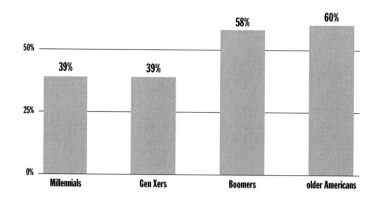

Table 1.20 Attitude toward Science, 2008

"Do you strongly agree, agree, disagree, or strongly disagree with the statement: Science makes our way of life change too fast."

(percent of people aged 18 or older responding by generation, 2008)

	strongly agree	agree	disagree	strongly disagree
Total people	**9.0%**	**38.8%**	**43.9%**	**8.3%**
Millennial generation (aged 18 to 31)	8.3	36.3	46.1	9.3
Generation X (aged 32 to 43)	8.4	39.4	44.9	7.3
Baby Boom (aged 44 to 62)	10.3	38.0	42.2	9.4
Older Americans (aged 63 or older)	7.6	43.4	43.4	5.7

Source: Survey Documentation and Analysis, Computer-assisted Survey Methods Program, University of California, Berkeley, General Social Surveys, 1972-2008 Cumulative Data Files, Internet site http://sda.berkeley.edu/cgi-bin32/hsda?harcsda+gss08; calculations by New Strategist

Table 1.21 Attitude toward Evolution, 2008

"True or false: Human beings, as we know them today, developed from earlier species of animals."

(percent of people aged 18 or older responding by generation, 2008)

	true	false
Total people	**50.9%**	**49.1%**
Millennial generation (aged 18 to 31)	62.1	37.9
Generation X (aged 32 to 43)	51.8	48.2
Baby Boom (aged 44 to 62)	47.8	52.2
Older Americans (aged 63 or older)	39.8	60.2

Source: Survey Documentation and Analysis, Computer-assisted Survey Methods Program, University of California, Berkeley, General Social Surveys, 1972-2008 Cumulative Data Files, Internet site http://sda.berkeley.edu/cgi-bin32/hsda?harcsda+gss08; calculations by New Strategist

Table 1.22 Religious Preference, 2008

"What is your religious preference?"

(percent of people aged 18 or older responding by generation, 2008)

	Protestant	Catholic	Jewish	none
Total people	**49.8%**	**25.1%**	**1.7%**	**16.8%**
Millennial generation (aged 18 to 31)	39.0	26.3	1.2	27.1
Generation X (aged 32 to 43)	39.1	28.1	2.9	18.9
Baby Boom (aged 44 to 62)	58.4	21.1	0.9	13.6
Older Americans (aged 63 or older)	60.1	27.3	2.6	7.2

Note: Figures will not sum to 100 percent because "other religion" is not shown.
Source: Survey Documentation and Analysis, Computer-assisted Survey Methods Program, University of California, Berkeley, General Social Surveys, 1972-2008 Cumulative Data Files, Internet site http://sda.berkeley.edu/cgi-bin32/hsda?harcsda+gss08; calculations by New Strategist

Table 1.23 Degree of Religiosity, 2008

"To what extent do you consider yourself a religious person?"

(percent of people aged 18 or older responding by generation, 2008)

	very religious	moderately religious	slightly religious	not religious
Total people	**18.2%**	**42.2%**	**23.4%**	**16.2%**
Millennial generation (aged 18 to 31)	12.1	33.1	28.1	26.7
Generation X (aged 32 to 43)	13.8	40.6	25.7	19.9
Baby Boom (aged 44 to 62)	20.1	45.9	22.1	11.9
Older Americans (aged 63 or older)	27.7	48.6	17.4	6.3

Source: Survey Documentation and Analysis, Computer-assisted Survey Methods Program, University of California, Berkeley, General Social Surveys, 1972-2008 Cumulative Data Files, Internet site http://sda.berkeley.edu/cgi-bin32/hsda?harcsda+gss08; calculations by New Strategist

Table 1.24 Belief in the Bible, 2008

"Which of these statements comes closest to describing your feelings about the Bible? 1) The Bible is the actual word of God and is to be taken literally, word for word; 2) The Bible is the inspired word of God but not everything in it should be taken literally, word for word; 3) The Bible is an ancient book of fables, legends, history, and moral precepts recorded by men."

(percent of people aged 18 or older responding by generation, 2008)

	word of God	inspired word	book of fables	other
Total people	**32.0%**	**47.0%**	**19.6%**	**1.4%**
Millennial generation (aged 18 to 31)	27.5	50.3	21.0	1.3
Generation X (aged 32 to 43)	30.8	46.3	20.3	2.6
Baby Boom (aged 44 to 62)	33.6	44.9	20.6	1.0
Older Americans (aged 63 or older)	36.0	48.1	15.0	1.0

Source: Survey Documentation and Analysis, Computer-assisted Survey Methods Program, University of California, Berkeley, General Social Surveys, 1972-2008 Cumulative Data Files, Internet site http://sda.berkeley.edu/cgi-bin32/hsda?harcsda+gss08; calculations by New Strategist

Table 1.25 Bible in the Public Schools, 2008

"The United States Supreme Court has ruled that no state or local government may require the reading of the Lord's Prayer or Bible verses in public schools. What are your views on this? Do you approve or disapprove of the court ruling?"

(percent of people aged 18 or older responding by generation, 2008)

	approve	disapprove
Total people	**41.8%**	**58.2%**
Millennial generation (aged 18 to 31)	52.8	47.2
Generation X (aged 32 to 43)	48.0	52.0
Baby Boom (aged 44 to 62)	36.2	63.8
Older Americans (aged 63 or older)	30.7	69.3

Source: Survey Documentation and Analysis, Computer-assisted Survey Methods Program, University of California, Berkeley, General Social Surveys, 1972-2008 Cumulative Data Files, Internet site http://sda.berkeley.edu/cgi-bin32/hsda?harcsda+gss08; calculations by New Strategist

Growing Tolerance of Sexual Behavior

Americans are growing more accepting of premarital sex and homosexuality.

The share of Americans who believe that premarital sex is not wrong at all grew from 43 percent in 1998 to 55 percent in 2008. While the majority of Boomers and younger generations see nothing wrong with premarital sex, the share is just 38 percent among older Americans.

When it comes to sexual relations between adults of the same sex, the trend of growing tolerance is apparent as well. Each successive generation is less likely to condemn homosexuality. The 52 percent majority of Millennials sees nothing wrong with same-sex sexual relations, but support dwindles to 45 percent among Xers, 34 percent among Boomers, and a mere 19 percent among older Americans.

■ Acceptance of gays and lesbians will grow as tolerant Millennials replace older, less tolerant generations in the population.

Most Millennials see nothing wrong with gays and lesbians

(percent of people aged 18 or older who see nothing wrong with sexual relations between two adults of the same sex, by generation, 2008)

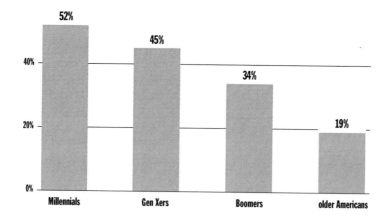

Table 1.26 Premarital Sex, 2008

"If a man and woman have sex relations before marriage, do you think it is always wrong, almost always wrong, wrong only sometimes, or not wrong at all?"

(percent of people aged 18 or older responding by generation, 2008)

	always wrong	almost always wrong	sometimes wrong	not wrong at all
Total people	**22.6%**	**7.2%**	**15.4%**	**54.8%**
Millennial generation (aged 18 to 31)	17.5	6.9	15.8	59.8
Generation X (aged 32 to 43)	21.0	4.9	17.7	56.5
Baby Boom (aged 44 to 62)	23.0	6.5	12.4	58.1
Older Americans (aged 63 or older)	31.0	11.7	18.9	38.4

Source: Survey Documentation and Analysis, Computer-assisted Survey Methods Program, University of California, Berkeley, General Social Surveys, 1972-2008 Cumulative Data Files, Internet site http://sda.berkeley.edu/cgi-bin32/hsda?harcsda+gss08; calculations by New Strategist

Table 1.27 Homosexual Relations, 2008

"What about sexual relations between two adults of the same sex?"

(percent of people aged 18 or older responding by generation, 2008)

	always wrong	almost always wrong	sometimes wrong	not wrong at all
Total people	**52.4%**	**3.1%**	**6.7%**	**37.8%**
Millennial generation (aged 18 to 31)	41.4	1.8	5.3	51.5
Generation X (aged 32 to 43)	47.0	4.3	3.9	44.8
Baby Boom (aged 44 to 62)	53.0	3.3	10.0	33.8
Older Americans (aged 63 or older)	72.6	2.8	5.4	19.2

Source: Survey Documentation and Analysis, Computer-assisted Survey Methods Program, University of California, Berkeley, General Social Surveys, 1972-2008 Cumulative Data Files, Internet site http://sda.berkeley.edu/cgi-bin32/hsda?harcsda+gss08; calculations by New Strategist

Television News Is Most Important

The Internet has jumped into the number two position.

Nearly half of Americans get most of their news from television, 22 percent from the Internet, and 20 percent from the newspaper. Together these three news outlets are the main source of news for 90 percent of the public. But there are big differences by generation. Millennials are far more likely than any other generation to depend on the Internet. Thirty-eight percent of Millennials say the Internet is their most important source of news versus 30 percent of Gen Xers, 15 percent of Boomers and just 5 percent of older Americans. The Millennial attachment to the Internet is so strong that it has boosted the Internet into second place as a news source.

When asked about their political leanings, Americans like to point to the moderate middle (39 percent). A slightly smaller 36 percent say they are conservative, and 26 percent identify themselves as liberal. Millennials are twice as likely as older Americans to hold liberal views. The share of self-described conservatives drops with each successive generation, from 45 percent among older Americans to 28 percent among Millennials. In fact, a larger share of Millennials is liberal than conservative—the only generation in which liberals outnumber conservatives.

■ Millennials depend more on the Internet than on television for the news.

News sources differ dramatically by generation

(percent of people aged 18 or older who turn to each source for the news, by generation, 2008)

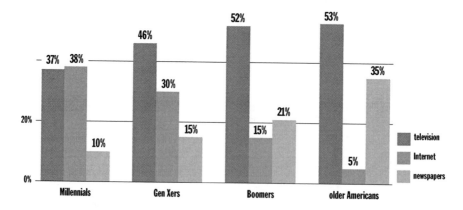

Table 1.28 Main Source of Information about Events in the News, 2008

"We are interested in how people get information about events in the news.
Where do you get most of your information about current news events?"

(percent of people aged 18 or older responding by generation, 2008)

	television	Internet	newspapers	radio	family, friends and colleagues	books, magazines, other
Total people	**47.5%**	**22.0%**	**19.6%**	**6.1%**	**2.8%**	**2.0%**
Millennial generation (aged 18 to 31)	36.8	38.3	9.8	8.4	5.9	0.8
Generation X (aged 32 to 43)	46.3	30.0	15.2	3.1	3.1	2.3
Baby Boom (aged 44 to 62)	52.4	14.8	21.5	7.6	1.5	2.2
Older Americans (aged 63 or older)	53.1	5.0	34.5	3.5	1.0	2.9

Source: Survey Documentation and Analysis, Computer-assisted Survey Methods Program, University of California, Berkeley, General Social Surveys, 1972-2008 Cumulative Data Files, Internet site http://sda.berkeley.edu/cgi-bin32/hsda?harcsda+gss08; calculations by New Strategist

Table 1.29 Political Leanings, 2008

"We hear a lot of talk these days about liberals and conservatives.
On a seven-point scale from extremely liberal (1) to extremely
conservative (7), where would you place yourself?"

(percent of people aged 18 or older responding by generation, 2008)

	1 extremely liberal	2 liberal	3 slightly liberal	4 moderate	5 slightly conservative	6 conservative	7 extremely conservative
Total people	**2.9%**	**12.2%**	**10.6%**	**38.6%**	**15.1%**	**16.7%**	**3.9%**
Millennial generation (aged 18 to 31)	3.0	16.1	15.3	37.6	13.9	12.2	2.0
Generation X (aged 32 to 43)	3.7	12.9	11.1	39.4	15.6	12.3	5.0
Baby Boom (aged 44 to 62)	2.1	11.1	10.2	38.4	15.9	18.1	4.1
Older Americans (aged 63 or older)	3.2	8.8	4.8	38.4	14.8	25.4	4.6

Source: Survey Documentation and Analysis, Computer-assisted Survey Methods Program, University of California, Berkeley, General Social Surveys, 1972-2008 Cumulative Data Files, Internet site http://sda.berkeley.edu/cgi-bin32/hsda?harcsda+gss08; calculations by New Strategist

Millennials and Gen Xers Are at Odds over Death Penalty

Overall opposition to capital punishment is growing.

Opposition to capital punishment is growing. In 1998, 27 percent of the public opposed the death penalty for persons convicted of murder. In 2008, the figure had increased to 32 percent. In a generational pattern rarely seen, support for the death penalty is strongest among Generation X (71 percent) and weakest among Millennials (63 percent).

The vast majority of Americans favors requiring a permit for gun ownership, and there is little variation by generation. Generation Xers are slightly more likely to favor gun permits than the other generations.

Support for legal abortion under certain circumstances is overwhelming. Nine out of 10 Americans approve of abortion if the women's health is in serious danger, and three-quarters if the pregnancy is the result of rape or there is a chance of serious defect in the baby. Economic and lifestyle reasons garner substantially lower approval ratings of 40 to 44 percent. Generally, there are only small differences in opinion by generation, but there are exceptions. Millennials are sharply less likely than the other generations to allow abortion because of a serious defect in the baby, for example. Boomers are much more accepting than other generations of abortion because a woman does not want more children. Older Americans are more likely than younger generations to want to outlaw abortion for economic and lifestyle reasons, but not for health reasons.

The two-thirds majority of Americans favor the right of the terminally ill to die with a doctor's assistance, but support for this measure has fallen slightly over the last decade. Support is strongest among Boomers, who are at an age when they may well see a terminally ill parent suffer, but it is weakest among older Americans themselves.

■ The generation gap between Boomers and older Americans is readily apparent on the issue of abortion for economic or lifestyle reasons.

Most do not favor allowing abortions for any reason

(percent of people aged 18 or older who favor legal abortion for any reason, by generation, 2008)

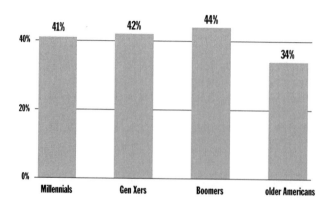

Table 1.30 Favor or Oppose Death Penalty for Murder, 2008

"Do you favor or oppose the death penalty for persons convicted of murder?"

(percent of people aged 18 or older responding by generation, 2008)

	favor	oppose
Total people	**67.6%**	**32.4%**
Millennial generation (aged 18 to 31)	62.8	37.2
Generation X (aged 32 to 43)	71.0	29.0
Baby Boom (aged 44 to 62)	68.0	32.0
Older Americans (aged 63 or older)	69.5	30.5

Source: Survey Documentation and Analysis, Computer-assisted Survey Methods Program, University of California, Berkeley, General Social Surveys, 1972-2008 Cumulative Data Files, Internet site http://sda.berkeley.edu/cgi-bin32/hsda?harcsda+gss08; calculations by New Strategist

Table 1.31 Favor or Oppose Gun Permits, 2008

"Would you favor or oppose a law which would require a person to obtain a police permit before he or she could buy a gun?"

(percent of people aged 18 or older responding by generation, 2008)

	favor	oppose
Total people	**79.1%**	**20.9%**
Millennial generation (aged 18 to 31)	78.3	21.7
Generation X (aged 32 to 43)	81.1	18.8
Baby Boom (aged 44 to 62)	78.4	21.6
Older Americans (aged 63 or older)	78.7	21.3

Source: Survey Documentation and Analysis, Computer-assisted Survey Methods Program, University of California, Berkeley, General Social Surveys, 1972-2008 Cumulative Data Files, Internet site http://sda.berkeley.edu/cgi-bin32/hsda?harcsda+gss08; calculations by New Strategist

Table 1.32 Support for Legal Abortion by Reason, 2008

"Please tell me whether or not you think it should be possible for a
pregnant woman to obtain a legal abortion if . . . "

(percent of people aged 18 or older responding yes by generation, 2008)

	her health is seriously endangered	pregnancy is the result of a rape	there is a serious defect in the baby	she cannot afford more children	she does not want more childen	she is single and does not want to marry the man	she wants it for any reason
Total people	**88.6%**	**75.6%**	**73.7%**	**42.3%**	**43.7%**	**40.3%**	**41.2%**
Millennial generation (aged 18 to 31)	85.5	75.8	64.1	43.9	41.5	38.8	41.2
Generation X (aged 32 to 43)	90.6	76.8	75.6	39.4	41.9	40.3	41.8
Baby Boom (aged 44 to 62)	90.4	74.6	78.1	46.2	50.0	43.3	44.5
Older Americans (aged 63 or older)	86.6	75.4	75.2	35.2	35.4	35.1	33.6

Source: Survey Documentation and Analysis, Computer-assisted Survey Methods Program, University of California, Berkeley, General Social Surveys, 1972-2008 Cumulative Data Files, Internet site http://sda.berkeley.edu/cgi-bin32/hsda?harcsda+gss08; calculations by New Strategist

Table 1.33 Doctor-Assisted Suicide, 2008

"When a person has a disease that cannot be cured, do you think
doctors should be allowed by law to end the patient's life by
some painless means if the patient and his family request it?"

(percent of people aged 18 or older responding by generation, 2008)

	yes	no
Total people	**66.2%**	**33.8%**
Millennial generation (aged 18 to 31)	63.7	36.3
Generation X (aged 32 to 43)	66.1	33.9
Baby Boom (aged 44 to 62)	69.9	30.1
Older Americans (aged 63 or older)	61.1	38.9

Source: Survey Documentation and Analysis, Computer-assisted Survey Methods Program, University of California, Berkeley, General Social Surveys, 1972-2008 Cumulative Data Files, Internet site http://sda.berkeley.edu/cgi-bin32/hsda?harcsda+gss08; calculations by New Strategist

2

Education

■ The oldest members of the Millennial generation have graduated from college and are embarking on a career. The youngest are still in high school. Consequently, the educational attainment of Millennials is rising rapidly.

■ Among Millennials aged 18 to 29, Asian women have the highest level of education and Hispanic men the lowest. Forty-two percent of Asian women and only 6 percent of Hispanic men in the age group have a bachelor's degree or more education.

■ School enrollment drops sharply among people in their early twenties. The 52 percent majority of people aged 20 are in school, but the figure falls to 23 percent by age 24.

■ Fewer Americans drop out of high school. Only 8.7 percent of people aged 16 to 24 in 2007 were neither high school graduates nor currently enrolled in school. Among Hispanic men, however, the high school dropout rate was a much larger 25 percent in 2007.

■ Few high school students are employed. The percentage of youths who are both going to school and employed fell from 31 percent in 2000 to 21 percent in 2007.

■ Younger Millennials may end up less educated than their older counterparts as the cost of college, combined with the economic downturn, takes a toll on college enrollment.

Many Millennials Are Still in School

Millennial women outdo their male counterparts in educational attainment.

Millennials spanned the broad age range from 14 to 31 in 2008. The older members of the generation have graduated from college and embarked on a career, but the youngest are still in school. Consequently, the educational attainment of Millennials is rising rapidly. Among 18-to-24-year-olds, just over one-half have college experience. The figure rises to 59 percent in the 25-to-29 age group. Women are further along than men. Fifty-five percent of 18-to-24-year-old women have college experience compared with only 46 percent of their male counterparts.

Among women aged 18 to 24, 11 percent have a bachelor's degree or more education. The figure is a smaller 8 percent among men in the age group. Since it takes, on average, six years to get a bachelor's degree today, it is little wonder so few in their early twenties have earned a college degree. Among 25-to-29-year-olds, nearly 35 percent of women and 27 percent of men have at least a bachelor's degree.

■ The greater educational attainment of Millennial women should help narrow the income gap between men and women in the years ahead.

Among Millennials, women are more likely to be college graduates

(percent of people aged 18 to 29 with a bachelor's degree or more education, by sex, 2008)

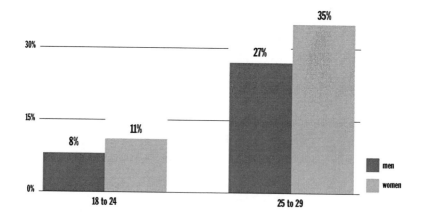

Table 2.1 Educational Attainment of Millennials, 2008

(number and percent distribution of total people aged 18 or older, and people aged 18 to 29, by highest level of education, 2008; numbers in thousands)

		aged 18 to 29		
	total 18 or older	total	18 to 24	25 to 29
Total people	**224,703**	**49,455**	**28,398**	**21,057**
Not a high school graduate	32,010	8,237	5,670	2,567
High school graduate	69,480	14,313	8,296	6,017
Some college, no degree	44,168	14,465	10,356	4,109
Associate's degree	18,589	3,295	1,407	1,888
Bachelor's degree	40,070	7,523	2,511	5,012
Master's degree	14,893	1,355	128	1,227
Professional degree	3,009	198	17	181
Doctoral degree	2,485	71	14	57
High school graduate or more	192,694	41,220	22,729	18,491
Some college or more	123,214	26,907	14,433	12,474
Associate's degree or more	79,046	12,442	4,077	8,365
Bachelor's degree or more	60,457	9,147	2,670	6,477
Total people	**100.0%**	**100.0%**	**100.0%**	**100.0%**
Not a high school graduate	14.2	16.7	20.0	12.2
High school graduate	30.9	28.9	29.2	28.6
Some college, no degree	19.7	29.2	36.5	19.5
Associate's degree	8.3	6.7	5.0	9.0
Bachelor's degree	17.8	15.2	8.8	23.8
Master's degree	6.6	2.7	0.5	5.8
Professional degree	1.3	0.4	0.1	0.9
Doctoral degree	1.1	0.1	0.0	0.3
High school graduate or more	85.8	83.3	80.0	87.8
Some college or more	54.8	54.4	50.8	59.2
Associate's degree or more	35.2	25.2	14.4	39.7
Bachelor's degree or more	26.9	18.5	9.4	30.8

Source: Bureau of the Census, Educational Attainment in the United States: 2008, detailed tables, Internet site http://www.census.gov/population/www/socdemo/education/cps2008.html; calculations by New Strategist

Table 2.2 Educational Attainment of Millennial Men, 2008

(number and percent distribution of total men aged 18 or older, and men aged 18 to 29, by highest level of education, 2008; numbers in thousands)

		aged 18 to 29		
	total 18 or older	total	18 to 24	25 to 29
Total men	**108,862**	**25,113**	**14,392**	**10,721**
Not a high school graduate	16,447	4,666	3,148	1,518
High school graduate	34,048	7,980	4557	3,423
Some college, no degree	20,735	6,983	4925	2,058
Associate's degree	8,091	1,504	655	849
Bachelor's degree	19,102	3,365	1060	2305
Master's degree	6,920	509	34	475
Professional degree	1,888	80	11	69
Doctoral degree	1,631	27	3	24
High school graduate or more	92,415	20,448	11,245	9,203
Some college or more	58,367	12,468	6,688	5,780
Associate's degree or more	37,632	5,485	1,763	3,722
Bachelor's degree or more	29,541	3,981	1,108	2,873
Total men	**100.0%**	**100.0%**	**100.0%**	**100.0%**
Not a high school graduate	15.1	18.6	21.9	14.2
High school graduate	31.3	31.8	31.7	31.9
Some college, no degree	19.0	27.8	34.2	19.2
Associate's degree	7.4	6.0	4.6	7.9
Bachelor's degree	17.5	13.4	7.4	21.5
Master's degree	6.4	2.0	0.2	4.4
Professional degree	1.7	0.3	0.1	0.6
Doctoral degree	1.5	0.1	0.0	0.2
High school graduate or more	84.9	81.4	78.1	85.8
Some college or more	53.6	49.6	46.5	53.9
Associate's degree or more	34.6	21.8	12.2	34.7
Bachelor's degree or more	27.1	15.9	7.7	26.8

Source: Bureau of the Census, Educational Attainment in the United States: 2008, detailed tables, Internet site http://www .census.gov/population/www/socdemo/education/cps2008.html; calculations by New Strategist

Table 2.3 Educational Attainment of Millennial Women, 2008

(number and percent distribution of total women aged 18 or older, and women aged 18 to 29, by highest level of education, 2008; numbers in thousands)

		aged 18 to 29		
	total 18 or older	total	18 to 24	25 to 29
Total women	**115,841**	**24,343**	**14,006**	**10,337**
Not a high school graduate	15,562	3,569	2,521	1,048
High school graduate	35,432	6,334	3740	2,594
Some college, no degree	23,433	7,482	5431	2,051
Associate's degree	10,498	1,791	752	1,039
Bachelor's degree	20,968	4,159	1451	2708
Master's degree	7,973	846	94	752
Professional degree	1,121	119	7	112
Doctoral degree	855	44	11	33
High school graduate or more	100,280	20,775	11,486	9,289
Some college or more	64,848	14,441	7,746	6,695
Associate's degree or more	41,415	6,959	2,315	4,644
Bachelor's degree or more	30,917	5,168	1,563	3,605
Total women	**100.0%**	**100.0%**	**100.0%**	**100.0%**
Not a high school graduate	13.4	14.7	18.0	10.1
High school graduate	30.6	26.0	26.7	25.1
Some college, no degree	20.2	30.7	38.8	19.8
Associate's degree	9.1	7.4	5.4	10.1
Bachelor's degree	18.1	17.1	10.4	26.2
Master's degree	6.9	3.5	0.7	7.3
Professional degree	1.0	0.5	0.0	1.1
Doctoral degree	0.7	0.2	0.1	0.3
High school graduate or more	86.6	85.3	82.0	89.9
Some college or more	56.0	59.3	55.3	64.8
Associate's degree or more	35.8	28.6	16.5	44.9
Bachelor's degree or more	26.7	21.2	11.2	34.9

Source: Bureau of the Census, Educational Attainment in the United States: 2008, detailed tables, Internet site http://www .census.gov/population/www/socdemo/education/cps2008.html; calculations by New Strategist

Asian Women Are the Best-Educated Millennials

Hispanic men are the least educated.

Among people aged 18 to 29, Asian women have the highest level of education. Already, 42 percent have a bachelor's degree or more. Asian men rank second in educational attainment, with 31 percent in the age group having a bachelor's degree or more.

Hispanics are the least educated among Millennials. Only 65 percent of Hispanic men and 71 percent of Hispanic women aged 18 to 29 are high school graduates. Just 8 percent of Hispanics in the age group have a bachelor's degree. Many Hispanics are immigrants from countries that provide little formal schooling.

■ Although the educational attainment of Millennials will rise as more of them complete high school and go to college, the gaps by race and Hispanic origin will persist.

Asians are far better educated than others

(percent of people aged 18 to 29 with college experience, by race and Hispanic origin, 2008)

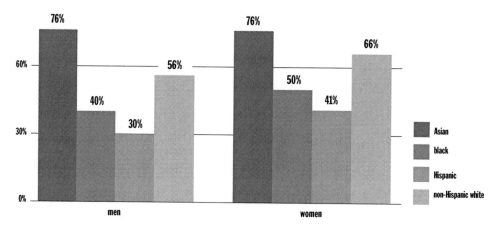

Table 2.4 Educational Attainment of Millennials by Race and Hispanic Origin, 2008

(number and percent distribution of people aged 18 to 29 by educational attainment, race, and Hispanic origin, 2008; numbers in thousands)

	total	Asian	black	Hispanic	non-Hispanic white
Total people aged 18 to 29	**49,455**	**2,482**	**7,287**	**9,286**	**30,069**
Not a high school graduate	8,237	196	1,422	3,007	3,533
High school graduate	14,313	402	2,556	3,047	8,202
Some college, no degree	14,465	826	2,068	2,053	9,399
Associate's degree	3,295	154	400	468	2,257
Bachelor's degree	7,523	646	695	616	5,554
Master's degree	1,355	215	123	75	940
Professional degree	198	25	14	15	145
Doctoral degree	71	20	7	6	38
High school graduate or more	41,220	2,288	5,863	6,280	26,535
Some college or more	26,907	1,886	3,307	3,233	18,333
Associate's degree or more	12,442	1,060	1,239	1,180	8,934
Bachelor's degree or more	9,147	906	839	712	6,677
Total people aged 18 to 29	**100.0%**	**100.0%**	**100.0%**	**100.0%**	**100.0%**
Not a high school graduate	16.7	7.9	19.5	32.4	11.7
High school graduate	28.9	16.2	35.1	32.8	27.3
Some college, no degree	29.2	33.3	28.4	22.1	31.3
Associate's degree	6.7	6.2	5.5	5.0	7.5
Bachelor's degree	15.2	26.0	9.5	6.6	18.5
Master's degree	2.7	8.7	1.7	0.8	3.1
Professional degree	0.4	1.0	0.2	0.2	0.5
Doctoral degree	0.1	0.8	0.1	0.1	0.1
High school graduate or more	83.3	92.2	80.5	67.6	88.2
Some college or more	54.4	76.0	45.4	34.8	61.0
Associate's degree or more	25.2	42.7	17.0	12.7	29.7
Bachelor's degree or more	18.5	36.5	11.5	7.7	22.2

Note: Asians and blacks are those who identify themselves as being of the race alone and those who identify themselves as being of the race in combination with other races. Non-Hispanic whites are those who identify themselves as being white alone and not Hispanic. Numbers do not add to total because not all races are shown and Hispanics may be of any race.
Source: Bureau of the Census, Educational Attainment in the United States: 2008, detailed tables, Internet site http://www .census.gov/population/www/socdemo/education/cps2008.html; calculations by New Strategist

Table 2.5 Educational Attainment of Millennial Men by Race and Hispanic Origin, 2008

(number and percent distribution of men aged 18 to 29 by educational attainment, race, and Hispanic origin, 2008; numbers in thousands)

	total	Asian	black	Hispanic	non-Hispanic white
Total men aged 18 to 29	**25,113**	**1,230**	**3,477**	**5,042**	**15,190**
Not a high school graduate	4,666	103	756	1,776	1,978
High school graduate	7,980	198	1,323	1,774	4,637
Some college, no degree	6,983	464	892	965	4,625
Associate's degree	1,504	83	166	202	1,043
Bachelor's degree	3,365	261	288	292	2,502
Master's degree	509	97	42	26	342
Professional degree	80	14	10	7	49
Doctoral degree	27	10	2	0	15
High school graduate or more	20,448	1,127	2,723	3,266	13,213
Some college or more	12,468	929	1,400	1,492	8,576
Associate's degree or more	5,485	465	508	527	3,951
Bachelor's degree or more	3,981	382	342	325	2,908
Total men aged 18 to 29	**100.0%**	**100.0%**	**100.0%**	**100.0%**	**100.0%**
Not a high school graduate	18.6	8.4	21.7	35.2	13.0
High school graduate	31.8	16.1	38.1	35.2	30.5
Some college, no degree	27.8	37.7	25.7	19.1	30.4
Associate's degree	6.0	6.7	4.8	4.0	6.9
Bachelor's degree	13.4	21.2	8.3	5.8	16.5
Master's degree	2.0	7.9	1.2	0.5	2.3
Professional degree	0.3	1.1	0.3	0.1	0.3
Doctoral degree	0.1	0.8	0.1	0.0	0.1
High school graduate or more	81.4	91.6	78.3	64.8	87.0
Some college or more	49.6	75.5	40.3	29.6	56.5
Associate's degree or more	21.8	37.8	14.6	10.5	26.0
Bachelor's degree or more	15.9	31.1	9.8	6.4	19.1

Note: Asians and blacks are those who identify themselves as being of the race alone and those who identify themselves as being of the race in combination with other races. Non-Hispanic whites are those who identify themselves as being white alone and not Hispanic. Numbers do not add to total because not all races are shown and Hispanics may be of any race.
Source: Bureau of the Census, Educational Attainment in the United States: 2008, detailed tables, Internet site http://www.census.gov/population/www/socdemo/education/cps2008.html; calculations by New Strategist

Table 2.6 Educational Attainment of Millennial Women by Race and Hispanic Origin, 2008

(number and percent distribution of women aged 18 to 29 by educational attainment, race, and Hispanic origin, 2008; numbers in thousands)

	total	Asian	black	Hispanic	non-Hispanic white
Total women aged 18 to 29	**129,847**	**1,251**	**3,811**	**4,245**	**14,878**
Not a high school graduate	18,083	91	669	1,230	1,556
High school graduate	39,172	204	1,233	1,274	3,565
Some college, no degree	28,864	362	1,177	1,088	4,774
Associate's degree	11,250	72	234	265	1,214
Bachelor's degree	22,419	385	407	323	3,052
Master's degree	8,067	116	82	49	597
Professional degree	1,128	11	5	8	96
Doctoral degree	866	10	5	6	23
High school graduate or more	111,766	1,160	3,143	3,013	13,321
Some college or more	72,594	956	1,910	1,739	9,756
Associate's degree or more	43,730	594	733	651	4,982
Bachelor's degree or more	32,480	522	499	386	3,768
Total women aged 18 to 29	**100.0%**	**100.0%**	**100.0%**	**100.0%**	**100.0%**
Not a high school graduate	13.9	7.3	17.6	29.0	10.5
High school graduate	30.2	16.3	32.4	30.0	24.0
Some college, no degree	22.2	28.9	30.9	25.6	32.1
Associate's degree	8.7	5.8	6.1	6.2	8.2
Bachelor's degree	17.3	30.8	10.7	7.6	20.5
Master's degree	6.2	9.3	2.2	1.2	4.0
Professional degree	0.9	0.9	0.1	0.2	0.6
Doctoral degree	0.7	0.8	–	0.1	0.2
High school graduate or more	86.1	92.7	82.5	71.0	89.5
Some college or more	55.9	76.4	50.1	41.0	65.6
Associate's degree or more	33.7	47.5	19.2	15.3	33.5
Bachelor's degree or more	25.0	41.7	13.1	9.1	25.3

Note: Asians and blacks are those who identify themselves as being of the race alone and those who identify themselves as being of the race in combination with other races. Non-Hispanic whites are those who identify themselves as being white alone and not Hispanic. Numbers do not add to total because not all races are shown and Hispanics may be of any race.
Source: Bureau of the Census, Educational Attainment in the United States: 2008, detailed tables, Internet site http://www .census.gov/population/www/socdemo/education/cps2008.html; calculations by New Strategist

Many Millennials Are Students

Nearly half of Millennials are still in school.

Among the nation's 76 million students in 2007, a substantial 28 million were aged 15 to 29 (Millennials were aged 13 to 30 in 2007). More than 90 percent of children aged 15, 16, or 17 are in school. The figure falls with age, but remains above 50 percent through age 20.

■ School enrollment will remain at close to record-high levels thanks to immigration and childbearing by the large Millennial generation.

School enrollment drops sharply among people in their early twenties

(percent of people aged 18 to 24 enrolled in school, by age, 2007)

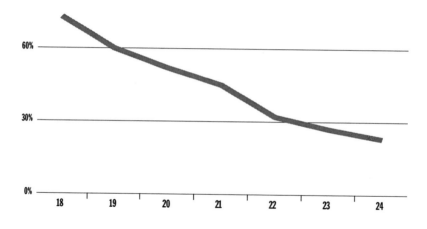

Table 2.7 School Enrollment by Age, 2007

(number of people aged 3 or older, and number and percent enrolled in school, by age, 2007; numbers in thousands)

	total	enrolled number	enrolled percent
Total people	**285,410**	**75,967**	**26.6%**
Under age 15	48,540	43,834	90.3
Aged 15 to 29	62,387	27,753	44.5
Aged 15	4,155	4,116	99.1
Aged 16	4,339	4,169	96.1
Aged 17	4,363	4,035	92.5
Aged 18	4,156	3,049	73.4
Aged 19	4,182	2,517	60.2
Aged 20	4,006	2,078	51.9
Aged 21	4,078	1,837	45.1
Aged 22	4,162	1,350	32.4
Aged 23	4,061	1,079	26.6
Aged 24	4,133	946	22.9
Aged 25 to 29	20,752	2,577	12.4
Aged 30 or older	174,484	4,377	2.5

Source: Bureau of the Census, School Enrollment—Social and Economic Characteristics of Students: October 2007, Internet site http://www.census.gov/population/www/socdemo/school/cps2007.html; calculations by New Strategist

Fewer Students Are Dropping Out of High School

The dropout rate is stubbornly high among Hispanics, however.

Among people aged 16 to 24 in 2007, only 8.7 percent were neither high school graduates nor currently enrolled in school, down from 10.9 percent in 2000. Since 2000, dropout rates have fallen for both men and women and for every racial and ethnic group.

Dropout rates remain high for Hispanics. While just 5.3 percent of non-Hispanic whites and 8.4 percent of non-Hispanic blacks aged 16 to 24 have dropped out of high school, a much larger 21.4 percent of Hispanics are high school dropouts. Among Hispanic men, the dropout rate was 24.7 percent in 2007, down from 31.8 in 2000 but still shockingly high. Among Hispanic women aged 16 to 24, a smaller 18.0 percent were high school dropouts in 2007, down from 23.5 percent in 2000.

■ The arrival of millions of poorly educated immigrants in the United States during the past decade explains the high dropout rate among Hispanics. Some did not, in fact, drop out of an American high school, but arrived in the United States without a high school diploma.

Non-Hispanic whites have the lowest dropout rate

(percent of people aged 16 to 24 who were neither enrolled in school nor high school graduates, by race and Hispanic origin, 2007)

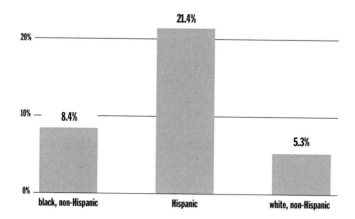

Table 2.8 High School Dropouts by Sex, Race, and Hispanic Origin, 2000 and 2007

(percentage of people aged 16 to 24 who were not enrolled in school and were not high school graduates by sex, race, and Hispanic origin, 2000 to 2007; percentage point change, 2000–07)

	2007	2000	percentage point change 2000–07
Total people	**8.7%**	**10.9%**	**–2.2**
Black	8.4	13.1	–4.7
Hispanic	21.4	27.8	–6.4
White	5.3	6.9	–1.6
Total men	**9.8**	**12.0**	**–2.2**
Black	8.0	15.3	–7.3
Hispanic	24.7	31.8	–7.1
White	6.0	7.0	–1.0
Total women	**7.7**	**9.9**	**–2.2**
Black	8.8	11.1	–2.3
Hispanic	18.0	23.5	–5.5
White	4.5	6.9	–2.4

Note: Whites and blacks include Hispanics.
Source: National Center for Education Statistics, Digest of Education Statistics 2008, Internet site http://nces.ed.gov/pubsearch/pubsinfo.asp?pubid=2009020; calculations by New Strategist

Few High School Students Have Jobs

Employment among high school students has declined over the years.

Among 16-to-17-year-olds, the 73 percent majority are enrolled in school and not employed. The percentage of youths who are both going to school and employed has fallen from 31 percent in 2000 to 21 percent in 2007. Fewer students have time for work because more are taking advanced placement courses and participating in community service and other extracurricular activities to boost their chances of getting into college.

The percentage of 18-to-19-year-olds who are juggling school and work has fallen slightly over the past few years, from 30 percent in 2000 to 26 percent in 2007.

In 2008, only 2.7 million of the nation's 9.7 million high school students aged 16 to 24 were in the labor force—or just 27.5 percent. The unemployment rate among high school students was a substantial 21.1 percent. Among 16-to-24-year-olds in college, the 54.1 percent majority are employed. Only 8.0 percent were unemployed.

■ In high school and college, women are more likely than men to be in the labor force.

The percentage of high school students with jobs has declined

(percent of high school students aged 16 to 17 who were employed, 2000 and 2007)

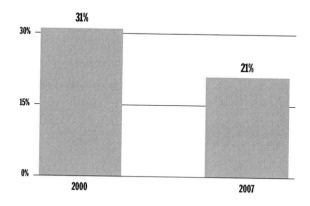

Table 2.9 Youth Employment during School Months, 2000 to 2007

(percent distribution of 16-to-19-year-olds by employment and school-enrollment status from January through May and Sepatmber through December of selected years, by age, 2000 to 2007)

	enrolled		not enrolled	
	employed	not employed	employed	not employed
Aged 16 to 17				
2007	21%	73%	2%	4%
2006	23	72	2	3
2005	23	72	2	3
2004	23	72	2	3
2003	24	71	2	3
2002	25	69	2	4
2001	28	65	3	4
2000	31	63	3	4
Aged 18 to 19				
2007	26	42	19	13
2006	28	40	20	13
2005	28	41	19	13
2004	27	41	19	13
2003	27	40	20	14
2002	28	37	21	14
2001	28	35	23	13
2000	30	34	24	12

Source: Bureau of Labor Statistics, Youth Enrollment and Employment during the School Year, Teressa L. Morisi, Monthly Labor Review, February 2008, Internet site http://www.bls.gov/opub/mlr/2008/02/art3abs.htm

Table 2.10 Employment Status of High School and College Students, 2008

(employment status of people aged 16 to 24 by selected demographic characteristics, 2008; numbers in thousands)

| | civilian noninstitutional population | civilian labor force | | | | |
| | | total | percent of population | employed | unemployed | |
					number	percent of labor force
TOTAL AGED 16 TO 24	**37,569**	**21,931**	**58.4%**	**19,020**	**2,911**	**13.3%**
Total enrolled in high school	**9,677**	**2,661**	**27.5**	**2,099**	**562**	**21.1**
Men	4,991	1,272	25.5	960	311	24.5
Women	4,686	1,389	29.6	1,139	251	18.0
Asian	349	66	18.9	57	9	13.6
Black	1,604	339	21.2	236	104	30.5
Hispanic	1,804	365	20.2	238	127	34.8
White	7,274	2,153	29.6	1,729	424	19.7
Total enrolled in college	**11,671**	**6,313**	**54.1**	**5,809**	**505**	**8.0**
Men	5,492	2,814	51.2	2,522	293	10.4
Women	6,179	3,499	56.6	3,287	212	6.1
Asian	680	238	35.1	223	16	6.6
Black	1,381	630	45.6	540	90	14.3
Hispanic	1,385	775	55.9	682	93	12.0
White	9,283	5,289	57.0	4,900	389	7.4

Source: Bureau of Labor Statistics, College Enrollment and Work Activity of 2008 High School Graduates, 2009, Internet site http://www.bls.gov/news.release/hsgec.toc.htm

SAT Scores Vary by Income and Parents' Education

The more educated the parent, the higher the child's score.

It is well known that scholastic aptitude test scores vary by race and Hispanic origin. Asians and whites get higher scores than blacks or Hispanics. It is also no surprise that students with the best grades get the highest scores. Students with an A+ grade point average (97 to 100) averaged a 615 out of 800 on the math section of the SAT in 2007–08, for example. Students with a B GPA (80 to 89) averaged a much lower 484 on the math section of the test.

SAT scores also vary by family income and parental education. Students with family incomes below $20,000 averaged a 456 on the math portion of the SAT in 2007–08 compared with a score of 570 among students with family incomes of $200,000 or more. Parental education also has a big impact on test scores. Among students with a parent who did not graduate from high school, the average SAT math score was 441. Among those whose parent had a graduate degree, the average math score was 565.

■ Affluent, educated parents can afford SAT prep courses for their children, which can boost test scores.

A parent's education influences a child's test score

(average SAT mathematics score by highest level of parental education, 2007–08)

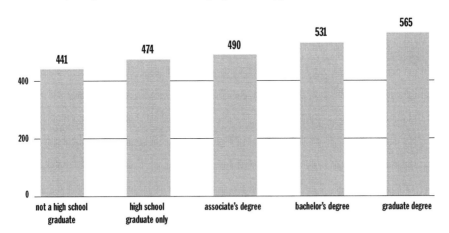

Table 2.11 SAT Scores by Selected Characteristics, 2007–08

(average SAT scores by selected characteristics, 2007–08)

	critical reading	mathematics	writing
TOTAL	**502**	**515**	**494**
Sex			
Men	504	533	488
Women	500	500	501
Race and Hispanic origin			
American Indian, Alaska Native	485	491	470
Asian or Pacific Islander	513	581	516
Black	430	426	424
Mexican American	454	463	447
Puerto Rican	456	453	445
Other Hispanic	455	461	448
White	528	537	518
High school grade point average			
A+ (97 to 100)	595	615	592
A (93 to 96)	559	578	555
A– (90 to 92)	529	547	523
B (80 to 89)	474	484	465
C (70 to 79)	421	423	408
D or F (below 70)	402	411	390
Family income			
Less than $20,000	434	456	430
$20,000 to $39,999	462	473	453
$40,000 o $59,999	488	496	477
$60,000 to $79,999	502	510	490
$80,000 to $99,999	514	525	504
$100,000 to $119,999	522	534	512
$120,000 to $139,999	526	537	517
$140,000 to $159,999	533	546	525
$160,000 to $199,999	535	548	529
$200,000 or more	554	570	552
Highest level of parental education			
Not a high school graduate	419	441	417
High school graduate	464	474	455
Associate's degree	482	490	471
Bachelor's degree	518	531	510
Graduate degree	553	565	546

Source: National Center for Education Statistics, Digest of Education Statistics 2008, Internet site http://nces.ed.gov/pubsearch/pubsinfo.asp?pubid=2009020; calculations by New Strategist

College Enrollment Rates Have Peaked

The cost of college is taking a toll on enrollment rates.

The rate at which high school graduates enroll in college was higher in 2007 than in 2000, but lower than in 2005. Two out of three men and women aged 16 to 24 who had graduated from high school in 2007 had enrolled in college (either two-year or four-year schools) within 12 months. Women's 68.3 percent enrollment rate in 2007 was 2 percentage points higher than their rate of 2000, but lower than the rates of 2004 and 2005. Men's college enrollment rate grew by 6 percentage points between 2000 and 2007, but was slightly below the rate of 2005.

The 2007 college enrollment rate of blacks and whites was below the all-time high reached in 2004 among blacks and 2005 among whites. An examination of enrollment rates by type of institution reveals that the decline in enrollment rates has been limited to four-year schools. In contrast, two-year schools are enjoying record enrollment rates.

Children from families with high incomes are much more likely to attend college than those from low- or middle-income families. In 2006, 81 percent of children from high-income families were enrolled in college. This enrollment rate was much higher than the 61 percent of children from middle-income families and the 51 percent of children from low-income families. Similarly, children whose parents have a college degree (who also tend to be more affluent) are far more likely to enroll in college than children whose parents are less educated.

■ The economic downturn is likely to spur an enrollment surge at less-expensive two-year schools and a drop in enrollment rates at four-year institutions.

The college enrollment rate peaked in 2005

(percent of people aged 16 to 24 who graduated from high school in the previous 12 months and were enrolled in college as of October of each year, 2000 to 2007)

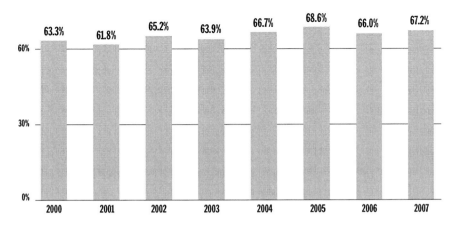

Table 2.12 College Enrollment Rates by Sex, 2000 to 2007

(percentage of people aged 16 to 24 who graduated from high school in the previous 12 months and were enrolled in college as of October, by sex, 2000 to 2007; percentage point change in enrollment rate, 2000–07)

	total	men	women
2007	67.2%	66.1%	68.3%
2006	66.0	65.8	66.1
2005	68.6	66.5	70.4
2004	66.7	61.4	71.5
2003	63.9	61.2	66.5
2002	65.2	62.1	68.4
2001	61.8	60.1	63.5
2000	63.3	59.9	66.2
Percentage point change			
2000 to 2007	3.9	6.2	2.1

Source: National Center for Education Statistics, Digest of Education Statistics 2008, Internet site http://nces.ed.gov/ pubsearch/pubsinfo.asp?pubid=2009020; calculations by New Strategist

Table 2.13 College Enrollment Rates by Race and Hispanic Origin, 2000 to 2007

(percent of people aged 16 to 24 who graduated from high school in the previous 12 months and were enrolled in college as of October, by race and Hispanic origin, 2000 to 2007; percentage point change in enrollment rate, 2000–07)

	total	non-Hispanic		Hispanic
		black	white	
2007	67.2%	55.7%	69.5%	–
2006	66.0	55.5	68.5	58.6%
2005	68.6	55.7	73.2	57.9
2004	66.7	62.5	68.8	58.1
2003	63.9	57.5	66.2	58.0
2002	65.2	59.4	69.1	54.6
2001	61.8	55.0	64.3	52.7
2000	63.3	54.9	65.7	49.0
Percentage point change				
2000 to 2007	3.9	0.8	3.8	9.6

Note: "–" means not available; Hispanic enrollment rates are a three-year moving average. Percentage point change in His-panic enrollment rate is the difference between 2000 and 2006 three-year moving averages.
Source: National Center for Education Statistics, Digest of Education Statistics 2008, Internet site http://nces.ed.gov/ pubsearch/pubsinfo.asp?pubid=2009020; calculations by New Strategist

Table 2.14 College Enrollment Rate by Sex and Type of Institution, 2000 to 2006

(percent of people aged 16 to 24 who graduated from high school in the previous 12 months and were enrolled in college as of October, by sex and type of institution, 2000 to 2006; percentage point change, 2000–06)

	men			women		
	total	two-year	four-year	total	two-year	four-year
2006	65.8%	24.9%	40.9%	66.1%	24.5%	41.7%
2005	66.5	24.7	41.8	70.4	23.4	47.0
2004	61.4	21.8	39.6	71.5	23.1	48.5
2003	61.2	21.9	39.3	66.5	21.0	45.5
2002	62.1	20.5	41.7	68.4	23.0	45.3
2001	60.1	18.6	41.1	63.5	20.7	42.9
2000	59.9	23.1	36.8	66.2	20.0	46.2
Percentage point change						
2000 to 2006	5.9	1.8	4.1	–0.1	4.5	–4.5

Source: National Center for Education Statistics, The Condition of Education, Internet site http://nces.ed.gov/programs/coe/2008/section3/indicator24.asp; calculations by New Strategist

Table 2.15 College Enrollment Rate by Family Income, 2000 to 2006

(percent of people aged 16 to 24 who graduated from high school in the previous 12 months and were enrolled in college as of October, by family income level, 2000 to 2006; percentage point change, 2000–06)

	total	family income level		
		low	middle	high
2006	66.0%	50.9%	61.4%	80.7%
2005	68.6	53.5	65.1	81.2
2004	66.7	47.8	63.3	80.1
2003	63.9	52.8	57.6	80.1
2002	65.2	56.4	60.7	78.2
2001	61.8	43.8	56.3	79.9
2000	63.3	49.7	59.5	76.9
Percentage point change				
2000 to 2006	2.7	1.2	1.9	3.8

Note: Low income refers to the bottom 20 percent of all family incomes, high income refers to the top 20 percent of all family incomes, and middle income refers to the 60 percent in between.
Source: National Center for Education Statistics, The Condition of Education, Internet site http://nces.ed.gov/programs/coe/2008/section3/indicator24.asp; calculations by New Strategist

Table 2.16 College Enrollment Rate by Parents' Education, 2000 to 2006

(percentage of people aged 16 to 24 who graduated from high school in the previous 12 months and were enrolled in college as of October, by highest level of parental education, 2000 to 2006; percentage point change, 2000–06)

| | total | parents' highest level of education | | | |
		less than high school	high school graduate	some college	bachelor's degree or more
2006	66.0%	43.0%	56.1%	67.0%	78.2%
2005	68.6	43.0	62.1	65.6	88.8
2004	66.7	40.2	53.8	67.0	85.9
2003	63.9	43.3	53.9	62.9	82.1
2002	65.2	43.3	51.9	65.9	82.6
2001	61.8	39.0	51.9	62.0	81.3
2000	63.3	44.4	51.8	63.8	81.2
Percentage point change					
2000 to 2006	2.7	–1.4	4.3	3.2	–3.0

Source: National Center for Education Statistics, The Condition of Education, Internet site http://nces.ed.gov/programs/coe/2008/section3/indicator24.asp; calculations by New Strategist

Six Million Families Have Children in College

High-income families are most likely to have a child in college.

Among the nation's 39 million families with school-aged children (5 to 24), more than 6 million have one or more children enrolled in college—or 16 percent. Not surprisingly the likelihood that a family is sending a child to college increases with income. Families with a household income of $75,000 or more are about three times as likely as families with incomes below $20,000 to have a child in college.

■ The economic downturn is likely to reduce the percentage of low- and middle-income families with children in college.

College is more likely for children from the most affluent families

(percent of families with children aged 5 to 24 who have one or more children enrolled in college, by household income, 2007)

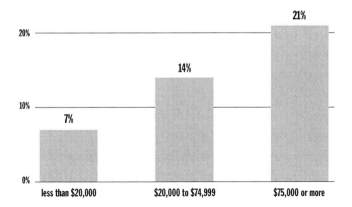

Table 2.17 Total Families with Children in College, 2007

(total number of families, number with dependent children aged 5 to 24, and number and percent with children enrolled in college by household income, 2007; numbers in thousands)

| | | | with one or more children enrolled in college | | |
	total	with children aged 5–24	number	percent of total families	percent of families with children 5–24
Total families	**79,095**	**38,743**	**6,104**	**7.7%**	**15.8%**
Less than $20,000	8,551	4,620	307	3.6	6.6
$20,000 to $74,999	32,735	15,713	2,137	6.5	13.6
$75,000 or more	20,704	10,689	2,294	11.1	21.5

Note: Numbers do sum to total because "not reported" is not shown.
Source: Bureau of the Census, School Enrollment—Social and Economic Characteristics of Students: October 2007, Detailed Tables, Internet site http://www.census.gov/population/www/socdemo/school/cps2007.html

Millennials Populate the Nation's Campuses

Four-year schools are more popular than two-year schools.

While the oldest Millennials have aged out of the prime college years and the youngest are not quite old enough to go to college yet, the broad middle populates the nation's campuses. (Millennials were aged 13 to 30 in 2007.) Millennial women outnumber their male counterparts in every type of college—two-year, four-year, and graduate school.

Nearly two of three college students under age 25 attend four-year schools. In the 25 to 34 age group, there is more diversity in the type of school attended: 25 percent are in two-year schools, 34 percent are in four-year schools, and the 41 percent plurality are in graduate school.

■ Among the nation's 18 million college students, 63 percent are under age 25.

Among Millennials, women outnumber men on college campuses

(percent distribution of college students aged 15 to 34, by age and sex, 2007)

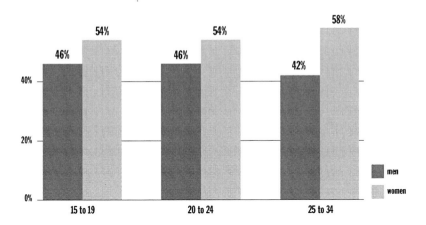

Table 2.18 College Students by Age and Sex, 2007

(number, percent, and percent distribution of people aged 15 or older enrolled in institutions of higher education, by type of institution, age, and sex, 2007; numbers in thousands)

	total	men total	men percent of total	women total	women percent of total
TOTAL COLLEGE STUDENTS					
Total students	**17,956**	**7,826**	**43.6%**	**10,130**	**56.4%**
Aged 15 to 19	4,261	1,980	46.5	2,281	53.5
Aged 20 to 24	7,086	3,253	45.9	3,834	54.1
Aged 25 to 34	3,838	1,625	42.3	2,212	57.6
Aged 35 or older	2,772	968	34.9	1,804	65.1
TWO-YEAR UNDERGRADUATE					
Total students	**4,813**	**2,061**	**42.8**	**2,753**	**57.2**
Aged 15 to 19	1,497	703	47.0	792	52.9
Aged 20 to 24	1,630	728	44.7	902	55.3
Aged 25 to 34	963	394	40.9	569	59.1
Aged 35 or older	725	236	32.6	488	67.3
FOUR-YEAR UNDERGRADUATE					
Total students	**9,550**	**4,345**	**45.5**	**5,207**	**54.5**
Aged 15 to 19	2,741	1,265	46.2	1,476	53.8
Aged 20 to 24	4,614	2,196	47.6	2,419	52.4
Aged 25 to 34	1,314	568	43.2	746	56.8
Aged 35 or older	881	315	35.8	565	64.1
GRADUATE SCHOOL					
Total students	**3,591**	**1,421**	**39.6**	**2,171**	**60.5**
Aged 15 to 19	24	12	50.0	13	54.2
Aged 20 to 24	841	329	39.1	513	61.0
Aged 25 to 34	1,560	663	42.5	898	57.6
Aged 35 or older	1,167	417	35.7	749	64.2

Source: Bureau of the Census, School Enrollment—Social and Economic Characteristics of Students: October 2007, Internet site http://www.census.gov/population/www/socdemo/school/cps2007.html; calculations by New Strategist

Table 2.19 College Students by Age, Type of School, and Attendance Status, 2007

(number, percent, and percent distribution of people aged 15 or older enrolled in institutions of higher education, by age, type of school, and attendance status, 2007; numbers in thousands)

	total	two-year school			four-year school			graduate school		
		number	share of total students in age group	percent distribution	number	share of total students in age group	percent distribution	number	share of total students in age group	percent distribution
TOTAL COLLEGE STUDENTS										
Total students	**17,956**	**4,813**	**26.8%**	**100.0%**	**9,550**	**53.2%**	**100.0%**	**3,591**	**20.0%**	**100.0%**
Aged 15 to 19	4,261	1,497	35.1	31.1	2,741	64.3	28.7	24	0.6	0.7
Aged 20 to 24	7,086	1,630	23.0	33.9	4,614	65.1	48.3	841	11.9	23.4
Aged 25 to 34	3,838	963	25.1	20.0	1,314	34.2	13.8	1,560	40.6	43.4
Aged 35 or older	2,772	725	26.2	15.1	881	31.8	9.2	1,167	42.1	32.5
TOTAL FULL-TIME STUDENTS										
Total students	**12,656**	**2,988**	**23.6**	**100.0**	**7,877**	**62.2**	**100.0**	**1,790**	**14.1**	**100.0**
Aged 15 to 19	3,902	1,276	32.7	42.7	2,603	66.7	33.0	23	0.6	1.3
Aged 20 to 24	5,767	1,051	18.2	35.2	4,087	70.9	51.9	627	10.9	35.0
Aged 25 to 34	2,100	442	21.0	14.8	842	40.1	10.7	815	38.8	45.5
Aged 35 or older	887	219	24.7	7.3	344	38.8	4.4	325	36.6	18.2
TOTAL PART-TIME STUDENTS										
Total students	**5,300**	**1,825**	**34.4**	**100.0**	**1,673**	**31.6**	**100.0**	**1,801**	**34.0**	**100.0**
Aged 15 to 19	359	221	61.6	12.1	138	38.4	8.2	1	0.3	0.1
Aged 20 to 24	1,319	579	43.9	31.7	527	40.0	31.5	214	16.2	11.9
Aged 25 to 34	1,738	521	30.0	28.5	472	27.2	28.2	745	42.9	41.4
Aged 35 or older	1,885	506	26.8	27.7	537	28.5	32.1	842	44.7	46.8

Source: Bureau of the Census, School Enrollment—Social and Economic Characteristics of Students: October 2007, Internet site http://www.census.gov/population/www/socdemo/school/cps2007.html; calculations by New Strategist

Most Degrees Are Earned in a Few Fields

Business, social sciences, health, and law dominate the academic degrees awarded.

It is a good bet that the great majority of those earning a college degree of some sort in 2006–07 were Millennials, a time period in which Millennials spanned the ages from 13 to 30. A look at the degrees they earned shows a few fields dominating each level of degree.

At the associate's degree level, liberal arts and sciences, general studies, and humanities was the most popular field. More than one-third of the associate's degrees awarded in 2006–07 were in this discipline. One in five associate's degrees was awarded in health professions and related clinical sciences, and 16 percent were in business.

At the bachelor's degree level, business was the preferred field in 2006–07, attracting 21 percent of graduates. The only other field in double digits was social sciences and history, in which 11 percent of all bachelor's degrees were awarded.

At the master's level, education was the field of choice for 29 percent, followed closely by business (25 percent). Together these two disciplines accounted for the 54 percent majority of all master's degrees awarded in 2006–07.

■ Almost half the students obtaining a first-professional degree in 2006–07 did so in the field of law.

One in five bachelor's degrees is in business

(percent distribution of bachelor's degrees conferred by field of study, 2006–07)

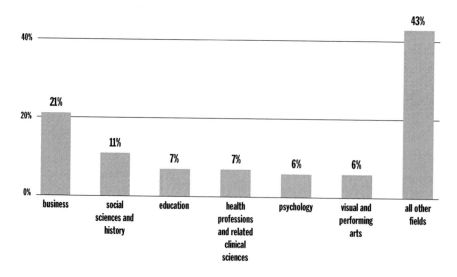

Table 2.20 Associate's Degrees Earned by Field of Study, 2006–07

(number and percent distribution of associate's degrees conferred by field of study, 2006–07)

	number	percent distribution
Total associate's degrees	**728,114**	**100.0%**
Agriculture and natural resources	5,838	0.8
Architecture and related services	517	0.1
Area, ethnic, cultural, and gender studies	164	0.0
Biological and biomedical sciences	2,060	0.3
Business	116,101	15.9
Communications, journalism, and related programs	2,609	0.4
Communications technologies	3,095	0.4
Computer and information sciences	27,712	3.8
Construction trades	3,895	0.5
Education	13,021	1.8
Engineering	2,136	0.3
Engineering technologies	29,199	4.0
English language and literature/letters	1,249	0.2
Family and consumer sciences	9,124	1.3
Foreign languages, literatures, and linguistics	1,207	0.2
Health professions and related clinical sciences	145,436	20.0
Legal professions and studies	10,391	1.4
Liberal arts and sciences, general studies, and humanities	250,030	34.3
Library science	84	0.0
Mathematics and statistics	827	0.1
Mechanics and repair technologies	15,432	2.1
Military technologies	781	0.1
Multi/interdisciplinary studies	15,838	2.2
Parks, recreation, leisure, and fitness studies	1,251	0.2
Philosophy and religious studies	375	0.1
Physical sciences and science technologies	3,404	0.5
Precision production	1,973	0.3
Psychology	2,213	0.3
Public administration and social service professions	4,338	0.6
Security and protective services	28,208	3.9
Social sciences and history	7,080	1.0
Theology and religious vocations	608	0.1
Transportation and materials moving	1,674	0.2
Visual and performing arts	20,244	2.8

Source: National Center for Education Statistics, Digest of Education Statistics 2008, Internet site http://nces.ed.gov/pubsearch/pubsinfo.asp?pubid=2009020; calculations by New Strategist

Table 2.21 Bachelor's Degrees Earned by Field of Study, 2006–07

(number and percent distribution of bachelor's degrees conferred by field of study, 2006–07)

	total	percent distribution
Total bachelor's degrees	**1,524,092**	**100.0%**
Agriculture and natural resources	23,133	1.5
Architecture and related services	9,717	0.6
Area, ethnic, cultural, and gender studies	8,194	0.5
Biological and biomedical sciences	75,151	4.9
Business	327,531	21.5
Communications, journalism, and related programs	74,783	4.9
Communications technologies	3,637	0.2
Computer and information sciences	42,170	2.8
Construction trades	129	0.0
Education	105,641	6.9
Engineering	67,092	4.4
Engineering technologies	14,588	1.0
English language and literature/letters	55,122	3.6
Family and consumer sciences	21,400	1.4
Foreign languages, literatures, and linguistics	20,275	1.3
Health professions and related clinical sciences	101,810	6.7
Legal professions and studies	3,596	0.2
Liberal arts and sciences, general studies, and humanities	44,255	2.9
Library science	82	0.0
Mathematics and statistics	14,954	1.0
Mechanics and repair technologies	263	0.0
Military technologies	168	0.0
Multi/interdisciplinary studies	33,792	2.2
Parks, recreation, leisure, and fitness studies	27,430	1.8
Philosophy and religious studies	11,969	0.8
Physical sciences and science technologies	21,073	1.4
Precision production	23	0.0
Psychology	90,039	5.9
Public administration and social service professions	23,147	1.5
Security and protective services	39,206	2.6
Social sciences and history	164,183	10.8
Theology and religious vocations	8,696	0.6
Transportation and materials moving	5,657	0.4
Visual and performing arts	85,186	5.6

Source: National Center for Education Statistics, Digest of Education Statistics 2008, Internet site http://nces.ed.gov/pubsearch/pubsinfo.asp?pubid=2009020; calculations by New Strategist

Table 2.22 Master's Degrees Earned by Field of Study, 2006–07

(number and percent distribution of master's degrees conferred by field of study, 2006–07)

	total	percent distribution
Total master's degrees	**604,607**	**100.0%**
Agriculture and natural resources	4,623	0.8
Architecture and related services	5,951	1.0
Area, ethnic, cultural, and gender studies	1,699	0.3
Biological and biomedical sciences	8,747	1.4
Business	150,211	24.8
Communications, journalism, and related programs	6,773	1.1
Communications technologies	499	0.1
Computer and information sciences	16,232	2.7
Education	176,572	29.2
Engineering	29,472	4.9
Engineering technologies	2,690	0.4
English language and literature/letters	8,742	1.4
Family and consumer sciences	2,080	0.3
Foreign languages, literatures, and linguistics	3,443	0.6
Health professions and related clinical sciences	54,531	9.0
Legal professions and studies	4,486	0.7
Liberal arts and sciences, general studies, and humanities	3,634	0.6
Library science	6,767	1.1
Mathematics and statistics	4,884	0.8
Military technologies	202	0.0
Multi/interdisciplinary studies	4,762	0.8
Parks, recreation, leisure, and fitness studies	4,110	0.7
Philosophy and religious studies	1,716	0.3
Physical sciences and science technologies	5,839	1.0
Precision production	5	0.0
Psychology	21,037	3.5
Public administration and social service professions	31,131	5.1
Security and protective services	4,906	0.8
Social sciences and history	17,665	2.9
Theology and religious vocations	6,446	1.1
Transportation and materials moving	985	0.2
Visual and performing arts	13,767	2.3

Source: National Center for Education Statistics, Digest of Education Statistics 2008, Internet site http://nces.ed.gov/pubsearch/pubsinfo.asp?pubid=2009020; calculations by New Strategist

Table 2.23 Doctoral Degrees Earned by Field of Study, 2006–07

(number and percent distribution of doctoral degrees conferred by field of study, 2006–07)

	total	percent distribution
Total doctoral degrees	**60,616**	**100.0%**
Agriculture and natural resources	1,272	2.1
Architecture and related services	178	0.3
Area, ethnic, cultural, and gender studies	233	0.4
Biological and biomedical sciences	6,354	10.5
Business	2,029	3.3
Communications, journalism, and related programs	479	0.8
Communications technologies	1	0.0
Computer and information sciences	1,595	2.6
Education	8,261	13.6
Engineering	8,062	13.3
Engineering technologies	61	0.1
English language and literature/letters	1,178	1.9
Family and consumer sciences	337	0.6
Foreign languages, literatures, and linguistics	1,059	1.7
Health professions and related clinical sciences	8,355	13.8
Legal professions and studies	143	0.2
Liberal arts and sciences, general studies, and humanities	77	0.1
Library science	52	0.1
Mathematics and statistics	1,351	2.2
Multi/interdisciplinary studies	1,093	1.8
Parks, recreation, leisure, and fitness studies	218	0.4
Philosophy and religious studies	637	1.1
Physical sciences and science technologies	4,846	8.0
Psychology	5,153	8.5
Public administration and social service professions	726	1.2
Security and protective services	85	0.1
Social sciences and history	3,844	6.3
Theology and religious vocations	1,573	2.6
Visual and performing arts	1,364	2.3

Source: National Center for Education Statistics, Digest of Education Statistics 2008, Internet site http://nces.ed.gov/pubsearch/ pubsinfo.asp?pubid=2009020; calculations by New Strategist

Table 2.24 First-Professional Degrees Earned by Field of Study, 2006–07

(number of first-professional degrees conferred by field of study, 2006–07)

	total	percent distribution
Total first-professional degrees	**90,064**	**100.0%**
Dentistry (D.D.S. or D.M.D.)	4,596	5.1
Medicine (M.D.)	15,730	17.5
Optometry (O.D.)	1,311	1.5
Osteopathic medicine (D.O.)	2,992	3.3
Pharmacy (Pharm.D.)	10,439	11.6
Podiatry (Pod.D., D.P., or D.P.M.)	331	0.4
Veterinary medicine (D.V.M.)	2,443	2.7
Chiropractic (D.C. or D.C.M.)	2,525	2.8
Naturopathic medicine	221	0.2
Law (LL.B. or J.D.)	43,486	48.3
Theology (M.Div., M.H.L., B.D., or Ord.)	5,990	6.7

Source: National Center for Education Statistics, Digest of Education Statistics 2008, Internet site http://nces.ed.gov/pubsearch/pubsinfo.asp?pubid=2009020; calculations by New Strategist

Many Young Adults Participate in Education for Job-Related Reasons

Life-long learning is becoming a necessity for job security.

As job security dwindles, many workers are turning to the educational system to try to stay on track. Overall, 27 percent of Americans aged 16 or older participated in work-related adult education in 2005 (the latest available data), while another 21 percent took personal interest courses and 5 percent were enrolled in part-time degree or diploma programs.

Participation in work-related adult education begins early, with 21 percent of 16-to-24-year-olds participating in 2005. The figure rises to 32 percent in the 25-to-34 age group. Among 16-to-24-year-olds, personal interest adult education courses are even more popular than work-related courses, with 27 percent participating in personal interest courses in 2005. From 9 to 11 percent of people aged 16 to 34 participated in a part-time degree or diploma program in 2005.

■ Many Americans who participate in work-related education are retraining themselves to compete in the increasingly global economy.

Work-related training peaks in the 45-to-54 age group

(percent of workers who participated in work-related adult education activities, by age, 2005)

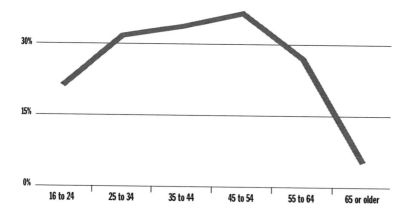

Table 2.25 Participation in Adult Education by Age, 2005

(percent of people aged 16 or older who participate in formal adult education activities, by age and type of adult education activity, 2005)

	total	percent participating in any activity	work-related courses	personal interest courses	part-time degree or diploma programs
Total people	**100.0%**	**44.4%**	**26.9%**	**21.4%**	**5.0%**
Aged 16 to 24	100.0	52.9	21.2	26.6	11.4
Aged 25 to 34	100.0	52.2	31.7	22.1	8.7
Aged 35 to 44	100.0	48.7	33.7	22.1	5.3
Aged 45 to 54	100.0	47.9	36.5	19.7	3.8
Aged 55 to 64	100.0	40.3	27.0	20.7	1.5
Aged 65 or older	100.0	22.9	5.2	18.8	0.3

Source: National Center for Education Statistics, The Condition of Education, Participation in Adult Education, Indicator 10 (2007), Internet site http://nces.ed.gov/programs/coe/2007/section1/indicator10.asp; calculations by New Strategist

3

Health

■ The 55 percent majority of Americans aged 18 or older are in "very good" or "excellent" health. The figure peaks at 63 percent in the 25-to-34 age group.

■ Americans have a weight problem, and young adults are no exception. The average man in his twenties weighs 188 pounds. The average woman in the age group weighs 156 pounds.

■ Among 15-to-19-year-olds, 57 percent of men and 62 percent of women are sexually experienced.

■ The Millennial generation dominates births. Women under age 30 in 2007 (the Millennial generation was aged 13 to 30 in that year) accounted for the 64 percent majority of births.

■ Among 18-to-24-year-olds, 28 percent do not have health insurance—a larger share than in any other age group. Among 25-to-34-year-olds, the figure is 26 percent.

■ People aged 15 to 24 visit a doctor only 1.7 times a year. This age group visits a doctor less often than any other in part because it is least likely to be covered by health insurance.

■ Accidents are the most important cause of death among 15-to-34-year-olds, accounting for 47 percent of deaths among 15-to-24-year-olds and 35 percent of deaths among 25-to-34-year-olds.

Most Young Adults Say Their Health Is Excellent or Very Good

The proportion of people who report very good or excellent health declines with age.

Overall, the 55 percent majority of Americans aged 18 or older say their health is "very good" or "excellent." Not surprisingly, the percentage who say their health is very good or excellent is higher among young adults than among middle-aged or older people. The figure peaks at 63 percent in the 25-to-34 age group, then falls with increasing age as chronic conditions become common.

Fewer than half of people aged 65 or older report excellent or very good health. Nevertheless, the proportion of respondents who say they are in poor health remains below 8 percent, regardless of age. Among people aged 65 or older, the proportion saying their health is excellent or very good (38 percent) surpasses the proportion saying their health is only "fair" or "poor" (25 percent).

■ Medical advances that allow people to manage chronic conditions should boost the proportions of people reporting excellent or very good health in the years ahead.

More than 60 percent of adults under age 45 say their health is excellent or very good

(percent of people aged 18 or older who say their health is excellent or very good, by age, 2008)

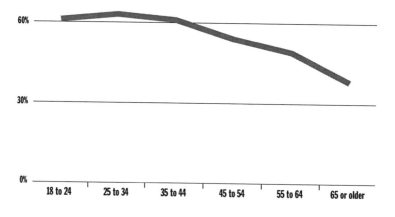

Table 3.1 Health Status by Age, 2008

(percent distribution of people aged 18 or older by self-reported health status, by age, 2008)

	total	excellent	very good	good	fair	poor
Total people	**100.0%**	**20.1%**	**34.9%**	**30.0%**	**10.6%**	**3.8%**
Aged 18 to 24	100.0	25.1	35.7	29.7	6.6	1.0
Aged 25 to 34	100.0	24.8	38.1	28.9	7.3	1.4
Aged 35 to 44	100.0	23.7	37.2	28.3	8.0	2.1
Aged 45 to 54	100.0	19.6	34.5	29.1	10.3	4.2
Aged 55 to 64	100.0	17.3	31.5	30.3	13.8	5.6
Aged 65 or older	100.0	11.4	26.7	34.1	18.0	7.4

Source: Centers for Disease Control and Prevention, Behavioral Risk Factor Surveillance System Prevalence Data, 2008, Internet site http://apps.nccd.cdc.gov/brfss/

Weight Problems Are the Norm Even for Young Adults

Most young men and women are overweight.

Americans have a weight problem, and young adults are no exception. The average man in his twenties weighs 188 pounds. The average woman in the age group weighs 156 pounds. Sixty-two percent of men and 51 percent of women aged 20 to 34 are overweight, and more than one in four are obese.

Although many people say they exercise, only 31 percent of adults participate in regular leisure-time physical activity, according to government data. The figure ranges from a high of 38 percent among 18-to-24-year-olds to a low of 17 percent among people aged 75 or older. Among 18-to-24-year-olds, more than one in three are physically inactive.

■ Most young adults lack the willpower to eat less or exercise more—fueling a diet and weight loss industry that never lacks for customers.

Most young adults weigh more than they should

(percent distribution of people aged 20 to 34 by weight status, by sex, 2003–06)

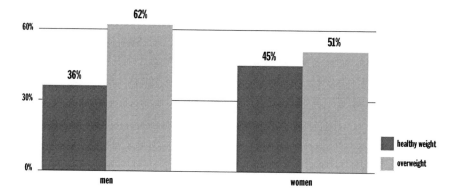

Table 3.2 Average Measured Weight by Age and Sex, 2003–06

(average weight in pounds of people aged 20 or older by age and sex, 2003–06)

	men	women
Total aged 20 or older	**194.7**	**164.7**
Aged 20 to 29	188.3	155.9
Aged 30 to 39	194.1	164.7
Aged 40 to 49	202.3	171.3
Aged 50 to 59	198.8	172.1
Aged 60 to 69	198.3	170.5
Aged 70 to 79	187.4	155.6
Aged 80 or older	168.1	142.2

Note: Data are based on measured weight of a sample of the civilian noninstitutionalized population.
Source: National Center for Health Statistics, Anthropometric Reference Data for Children and Adults: United States, 2003–2006, National Health Statistics Reports, Number 10, 2008, Internet site http://www.cdc.gov/nchs/products/pubs/pubd/nhsr/nhsr.htm; calculations by New Strategist

Table 3.3 Weight Status by Sex and Age, 2003–06

(percent distribution of people aged 20 or older by weight status, sex, and age, 2003–06)

	total	healthy weight	overweight total	obese
TOTAL PEOPLE	**100.0%**	**31.4%**	**66.9%**	**34.1%**
Total men	**100.0**	**26.1**	**72.6**	**33.1**
Aged 20 to 34	100.0	35.9	61.6	26.2
Aged 35 to 44	100.0	24.1	75.2	37.0
Aged 45 to 54	100.0	20.8	78.5	34.6
Aged 55 to 64	100.0	19.3	79.7	39.3
Aged 65 to 74	100.0	21.2	78.0	33.0
Aged 75 or older	100.0	33.1	65.8	24.0
Total women	**100.0**	**36.6**	**61.2**	**35.2**
Aged 20 to 34	100.0	45.1	50.9	28.4
Aged 35 to 44	100.0	37.6	60.7	36.1
Aged 45 to 54	100.0	31.1	67.3	40.0
Aged 55 to 64	100.0	29.5	69.6	41.0
Aged 65 to 74	100.0	28.5	70.5	36.4
Aged 75 or older	100.0	35.4	62.6	24.2

Note: Data are based on measured height and weight of a sample of the civilian noninstitutionalized population. Overweight is defined as a body mass index of 25 or higher. Obesity is defined as a body mass index of 30 or higher. Body mass index is calculated by dividing weight in kilograms by height in meters squared.
Source: National Center for Health Statistics, Health United States, 2008, Internet site http://www.cdc.gov/nchs/hus.htm

Table 3.4 Leisure-Time Physical Activity Level by Sex and Age, 2006

(percent distribution of people aged 18 or older by leisure-time physical activity level, by sex and age, 2006)

	total	physically inactive	at least some physical activity	regular physical activity
TOTAL PEOPLE	**100.0%**	**39.5%**	**29.6%**	**30.9%**
Aged 18 to 24	100.0	34.8	27.1	38.1
Aged 25 to 44	100.0	35.0	31.6	33.4
Aged 45 to 54	100.0	38.2	30.7	31.1
Aged 55 to 64	100.0	41.9	30.9	27.2
Aged 65 to 74	100.0	48.0	25.8	26.2
Aged 75 or older	100.0	59.6	23.1	17.3
Total men	**100.0**	**38.5**	**27.4**	**33.1**
Aged 18 to 44	100.0	34.2	28.8	36.9
Aged 45 to 54	100.0	39.0	28.4	32.7
Aged 55 to 64	100.0	41.1	30.6	28.2
Aged 65 to 74	100.0	46.9	25.0	28.2
Aged 75 or older	100.0	52.1	26.6	21.4
Total women	**100.0**	**40.3**	**30.7**	**29.0**
Aged 18 to 44	100.0	35.6	32.0	32.4
Aged 45 to 54	100.0	37.5	33.0	29.5
Aged 55 to 64	100.0	42.6	31.1	26.3
Aged 65 to 74	100.0	49.0	26.5	24.5
Aged 75 or older	100.0	64.4	20.8	14.7

Note: "Physically inactive" are those with no sessions of light-to-moderate or vigorous leisure-time physical activity of at least 10 minutes duration during past week. "At least some physical activity" includes those with at least one light-to-moderate or vigorous leisure-time physical activity of at least 10 minutes duration during past week, but who did not meet the definition for regular leisure-time activity. "Regular physical activity" includes those who did three or more sessions per week of vigorous activity lasting at least 20 minutes or five or more sessions per week of light-to-moderate activity lasting at least 30 minutes.
Source: National Center for Health Statistics, Health United States, 2008, Internet site http://www.cdc.gov/nchs/hus.htm

Americans Report on Their Sexual Behavior

For most, sexual activity is limited to one partner.

Every few years the federal government fields the National Survey of Family Growth, which examines the sexual behavior, contraceptive use, and childbearing patterns of Americans aged 15 to 44. Results from the latest survey, taken in 2002, have been released by the National Center for Health Statistics.

Overall 90 percent of men and 91 percent of women aged 180. to 44 have had at least one opposite-sex partner in their lifetime. Even among 15-to-19-year-olds, 57 percent of men and 62 percent of women are sexually experienced. Men aged 15 to 44 have had a median of 5.6 opposite-sex partners in their lifetime, the figure peaking at 8.2 among men aged 40 to 44. Women have had a median of 3.3 partners in their lifetime, with a peak of 3.8 to 3.9 partners among women aged 30 or older. Among those with an opposite-sex partner in the past year, most had only one.

Ninety percent of men and women aged 15 to 44 identify themselves as heterosexual. Only 2 percent of men and 1 percent of women say they are homosexual. But 6 percent of men and 11 percent of women say they have had sexual activity with a same-sex partner in their lifetime (the 2002 survey questions regarding same-sex activity were worded differently for men and women, a factor that may explain the different percentages reporting same-sex activity).

■ Twenty-three percent of men and 9 percent of women report having had 15 or more opposite-sex partners in their lifetime.

Most Americans aged 18 or older are sexually active

(percent of people aged 15 to 44 who have had at least one opposite-sex partner during the past 12 months, by sex and age, 2002)

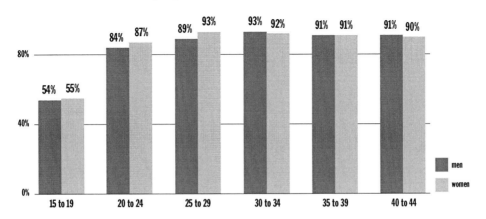

Table 3.5 Lifetime Sexual Activity of 15-to-44-Year-Olds by Sex, 2002

(number of people aged 15 to 44 and percent distribution by sexual experience with opposite-sex partners during lifetime, by sex and age, 2002; numbers in thousands)

	total		number of opposite-sex partners in lifetime							
	number	percent	none	1 or more	1	2	3 to 6	7 to 14	15 or more	median
Total men aged 15 to 44	**61,147**	**100.0%**	**9.6**	**90.4**	**12.5**	**8.0**	**27.2**	**19.5**	**23.2**	**5.6**
Aged 15 to 19	10,208	100.0	43.5	56.6	23.4	9.0	17.0	4.9	2.3	1.6
Aged 20 to 24	9,883	100.0	9.9	90.1	15.7	11.6	33.1	13.9	15.8	3.8
Aged 25 to 29	9,226	100.0	5.0	94.9	10.0	8.7	29.3	23.1	23.8	5.9
Aged 30 to 34	10,138	100.0	3.0	97.0	10.7	6.9	28.4	21.9	29.1	6.4
Aged 35 to 39	10,557	100.0	2.1	97.9	8.9	7.0	27.9	25.4	28.7	6.9
Aged 40 to 44	11,135	100.0	1.9	98.2	8.8	5.4	25.6	24.2	34.2	8.2
Total women aged 15 to 44	**61,561**	**100.0**	**8.6**	**91.4**	**22.5**	**10.8**	**32.6**	**16.3**	**9.2**	**3.3**
Aged 15 to 19	9,834	100.0	37.8	62.2	27.2	9.0	19.1	5.0	1.9	1.4
Aged 20 to 24	9,840	100.0	8.9	91.1	24.6	13.0	32.2	14.4	6.9	2.8
Aged 25 to 29	9,249	100.0	2.5	97.5	22.5	11.7	31.3	20.1	11.9	3.5
Aged 30 to 34	10,272	100.0	1.9	98.0	20.5	9.4	38.8	18.0	11.3	3.8
Aged 35 to 39	10,853	100.0	1.1	98.9	20.2	11.2	35.8	20.5	11.2	3.9
Aged 40 to 44	11,512	100.0	1.4	98.6	20.4	10.5	37.4	19.1	11.2	3.8

Source: National Center for Health Statistics, Sexual Behavior and Selected Health Measures: Men and Women 15–44 Years of Age, United States, 2002, Advance Data, No. 362, 2005, Internet site http://www.cdc.gov/nchs/nsfg.htm

Table 3.6 Past Year Sexual Activity of 15-to-44-Year-Olds by Sex, 2002

(percent distribution of people aged 15 to 44 by sexual experience with opposite-sex partners during the past 12 months, and percent distribution by number of opposite partners in past 12 months, by sex and age, 2002; numbers in thousands)

	total	no opposite-sex partners in past year	one or more opposite-sex partners in past year
Sexual activity in past year			
Total men	**100.0%**	**16.4%**	**83.6%**
Aged 15 to 19	100.0	46.2	53.8
Aged 20 to 24	100.0	15.6	84.4
Aged 25 to 29	100.0	11.4	88.6
Aged 30 to 34	100.0	7.4	92.7
Aged 35 to 39	100.0	9.3	90.8
Aged 40 to 44	100.0	9.0	91.1
Total women	**100.0**	**15.3**	**84.7**
Aged 15 to 19	100.0	44.8	55.3
Aged 20 to 24	100.0	13.4	86.7
Aged 25 to 29	100.0	6.9	93.0
Aged 30 to 34	100.0	7.9	92.1
Aged 35 to 39	100.0	9.2	90.8
Aged 40 to 44	100.0	10.5	89.5

	total with one or more	one	two	three or more	not reported
Number of sex partners in past year					
Total men	**100.0%**	**75.0%**	**9.6%**	**12.4%**	**3.0%**
Aged 15 to 19	100.0	56.3	21.9	19.9	1.9
Aged 20 to 24	100.0	58.4	15.0	22.9	3.7
Aged 25 to 29	100.0	75.7	7.4	14.1	2.7
Aged 30 to 34	100.0	80.7	7.3	9.4	2.6
Aged 35 to 39	100.0	84.6	5.5	7.5	2.4
Aged 40 to 44	100.0	83.9	6.0	5.8	4.3
Total women	**100.0**	**80.5**	**9.0**	**8.0**	**2.5**
Aged 15 to 19	100.0	58.2	17.5	20.4	3.8
Aged 20 to 24	100.0	70.2	14.5	13.3	2.0
Aged 25 to 29	100.0	81.6	10.1	6.1	2.2
Aged 30 to 34	100.0	86.5	6.1	5.4	2.0
Aged 35 to 39	100.0	86.2	6.7	4.8	2.2
Aged 40 to 44	100.0	88.7	3.8	4.1	3.4

Source: National Center for Health Statistics, Sexual Behavior and Selected Health Measures: Men and Women 15–44 Years of Age, United States, 2002, Advance Data, No. 362, 2005, Internet site http://www.cdc.gov/nchs/nsfg.htm; calculations by New Strategist

Table 3.7 Sexual Orientation of 18-to-44-Year-Olds, 2002

(number of people aged 18 to 44 and percent distribution by sexual orientation, by sex and age, 2002; numbers in thousands)

	total		sexual orientation				
	number	percent	heterosexual	homosexual	bisexual	something else	did not report
Total men 18 to 44	**55,399**	**100.0%**	**90.2%**	**2.3%**	**1.8%**	**3.9%**	**1.8%**
Aged 18 to 19	4,460	100.0	91.3	1.7	1.4	3.5	2.1
Aged 20 to 24	9,883	100.0	91.0	2.3	2.0	3.5	1.3
Aged 25 to 29	9,226	100.0	87.3	2.8	0.9	5.7	3.3
Aged 30 to 34	10,138	100.0	91.1	2.0	1.7	4.0	1.2
Aged 35 to 44	21,692	100.0	90.3	2.4	2.2	3.5	1.6
Total women 18 to 44	**55,742**	**100.0**	**90.3**	**1.3**	**2.8**	**3.8**	**1.8**
Aged 18 to 19	4,015	100.0	84.2	0.9	7.4	5.7	1.9
Aged 20 to 24	9,840	100.0	90.0	0.8	3.5	4.4	1.3
Aged 25 to 29	9,249	100.0	89.9	1.5	2.8	2.8	3.1
Aged 30 to 34	10,272	100.0	91.2	1.3	2.1	3.8	1.6
Aged 35 to 44	22,365	100.0	91.4	1.5	2.0	3.5	1.6

Source: National Center for Health Statistics, Sexual Behavior and Selected Health Measures: Men and Women 15–44 Years of Age, United States, 2002, Advance Data, No. 362, 2005, Internet site http://www.cdc.gov/nchs/nsfg.htm

Table 3.8 Lifetime Same-Sex Sexual Activity of 15-to-44-Year-Olds, 2002

(percent of people aged 15 to 44 reporting any sexual activity with same-sex partners in their lifetime, by age and sex, 2002)

	men	women
Total aged 15 to 44	**6.0%**	**11.2%**
Aged 15 to 19	4.5	10.6
Aged 20 to 24	5.5	14.2
Aged 25 to 29	5.7	14.1
Aged 30 to 34	6.2	9.1
Aged 35 to 39	8.0	12.3
Aged 40 to 44	6.0	7.8

Note: The question about same-sex sexual contact was worded differently for men and women. Women were asked whether they had ever had a sexual experience of any kind with another female. Men were asked whether they had performed any of four specific sexual acts with another male. The question asked of women may have elicited more yes answers than the questions asked of men.
Source: National Center for Health Statistics, Sexual Behavior and Selected Health Measures: Men and Women 15–44 Years of Age, United States, 2002, Advance Data, No. 362, 2005, Internet site http://www.cdc.gov/nchs/nsfg.htm

Birth Rate Has Fallen among Women under Age 30

Rate has increased among women aged 30 or older.

Between 1990 and 2006, the birth rate fell for women under age 30. The biggest decline occurred among teenagers, the number of births per 1,000 women aged 15 to 19 falling by 20 percent. The birth rate among 20-to-29-year-olds fell 6 percent during those years. Interestingly, the birth rate among 25-to-29-year old women bottomed out in 1997 and has been rising since then.

The birth rate has climbed substantially among women aged 30 or older since 1990. Behind the increase is catch-up childbearing by women who had postponed starting a family while they went to college and embarked on a career.

■ One reason for the recent rise in the birth rate among women aged 25 to 29 is the growing Hispanic population.

Birth rate peaks in the 25-to-29 age group

(births per 1,000 women in age group, 2006)

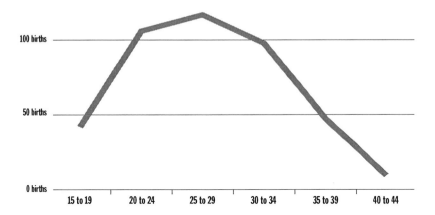

Table 3.9 Birth Rate by Age, 1990 to 2006

(number of live births per 1,000 women in age group, 1990 to 2006; percent change in rate, 1990–2000 and 2000–06)

	total	15 to 19	20 to 24	25 to 29	30 to 34	35 to 39	40 to 44	45 to 49
2006	68.5	41.9	105.9	116.7	97.7	47.3	9.4	0.6
2005	66.7	40.5	102.2	115.5	95.8	46.3	9.1	0.6
2004	66.3	41.1	101.7	115.5	95.3	45.4	8.9	0.5
2003	66.1	41.6	102.6	115.6	95.1	43.8	8.7	0.5
2002	64.8	43.0	103.6	113.6	91.5	41.4	8.3	0.5
2001	65.3	45.3	106.2	113.4	91.9	40.6	8.1	0.5
2000	65.9	47.7	109.7	113.5	91.2	39.7	8.0	0.5
1999	64.4	48.8	107.9	111.2	87.1	37.8	7.4	0.4
1998	64.3	50.3	108.4	110.2	85.2	36.9	7.4	0.4
1997	63.6	51.3	107.3	108.3	83.0	35.7	7.1	0.4
1996	64.1	53.5	107.8	108.6	82.1	34.9	6.8	0.3
1995	64.6	56.0	107.5	108.8	81.1	34.0	6.6	0.3
1994	65.9	58.2	109.2	111.0	80.4	33.4	6.4	0.3
1993	67.0	59.0	111.3	113.2	79.9	32.7	6.1	0.3
1992	68.4	60.3	113.7	115.7	79.6	32.3	5.9	0.3
1991	69.3	61.8	115.3	117.2	79.2	31.9	5.5	0.2
1990	70.9	59.9	116.5	120.2	80.8	31.7	5.5	0.2
Percent change								
2000 to 2006	3.9%	–12.2%	–3.5%	2.8%	7.1%	19.1%	17.5%	20.0%
1990 to 2000	–7.1	–20.4	–5.8	–5.6	12.9	25.2	45.5	150.0

Source: National Center for Health Statistics, Births: Final Data for 2006, National Vital Statistics Reports, Vol. 57, No. 7, 2009, Internet site http://www.cdc.gov/nchs/births.htm; calculations by New Strategist

Most Women Are Mothers by Age 30

Among women aged 15 to 44, the largest share has had two children.

The proportion of women who have never had a child falls from 93 percent among 15-to-19-year-olds to a much smaller (but still substantial) 19 percent among women aged 35 to 39. Overall, 55 percent of women aged 15 to 44 have had at least one child. The largest share (22 percent) have had two.

Six percent of women aged 15 to 44 had a baby in the past year, according to a 2006 survey. Women aged 25 to 29 are most likely to have had a baby in the past year, with 10 percent giving birth. By race and Hispanic origin, Hispanics are most likely to have had a baby in the past year, at 8 percent. Six percent of native-born women aged 15 to 44 had a child in the past year. Among foreign-born women, the figure is a larger 8 percent.

■ The two-child family has been the norm in the United States for several decades.

Most women aged 25 or older have had at least one child

(percent of women aged 15 to 44 who have had one or more children, by age, 2006)

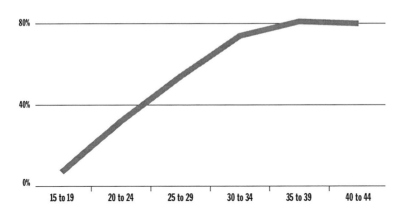

Table 3.10 Number of Children Born to Women Aged 15 to 44, 2006

(total number of women aged 15 to 44, and percent distribution by number of children ever borne, by age, 2006; numbers in thousands)

	total		number of children							
	number	percent	none	one or more	one	two	three	four	five or six	seven or more
Total aged 15 to 44	**61,683**	**100.0%**	**45.1%**	**54.9%**	**17.0%**	**21.7%**	**10.8%**	**3.7%**	**1.4%**	**0.3%**
Aged 15 to 19	10,269	100.0	93.3	6.7	4.5	1.5	0.5	0.2	0.0	0.0
Aged 20 to 24	10,079	100.0	68.6	31.6	18.8	9.3	2.7	0.6	0.1	0.1
Aged 25 to 29	10,004	100.0	45.6	54.4	22.9	19.4	8.5	2.8	0.7	0.1
Aged 30 to 34	9,647	100.0	26.2	73.9	21.8	29.3	15.3	5.3	1.9	0.3
Aged 35 to 39	10,450	100.0	18.9	81.0	17.6	35.4	18.5	6.5	2.5	0.5
Aged 40 to 44	11,235	100.0	20.4	79.7	16.9	34.4	18.5	6.4	3.0	0.5

Source: Bureau of the Census, Fertility of American Women, Current Population Survey—June 2006, Detailed Tables, Internet site http://www.census.gov/population/www/socdemo/fertility/cps2006.html; calculations by New Strategist

Table 3.11 Women Giving Birth in the Past Year, 2006

(total number of women aged 15 to 44, number and percent who gave birth in the past year, and number and percent who had a first birth in past year, by age, 2006; numbers in thousands)

	total	gave birth in past year		first birth in past year	
		number	percent	number	percent
TOTAL AGED 15 TO 44	**61,683**	**3,974**	**6.4%**	**1,551**	**2.5%**
Age					
Aged 15 to 19	10,269	417	4.1	243	2.4
Aged 20 to 24	10,079	935	9.3	483	4.8
Aged 25 to 29	10,004	1,046	10.5	401	4.0
Aged 30 to 34	9,647	888	9.2	277	2.9
Aged 35 to 39	10,450	579	5.5	121	1.2
Aged 40 to 44	11,235	109	1.0	26	0.2
Race and Hispanic origin					
Asian	3,391	202	6.0	88	2.6
Black	9,272	538	5.8	218	2.4
Hispanic	10,099	830	8.2	309	3.1
Non-Hispanic white	38,532	2,383	6.2	923	2.4
Nativity status					
Native born	52,002	3,203	6.2	1,237	2.4
Foreign born	9,681	771	8.0	314	3.2
Region					
Northeast	11,176	667	6.0	262	2.3
Midwest	13,557	905	6.7	356	2.6
South	22,546	1,406	6.2	560	2.5
West	14,404	996	6.9	373	2.6

Note: Numbers by race and Hispanic origin do not add to total because Asians and blacks include those who identified themselves as being of the race alone and those who identified themselves as being of the race in combination with other races, and because Hispanics may be of any race. Non-Hispanic whites are those who identified themselves as being white alone and not Hispanic.

Source: Bureau of the Census, Fertility of American Women, Current Population Survey—June 2006, Detailed Tables, Internet site http://www.census.gov/population/www/socdemo/fertility/cps2006.html; calculations by New Strategist

The Millennial Generation Now Dominates Births

Nearly two-thirds of babies are born to women under age 30.

Despite an increase in the number of older mothers during the past few decades, the great majority of women who give birth are in their teens and twenties. Women under age 30 accounted for the 64 percent majority of births in 2007 (the Millennial generation was aged 13 to 30 in that year).

Among blacks and Hispanics, the Millennial generation accounts for fully 70 to 74 percent of births. For non-Hispanic whites, women under age 30 account for a smaller 60 percent of births. Among Asians, the figure is just 44 percent. Many Asian women postpone childbearing until they are in their thirties because most spend much of their twenties in college.

Among women under age 20 who gave birth in 2007, the great majority was having a first child. Among women aged 20 to 29, however, fewer than half of those who gave birth in 2007 were having a first child.

■ The Millennial generation has replaced Generation X as the dominant group entering parenthood.

Millennials are the majority of new mothers

(percent distribution of births by age of mother, 2007)

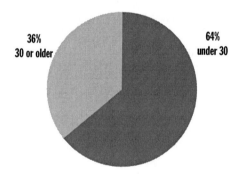

36%
30 or older

64%
under 30

Table 3.12 Births by Age, Race, and Hispanic Origin, 2007

(number and percent distribution of births by age, race, and Hispanic origin of mother, 2007)

	total	American Indian	Asian	non-Hispanic black	Hispanic	non-Hispanic white
Total births	**4,317,119**	**49,284**	**254,734**	**627,230**	**1,061,970**	**2,312,473**
Under age 15	6,218	120	92	2,326	2,407	1,269
Aged 15 to 19	445,045	8,925	8,022	106,224	148,453	173,104
Aged 20 to 24	1,082,837	16,759	32,309	200,273	305,107	526,943
Aged 25 to 29	1,208,504	12,420	71,465	157,173	287,730	676,599
Aged 30 to 34	962,179	7,052	86,949	97,332	201,212	566,197
Aged 35 to 39	499,916	3,265	46,379	50,614	95,694	301,666
Aged 40 to 44	105,071	704	8,879	12,428	20,273	62,152
Aged 45 to 54	7,349	38	639	860	1,095	4,544

PERCENT DISTRIBUTION BY RACE AND HISPANIC ORIGIN

Total births	**100.0%**	**1.1%**	**5.9%**	**14.5%**	**24.6%**	**53.6%**
Under age 15	100.0	1.9	1.5	37.4	38.7	20.4
Aged 15 to 19	100.0	2.0	1.8	23.9	33.4	38.9
Aged 20 to 24	100.0	1.5	3.0	18.5	28.2	48.7
Aged 25 to 29	100.0	1.0	5.9	13.0	23.8	56.0
Aged 30 to 34	100.0	0.7	9.0	10.1	20.9	58.8
Aged 35 to 39	100.0	0.7	9.3	10.1	19.1	60.3
Aged 40 to 44	100.0	0.7	8.5	11.8	19.3	59.2
Aged 45 to 54	100.0	0.5	8.7	11.7	14.9	61.8

PERCENT DISTRIBUTION BY AGE

Total births	**100.0%**	**100.0%**	**100.0%**	**100.0%**	**100.0%**	**100.0%**
Under age 15	0.1	0.2	0.0	0.4	0.2	0.1
Aged 15 to 19	10.3	18.1	3.1	16.9	14.0	7.5
Aged 20 to 24	25.1	34.0	12.7	31.9	28.7	22.8
Aged 25 to 29	28.0	25.2	28.1	25.1	27.1	29.3
Aged 30 to 34	22.3	14.3	34.1	15.5	18.9	24.5
Aged 35 to 39	11.6	6.6	18.2	8.1	9.0	13.0
Aged 40 to 44	2.4	1.4	3.5	2.0	1.9	2.7
Aged 45 to 54	0.2	0.1	0.3	0.1	0.1	0.2

Note: Births by race and Hispanic origin do not add to total because Hispanics may be of any race and "not stated" is not shown.
Source: National Center for Health Statistics, Births: Preliminary Data for 2007, National Vital Statistics Reports, Vol. 57, No. 12, 2009, Internet site http://www.cdc.gov/nchs/products/nvsr.htm#57_12; calculations by New Strategist

Table 3.13 Births by Age of Mother and Birth Order, 2007

(number and percent distribution of births by age of mother and birth order, 2007)

	total	first child	second child	third child	fourth or later child
Total births	**4,317,119**	**1,726,523**	**1,364,048**	**722,883**	**483,766**
Under age 15	6,218	6,088	99	2	1
Aged 15 to 19	445,045	357,092	73,891	10,863	1,472
Aged 20 to 24	1,082,837	524,240	359,732	141,942	52,063
Aged 25 to 29	1,208,504	432,011	400,000	230,640	140,490
Aged 30 to 34	962,179	270,057	334,881	201,033	151,655
Aged 35 to 39	499,916	112,833	163,927	114,878	105,601
Aged 40 to 44	105,071	22,322	29,721	22,220	30,175
Aged 45 to 54	7,349	1,881	1,797	1,307	2,310

PERCENT DISTRIBUTION BY BIRTH ORDER

	total	first child	second child	third child	fourth or later child
Total births	**100.0%**	**40.0%**	**31.6%**	**16.7%**	**11.2%**
Under age 15	100.0	97.9	1.6	0.0	0.0
Aged 15 to 19	100.0	80.2	16.6	2.4	0.3
Aged 20 to 24	100.0	48.4	33.2	13.1	4.8
Aged 25 to 29	100.0	35.7	33.1	19.1	11.6
Aged 30 to 34	100.0	28.1	34.8	20.9	15.8
Aged 35 to 39	100.0	22.6	32.8	23.0	21.1
Aged 40 to 44	100.0	21.2	28.3	21.1	28.7
Aged 45 to 54	100.0	25.6	24.5	17.8	31.4

PERCENT DISTRIBUTION BY AGE

	total	first child	second child	third child	fourth or later child
Total births	**100.0%**	**100.0%**	**100.0%**	**100.0%**	**100.0%**
Under age 15	0.1	0.4	0.0	0.0	0.0
Aged 15 to 19	10.3	20.7	5.4	1.5	0.3
Aged 20 to 24	25.1	30.4	26.4	19.6	10.8
Aged 25 to 29	28.0	25.0	29.3	31.9	29.0
Aged 30 to 34	22.3	15.6	24.6	27.8	31.3
Aged 35 to 39	11.6	6.5	12.0	15.9	21.8
Aged 40 to 44	2.4	1.3	2.2	3.1	6.2
Aged 45 to 54	0.2	0.1	0.1	0.2	0.5

Note: Numbers do not add to total because "not stated" is not shown.
Source: National Center for Health Statistics, Births: Preliminary Data for 2007, National Vital Statistics Reports, Vol. 57, No. 12, 2009, Internet site http://www.cdc.gov/nchs/products/nvsr.htm#57_12; calculations by New Strategist

Many Millennial Mothers Are Not Married

Out-of-wedlock births fall with age.

Nearly 40 percent of babies born in 2007 had a mother who was not married. There are sharp differences by age in the percentage of new mothers who are not married, however. The younger the woman, the more likely she is to give birth out of wedlock.

Among babies born to women under age 25 in 2007, most were born to single mothers. The figure falls to 32 percent in the 25-to-29 age group. Among babies born to women aged 30 or older, from 17 to 20 percent had a single mother.

■ Out-of-wedlock childbearing has increased enormously over the past few decades and has become common even among older mothers.

Sixty percent of babies born to women aged 20 to 24 are out of wedlock

(percent of babies born to unmarried women, by age of mother, 2007)

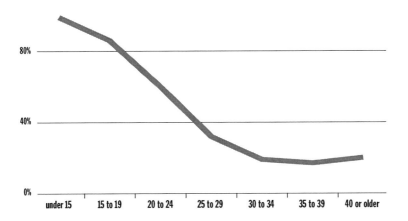

Table 3.14 Births to Unmarried Women by Age, 2007

(total number of births and number and percent to unmarried women, by age of mother, 2007)

| | total | unmarried women | | |
		number	percent distribution	percent of total
Total births	**4,317,119**	**1,714,643**	**100.0%**	**39.7%**
Under age 15	6,218	6,142	0.4	98.8
Aged 15 to 19	445,045	380,560	22.2	85.5
Aged 20 to 24	1,082,837	644,591	37.6	59.5
Aged 25 to 29	1,208,504	389,169	22.7	32.2
Aged 30 to 34	962,179	185,425	10.8	19.3
Aged 35 to 39	499,916	86,343	5.0	17.3
Aged 40 to 54	112,420	22,411	1.3	19.9

Source: National Center for Health Statistics, Births: Preliminary Data for 2007, National Vital Statistics Reports, Vol. 57, No. 12, 2009, Internet site http://www.cdc.gov/nchs/products/nvsr.htm#57_12; calculations by New Strategist

Caesarean Deliveries Are Common among Women of All Ages

The rate is highest among older women, however.

Delayed childbearing can have an unanticipated cost. The older a woman is when she has a child, the greater the likelihood of complications that necessitate Caesarean delivery.

Among babies born in 2006, fully 31 percent were delivered by Caesarean section. The figure ranges from only 22 percent of babies born to women under age 20 to 41 percent of babies born to women aged 35 to 39 and nearly half (47 percent) of those born to women aged 40 or older.

■ As women delay childbearing, the rate of Caesarean delivery increases. With new fertility technologies enabling more women to have children later in life, the rate is likely to rise further.

Younger mothers are least likely to require a Caesarean delivery

(percent of births delivered by Caesarean section, by age of mother, 2006)

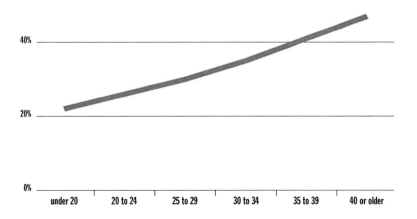

Table 3.15 Births by Age and Method of Delivery, 2006

(number and percent distribution of births by age of mother and method of delivery, 2006)

	total births	vaginal	Caesarean
Total births	**4,265,555**	**2,929,590**	**1,321,054**
Under age 20	441,832	342,977	97,806
Aged 20 to 24	1,080,437	792,028	285,227
Aged 25 to 29	1,181,899	826,822	351,002
Aged 30 to 34	950,258	615,784	330,783
Aged 35 to 39	498,616	293,352	202,987
Aged 40 or older	112,513	58,627	53,249

PERCENT DISTRIBUTION BY METHOD OF DELIVERY

Total births	**100.0%**	**68.7%**	**31.0%**
Under age 20	100.0	77.6	22.1
Aged 20 to 24	100.0	73.3	26.4
Aged 25 to 29	100.0	70.0	29.7
Aged 30 to 34	100.0	64.8	34.8
Aged 35 to 39	100.0	58.8	40.7
Aged 40 or older	100.0	52.1	47.3

PERCENT DISTRIBUTION BY AGE

Total births	**100.0%**	**100.0%**	**100.0%**
Under age 20	10.4	11.7	7.4
Aged 20 to 24	25.3	27.0	21.6
Aged 25 to 29	27.7	28.2	26.6
Aged 30 to 34	22.3	21.0	25.0
Aged 35 to 39	11.7	10.0	15.4
Aged 40 or older	2.6	2.0	4.0

Note: Numbers do not add to total because "not stated" is not shown.
Source: National Center for Health Statistics, Births: Final Data for 2006, National Vital Statistics Reports, Vol. 57, No. 7, 2009, Internet site http://www.cdc.gov/nchs/births.htm; calculations by New Strategist

Cigarette Smoking Is above Average among Millennials

Many young adults have smoked cigarettes in the past month.

Cigarette smoking has been declining in the population as a whole, but among young adults it remains stubbornly high. Overall, 24 percent of people aged 12 or older have smoked a cigarette in the past month, according to a 2007 survey. The proportion surpasses the national average among 18-year-olds and peaks at 40 percent among 22-year-olds.

A separate government survey shows that 23 to 24 percent of people ranging in age from 18 to 34 are current smokers. Among 18-to-24-year-olds, 70 percent say they have never smoked. The figure drops to just 58 percent in the 25-to-34 age group.

■ Although smoking is becoming less common, many young adults experiment with cigarettes and some will become lifelong smokers.

A large share of Millennials smoke cigarettes

(percent distribution of people aged 18 to 34 by cigarette smoking status, 2007)

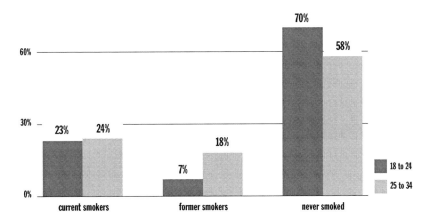

Table 3.16 Cigarette Smoking among People Aged 12 or Older, 2007

(percent of people aged 12 or older reporting any, past year, and past month use of cigarettes, 2007)

	ever smoked	smoked in past year	smoked in past month
Total people	**65.3%**	**28.5%**	**24.2%**
Aged 12 to 17	23.7	15.7	9.8
Aged 18	51.5	38.7	29.7
Aged 19	60.5	45.5	33.2
Aged 20	64.0	44.9	35.7
Aged 21	64.6	45.1	37.1
Aged 22	67.7	49.4	40.3
Aged 23	71.0	48.4	39.8
Aged 24	71.0	47.4	39.5
Aged 25	71.4	42.8	35.7
Aged 26 to 29	70.1	41.4	35.7
Aged 30 to 34	68.3	36.0	31.5
Aged 35 to 39	70.0	32.9	28.5
Aged 40 to 44	70.5	30.3	26.6
Aged 45 to 49	74.9	32.3	29.6
Aged 50 to 54	75.2	29.7	26.7
Aged 55 to 59	73.6	24.6	22.0
Aged 60 to 64	76.3	20.5	18.8
Aged 65 or older	65.1	10.8	9.0

Source: SAMHSA, Office of Applied Studies, National Survey on Drug Use and Health, 2007, Internet site http://www.oas .samhsa.gov/nsduh/2k7nsduh/2k7Results.pdf

Table 3.17 Cigarette Smoking Status by Age, 2008

(percent distribution of people aged 18 or older by age and cigarette smoking status, 2008)

		current smokers				
	total	total	smoke every day	smoke some days	former smoker	never smoked
Total people	**100.0%**	**18.2%**	**13.4%**	**4.8%**	**25.2%**	**55.3%**
Aged 18 to 24	100.0	23.0	15.8	7.2	7.2	70.0
Aged 25 to 34	100.0	23.5	16.8	6.7	17.6	58.4
Aged 35 to 44	100.0	20.0	14.9	5.1	18.7	60.6
Aged 45 to 54	100.0	20.5	16.0	4.5	25.2	52.4
Aged 55 to 64	100.0	16.4	12.4	4.0	35.0	46.6
Aged 65 or older	100.0	8.0	6.0	2.0	42.9	48.8

Source: Centers for Disease Control and Prevention, Behavioral Risk Factor Surveillance System Prevalence Data, 2008, Internet site http://apps.nccd.cdc.gov/brfss/index.asp; calculations by New Strategist

Most Young Adults Have Had a Drink in the Past Month

Drinking peaks among 21-year-olds.

More than half of Americans aged 12 or older have had an alcoholic beverage in the past month. The figure peaks at 72 percent among 21-year-olds, perhaps in celebration of the fact that they have reached legal drinking age. Few young adults wait until their 21st birthday before they have a drink, however. The majority of 19- and 20-year-olds have had alcohol in the past month.

Many young adults take part in binge drinking, meaning they have had five or more drinks on one occasion in the past month. More than one in 10 people ranging in age from 19 to 29 have participated in heavy drinking during the past month—meaning they have binged at least five times during the month.

In another government survey asking people aged 18 or older whether they have had a drink in the past 30 days, half of 18-to-24-year-olds say yes. The figure rises to 61 percent in the 25-to-34 age group.

■ Among young adults, heavy drinking is a bigger problem than drug use.

Most young adults do not wait for legal drinking age

(percent of people aged 18 to 24 who have had an alcoholic drink in the past 30 days, by age, 2007)

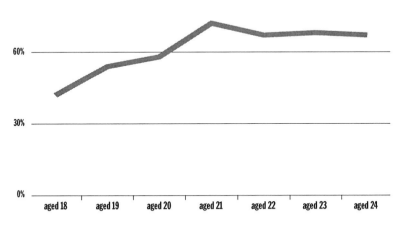

Table 3.18 Alcohol Use by People Aged 12 or Older, 2007

(percent of people aged 12 or older who drank alcoholic beverages during the past month, by level of alcohol use, 2007)

	drank at any time during past month	binge drinking during past month	heavy drinking during past month
Total people	**51.1%**	**23.3%**	**6.9%**
Aged 18	41.8	28.9	9.6
Aged 19	53.7	38.8	14.1
Aged 20	57.8	40.3	15.8
Aged 21	71.8	50.1	17.9
Aged 22	66.5	46.9	16.9
Aged 23	68.4	45.3	16.2
Aged 24	67.4	44.3	15.6
Aged 25	67.3	42.7	12.6
Aged 26 to 29	63.2	37.9	10.5
Aged 30 to 34	62.1	32.6	9.0
Aged 35 to 39	59.1	28.4	8.5
Aged 40 to 44	60.9	27.9	7.3
Aged 45 to 49	58.3	23.9	7.8
Aged 50 to 54	57.0	21.5	6.3
Aged 55 to 59	52.0	15.9	4.5
Aged 60 to 64	47.6	12.1	2.9
Aged 65 or older	38.1	7.6	1.4

Note: "Binge drinking" is defined as having five or more drinks on the same occasion on at least one day in the 30 days prior to the survey. "Heavy drinking" is having five or more drinks on the same occasion on each of five or more days in 30 days prior to the survey.
Source: SAMHSA, Office of Applied Studies, National Survey on Drug Use and Health, 2007, Internet site http://www.oas.samhsa.gov/nsduh/2k7nsduh/2k7Results.pdf

Table 3.19 Alcohol Use by Age, 2008

(percent distribution of people aged 18 or older by whether they have had at least one drink of alcohol within the past 30 days, by age, 2008)

	total	yes	no
Total people	**100.0%**	**54.4%**	**45.5%**
Aged 18 to 24	100.0	49.9	50.0
Aged 25 to 34	100.0	60.5	39.4
Aged 35 to 44	100.0	60.5	39.4
Aged 45 to 54	100.0	58.4	41.5
Aged 55 to 64	100.0	53.4	46.5
Aged 65 or older	100.0	40.6	59.3

Source: Centers for Disease Control and Prevention, Behavioral Risk Factor Surveillance System Prevalence Data, 2008, Internet site http://apps.nccd.cdc.gov/brfss/index.asp

Drug Use Is Prevalent among Young Adults

At least one in five 18-to-22-year-olds has used an illicit drug in the past month.

Among Americans aged 12 or older, only 8 percent have used an illicit drug in the past month. Young adults are much more likely to be current drug users than the average person. Among 18-to-22-year-olds, the prevalence of illicit drug use in the past month ranges from 20 to 23 percent. For many, if not most, the illicit drug is marijuana.

Marijuana is widely used by young adults, and even the middle aged are likely to have used marijuana. The majority or near majority of people ranging in age from 20 to 54 have used marijuana at some point in their lives. Among people aged 18 to 25, from 13 to 19 percent have used marijuana in the past month.

■ Although many Americans have used marijuana, support for legalizing the drug remains low.

Many young adults use marijuana

(percent of people aged 18 to 24 who have used marijuana in the past month, by age, 2007)

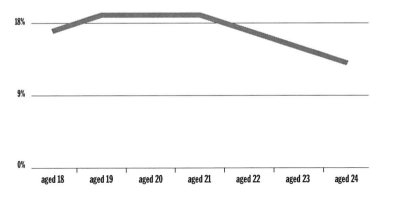

Table 3.20 Illicit Drug Use by People Aged 12 or Older, 2007

(percent of people aged 12 or older who ever used any illicit drug, who used an illicit drug in the past year, and who used an illicit drug in the past month, by age, 2007)

	ever used	used in past year	used in past month
Total people	**46.1%**	**14.4%**	**8.0%**
Aged 12 to 17	26.2	18.7	9.5
Aged 18	46.9	34.8	20.7
Aged 19	53.3	36.6	22.3
Aged 20	57.1	36.6	22.0
Aged 21	60.3	37.6	23.1
Aged 22	59.6	32.8	20.0
Aged 23	62.7	31.6	17.5
Aged 24	62.1	28.7	16.1
Aged 25	60.1	25.4	15.4
Aged 26 to 29	57.8	23.0	12.8
Aged 30 to 34	55.5	16.9	9.4
Aged 35 to 39	56.1	13.9	7.3
Aged 40 to 44	58.6	13.1	7.0
Aged 45 to 49	61.0	11.9	7.2
Aged 50 to 54	58.9	10.6	5.7
Aged 55 to 59	51.6	8.0	4.1
Aged 60 to 64	35.0	4.4	1.9
Aged 65 or older	10.7	1.0	0.7

Note: Illicit drugs include marijuana, hashish, cocaine (including crack), heroin, hallucinogens, inhalants, or any prescription-type psychotherapeutic used nonmedically.
Source: SAMHSA, Office of Applied Studies, National Survey on Drug Use and Health, 2007, Internet site http://www.oas .samhsa.gov/nsduh/2k7nsduh/2k7Results.pdf

Table 3.21 Marijuana Use by People Aged 12 or Older, 2007

(percent of people aged 12 or older who ever used marijuana, who used marijuana in the past year, and who used marijuana in the past month, by age, 2007)

	ever used	used in past year	used in past month
Total people	**40.6%**	**10.1%**	**5.8%**
Aged 12 to 17	16.2	12.5	6.7
Aged 18	39.5	28.3	17.1
Aged 19	46.8	31.4	18.9
Aged 20	50.8	31.5	19.2
Aged 21	53.8	31.0	18.9
Aged 22	53.1	27.4	16.7
Aged 23	57.0	25.1	14.6
Aged 24	55.2	23.0	12.7
Aged 25	52.8	20.3	12.5
Aged 26 to 29	52.0	17.4	9.8
Aged 30 to 34	48.8	11.1	6.3
Aged 35 to 39	49.8	8.9	5.4
Aged 40 to 44	53.5	8.0	4.5
Aged 45 to 49	56.9	7.9	4.9
Aged 50 to 54	54.8	6.7	3.8
Aged 55 to 59	46.2	4.4	2.1
Aged 60 to 64	29.6	1.9	0.6
Aged 65 or older	8.4	0.3	0.2

Source: SAMHSA, Office of Applied Studies, National Survey on Drug Use and Health, 2007, Internet site http://oas.samhsa .gov/NSDUH/2k7NSDUH/tabs/Sect1peTabs1to46.htm#Tab1.1A

Millennials Are Most Likely to Lack Health Insurance

More than one in four has no insurance.

People aged 18 to 24 are most likely to be without health insurance. Entering the workforce at the age of 18, or graduating from college at the age of 21, usually means health insurance coverage is no longer available through a parent's plan. This partly explains why a substantial 28 percent of the nation's 18-to-24-year-olds lack health insurance. Among 25-to-34-year-olds, the figure is not much better, with 26 percent lacking health insurance.

Most Americans obtain health insurance coverage through their employer. But among 18-to-24-year-olds, only 48 percent had employment-based coverage and just 19 percent had coverage through their own employer. In the 25-to-34 age group, the percentage with employment-based coverage increases to 61 percent, but fewer than half have coverage through their own employer. Among all 18-to-44-year-olds without health insurance in 2007, the single biggest reason for not having coverage was the high cost, cited by 49 percent.

■ The economic downturn is likely to increase the percentage of Millennials without health insurance.

Many Americans do not have health insurance coverage

(percent of people aged 18 or older without health insurance, by age, 2007)

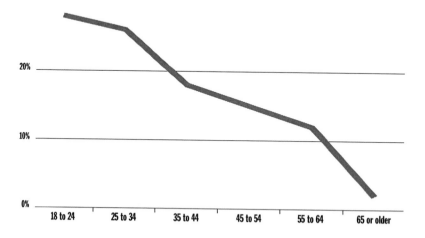

Table 3.22 Health Insurance Coverage by Age, 2007

(number and percent distribution of people by age and health insurance coverage status, 2007; numbers in thousands)

		with health insurance			
	total	total	private	government	not covered
Total people	**299,106**	**253,449**	**201,991**	**83,031**	**45,657**
Under age 18	74,403	66,254	47,750	23,041	8,149
Aged 18 to 24	28,398	20,407	17,074	4,428	7,991
Aged 25 to 34	40,146	29,817	26,430	4,539	10,329
Aged 35 to 44	42,132	34,415	31,067	4,546	7,717
Aged 45 to 54	43,935	37,161	33,350	5,363	6,774
Aged 55 to 64	33,302	29,291	25,114	6,651	4,011
Aged 65 or older	36,790	36,103	21,206	34,464	686
PERCENT DISTRIBUTION BY COVERAGE STATUS					
Total people	**100.0%**	**84.7%**	**67.5%**	**27.8%**	**15.3%**
Under age 18	100.0	89.0	64.2	31.0	11.0
Aged 18 to 24	100.0	71.9	60.1	15.6	28.1
Aged 25 to 34	100.0	74.3	65.8	11.3	25.7
Aged 35 to 44	100.0	81.7	73.7	10.8	18.3
Aged 45 to 54	100.0	84.6	75.9	12.2	15.4
Aged 55 to 64	100.0	88.0	75.4	20.0	12.0
Aged 65 or older	100.0	98.1	57.6	93.7	1.9
PERCENT DISTRIBUTION BY AGE					
Total people	**100.0%**	**100.0%**	**100.0%**	**100.0%**	**100.0%**
Under age 18	24.9	26.1	23.6	27.7	17.8
Aged 18 to 24	9.5	8.1	8.5	5.3	17.5
Aged 25 to 34	13.4	11.8	13.1	5.5	22.6
Aged 35 to 44	14.1	13.6	15.4	5.5	16.9
Aged 45 to 54	14.7	14.7	16.5	6.5	14.8
Aged 55 to 64	11.1	11.6	12.4	8.0	8.8
Aged 65 or older	12.3	14.2	10.5	41.5	1.5

Note: Numbers may not add to total because some people have more than one type of health insurance coverage.
Source: Bureau of the Census, Health Insurance, Table HI01, Internet site http://pubdb3.census.gov/macro/032008/health/toc
.htm; calculations by New Strategist

Table 3.23 Private Health Insurance Coverage by Age, 2007

(number and percent distribution of people by age and private health insurance coverage status, 2007; numbers in thousands)

| | | with private health insurance | | | |
| | | total | employment based | | |
	total	total	total	own	direct purchase
Total people	**299,106**	**201,991**	**177,446**	**93,774**	**26,673**
Under age 18	74,403	47,750	44,252	227	3,930
Aged 18 to 24	28,398	17,074	13,747	5,386	1,635
Aged 25 to 34	40,146	26,430	24,505	19,005	2,347
Aged 35 to 44	42,132	31,067	29,009	20,616	2,687
Aged 45 to 54	43,935	33,350	30,805	22,486	3,292
Aged 55 to 64	33,302	25,114	22,569	16,612	3,237
Aged 65 or older	36,790	21,206	12,558	9,442	9,546
PERCENT DISTRIBUTION BY COVERAGE STATUS					
Total people	**100.0%**	**67.5%**	**59.3%**	**31.4%**	**8.9%**
Under age 18	100.0	64.2	59.5	0.3	5.3
Aged 18 to 24	100.0	60.1	48.4	19.0	5.8
Aged 25 to 34	100.0	65.8	61.0	47.3	5.8
Aged 35 to 44	100.0	73.7	68.9	48.9	6.4
Aged 45 to 54	100.0	75.9	70.1	51.2	7.5
Aged 55 to 64	100.0	75.4	67.8	49.9	9.7
Aged 65 or older	100.0	57.6	34.1	25.7	25.9
PERCENT DISTRIBUTION BY AGE					
Total people	**100.0%**	**100.0%**	**100.0%**	**100.0%**	**100.0%**
Under age 18	24.9	23.6	24.9	0.2	14.7
Aged 18 to 24	9.5	8.5	7.7	5.7	6.1
Aged 25 to 34	13.4	13.1	13.8	20.3	8.8
Aged 35 to 44	14.1	15.4	16.3	22.0	10.1
Aged 45 to 54	14.7	16.5	17.4	24.0	12.3
Aged 55 to 64	11.1	12.4	12.7	17.7	12.1
Aged 65 or older	12.3	10.5	7.1	10.1	35.8

Note: Numbers may not add to total because some people have more than one type of health insurance coverage.
Source: Bureau of the Census, Health Insurance, Table HI01, Internet site http://pubdb3.census.gov/macro/032008/health/toc .htm; calculations by New Strategist

Table 3.24 Government Health Insurance Coverage by Age, 2007

(number and percent distribution of people by age and government health insurance coverage status, 2007; numbers in thousands)

| | | with government health insurance | | | |
	total	total	Medicaid	Medicare	military
Total people	**299,106**	**83,031**	**39,554**	**41,375**	**10,955**
Under age 18	74,403	23,041	20,899	518	2,101
Aged 18 to 24	28,398	4,428	3,563	180	823
Aged 25 to 34	40,146	4,539	3,237	501	1,047
Aged 35 to 44	42,132	4,546	3,027	924	1,016
Aged 45 to 54	43,935	5,363	3,103	1,795	1,285
Aged 55 to 64	33,302	6,651	2,462	3,179	2,079
Aged 65 or older	36,790	34,464	3,263	34,278	2,604
PERCENT DISTRIBUTION BY COVERAGE STATUS					
Total people	**100.0%**	**27.8%**	**13.2%**	**13.8%**	**3.7%**
Under age 18	100.0	31.0	28.1	0.7	2.8
Aged 18 to 24	100.0	15.6	12.5	0.6	2.9
Aged 25 to 34	100.0	11.3	8.1	1.2	2.6
Aged 35 to 44	100.0	10.8	7.2	2.2	2.4
Aged 45 to 54	100.0	12.2	7.1	4.1	2.9
Aged 55 to 64	100.0	20.0	7.4	9.5	6.2
Aged 65 or older	100.0	93.7	8.9	93.2	7.1
PERCENT DISTRIBUTION BY AGE					
Total people	**100.0%**	**100.0%**	**100.0%**	**100.0%**	**100.0%**
Under age 18	24.9	27.7	52.8	1.3	19.2
Aged 18 to 24	9.5	5.3	9.0	0.4	7.5
Aged 25 to 34	13.4	5.5	8.2	1.2	9.6
Aged 35 to 44	14.1	5.5	7.7	2.2	9.3
Aged 45 to 54	14.7	6.5	7.8	4.3	11.7
Aged 55 to 64	11.1	8.0	6.2	7.7	19.0
Aged 65 or older	12.3	41.5	8.2	82.8	23.8

Note: Numbers may not add to total because some people have more than one type of health insurance coverage.
Source: Bureau of the Census, Health Insurance, Table HI01, Internet site http://pubdb3.census.gov/macro/032008/health/toc .htm; calculations by New Strategist

Table 3.25 People Aged 18 to 44 by Health Insurance Coverage Status and Reason for No Coverage, 2007

(number and percent distribution of people aged 18 to 44 by health insurance coverage status and reasons for lack of coverage, 2007)

	number	percent
HEALTH INSURANCE STATUS		
Total people aged 18 to 44	**110,890**	**100.0%**
With health insurance	84,711	76.4
Without health insurance	26,179	23.6
REASON FOR LACK OF HEALTH INSURANCE		
People aged 18 to 44 without health insurance	**26,179**	**100.0**
Cost	12,775	48.8
Lost job or change in employment	5,916	22.6
Employer didn't offer insurance/company refused	4,372	16.7
Ineligible due to age/left school	3,272	12.5
Medicaid stopped	2,801	10.7
Change in marital status or death of parent	550	2.1
Other reason	1,545	5.9

Note: Numbers do not sum to total because "unknown" is not shown and people could report more than one reason.
Source: National Center for Health Statistics, Summary Health Statistics for the U.S. Population: National Health Interview Survey, 2007, Vital and Health Statistics, Series 10, No. 238, 2008, Internet site http://www.cdc.gov/nchs/nhis.htm; calculations by New Strategist

Table 3.26 Spending on Health Care by Age, 2006

(percent of people with health care expense, median expense per person, total expenses, and percent distribution of total expenses by source of payment, by age, 2006)

	total (thousands)	percent with expense	median expense per person	total expenses	
				amount (millions)	percent distribution
Total people	**299,267**	**84.6%**	**$1,185**	**$1,033,056**	**100.0%**
Under age 18	74,106	85.4	462	98,789	9.6
Aged 18 to 29	49,243	73.5	685	79,302	7.7
Aged 30 to 39	39,719	78.5	1,017	94,457	9.1
Aged 40 to 49	44,328	83.8	1,100	129,809	12.6
Aged 50 to 59	39,458	90.0	2,220	207,157	20.1
Aged 60 to 64	14,433	91.8	2,855	90,222	8.7
Aged 65 or older	37,980	96.7	4,215	333,320	32.3

PERCENT DISTRIBUTION BY SOURCE OF PAYMENT

	total	out of pocket	private insurance	Medicare	Medicaid	other
Total people	**100.0%**	**19.0%**	**41.7%**	**23.5%**	**8.7%**	**7.1%**
Under age 18	100.0	20.5	50.7	0.5	23.7	4.6
Aged 18 to 29	100.0	24.8	46.3	0.8	20.0	8.1
Aged 30 to 39	100.0	19.5	62.3	3.0	8.3	6.8
Aged 40 to 49	100.0	20.3	55.3	6.1	10.0	8.3
Aged 50 to 59	100.0	19.6	57.6	8.9	7.0	6.9
Aged 60 to 64	100.0	22.1	52.2	10.7	7.8	7.2
Aged 65 or older	100.0	15.2	14.1	60.9	2.4	7.3

Note: "Other" insurance includes Department of Veterans Affairs (except Tricare), American Indian Health Service, state and local clinics, worker's compensation, homeowner's and automobile insurance, etc.
Source: Agency for Healthcare Research and Quality, Medical Expenditure Panel Survey, 2006, Internet site http://www.meps .ahrq.gov/mepsweb/data_stats/quick_tables_results.jsp?component=1&subcomponent=0&tableSeries=1&year=-1&SearchMet hod=1&Action=Search; calculations by New Strategist

Health Problems Are Few in the 18-to-44 Age Group

Lower back pain is by far the most common health condition in the age group.

Twenty-two percent of Americans aged 18 to 44 have experienced lower back pain for at least one full day in the past three months, making it the most common health condition in the age group. Migraines or severe headaches are second, with 15 percent having the problem. Chronic joint symptoms are third, with 13 percent reporting this problem.

The 18-to-44 age group accounts for more than half of those who have ever had asthma, and they are nearly half of those who still have asthma. They account for 60 percent of those with migraines or severe headaches.

■ As the Millennial generation ages into its thirties and forties, the percentage with health problems will rise.

Headaches are the second most common health problem among 18-to-44-year-olds

(percent of people aged 18 to 44 with health condition, 2007)

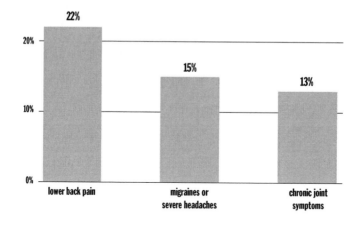

Table 3.27 Health Conditions among People Aged 18 to 44, 2007

(number of people aged 18 or older and aged 18 to 44 with selected health conditions, by type of condition, 2007; numbers in thousands)

		aged 18 to 44		
	total	18 to 44	percent with condition	share of total
TOTAL PEOPLE 18 OR OLDER	223,181	110,890	100.0%	49.7
Selected circulatory diseases				
Heart disease, all types	25,095	4,591	4.1	18.3
Coronary	13,674	1,041	0.9	7.6
Hypertension	52,920	9,094	8.2	17.2
Stroke	5,426	285	0.3	5.3
Selected respiratory conditions				
Emphysema	3,736	226	0.2	6.0
Asthma, ever	24,402	12,996	11.7	53.3
Asthma, still	16,177	7,996	7.2	49.4
Hay fever	16,882	7,420	6.7	44.0
Sinusitis	25,953	10,261	9.3	39.5
Chronic bronchitis	7,604	2,515	2.3	33.1
Selected types of cancer				
Any cancer	16,370	2,085	1.9	12.7
Breast cancer	2,630	178	0.2	6.8
Cervical cancer	1,011	437	0.4	43.2
Prostate cancer	2,037	0	0.0	0.0
Other selected diseases and conditions				
Diabetes	17,273	2,432	2.2	14.1
Ulcers	14,501	4,616	4.2	31.8
Kidney disease	3,343	759	0.7	22.7
Liver disease	2,649	749	0.7	28.3
Arthritis	46,429	7,810	7.0	16.8
Chronic joint symptoms	53,945	14,776	13.3	27.4
Migraines or severe headaches	27,364	16,427	14.8	60.0
Pain in neck	29,019	11,833	10.7	40.8
Pain in lower back	57,070	24,555	22.1	43.0
Pain in face or jaw	9,062	4,649	4.2	51.3
Selected sensory problems				
Hearing	33,318	6,597	5.9	19.8
Vision	22,378	7,596	6.9	33.9
Absence of all natural teeth	16,997	2,066	1.9	12.2

Note: The conditions shown are those that have ever been diagnosed by a doctor, except as noted. Hay fever, sinusitis, and chronic bronchitis have been diagnosed in the past 12 months. Kidney and liver diseases have been diagnosed in the past 12 months and exclude kidney stones, bladder infections, and incontinence. Chronic joint symptoms are shown if respondent had pain, aching, or stiffness in or around a joint (excluding back and neck) and the condition began more than three months ago. Migraines, and pain in neck, lower back, face, or jaw are shown only if pain lasted a whole day or more.
Source: National Center for Health Statistics, Summary Health Statistics for U.S. Adults: National Health Interview Survey, 2007, Vital and Health Statistics, Series 10, No. 240, 2008, Internet site http://www.cdc.gov/nchs/nhis.htm

Many Americans Turn to Alternative Medicine

More than one-third of young adults use alternative therapies.

Alternative medicine is big business. In 2007, fully 38 percent of Americans aged 18 or older used a complementary or alternative medicine or therapy, according to a study by the National Center for Health Statistics. Alternative treatments range from popular regimens such as the South Beach diet to chiropractic care, yoga, and acupuncture.

Middle-aged adults are most likely to use alternative medicine. Forty-four percent of people aged 50 to 59 used alternative medicine in 2007. Among Millennials (under age 30), 36 percent used alternative medicine in the past year—16 percent used biologically based therapies (which include special diets) and an even larger 21 percent used mind-body therapy (which includes meditation and yoga).

■ The use of alternative medicine declines in the older age groups as health problems become more severe.

The use of alternative medicine peaks in middle age

(percent of people aged 18 or older who have used alternative medicine in the past 12 months, by age, 2007)

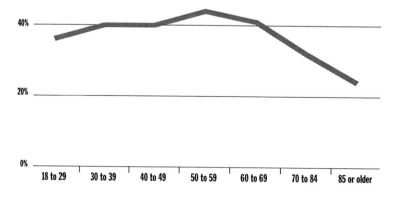

Table 3.28 Adults Who Use Complementary and Alternative Medicine by Age, 2007

(percent of people aged 18 or older who used complementary or alternative medicine in the past 12 months, by age, 2007)

	any use	biologically based therapies	mind-body therapies	alternative medical systems	manipulative and body-based therapies
Total adults	**38.3%**	**19.9%**	**19.2%**	**3.4%**	**15.2%**
Aged 18 to 29	36.3	15.9	21.3	3.2	15.1
Aged 30 to 39	39.6	19.8	19.9	3.6	17.2
Aged 40 to 49	40.1	20.4	19.7	4.6	17.4
Aged 50 to 59	44.1	24.2	22.9	4.9	17.3
Aged 60 to 69	41.0	25.4	17.3	2.8	13.8
Aged 70 to 84	32.1	19.3	11.9	1.8	9.9
Aged 85 or older	24.2	13.7	9.8	1.9	7.0

Definitions: Biologically based therapies include chelation therapy nonvitamin, nonmineral, natural products and diet-based therapies. Mind-body therapies include biofeedback; meditation; guided imagery; progressive relaxation; deep breathing exercises; hypnosis; yoga; tai chi; and qi gong. Alternative medical systems include acupuncture; ayurveda; homeopathic treatment; naturopathy; and traditional healers. Manipulative body-based therapies include chiropractic or osteopathic manipulation; massage; and movement therapies.
Source: National Center for Health Statistics, Complementary and Alternative Medicine Use Among Adults and Children: United States, 2007, National Health Statistics Report, No. 12, 2008, Internet site http://nccam.nih.gov/news/camstats/2007/index.htm

Nearly 1 Million Americans Have Been Diagnosed with AIDS

For most, the diagnosis occurred when they were aged 30 or older.

As of 2006, nearly 1 million people had been diagnosed with AIDS in the United States. Few are diagnosed younger than age 30. As of 2006, only 17 percent had been diagnosed before age 30. Nevertheless, those diagnosed with AIDS in their thirties or older often contracted the illness as young adults.

Although new drug treatments have lowered mortality rates from AIDS, the cost of treatment can be prohibitive.

■ The AIDS epidemic has boosted the use of condoms among teens and young adults.

Few are diagnosed with AIDS before age 30

(percent distribution of cumulative number of AIDS cases by age at diagnosis, through 2006)

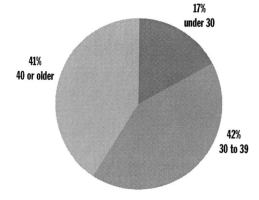

17%
under 30

41%
40 or older

42%
30 to 39

Table 3.29 Cumulative Number of AIDS Cases by Sex and Age, through 2006

(cumulative number and percent distribution of AIDS cases by sex and age at diagnosis, through 2006)

	number	percent distribution
TOTAL CASES	**982,498**	**100.0%**
Sex		
Males aged 13 or older	783,786	79.8
Females aged 13 or older	189,566	19.3
Age		
Under age 13	9,156	0.9
Aged 13 to 14	1,078	0.1
Aged 15 to 19	5,626	0.6
Aged 20 to 24	36,225	3.7
Aged 25 to 29	117,099	11.9
Aged 30 to 34	197,530	20.1
Aged 35 to 39	213,573	21.7
Aged 40 to 44	170,531	17.4
Aged 45 to 49	107,207	10.9
Aged 50 to 54	59,907	6.1
Aged 55 to 59	32,190	3.3
Aged 60 to 64	17,303	1.8
Aged 65 or older	15,074	1.5

Source: Centers for Disease Control and Prevention, Cases of HIV/AIDS and AIDS, Internet site http://www.cdc.gov/hiv/topics/surveillance/resources/reports/2006report/table3.htm

Young Adults Are Least Likely to See a Doctor

People aged 15 to 24 visit doctors fewer than two times a year, on average.

In 2006, Americans visited physicians a total of 902 million times. People aged 15 to 24 accounted for only 8 percent of physician visits. They visited a doctor only 1.7 times during the year, on average. This age group visits a doctor less often than any other in part because it is least likely to be covered by health insurance.

People aged 15 to 24 account for 12 percent of hospital outpatient visitors. Most visit the outpatient department because of an acute health problem. The 15-to-24 age group accounts for a larger 16 percent share of visits to hospital emergency departments. This is the age group whose emergency visits are least likely to be deemed a true emergency. Many head to the emergency room because they lack health insurance and have no other source of health care.

When people visiting a doctor or health care clinic are asked to rate the care they receive, fewer than half give it the highest rating (a 9 or 10 on a scale of 0 to 10). The proportion rating their experience a 9 or 10 rises with age to a peak of 62 percent among Medicare recipients (people aged 65 or older). Only 39 to 45 percent of people aged 18 to 29 give the health care they received the highest rating.

■ Among people aged 15 to 24, women visit a doctor much more frequently than men because of pregnancy and childbirth.

People aged 15 to 24 see a doctor less frequently than any other age group

(average number of physician visits per person per year, by age, 2006)

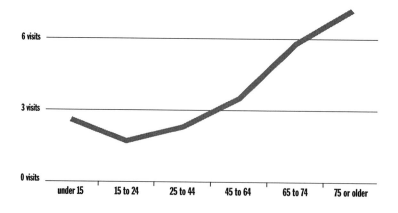

Table 3.30 Physician Office Visits by Sex and Age, 2006

(total number, percent distribution, and number of physician office visits per person per year, by sex and age, 2006; numbers in thousands)

	total	percent distribution	average visits per year
TOTAL VISITS	**901,954**	**100.0%**	**3.1**
Under age 15	157,906	17.5	2.6
Aged 15 to 24	72,411	8.0	1.7
Aged 25 to 44	185,305	20.5	2.3
Aged 45 to 64	256,494	28.4	3.5
Aged 65 to 74	108,063	12.0	5.8
Aged 75 or older	121,774	13.5	7.2
Visits by females	**533,292**	**59.1**	**3.6**
Under age 15	76,300	8.5	2.6
Aged 15 to 24	49,641	5.5	2.4
Aged 25 to 44	122,261	13.6	3.0
Aged 45 to 64	149,778	16.6	3.9
Aged 65 to 74	60,699	6.7	6.0
Aged 75 or older	74,613	8.3	7.3
Visits by males	**368,662**	**40.9**	**2.6**
Under age 15	81,607	9.0	2.6
Aged 15 to 24	22,770	2.5	1.1
Aged 25 to 44	63,044	7.0	1.6
Aged 45 to 64	106,716	11.8	3.0
Aged 65 to 74	47,364	5.3	5.5
Aged 75 or older	47,161	5.2	7.1

Source: National Center for Health Statistics, National Ambulatory Medical Care Survey: 2006 Summary, National Health Statistics Report, No. 3, 2008, Internet site http://www.cdc.gov/nchs/about/major/ahcd/adata.htm

Table 3.31 Hospital Outpatient Department Visits by Age and Reason, 2006

(number and percent distribution of visits to hospital outpatient departments by age and major reason for visit, 2006; numbers in thousands)

	total		major reason for visit						
	number	percent distribution	total	acute problem	chronic problem, routine	chronic problem, flare-up	pre- or post-surgery	preventive care	unknown
Total visits	102,208	100.0%	100.0%	36.7%	31.1%	6.8%	4.3%	19.4%	1.7%
Under age 15	19,864	19.4	100.0	48.9	17.6	3.7	2.0	24.8	2.8
Aged 15 to 24	12,012	11.8	100.0	38.9	16.0	4.7	3.5	34.8	2.1
Aged 25 to 44	25,104	24.6	100.0	37.3	27.2	7.0	4.3	22.6	1.5
Aged 45 to 64	28,707	28.1	100.0	32.2	41.4	8.4	5.4	11.5	1.1
Aged 65 or older	16,522	16.2	100.0	27.4	46.2	8.8	5.9	10.3	1.4

Source: National Center for Health Statistics, National Hospital Ambulatory Medical Care Survey: 2006 Outpatient Department Summary, National Health Statistics Reports, No. 4, 2008, Internet site http://www.cdc.gov/nchs/about/major/ahcd/adata .htm; calculations by New Strategist

Table 3.32 Emergency Department Visits by Age and Urgency of Problem, 2006

(number of visits to emergency rooms and percent distribution by urgency of problem, by age, 2006; numbers in thousands)

	total		percent distribution by urgency of problem						
	number	percent distribution	total	immediate	emergent	urgent	semiurgent	nonurgent	unknown
Total visits	119,191	100.0%	100.0%	5.1%	10.8%	36.6%	22.0%	12.1%	13.4%
Under age 15	21,876	18.4	100.0	3.1	7.8	35.0	25.6	14.6	13.9
Aged 15 to 24	19,525	16.4	100.0	4.1	8.4	34.3	24.7	14.3	14.1
Aged 25 to 44	35,034	29.4	100.0	4.3	10.1	36.4	22.7	12.9	13.6
Aged 45 to 64	25,466	21.4	100.0	5.9	12.8	37.1	20.0	11.1	13.2
Aged 65 or older	17,290	14.5	100.0	9.2	15.4	41.3	15.5	6.7	11.9

Note: "Immediate" is a visit in which the patient should be seen immediately. "Emergent" is a visit in which the patient should be seen within 1 to 14 minutes; "urgent" is a visit in which the patient should be seen within 15 to 60 minutes; "semiurgent" is a visit in which the patient should be seen within 61 to 120 minutes; "nonurgent" is a visit in which the patient should be seen within 121 minutes to 24 hours; "unknown" is a visit with no mention of immediacy or triage or the patient was dead on arrival.

Source: National Center for Health Statistics, National Hospital Ambulatory Medical Care Survey: 2006 Emergency Department Summary, National Health Statistics Reports, No. 7, 2008, Internet site http://www.cdc.gov/nchs/about/major/ahcd/adata .htm

Table 3.33 Rating of Health Care Received from Doctor's Office or Clinic, 2006

(number of people aged 18 or older visiting a doctor or health care clinic in past 12 months, and percent distribution by rating for health care received on a scale from 0 (worst) to 10 (best), by age, 2006; people in thousands)

	with health care visit		rating		
	number	percent	9 to 10	7 to 8	0 to 6
Total people	**140,898**	**100.0%**	**49.3%**	**35.8%**	**13.9%**
Aged 18 to 24	14,039	100.0	45.4	38.7	15.1
Aged 25 to 29	10,235	100.0	38.7	42.4	18.4
Aged 30 to 39	23,007	100.0	43.8	41.3	14.0
Aged 40 to 49	26,565	100.0	45.6	37.6	16.2
Aged 50 to 59	27,436	100.0	48.1	37.0	14.0
Aged 60 to 64	10,666	100.0	54.8	32.6	12.1
Aged 65 or older	28,951	100.0	61.9	26.1	10.2

Source: Agency for Healthcare Research and Quality, Medical Expenditure Panel Survey, 2006, Internet site http://www.meps .ahrq.gov/mepsweb/data_stats/quick_tables_results.jsp?component=1&subcomponent=0&tableSeries=3&year=-1&SearchMet hod=1&Action=Search; calculations by New Strategist

Most Deaths of Young Adults Are Preventable

Accidents are the leading killers of 15-to-34-year-olds.

When young adults die, it is often preventable. Accidents are the most important cause of death among 15-to-34-year-olds, accounting for 47 percent of deaths among 15-to-24-year-olds and 35 percent of deaths among 25-to-34-year-olds. Homicide ranks second among 15-to-24-year-olds, and suicide is third. Among 25-to-34-year-olds, suicide is second and homicide is third. HIV infection ranks eighth as a cause of death among 15-to-24-year-olds and a higher sixth among 25-to-34-year-olds.

Although more could be done to reduce deaths among young adults, some progress has been made. The life expectancy of Americans continues to rise. At birth, Americans can expect to live 77.7 years. At age 25, life expectancy is another 53.9 years.

■ As Millennials age, heart disease and cancer will become increasingly important causes of death.

Accidents are the most important cause of death among people aged 15 to 34

(percent of deaths due to the three most important causes of death among people aged 15 to 34, 2006)

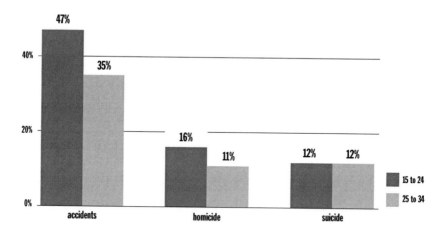

Table 3.34 Leading Causes of Death for People Aged 15 to 24, 2006

(number and percent distribution of deaths accounted for by the 10 leading causes of death for people aged 15 to 24, 2006)

		number	percent distribution
	All causes	**34,887**	**100.0%**
1.	Accidents (unintentional injuries) (5)	16,229	46.5
2.	Homicide (15)	5,717	16.4
3.	Suicide (11)	4,189	12.0
4.	Malignant neoplasms (cancer) (2)	1,644	4.7
5.	Diseases of the heart (1)	1,076	3.1
6.	Congenital malformations, deformations	460	1.3
7.	Cerebrovascular diseases (3)	210	0.6
8.	Human immunodeficiency virus infection	206	0.6
9.	Influenza and pneumonia (8)	184	0.5
10.	Pregnancy and childbirth	179	0.5
	All other causes	4,793	13.7

Note: Number in parentheses shows rank for all Americans if the cause of death is among top 15.
Source: National Center for Health Statistics, Deaths: Final Data for 2006, National Vital Statistics Reports, Vol. 57, No. 14, 2009, Internet site http://www.cdc.gov/nchs/products/nvsr.htm#vol57; calculations by New Strategist

Table 3.35 Leading Causes of Death for People Aged 25 to 34, 2006

(number and percent distribution of deaths accounted for by the 10 leading causes of death for people aged 25 to 34, 2006)

		number	percent distribution
	All causes	**42,952**	**100.0%**
1.	Accidents (unintentional injuries) (5)	14,954	34.8
2.	Suicide (11)	4,985	11.6
3.	Homicide (15)	4,725	11.0
4.	Malignant neoplasms (cancer) (2)	3,656	8.5
5.	Diseases of the heart (1)	3,307	7.7
6.	Human immunodeficiency virus infection	1,182	2.8
7.	Diabetes mellitus (6)	673	1.6
8.	Cerebrovascular diseases (3)	527	1.2
9.	Congenital malformations, deformations	437	1.0
10.	Influenza and pneumonia (8)	335	0.8
	All other causes	8,171	19.0

Note: Number in parentheses shows rank for all Americans if the cause of death is among top 15.
Source: National Center for Health Statistics, Deaths: Final Data for 2006, National Vital Statistics Reports, Vol. 57, No. 14, 2009, Internet site http://www.cdc.gov/nchs/products/nvsr.htm#vol57; calculations by New Strategist

Table 3.36 Life Expectancy by Age and Sex, 2006

(expected years of life remaining at selected ages, by sex, 2006)

	total	females	males
At birth	77.7	80.2	75.1
Aged 1	77.2	79.7	74.7
Aged 5	73.3	75.8	70.8
Aged 10	68.4	70.8	65.8
Aged 15	63.4	65.9	60.9
Aged 20	58.6	61.0	56.1
Aged 25	53.9	56.1	51.5
Aged 30	49.2	51.3	46.9
Aged 35	44.4	46.4	42.2
Aged 40	39.7	41.7	37.6
Aged 45	35.2	37.0	33.1
Aged 50	30.7	32.5	28.8
Aged 55	26.5	28.0	24.7
Aged 60	22.4	23.8	20.7
Aged 65	18.5	19.7	17.0
Aged 70	14.9	15.9	13.6
Aged 75	11.6	12.3	10.5
Aged 80	8.7	9.3	7.8
Aged 85	6.4	6.8	5.7
Aged 90	4.6	4.8	4.1
Aged 95	3.2	3.3	2.9
Aged 100	2.3	2.3	2.0

Source: National Center for Health Statistics, Deaths: Final Data for 2006, National Vital Statistics Reports, Vol. 57, No. 14, 2009, Internet site http://www.cdc.gov/nchs/products/nvsr.htm#vol57; calculations by New Strategist

4

Housing

■ The homeownership rate fell between 2004 and 2008, but it declined the least among householders aged 25 to 29 (Millennials were aged 15 to 31 in 2008).

■ Less than half of Millennials have made the transition from renting to home owning. Only one-third of householders under age 30 were homeowners in 2008. Among householders under age 25, just 24 percent were homeowners.

■ Most (57 percent) of householders under age 25 live in apartment buildings, as do 42 percent of householders aged 25 to 29.

■ Because of their age, many Millennial couples are still renters rather than homeowners. This means they avoided the high prices of the housing bubble. Consequently, Millennials may enjoy lower housing costs throughout their lives.

■ Young adults are far more likely than their elders to move from one home to another. Only 7 percent of people aged 35 or older moved between 2007 and 2008, but among people aged 20 to 29, the percentage was a much higher 25 to 27 percent.

Homeownership Rate Has Declined

Since 2004, the rate has fallen the least among 25-to-29-year-olds.

The homeownership rate in the United States reached a peak of 69.0 percent in 2004. Since then, the rate has fallen by 1.2 percentage points, to 67.8 percent in 2008, as the housing market collapsed. Householders aged 25 to 29 experienced the smallest decline in homeownership, their rate falling by just 0.2 percentage points to 40.0 percent during those years. Householders under age 25 saw their rate decline by a larger 1.6 percentage points, dropping to 23.6 percent.

In 2008, the overall homeownership rate was 0.4 percentage points greater than in 2000. But for householders under age 30 (Millennials were aged 14 to 31 in 2008), homeownership was 1.9 percentage points higher in 2008 than in 2000. Every other age group lost ground during those years.

■ If the housing market stabilizes, the homeownership rate of Millennials should increase as they grow older.

After peaking in 2004, homeownership rate is down

(homeownership rate for householders under age 30, by age, 2004 and 2008)

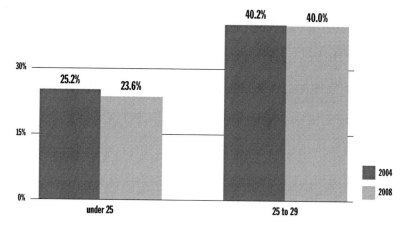

Table 4.1 Homeownership by Age of Householder, 2000 to 2008

(percentage of householders who own their home by age of householder, 2000 to 2008; percentage point change, 2004–08, and 2000–08)

	2008	2004	2000	percentage point change 2004–08	2000–08
Total households	**67.8%**	**69.0%**	**67.4%**	**−1.2**	**0.4**
Under age 25	23.6	25.2	21.7	−1.6	1.9
Aged 25 to 29	40.0	40.2	38.1	−0.2	1.9
Aged 30 to 34	53.5	57.4	54.6	−3.9	−1.1
Aged 35 to 39	64.6	66.2	65.0	−1.6	−0.4
Aged 40 to 44	69.4	71.9	70.6	−2.5	−1.2
Aged 45 to 54	75.0	77.2	76.5	−2.2	−1.5
Aged 55 to 64	80.1	81.7	80.3	−1.6	−0.2
Aged 65 or older	80.1	81.1	80.4	−1.0	−0.3

Source: Bureau of the Census, Housing Vacancies and Homeownership Survey, Internet site http://www.census.gov/hhes/www/ housing/hvs/annual08/ann08ind.html; calculations by New Strategist

Homeownership Rises with Age

Most householders under age 30 are not yet homeowners.

Less than half of Millennials have made the transition from renting to home owning. Only one-third of householders under age 30 were homeowners in 2008 (Millennials were aged 14 to 31 in that year). Among householders under age 25, just 24 percent were homeowners. The homeownership rate rises to 40 percent among householders aged 25 to 29.

Overall, two-thirds of households headed by Millennials are renters. People under age 30 account for 29 percent of the nation's renters and only 7 percent of homeowners.

■ The Millennial generation has replaced the smaller Generation X in the young-adult age group, giving the rental market a boost.

Homeownership is not yet the norm among Millennials

(percent distribution of householders under age 30 by homeownership status, 2008)

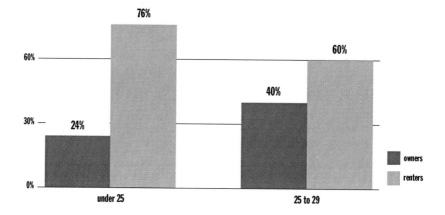

Table 4.2 Owners and Renters by Age of Householder, 2008

(number and percent distribution of householders by homeownership status, and owner and renter share of total, by age of householder, 2008; numbers in thousands)

	total	owners			renters		
		number	percent distribution	share of total	number	percent distribution	share of total
Total households	**111,409**	**75,566**	**100.0%**	**67.8%**	**35,843**	**100.0%**	**32.2%**
Under age 30	15,366	5,123	6.8	33.3	10,244	28.6	66.7
Under age 25	6,272	1,482	2.0	23.6	4,790	13.4	76.4
Aged 25 to 29	9,094	3,641	4.8	40.0	5,453	15.2	60.0
Aged 30 to 34	9,343	4,998	6.6	53.5	4,346	12.1	46.5
Aged 35 to 44	21,524	14,425	19.1	67.0	7,098	19.8	33.0
Aged 45 to 54	23,382	17,537	23.2	75.0	5,845	16.3	25.0
Aged 55 to 64	18,818	15,069	19.9	80.1	3,748	10.5	19.9
Aged 65 or older	22,976	18,414	24.4	80.1	4,562	12.7	19.9

Source: Bureau of the Census, Housing Vacancies and Homeownership Survey, Internet site http://www.census.gov/hhes/www/housing/hvs/historic/index.html; calculations by New Strategist

Married Couples Are Most Likely to Be Homeowners

Two incomes make homes more affordable.

The homeownership rate among all married couples stood at 83.4 percent in 2008, much higher than the 67.8 percent rate for all households. Among Millennial couples (Millennials were aged 14 to 31 in 2008), the homeownership rate ranges from 37.3 percent among couples under age 25 to the 58.7 percent majority of couples aged 25 to 29.

Homeownership is much lower for other types of households and lowest among female-headed families. Only 23 to 24 percent of families headed by female householders under age 30 are homeowners. Among women under age 25 who live alone, just 11 percent own a home.

■ Most Millennials were too young to buy homes during the housing bubble. As they enter the housing market in the next few years, they will find homes much more affordable than they would have a few years ago.

More than 50 percent of couples aged 25 to 29 own their home

(percent of married-couple householders who own their home, by age, 2008)

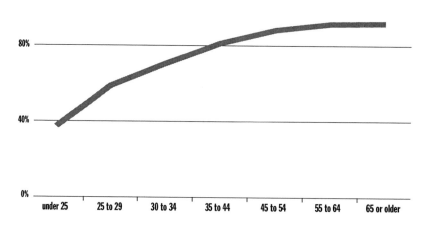

Table 4.3 Homeownership Rate by Age of Householder and Type of Household, 2008

(percent of households that own their home, by age of householder and type of household, 2008)

| | | family households | | | people living alone | |
	total	married couples	female householder, no spouse present	male householder, no spouse present	females	males
Total households	**67.8%**	**83.4%**	**49.5%**	**57.6%**	**58.6%**	**50.6%**
Under age 25	23.6	37.3	23.4	41.7	11.2	16.7
Aged 25 to 29	40.0	58.7	24.0	40.2	24.1	30.0
Aged 30 to 34	53.5	70.3	30.7	44.9	34.0	36.1
Aged 35 to 44	67.0	81.2	45.2	56.5	47.5	45.6
Aged 45 to 54	75.0	88.2	60.1	69.4	55.0	53.9
Aged 55 to 64	80.1	91.4	66.7	76.1	66.0	60.2
Aged 65 or older	80.1	91.7	81.2	81.2	69.4	68.2

Source: Bureau of the Census, Housing Vacancies and Homeownership Survey, Internet site http://www.census.gov/hhes/www/housing/hvs/annual08/ann08ind.html

Few Millennials, Regardless of Race, Are Homeowners

Hispanics are more likely than blacks to own a home.

The homeownership rate of blacks and Hispanics is well below average. The overall homeownership rate stood at 68.3 percent in 2007 (the latest data available by age, race, and Hispanic origin). Among blacks, the rate was a smaller 46.7 percent. The Hispanic rate was slightly greater at 50.5 percent.

Homeownership rates range from 14.8 to 19.5 percent among black householders under age 30. Among Hispanics, the rate reaches 31.6 percent in the 25-to-29 age group. The homeownership rate does not rise above 50 percent among black householders until the 45-to-54 age group. Among Hispanics, the rate surpasses 50 percent in the 35-to-44 age group.

■ Blacks are less likely than Hispanics to be homeowners because married couples head a smaller share of black households.

Thirty-two percent of Hispanic householders aged 25 to 29 own their home

(homeownership rate of total householders and householders under age 30, by race and Hispanic origin, 2007)

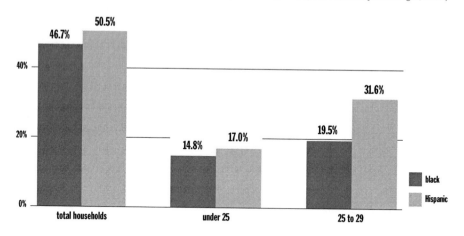

Table 4.4 Black and Hispanic Homeownership Rate by Age, 2007

(percent of total, black, and Hispanic households that own their home, by age of householder, 2007)

	total	black	Hispanic
Total households	**68.3%**	**46.7%**	**50.5%**
Under age 25	23.3	14.8	17.0
Aged 25 to 29	41.6	19.5	31.6
Aged 30 to 34	54.7	28.7	41.3
Aged 35 to 44	67.9	44.8	53.5
Aged 45 to 54	75.6	55.1	61.1
Aged 55 to 64	80.7	60.6	64.2
Aged 65 to 74	82.2	64.2	67.4
Aged 75 or older	77.5	66.4	63.7

Note: Blacks include only those who identify themselves as being black alone. Hispanics may be of any race.
Source: Bureau of the Census, American Housing Survey for the United States: 2007, Internet site http://www.census.gov/hhes/www/housing/ahs/ahs07/ahs07.html; calculations by New Strategist

Few Young Adults Live in a Single-Family Home

The majority of the youngest adults live in apartment buildings.

Most American households (65 percent) live in detached, single-family homes. But there is great variation by age. While the majority of householders aged 30 or older live in this type of home, the figure is only 40 percent among those under age 30. The under-30 age group accounts for only 8 percent of householders living in single-family, detached homes.

Fifty-seven percent of householders under age 25 live in apartment buildings, as do 42 percent of householders aged 25 to 29. The share living in an apartment building drops to 32 percent in the 30-to-34 age group. Householders under age 30 account for 28 percent of the nation's apartment dwellers.

Six percent of householders live in a mobile home, a proportion that does not vary much by age. Householders under age 30 account for 12 percent of mobile home householders.

■ As the number of young adults grows with the aging of the Millennial generation, the demand for apartments is likely to be strong.

Young adults are most likely to live in apartments

(percent of households living in multi-unit buildings, by age of householder, 2007)

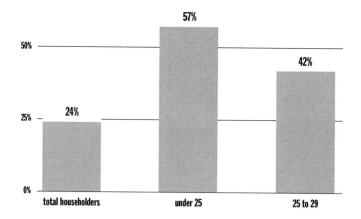

Table 4.5 Number of Units in Structure by Age of Householder, 2007

(number and percent distribution of households by age of householder and number of units in structure, 2007; numbers in thousands)

	total	one, detached	one, attached	multi-unit dwellings total	2 to 4	5 to 9	10 to 19	20 to 49	50 or more	mobile homes
Total households	**110,692**	**71,435**	**6,083**	**26,256**	**8,790**	**5,258**	**4,697**	**3,645**	**3,866**	**6,919**
Under age 30	15,082	6,011	951	7,285	2,319	1,712	1,613	1,048	592	834
Under age 25	6,273	1,971	357	3,595	1,091	900	880	476	248	349
Aged 25 to 29	8,809	4,040	594	3,690	1,228	812	733	572	344	485
Aged 30 to 34	9,571	5,263	643	3,058	1,058	677	601	459	262	607
Aged 35 to 44	21,756	14,644	1,146	4,705	1,707	986	857	684	470	1,262
Aged 45 to 54	23,208	16,683	1,153	3,906	1,440	760	724	484	497	1,467
Aged 55 to 64	18,211	13,125	1,033	2,832	1,020	499	440	351	521	1,222
Aged 65 or older	22,865	15,710	1,157	4,470	1,246	622	461	617	1,524	1,528
Median age	49	51	48	41	41	37	37	40	57	50

PERCENT DISTRIBUTION BY AGE OF HOUSEHOLDER

	total	one, detached	one, attached	multi-unit dwellings total	2 to 4	5 to 9	10 to 19	20 to 49	50 or more	mobile homes
Total households	**100.0%**	**100.0%**	**100.0%**	**100.0%**	**100.0%**	**100.0%**	**100.0%**	**100.0%**	**100.0%**	**100.0%**
Under age 30	13.6	8.4	15.6	27.7	26.4	32.6	34.3	28.8	15.3	12.1
Under age 25	5.7	2.8	5.9	13.7	12.4	17.1	18.7	13.1	6.4	5.0
Aged 25 to 29	8.0	5.7	9.8	14.1	14.0	15.4	15.6	15.7	8.9	7.0
Aged 30 to 34	8.6	7.4	10.6	11.6	12.0	12.9	12.8	12.6	6.8	8.8
Aged 35 to 44	19.7	20.5	18.8	17.9	19.4	18.8	18.2	18.8	12.2	18.2
Aged 45 to 54	21.0	23.4	19.0	14.9	16.4	14.5	15.4	13.3	12.9	21.2
Aged 55 to 64	16.5	18.4	17.0	10.8	11.6	9.5	9.4	9.6	13.5	17.7
Aged 65 or older	20.7	22.0	19.0	17.0	14.2	11.8	9.8	16.9	39.4	22.1

PERCENT DISTRIBUTION BY UNITS IN STRUCTURE

	total	one, detached	one, attached	multi-unit dwellings total	2 to 4	5 to 9	10 to 19	20 to 49	50 or more	mobile homes
Total households	**100.0%**	**64.5%**	**5.5%**	**23.7%**	**7.9%**	**4.8%**	**4.2%**	**3.3%**	**3.5%**	**6.3%**
Under age 30	100.0	39.9	6.3	48.3	15.4	11.4	10.7	6.9	3.9	5.5
Under age 25	100.0	31.4	5.7	57.3	17.4	14.3	14.0	7.6	4.0	5.6
Aged 25 to 29	100.0	45.9	6.7	41.9	13.9	9.2	8.3	6.5	3.9	5.5
Aged 30 to 34	100.0	55.0	6.7	32.0	11.1	7.1	6.3	4.8	2.7	6.3
Aged 35 to 44	100.0	67.3	5.3	21.6	7.8	4.5	3.9	3.1	2.2	5.8
Aged 45 to 54	100.0	71.9	5.0	16.8	6.2	3.3	3.1	2.1	2.1	6.3
Aged 55 to 64	100.0	72.1	5.7	15.6	5.6	2.7	2.4	1.9	2.9	6.7
Aged 65 or older	100.0	68.7	5.1	19.5	5.4	2.7	2.0	2.7	6.7	6.7

Source: Bureau of the Census, American Housing Survey for the United States: 2007, Internet site http://www.census.gov/hhes/ www/housing/ahs/ahs07/ahs07.html; calculations by New Strategist

Many Young Homeowners Live in New Homes

Few older homeowners are in newly built homes.

New homes are the province of the young. Overall, only 6 percent of homeowners live in a new home—one built in the past four years. The share is much greater among young homeowners, however. Eleven percent of homeowners under age 25 live in a new home, as do 14 percent of those aged 25 to 29. In contrast, only 3 to 5 percent of homeowners aged 45 or older have a new home. Older homeowners tend to live in homes they have owned for many years. Even if new at the time they bought the home, it has aged along with the owner.

Overall, 3 percent of renters are in housing units built in the past four years. The proportion is slightly higher among renters under age 30.

■ The Millennial generation accounts for 14 percent of homeowners who live in a house built in the past four years.

Many homeowners under age 30 live in new homes

(percent of homeowners who live in a home built in the past four years, by age of householder, 2007)

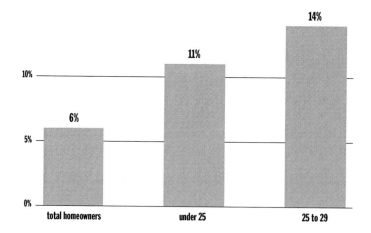

Table 4.6 Owners and Renters of New Homes by Age of Householder, 2007

(number of total occupied housing units, number and percent built in the past four years, and percent distribution of new units by housing tenure and age of householder, 2007; numbers in thousands)

	total	new homes number	new homes percent of total	new homes percent distribution
Total households	**110,692**	**5,747**	**5.2%**	**100.0%**
Under age 30	15,082	1,025	6.8	17.8
Under age 25	6,273	335	5.3	5.8
Aged 25 to 29	8,809	690	7.8	12.0
Aged 30 to 34	9,571	835	8.7	14.5
Aged 35 to 44	21,756	1,536	7.1	26.7
Aged 45 to 54	23,208	1,056	4.6	18.4
Aged 55 to 64	18,211	683	3.8	11.9
Aged 65 or older	22,865	611	2.7	10.6
Total owner households	**75,647**	**4,710**	**6.2**	**100.0**
Under age 30	5,126	679	13.2	14.4
Under age 25	1,462	164	11.2	3.5
Aged 25 to 29	3,664	515	14.1	10.9
Aged 30 to 34	5,235	675	12.9	14.3
Aged 35 to 44	14,781	1,318	8.9	28.0
Aged 45 to 54	17,539	935	5.3	19.9
Aged 55 to 64	14,695	616	4.2	13.1
Aged 65 or older	18,271	487	2.7	10.3
Total renter households	**35,045**	**1,036**	**3.0**	**100.0**
Under age 30	9,955	347	3.5	33.5
Under age 25	4,810	171	3.6	16.5
Aged 25 to 29	5,145	176	3.4	17.0
Aged 30 to 34	4,336	160	3.7	15.4
Aged 35 to 44	6,975	217	3.1	20.9
Aged 45 to 54	5,669	121	2.1	11.7
Aged 55 to 64	3,516	67	1.9	6.5
Aged 65 or older	4,593	124	2.7	12.0

Source: Bureau of the Census, American Housing Survey for the United States: 2007, Internet site http://www.census.gov/hhes/ www/housing/ahs/ahs07/ahs07.html; calculations by New Strategist

Housing Costs Are Lower for Millennial Couples

Those who avoided the inflated prices of the housing bubble may enjoy lower costs throughout their lives.

Monthly housing costs for the average household in 2007 stood at $843, including utilities. For homeowners, median monthly housing cost was $927 including mortgages, and for renters the figure was a smaller $755.

Housing costs are highest for married-couple homeowners aged 35 to 44, not only because their homes are larger than average to make room for children but also because many are recent buyers who bought homes during the housing bubble. Because of their age, many Millennial couples are still renters rather than homeowners. This means they avoided the high prices of the housing bubble. When they do buy a home, they are likely to pay less than many Generation Xers and Baby Boomers who bought at the price peak. Consequently, Millennials may enjoy lower housing costs throughout their lives.

■ Housing costs are lower among couples aged 65 or older because most have paid off their mortgage.

Millennial couples pay less for housing than Gen Xers and Boomers

(median monthly housing costs for married couples, by age of householder, 2007)

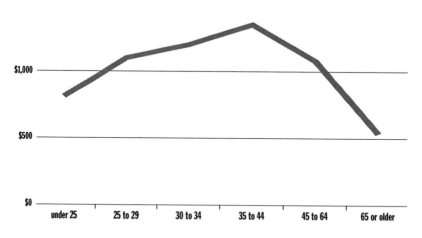

Table 4.7 Median Monthly Housing Costs among Married Couples by Age of Householder, 2007

(median monthly housing costs and indexed costs among married couples by age of householder and housing tenure, 2007)

	median monthly cost			indexed cost		
	total	owners	renters	total	owners	renters
TOTAL HOUSEHOLDS	**$843**	**$927**	**$755**	**100**	**110**	**90**
Total married couples	**1,026**	**1,088**	**878**	**122**	**129**	**104**
Under age 25	810	979	716	96	116	85
Aged 25 to 29	1,100	1,286	871	130	153	103
Aged 30 to 34	1,200	1,366	897	142	162	106
Aged 35 to 44	1,349	1,466	937	160	174	111
Aged 45 to 64	1,078	1,113	895	128	132	106
Aged 65 or older	536	514	814	64	61	97

Note: Housing costs include utilities, mortgages, real estate taxes, property insurance, and regime fees. The index is calculated by dividing median monthly housing costs for each household type by the median cost for total households and multiplying by 100.
Source: Bureau of the Census, American Housing Survey for the United States: 2007, Internet site http://www.census.gov/hhes/www/housing/ahs/ahs07/ahs07.html; calculations by New Strategist

The Homes of the Youngest Adults Are below Average in Value

The Millennial generation may have lucked out in the housing market.

The median value of America's owned homes stood at $191,471 in 2007. Median home value among the nation's married couples is an even higher $220,607. Home values peak among couples aged 35 to 44, at a median of $244,492. Many of those homes are worth far less today, however, because of the bursting of the housing bubble.

The value of the homes owned by married couples under age 30 is well below average because many are small starter homes. Among couples aged 25 to 29, median home value stood at $168,736 in 2007. For couples under age 25, median home value was an even lower $138,617. Since most Millennials are not overinvested in the housing market, they may find themselves well positioned to move up into larger homes now that housing prices are lower.

■ Home values have been falling and are significantly lower than the 2007 figures shown in this table.

Home values were highest for 35-to-44-year-old couples in 2007

(median value of homes owned by married couples, by age of householder, 2007)

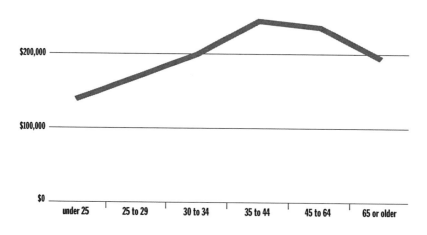

Table 4.8 Value of Owner-Occupied Homes among Married Couples by Age of Householder, 2007

(number of total and married-couple homeowners by value of home, median value of home, and indexed median value, by age of householder, 2007)

	number (in 000s)	under $100,000	$100,000– $149,999	$150,000– $199,999	$200,000– $299,999	$300,000– $399,999	$400,000– $499,999	$500,000– $749,999	$750,000 or more	median value of home ($)	indexed median value
TOTAL HOMEOWNERS	**75,647**	**18,779**	**11,048**	**9,643**	**13,132**	**8,060**	**4,740**	**6,234**	**4,013**	**191,471**	**100**
Married couples	**46,570**	**9227**	**6,282**	**5,992**	**8,660**	**5,664**	**3,348**	**4,443**	**2,955**	**220,607**	**115**
Under age 25	540	176	122	55	66	55	17	37	11	138,617	72
Aged 25 to 29	2,133	494	438	359	415	257	72	89	10	168,736	88
Aged 30 to 34	3,456	709	500	525	739	357	234	264	128	199,431	104
Aged 35 to 44	10,245	1560	1,331	1,334	2,020	1,375	852	1,073	701	244,492	128
Aged 45 to 64	21,119	4048	2,655	2,502	3,795	2,714	1,568	2,274	1,564	235,723	123
Aged 65 or older	9,078	2242	1,237	1,216	1,625	906	605	706	541	193,584	101

Source: Bureau of the Census, American Housing Survey for the United States: 2007, Internet site http://www.census.gov/hhes/ www/housing/ahs/ahs07/ahs07.html; calculations by New Strategist

Twentysomethings Are Most Likely to Move

More than one in four move each year.

Young adults are far more likely than their elders to move from one home to another. Only 7 percent of people aged 35 or older moved between 2007 and 2008, but among people aged 20 to 29, the percentage was a much higher 25 to 27 percent.

Most movers stay within the same county. Only 13 percent cross state lines. Among movers under age 30, as for all movers, housing is the primary reason for moving, but family reasons rank a close second. Many young adults move because they are going to or coming from college.

■ Americans are moving less than they once did. Several factors are behind the lower mobility rate including the economic downturn and the aging of the population.

Mobility rate is high among people aged 20 to 29

(percent of people who moved between March 2007 and March 2008, by age)

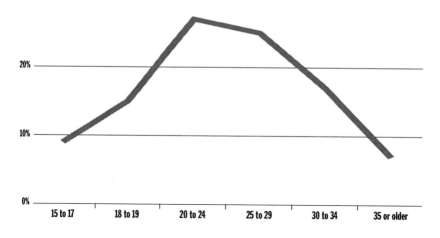

Table 4.9 Geographic Mobility by Age and Type of Move, 2007–08

(total number of people aged 1 or older, and number and percent who moved between March 2007 and March 2008, by age and type of move; numbers in thousands)

	total	total movers	same county	different county, same state	different state total	different state same region	different state different region	movers from abroad
Total, aged 1 or older	**294,851**	**35,166**	**23,013**	**6,282**	**4,727**	**2,248**	**2,479**	**1,145**
Under age 15	56,704	7,613	5,345	1,123	943	456	487	199
Aged 15 to 29	62,900	13,285	8,628	2,455	1,705	824	881	495
Aged 15 to 17	13,445	1,196	840	158	148	88	60	48
Aged 18 to 19	7,869	1,161	743	232	133	80	53	54
Aged 20 to 24	20,529	5,643	3,691	1,060	703	328	375	188
Aged 25 to 29	21,057	5,285	3,354	1,005	721	328	393	205
Aged 30 to 34	19,089	3,321	2,066	597	504	229	275	154
Aged 35 or older	156,158	10,949	6,975	2,104	1,575	741	834	295

PERCENT DISTRIBUTION BY MOBILITY STATUS

	total	total movers	same county	different county, same state	different state total	different state same region	different state different region	movers from abroad
Total, aged 1 or older	**100.0%**	**11.9%**	**7.8%**	**2.1%**	**1.6%**	**0.8%**	**0.8%**	**0.4%**
Under age 15	100.0	13.4	9.4	2.0	1.7	0.8	0.9	0.4
Aged 15 to 29	100.0	21.1	13.7	3.9	2.7	1.3	1.4	0.8
Aged 15 to 17	100.0	8.9	6.2	1.2	1.1	0.7	0.4	0.4
Aged 18 to 19	100.0	14.8	9.4	2.9	1.7	1.0	0.7	0.7
Aged 20 to 24	100.0	27.5	18.0	5.2	3.4	1.6	1.8	0.9
Aged 25 to 29	100.0	25.1	15.9	4.8	3.4	1.6	1.9	1.0
Aged 30 to 34	100.0	17.4	10.8	3.1	2.6	1.2	1.4	0.8
Aged 35 or older	100.0	7.0	4.5	1.3	1.0	0.5	0.5	0.2

PERCENT DISTRIBUTION OF MOVERS BY TYPE OF MOVE

	total	total movers	same county	different county, same state	different state total	different state same region	different state different region	movers from abroad
Total, aged 1 or older	–	**100.0%**	**65.4%**	**17.9%**	**13.4%**	**6.4%**	**7.0%**	**3.3%**
Under age 15	–	100.0	70.2	14.8	12.4	6.0	6.4	2.6
Aged 15 to 29	–	100.0	64.9	18.5	12.8	6.2	6.6	3.7
Aged 15 to 17	–	100.0	70.2	13.2	12.4	7.4	5.0	4.0
Aged 18 to 19	–	100.0	64.0	20.0	11.5	6.9	4.6	4.7
Aged 20 to 24	–	100.0	65.4	18.8	12.5	5.8	6.6	3.3
Aged 25 to 29	–	100.0	63.5	19.0	13.6	6.2	7.4	3.9
Aged 30 to 34	–	100.0	62.2	18.0	15.2	6.9	8.3	4.6
Aged 35 or older	–	100.0	63.7	19.2	14.4	6.8	7.6	2.7

Note: "–" means not applicable.
Source: Bureau of the Census, Geographic Mobility: 2007 to 2008, Detailed Tables, Internet site http://www.census.gov/population/www/socdemo/migrate/cps2008.html; calculations by New Strategist

Table 4.10 Reason for Moving among People Aged 16 to 19, 2007–08

(number and percent distribution of movers aged 16 to 19 by primary reason for move and share of total movers between March 2007 and March 2008, by age; numbers in thousands)

	total movers	movers aged 16 to 19		
		number	percent distribution	share of total
TOTAL MOVERS	35,167	1,960	100.0%	5.6%
Family reasons	10,738	681	34.7	6.3
Change in marital status	1,987	71	3.6	3.6
To establish own household	3,682	257	13.1	7.0
Other familiy reasons	5,069	353	18.0	7.0
Employment reasons	7,352	301	15.4	4.1
New job or job transfer	2,940	83	4.2	2.8
To look for work or lost job	794	53	2.7	6.7
To be closer to work/easier commute	2,183	104	5.3	4.8
Retired	140	4	0.2	2.9
Other job-related reason	1,295	57	2.9	4.4
Housing reasons	14,098	710	36.2	5.0
Wanted own home, not rent	2,033	59	3.0	2.9
Wanted better home/apartment	4,866	259	13.2	5.3
Wanted beter neighborhood	1,778	87	4.4	4.9
Wanted cheaper housing	2,872	153	7.8	5.3
Other housing reasons	2,549	152	7.8	6.0
Other reasons	2,978	268	13.7	9.0
To attend or leave college	872	131	6.7	15.0
Change of climate	212	3	0.2	1.4
Health reasons	460	18	0.9	3.9
Natural disaster	61	2	0.1	3.3
Other reasons	1,373	114	5.8	8.3

Source: Bureau of the Census, Geographic Mobility: 2007 to 2008, Detailed Tables, Internet site http://www.census.gov/ population/www/socdemo/migrate/cps2008.html; calculations by New Strategist"

Table 4.11 Reason for Moving among People Aged 20 to 24, 2007–08

(number and percent distribution of movers aged 20 to 24 by primary reason for move and share of total movers between March 2007 and March 2008, by age; numbers in thousands)

	total movers	movers aged 20 to 24		
		number	percent distribution	share of total
TOTAL MOVERS	**35,167**	**5,642**	**100.0%**	**16.0%**
Family reasons	**10,738**	**1,852**	**32.8**	**17.2**
Change in marital status	1,987	229	4.1	11.5
To establish own household	3,682	976	17.3	26.5
Other family reasons	5,069	647	11.5	12.8
Employment reasons	**7,352**	**1,147**	**20.3**	**15.6**
New job or job transfer	2,940	479	8.5	16.3
To look for work or lost job	794	120	2.1	15.1
To be closer to work/easier commute	2,183	384	6.8	17.6
Retired	140	5	0.1	3.6
Other job-related reason	1,295	159	2.8	12.3
Housing reasons	**14,098**	**1,932**	**34.2**	**13.7**
Wanted own home, not rent	2,033	277	4.9	13.6
Wanted better home/apartment	4,866	641	11.4	13.2
Wanted better neighborhood	1,778	223	4.0	12.5
Wanted cheaper housing	2,872	462	8.2	16.1
Other housing reasons	2,549	329	5.8	12.9
Other reasons	**2,978**	**711**	**12.6**	**23.9**
To attend or leave college	872	417	7.4	47.8
Change of climate	212	16	0.3	7.5
Health reasons	460	25	0.4	5.4
Natural disaster	61	6	0.1	9.8
Other reasons	1,373	247	4.4	18.0

Source: Bureau of the Census, Geographic Mobility: 2007 to 2008, Detailed Tables, Internet site http://www.census.gov/population/www/socdemo/migrate/cps2008.html; calculations by New Strategist

Table 4.12 Reason for Moving among People Aged 25 to 29, 2007–08

(number and percent distribution of movers aged 25 to 29 by primary reason for move and share of total movers between March 2007 and March 2008, by age; numbers in thousands)

	total movers	movers aged 25 to 29		
		number	percent distribution	share of total
TOTAL MOVERS	35,167	5,285	100.0%	15.0%
Family reasons	10,738	1,607	30.4	15.0
Change in marital status	1,987	309	5.8	15.6
To establish own household	3,682	695	13.2	18.9
Other family reasons	5,069	603	11.4	11.9
Employment reasons	7,352	1,230	23.3	16.7
New job or job transfer	2,940	560	10.6	19.0
To look for work or lost job	794	98	1.9	12.3
To be closer to work/easier commute	2,183	375	7.1	17.2
Retired	140	0	0.0	0.0
Other job-related reason	1,295	197	3.7	15.2
Housing reasons	14,098	2,018	38.2	14.3
Wanted own home, not rent	2,033	375	7.1	18.4
Wanted better home/apartment	4,866	683	12.9	14.0
Wanted better neighborhood	1,778	235	4.4	13.2
Wanted cheaper housing	2,872	414	7.8	14.4
Other housing reasons	2,549	311	5.9	12.2
Other reasons	2,978	430	8.1	14.4
To attend or leave college	872	145	2.7	16.6
Change of climate	212	12	0.2	5.7
Health reasons	460	35	0.7	7.6
Natural disaster	61	8	0.2	13.1
Other reasons	1,373	230	4.4	16.8

Source: Bureau of the Census, Geographic Mobility: 2007 to 2008, Detailed Tables, Internet site http://www.census.gov/population/www/socdemo/migrate/cps2008.html; calculations by New Strategist

Income

■ The median income of the average household fell 0.6 percent between 2000 and 2007, after adjusting for inflation. Among householders under age 35, the decline was a much larger 5 percent. (Millennials were aged 13 to 30 in 2007.)

■ Householders aged 15 to 24 had a median income of $31,790 in 2007, well below the $50,233 overall median. Within the age group, black householders have the lowest median income by far, while Asians and non-Hispanic whites have the highest.

■ In most age groups, married couples are the most affluent household type. Among households headed by people under age 25, however, the median income of male-headed families is higher than that of married couples.

■ The median incomes of men and women under age 25 are low—$11,209 and $8,959, respectively, in 2007—because many in the age group are in college and few work full-time.

■ Children and young adults are much more likely to be poor than middle-aged or older adults. While 12.5 percent of all Americans were poor in 2007, the poverty rate among the Millennial generation was a larger 15.2 percent.

Incomes of Millennial Householders Are below Their Peak

Young adults have gained ground since 1990, however.

The median income of the average household fell 0.6 percent between 2000 and 2007, after adjusting for inflation. Among householders under age 25, the decline was a much larger 5.2 percent. (Millennials were aged 13 to 30 in 2007.) Householders aged 25 to 34 saw their median income decline by 4.6 percent. The lackluster recovery following the recession of 2001 limited the earnings of young adults—statistics that do not reflect the economic downturn of 2008.

Despite the decline since 2000, the median income of householders under age 35 was higher in 2007 than in 1990, and the gain experienced by young adults exceeded that of the average household during those years. The median income of householders under age 25 was 15 percent greater in 2007 than in 1990, after adjusting for inflation, compared with a 9 percent gain for the average household. The median income of households headed by 25-to-34-year-olds rose 9 percent between 1990 and 2007.

■ The economic downturn probably has pushed the incomes of Millennials well below the levels recorded in the 2007 statistics.

Young adults have seen their incomes fall since 2000

(median income of households headed by people aged 15 to 34, 1990, 2000, and 2007; in 2007 dollars)

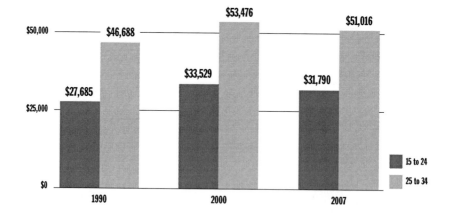

Table 5.1 Median Income of Households Headed by People under Age 35, 1990 to 2007

(median income of total households and households headed by people aged 15 to 34, and index of age group to total, 1990 to 2007; percent change for selected years; in 2007 dollars)

	total households	15 to 24	index, 15–24 to total	25 to 34	index, 25–34 to total
2007	$50,233	$31,790	63	$51,016	102
2006	49,568	31,815	64	50,559	102
2005	49,202	30,556	62	50,321	102
2004	48,665	30,269	62	49,907	103
2003	48,835	30,498	62	50,482	103
2002	48,878	32,073	66	52,244	107
2001	49,455	33,022	67	52,796	107
2000	50,557	33,529	66	53,476	106
1999	50,641	31,294	62	52,376	103
1998	49,397	29,934	61	50,901	103
1997	47,665	29,089	61	49,171	103
1996	46,704	28,210	60	47,225	101
1995	46,034	28,341	62	46,879	102
1994	44,636	26,756	60	45,863	103
1993	44,143	27,317	62	44,200	100
1992	44,359	25,575	58	45,232	102
1991	44,726	27,188	61	45,789	102
1990	46,049	27,685	60	46,688	101
Percent change					
2000 to 2007	–0.6%	–5.2%	–	–4.6%	–
1990 to 2007	9.1	14.8	–	9.3	–

Note: The index is calculated by dividing the median income of the age group by the national median and multiplying by 100. "–" means not applicable.
Source: Bureau of the Census, Current Population Survey Annual Social and Economic Supplements, Internet site http://www .census.gov/hhes//www/income/histinc/inchhtoc.html; calculations by New Strategist

Household Income Differs Sharply by Race and Hispanic Origin

Among householders under age 25, blacks have the lowest incomes.

Householders aged 15 to 24 had a median income of $31,790 in 2007, well below the $50,233 over-all median. Within the age group, black householders have the lowest incomes by far—a median of just $20,753. Asians and non-Hispanic whites have the highest median household income in the age group—over $35,000. The Hispanic median is $31,628.

Household income rises substantially in the 25-to-29 age group as young men and women marry and more households have two incomes. At $47,358, the median income of householders aged 25 to 29 is just below the overall median. Asians have the highest median income within the 25-to-29 age group, a comfortable $60,165.

■ Differences in household income among young adults by race and Hispanic origin are due to differences in household composition and educational attainment.

Asians and non-Hispanic whites have the highest incomes

(median income of householders aged 15 to 29, by race and Hispanic origin, 2007)

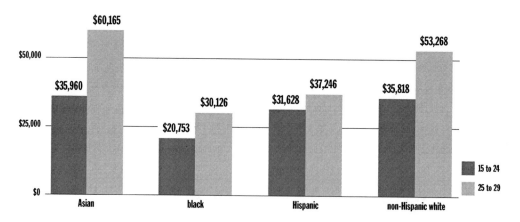

Table 5.2 Income of Households Headed by People under Age 30, 2007: Total Households

(number and percent distribution of total households and households headed by people under age 30, by household income, 2007; households in thousands as of 2008)

	total	15 to 24	25 to 29
Total households	**116,783**	**6,554**	**9,400**
Under $10,000	8,455	900	611
$10,000 to $19,999	13,778	1,051	886
$20,000 to $29,999	13,115	1,092	1,166
$30,000 to $39,999	12,006	921	1,160
$40,000 to $49,999	10,733	743	1,120
$50,000 to $59,999	9,565	595	942
$60,000 to $69,999	8,009	341	786
$70,000 to $79,999	7,006	274	652
$80,000 to $89,999	5,788	165	496
$90,000 to $99,999	4,741	120	364
$100,000 or more	23,586	351	1,217
Median income	$50,233	$31,790	$47,358
Total households	**100.0%**	**100.0%**	**100.0%**
Under $10,000	7.2	13.7	6.5
$10,000 to $19,999	11.8	16.0	9.4
$20,000 to $29,999	11.2	16.7	12.4
$30,000 to $39,999	10.3	14.1	12.3
$40,000 to $49,999	9.2	11.3	11.9
$50,000 to $59,999	8.2	9.1	10.0
$60,000 to $69,999	6.9	5.2	8.4
$70,000 to $79,999	6.0	4.2	6.9
$80,000 to $89,999	5.0	2.5	5.3
$90,000 to $99,999	4.1	1.8	3.9
$100,000 or more	20.2	5.4	12.9

Source: Bureau of the Census, 2008 Current Population Survey Annual Social and Economic Supplement, Internet site http://www.census.gov/hhes/www/macro/032008/hhinc/new02_001.htm; calculations by New Strategist

Table 5.3 Income of Households Headed by People under Age 30, 2007: Asian Households

(number and percent distribution of total Asian households and Asian households headed by people under age 30, by household income, 2007; households in thousands as of 2008)

	total	15 to 24	25 to 29
Total Asian households	**4,715**	**248**	**448**
Under $10,000	311	34	37
$10,000 to $19,999	365	32	31
$20,000 to $29,999	388	37	44
$30,000 to $39,999	357	30	39
$40,000 to $49,999	372	23	37
$50,000 to $59,999	336	20	36
$60,000 to $69,999	327	20	35
$70,000 to $79,999	307	16	31
$80,000 to $89,999	243	8	29
$90,000 to $99,999	240	4	36
$100,000 or more	1,468	26	94
Median income	$65,876	$35,960	$60,165
Total Asian households	**100.0%**	**100.0%**	**100.0%**
Under $10,000	6.6	13.7	8.3
$10,000 to $19,999	7.7	12.9	6.9
$20,000 to $29,999	8.2	14.9	9.8
$30,000 to $39,999	7.6	12.1	8.7
$40,000 to $49,999	7.9	9.3	8.3
$50,000 to $59,999	7.1	8.1	8.0
$60,000 to $69,999	6.9	8.1	7.8
$70,000 to $79,999	6.5	6.5	6.9
$80,000 to $89,999	5.2	3.2	6.5
$90,000 to $99,999	5.1	1.6	8.0
$100,000 or more	31.1	10.5	21.0

Note: Asians include those who identify themselves as being of the race alone and those who identify themselves as being of the race in combination with other races.
Source: Bureau of the Census, 2008 Current Population Survey Annual Social and Economic Supplement, Internet site http:// www.census.gov/hhes/www/macro/032008/hhinc/new02_001.htm; calculations by New Strategist

Table 5.4 Income of Households Headed by People under Age 30, 2007: Black Households

(number and percent distribution of total black households and black households headed by people under age 30, by household income, 2007; households in thousands as of 2008)

	total	15 to 24	25 to 29
Total black households	**14,976**	**1,182**	**1,336**
Under $10,000	2,256	320	203
$10,000 to $19,999	2,444	257	226
$20,000 to $29,999	1,988	190	236
$30,000 to $39,999	1,746	153	176
$40,000 to $49,999	1,379	69	118
$50,000 to $59,999	1,161	73	82
$60,000 to $69,999	867	34	73
$70,000 to $79,999	683	27	64
$80,000 to $89,999	549	12	46
$90,000 to $99,999	403	10	15
$100,000 or more	1,500	35	96
Median income	$34,091	$20,753	$30,126
Total black households	**100.0%**	**100.0%**	**100.0%**
Under $10,000	15.1	27.1	15.2
$10,000 to $19,999	16.3	21.7	16.9
$20,000 to $29,999	13.3	16.1	17.7
$30,000 to $39,999	11.7	12.9	13.2
$40,000 to $49,999	9.2	5.8	8.8
$50,000 to $59,999	7.8	6.2	6.1
$60,000 to $69,999	5.8	2.9	5.5
$70,000 to $79,999	4.6	2.3	4.8
$80,000 to $89,999	3.7	1.0	3.4
$90,000 to $99,999	2.7	0.8	1.1
$100,000 or more	10.0	3.0	7.2

Note: Blacks include those who identify themselves as being of the race alone and those who identify themselves as being of the race in combination with other races.
Source: Bureau of the Census, 2008 Current Population Survey Annual Social and Economic Supplement, Internet site http://www.census.gov/hhes/www/macro/032008/hhinc/new02_001.htm; calculations by New Strategist

Table 5.5 Income of Households Headed by People under Age 30, 2007: Hispanic Households

(number and percent distribution of total Hispanic households and Hispanic households headed by people under age 30, by household income, 2007; households in thousands as of 2008)

	total	15 to 24	25 to 29
Total Hispanic households	**13,339**	**1,182**	**1,601**
Under $10,000	1,184	126	112
$10,000 to $19,999	1,901	220	173
$20,000 to $29,999	1,961	202	297
$30,000 to $39,999	1,787	190	277
$40,000 to $49,999	1,387	137	197
$50,000 to $59,999	1,119	92	146
$60,000 to $69,999	921	58	110
$70,000 to $79,999	758	57	89
$80,000 to $89,999	534	25	56
$90,000 to $99,999	401	25	37
$100,000 or more	1,385	49	105
Median income	$38,679	$31,628	$37,246
Total Hispanic households	**100.0%**	**100.0%**	**100.0%**
Under $10,000	8.9	10.7	7.0
$10,000 to $19,999	14.3	18.6	10.8
$20,000 to $29,999	14.7	17.1	18.6
$30,000 to $39,999	13.4	16.1	17.3
$40,000 to $49,999	10.4	11.6	12.3
$50,000 to $59,999	8.4	7.8	9.1
$60,000 to $69,999	6.9	4.9	6.9
$70,000 to $79,999	5.7	4.8	5.6
$80,000 to $89,999	4.0	2.1	3.5
$90,000 to $99,999	3.0	2.1	2.3
$100,000 or more	10.4	4.1	6.6

Source: Bureau of the Census, 2008 Current Population Survey Annual Social and Economic Supplement, Internet site http://www.census.gov/hhes/www/macro/032008/hhinc/new02_001.htm; calculations by New Strategist

Table 5.6 Income of Households Headed by People under Age 30, 2007: Non-Hispanic White Households

(number and percent distribution of total non-Hispanic white households and non-Hispanic white households headed by people under age 30, by household income, 2007; households in thousands as of 2008)

	total	15 to 24	25 to 29
Total non-Hispanic white households	**82,765**	**3,918**	**5,942**
Under $10,000	4,607	416	262
$10,000 to $19,999	8,971	550	442
$20,000 to $29,999	8,639	649	581
$30,000 to $39,999	8,017	549	664
$40,000 to $49,999	7,479	506	743
$50,000 to $59,999	6,854	408	670
$60,000 to $69,999	5,836	230	556
$70,000 to $79,999	5,213	171	467
$80,000 to $89,999	4,419	119	366
$90,000 to $99,999	3,664	79	277
$100,000 or more	19,062	240	914
Median income	$54,920	$35,818	$53,268
Total non-Hispanic white households	**100.0%**	**100.0%**	**100.0%**
Under $10,000	5.6	10.6	4.4
$10,000 to $19,999	10.8	14.0	7.4
$20,000 to $29,999	10.4	16.6	9.8
$30,000 to $39,999	9.7	14.0	11.2
$40,000 to $49,999	9.0	12.9	12.5
$50,000 to $59,999	8.3	10.4	11.3
$60,000 to $69,999	7.1	5.9	9.4
$70,000 to $79,999	6.3	4.4	7.9
$80,000 to $89,999	5.3	3.0	6.2
$90,000 to $99,999	4.4	2.0	4.7
$100,000 or more	23.0	6.1	15.4

Note: Non-Hispanic whites are those who identify themselves as being white alone and not Hispanic.
Source: Bureau of the Census, 2008 Current Population Survey Annual Social and Economic Supplement, Internet site http:// www.census.gov/hhes/www/macro/032008/hhinc/new02_001.htm; calculations by New Strategist

Married Couples Have Above-Average Incomes

Among householders under age 25, the median income of male-headed families is slightly higher than that of married couples, however.

In most age groups married couples are the most affluent household type. Among households headed by people aged 15 to 24, however, the $43,188 median income of male-headed families is higher than the $40,706 median of married couples. Female-headed family households in the age group had a median income of just $23,008, while women who live alone had the lowest incomes, a median of just $19,292.

Male-headed families often have more than one working adult in the household, which boosts income. While most married couples also have more than one earner in the household, among young couples a relatively large proportion has a stay-at-home wife. Many of these couples have young children, and the wife is taking care of the kids rather than working outside the home—lowering household income.

In the 25-to-29 age group, the incomes of married couples soar as dual earners become more common. The median income of married couples aged 25 to 29 stood at $60,847 in 2007, well above that of any other household type.

■ Young adult households are diverse, many having at best one earner, which limits their incomes.

Women who live alone have the lowest incomes

(median income of householders aged 25 to 29, by household type, 2007)

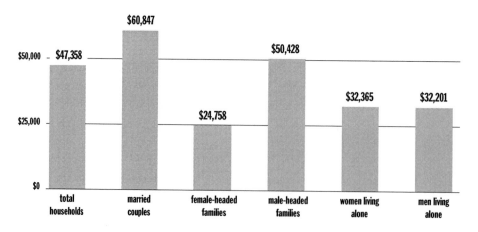

Table 5.7 Income of Households by Household Type, 2007: Aged 15 to 24

(number and percent distribution of households headed by people aged 15 to 24, by household income and household type, 2007; households in thousands as of 2008)

| | | family households | | | nonfamily households | | | |
| | | | | | female householder | | male householder | |
	total	married couples	female hh, no spouse present	male hh, no spouse present	total	living alone	total	living alone
Total households headed by 15-to-24-year-olds	**6,554**	**1,224**	**1,318**	**817**	**1,527**	**805**	**1,668**	**844**
Under $10,000	900	53	319	49	261	207	216	158
$10,000 to $19,999	1,051	136	282	87	286	206	260	196
$20,000 to $29,999	1,092	181	176	110	302	191	319	229
$30,000 to $39,999	921	226	152	120	191	69	232	108
$40,000 to $49,999	743	186	99	97	165	80	198	70
$50,000 to $59,999	595	155	82	71	123	43	164	46
$60,000 to $69,999	341	98	37	62	59	6	86	16
$70,000 to $79,999	274	84	40	60	50	1	39	3
$80,000 to $89,999	165	21	31	33	28	0	52	10
$90,000 to $99,999	120	26	20	22	20	0	33	0
$100,000 or more	351	57	80	105	41	0	67	9
Median income	$31,790	$40,706	$23,008	$43,188	$26,665	$19,292	$30,989	$22,507
Total households headed by 15-to-24-year-olds	**100.0%**	**100.0%**	**100.0%**	**100.0%**	**100.0%**	**100.0%**	**100.0%**	**100.0%**
Under $10,000	13.7	4.3	24.2	6.0	17.1	25.7	12.9	18.7
$10,000 to $19,999	16.0	11.1	21.4	10.6	18.7	25.6	15.6	23.2
$20,000 to $29,999	16.7	14.8	13.4	13.5	19.8	23.7	19.1	27.1
$30,000 to $39,999	14.1	18.5	11.5	14.7	12.5	8.6	13.9	12.8
$40,000 to $49,999	11.3	15.2	7.5	11.9	10.8	9.9	11.9	8.3
$50,000 to $59,999	9.1	12.7	6.2	8.7	8.1	5.3	9.8	5.5
$60,000 to $69,999	5.2	8.0	2.8	7.6	3.9	0.7	5.2	1.9
$70,000 to $79,999	4.2	6.9	3.0	7.3	3.3	0.1	2.3	0.4
$80,000 to $89,999	2.5	1.7	2.4	4.0	1.8	0.0	3.1	1.2
$90,000 to $99,999	1.8	2.1	1.5	2.7	1.3	0.0	2.0	0.0
$100,000 or more	5.4	4.7	6.1	12.9	2.7	0.0	4.0	1.1

Note: "hh" is short for householder.
Source: Bureau of the Census, 2008 Current Population Survey Annual Social and Economic Supplement, Internet site http://www.census.gov/hhes/www/macro/032008/hhinc/new02_000.htm; calculations by New Strategist

Table 5.8 Income of Households by Household Type, 2007: Aged 25 to 29

(number and percent distribution of households headed by people aged 25 to 29, by income and household type, 2007; households in thousands as of 2008)

| | total | family households | | | nonfamily households | | | |
| | | married couples | female hh, no spouse present | male hh, no spouse present | female householder | | male householder | |
					total	living alone	total	living alone
Total households headed by 25-to-29-year-olds	**9,400**	**3,753**	**1,466**	**650**	**1,457**	**922**	**2,074**	**1,245**
Under $10,000	611	60	269	22	126	115	133	116
$10,000 to $19,999	886	160	329	60	141	125	198	161
$20,000 to $29,999	1,166	328	257	78	203	168	302	247
$30,000 to $39,999	1,160	402	153	89	200	162	316	241
$40,000 to $49,999	1,120	459	138	73	201	148	249	131
$50,000 to $59,999	942	423	85	76	130	68	226	144
$60,000 to $69,999	786	409	52	67	109	42	151	66
$70,000 to $79,999	652	401	39	45	70	25	97	37
$80,000 to $89,999	496	266	47	30	62	13	92	36
$90,000 to $99,999	364	187	26	12	49	17	89	16
$100,000 or more	1,217	662	73	97	163	37	223	49
Median income	$47,358	$60,847	$24,758	$50,428	$41,956	$32,365	$42,359	$32,201
Total households headed by 25-to-29-year-olds	**100.0%**	**100.0%**	**100.0%**	**100.0%**	**100.0%**	**100.0%**	**100.0%**	**100.0%**
Under $10,000	6.5	1.6	18.3	3.4	8.6	12.5	6.4	9.3
$10,000 to $19,999	9.4	4.3	22.4	9.2	9.7	13.6	9.5	12.9
$20,000 to $29,999	12.4	8.7	17.5	12.0	13.9	18.2	14.6	19.8
$30,000 to $39,999	12.3	10.7	10.4	13.7	13.7	17.6	15.2	19.4
$40,000 to $49,999	11.9	12.2	9.4	11.2	13.8	16.1	12.0	10.5
$50,000 to $59,999	10.0	11.3	5.8	11.7	8.9	7.4	10.9	11.6
$60,000 to $69,999	8.4	10.9	3.5	10.3	7.5	4.6	7.3	5.3
$70,000 to $79,999	6.9	10.7	2.7	6.9	4.8	2.7	4.7	3.0
$80,000 to $89,999	5.3	7.1	3.2	4.6	4.3	1.4	4.4	2.9
$90,000 to $99,999	3.9	5.0	1.8	1.8	3.4	1.8	4.3	1.3
$100,000 or more	12.9	17.6	5.0	14.9	11.2	4.0	10.8	3.9

Note: "hh" is short for householder.
Source: Bureau of the Census, 2008 Current Population Survey Annual Social and Economic Supplement, Internet site http://www.census.gov/hhes/www/macro/032008/hhinc/new02_000.htm; calculations by New Strategist

Men under Age 35 Have Seen Incomes Decline since 2000

The incomes of their female counterparts have grown, however.

Between 2000 and 2007, men aged 15 to 24 saw their median income fall 2.5 percent, after adjusting for inflation. Women of the same age experienced a 1.1 percent gain in median income during those years. Men aged 25 to 34 experienced a much sharper decline, their inflation-adjusted median income falling by 9.8 percent between 2000 and 2007. Their female counterparts enjoyed a 2.1 percent rise in median income.

Despite the decline since 2000 in the median income of young men, the median income of young men and women was substantially greater in 2007 than in 1990. For men aged 15 to 24, median income grew 15 percent during those years, after adjusting for inflation. Those aged 25 to 34, however, did not see any increase. Among women aged 15 to 24, median income rose 19 percent between 1990 and 2007, and for those aged 25 to 34 it increased by an even larger 34 percent.

■ The median income of men and women under age 25 is low because many are going to school and working part-time or not at all. As these young adults earn their degree, their incomes will rise.

The incomes of young men and women are low because many work part-time

(median income of people aged 15 to 24, by sex, 2007)

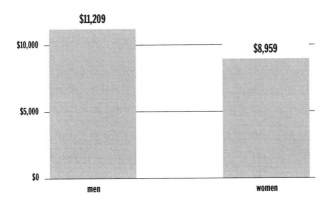

Table 5.9 Median Income of Men under Age 35, 1990 to 2007

(median income of men aged 15 or older and aged 15 to 34, and index of age group to total, 1990 to 2007; percent change for selected years; in 2007 dollars)

	total men	15 to 24	index, 15–24 to total	25 to 34	index, 25–34 to total
2007	$33,196	$11,209	34	$32,875	99
2006	33,180	11,275	34	33,043	100
2005	33,217	11,119	33	33,096	100
2004	33,497	11,067	33	34,020	102
2003	33,743	11,230	33	34,454	102
2002	33,698	11,113	33	35,356	105
2001	34,082	10,893	32	35,732	105
2000	34,126	11,494	34	36,427	107
1999	33,963	10,391	31	36,556	108
1998	33,654	10,404	31	35,718	106
1997	32,475	9,619	30	33,485	103
1996	31,363	9,159	29	33,133	106
1995	30,480	9,339	31	31,894	105
1994	30,049	9,751	32	31,275	104
1993	29,817	9,084	30	30,983	104
1992	29,617	9,118	31	31,126	105
1991	30,389	9,325	31	32,061	106
1990	31,208	9,718	31	32,900	105
Percent change					
2000 to 2007	−2.7%	−2.5%	–	−9.8%	–
1990 to 2007	6.4	15.3	–	−0.1	–

Note: The index is calculated by dividing the median income of the age group by the national median and multiplying by 100. "–" means not applicable.

Source: Bureau of the Census, data from the Current Population Survey Annual Demographic Supplements, Internet site http://www.census.gov/hhes/www/income/histinc/p08AR.html; calculations by New Strategist

Table 5.10 Median Income of Women under Age 35, 1990 to 2007

(median income of women aged 15 or older and aged 15 to 34, and index of age group to total, 1990 to 2007; percent change for selected years; in 2007 dollars)

	total women	15 to 24	index, 15–24 to total	25 to 34	index, 25–34 to total
2007	$20,922	$8,959	43	$25,884	124
2006	20,582	8,898	43	24,865	121
2005	19,729	8,730	44	24,231	123
2004	19,393	8,456	44	24,223	125
2003	19,457	8,382	43	24,793	127
2002	19,376	8,739	45	24,951	129
2001	19,458	8,745	45	25,148	129
2000	19,340	8,862	46	25,344	131
1999	19,044	8,310	44	24,027	126
1998	18,331	8,300	45	23,193	127
1997	17,650	8,169	46	22,731	129
1996	16,863	7,739	46	21,560	128
1995	16,387	7,173	44	21,016	128
1994	15,863	7,620	48	20,591	130
1993	15,608	7,561	48	19,765	127
1992	15,513	7,486	48	19,737	127
1991	15,553	7,716	50	19,247	124
1990	15,486	7,539	49	19,360	125
Percent change					
2000 to 2007	8.2%	1.1%	–	2.1%	–
1990 to 2007	35.1	18.8	–	33.7	–

Note: The index is calculated by dividing the median income of the age group by the national median and multiplying by 100. "–" means not applicable.
Source: Bureau of the Census, data from the Current Population Survey Annual Demographic Supplements, Internet site http:// www.census.gov/hhes/www/income/histinc/p08AR.html; calculations by New Strategist

Incomes of Millennial Men Are Low

Their incomes are low because few work full-time.

The median income of men aged 15 to 24 stood at just $11,209 in 2007, but that of men aged 25 to 29 was a much higher $30,281. (Millennials were aged 13 to 30 in 2007.) Behind the low figure for the younger group lies the fact that few men of that age work full-time—only 23 percent are full-time workers versus 54 percent of all men aged 15 or older. A much larger 66 percent of men aged 25 to 29 work full-time, hence their higher incomes.

Among men aged 15 to 24, Hispanics have the highest median income ($14,886) because they are most likely to work full-time. Among the 30 percent with full-time jobs, median income was $21,459 in 2007. Only 14 percent of Asian men under age 25 work full-time because most are in college, which explains their modest median income of $10,652. The median income of non-Hispanic white men aged 15 to 24 is an almost identical $10,683; they too are likely to be in college—only 23 percent work full-time. Black men under age 25 have the lowest income, just $9,996 in 2007. Only 19 percent of black men in the age group work full-time, and their median income stood at $22,181 in 2007.

■ Men's incomes rise steeply as they enter their late twenties and the majority gets full-time jobs.

Among young men, Hispanics have the highest incomes

(median income of men aged 15 to 24, by race and Hispanic origin, 2007)

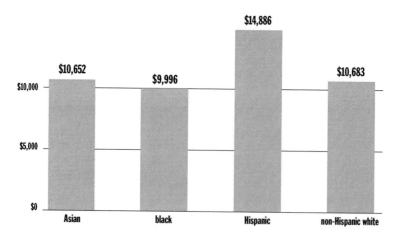

Table 5.11 Income of Men under Age 30, 2007: Total Men

(number and percent distribution of men aged 15 or older and under age 30 by income, 2007; median income by work status, and percent working year-round, full-time; men in thousands as of 2008)

	total	15 to 24	25 to 29
TOTAL MEN	**115,678**	**21,208**	**10,721**
Without income	**10,889**	**7,066**	**758**
With income	**104,789**	**14,142**	**9,963**
Under $10,000	13,989	6,516	1,083
$10,000 to $19,999	16,953	3,292	1,757
$20,000 to $29,999	15,483	2,286	2,059
$30,000 to $39,999	13,877	1,115	1,751
$40,000 to $49,999	10,420	460	1,125
$50,000 to $59,999	8,291	219	850
$60,000 to $69,999	5,814	81	455
$70,000 to $79,999	4,677	66	305
$80,000 to $89,999	3,066	36	149
$90,000 to $99,999	2,273	5	123
$100,000 or more	9,949	67	304
Median income of men with income	$33,196	$11,209	$30,281
Median income of full-time workers	46,224	23,745	35,900
Percent working full-time	54.5%	22.8%	66.3%
TOTAL MEN	**100.0%**	**100.0%**	**100.0%**
Without income	**9.4**	**33.3**	**7.1**
With income	**90.6**	**66.7**	**92.9**
Under $10,000	12.1	30.7	10.1
$10,000 to $19,999	14.7	15.5	16.4
$20,000 to $29,999	13.4	10.8	19.2
$30,000 to $39,999	12.0	5.3	16.3
$40,000 to $49,999	9.0	2.2	10.5
$50,000 to $59,999	7.2	1.0	7.9
$60,000 to $69,999	5.0	0.4	4.2
$70,000 to $79,999	4.0	0.3	2.8
$80,000 to $89,999	2.7	0.2	1.4
$90,000 to $99,999	2.0	0.0	1.1
$100,000 or more	8.6	0.3	2.8

Source: Bureau of the Census, 2008 Current Population Survey Annual Social and Economic Supplement, Internet site http:// www.census.gov/hhes/www/macro/032008/perinc/new01_000.htm; calculations by New Strategist

Table 5.12 Income of Men under Age 30, 2007: Asian Men

(number and percent distribution of Asian men aged 15 or older and under age 30 by income, 2007; median income by work status, and percent working year-round, full-time; men in thousands as of 2008)

	total	15 to 24	25 to 29
TOTAL ASIAN MEN	**5,414**	**969**	**562**
Without income	**705**	**411**	**56**
With income	**4,709**	**558**	**506**
Under $10,000	639	259	57
$10,000 to $19,999	645	145	72
$20,000 to $29,999	646	94	93
$30,000 to $39,999	536	31	69
$40,000 to $49,999	426	10	61
$50,000 to $59,999	338	4	56
$60,000 to $69,999	278	5	19
$70,000 to $79,999	276	2	32
$80,000 to $89,999	156	3	13
$90,000 to $99,999	144	1	11
$100,000 or more	625	3	21
Median income of men with income	$36,729	$10,652	$34,503
Median income of full-time workers	51,001	25,367	41,837
Percent working full-time	58.5%	14.0%	64.9%
TOTAL ASIAN MEN	**100.0%**	**100.0%**	**100.0%**
Without income	**13.0**	**42.4**	**10.0**
With income	**87.0**	**57.6**	**90.0**
Under $10,000	11.8	26.7	10.1
$10,000 to $19,999	11.9	15.0	12.8
$20,000 to $29,999	11.9	9.7	16.5
$30,000 to $39,999	9.9	3.2	12.3
$40,000 to $49,999	7.9	1.0	10.9
$50,000 to $59,999	6.2	0.4	10.0
$60,000 to $69,999	5.1	0.5	3.4
$70,000 to $79,999	5.1	0.2	5.7
$80,000 to $89,999	2.9	0.3	2.3
$90,000 to $99,999	2.7	0.1	2.0
$100,000 or more	11.5	0.3	3.7

Note: Asians include those who identify themselves as being of the race alone and those who identify themselves as being of the race in combination with other races.
Source: Bureau of the Census, 2008 Current Population Survey Annual Social and Economic Supplement, Internet site http://www.census.gov/hhes/www/macro/032008/perinc/new01_000.htm; calculations by New Strategist

Table 5.13 Income of Men under Age 30, 2007: Black Men

(number and percent distribution of black men aged 15 or older and under age 30 by income, 2007; median income by work status, and percent working year-round, full-time; men in thousands as of 2008)

	total	15 to 24	25 to 29
TOTAL BLACK MEN	**13,370**	**3,233**	**1,384**
Without income	**2,389**	**1,452**	**236**
With income	**10,981**	**1,781**	**1,148**
Under $10,000	2,307	891	217
$10,000 to $19,999	2,145	416	273
$20,000 to $29,999	1,691	243	208
$30,000 to $39,999	1,559	135	195
$40,000 to $49,999	997	43	95
$50,000 to $59,999	747	42	51
$60,000 to $69,999	482	2	28
$70,000 to $79,999	345	1	33
$80,000 to $89,999	196	0	18
$90,000 to $99,999	122	0	5
$100,000 or more	390	8	24
Median income of men with income	$25,792	$9,996	$24,218
Median income of full-time workers	36,780	22,181	30,895
Percent working full-time	46.1%	18.8%	51.2%
TOTAL BLACK MEN	**100.0%**	**100.0%**	**100.0%**
Without income	**17.9**	**44.9**	**17.1**
With income	**82.1**	**55.1**	**82.9**
Under $10,000	17.3	27.6	15.7
$10,000 to $19,999	16.0	12.9	19.7
$20,000 to $29,999	12.6	7.5	15.0
$30,000 to $39,999	11.7	4.2	14.1
$40,000 to $49,999	7.5	1.3	6.9
$50,000 to $59,999	5.6	1.3	3.7
$60,000 to $69,999	3.6	0.1	2.0
$70,000 to $79,999	2.6	0.0	2.4
$80,000 to $89,999	1.5	0.0	1.3
$90,000 to $99,999	0.9	0.0	0.4
$100,000 or more	2.9	0.2	1.7

Note: Blacks include those who identify themselves as being of the race alone and those who identify themselves as being of the race in combination with other races.
Source: Bureau of the Census, 2008 Current Population Survey Annual Social and Economic Supplement, Internet site http://www.census.gov/hhes/www/macro/032008/perinc/new01_000.htm; calculations by New Strategist

Table 5.14 Income of Men under Age 30, 2007: Hispanic Men

(number and percent distribution of Hispanic men aged 15 or older and under age 30 by income, 2007; median income by work status, and percent working year-round, full-time; men in thousands as of 2008)

	total	15 to 24	25 to 29
TOTAL HISPANIC MEN	**16,837**	**3,842**	**2,413**
Without income	**2,228**	**1,474**	**170**
With income	**14,609**	**2,368**	**2,243**
Under $10,000	2,135	838	262
$10,000 to $19,999	3,548	741	600
$20,000 to $29,999	3,168	492	603
$30,000 to $39,999	2,143	175	348
$40,000 to $49,999	1,209	70	197
$50,000 to $59,999	809	32	80
$60,000 to $69,999	513	4	68
$70,000 to $79,999	330	11	33
$80,000 to $89,999	201	1	11
$90,000 to $99,999	127	0	8
$100,000 or more	425	5	31
Median income of men with income	$24,451	$14,886	$23,058
Median income of full-time workers	30,454	21,459	26,458
Percent working full-time	58.0%	29.5%	68.0%
TOTAL HISPANIC MEN	**100.0%**	**100.0%**	**100.0%**
Without income	**13.2**	**38.4**	**7.0**
With income	**86.8**	**61.6**	**93.0**
Under $10,000	12.7	21.8	10.9
$10,000 to $19,999	21.1	19.3	24.9
$20,000 to $29,999	18.8	12.8	25.0
$30,000 to $39,999	12.7	4.6	14.4
$40,000 to $49,999	7.2	1.8	8.2
$50,000 to $59,999	4.8	0.8	3.3
$60,000 to $69,999	3.0	0.1	2.8
$70,000 to $79,999	2.0	0.3	1.4
$80,000 to $89,999	1.2	0.0	0.5
$90,000 to $99,999	0.8	0.0	0.3
$100,000 or more	2.5	0.1	1.3

Source: Bureau of the Census, 2008 Current Population Survey Annual Social and Economic Supplement, Internet site http://www.census.gov/hhes/www/macro/032008/perinc/new01_000.htm; calculations by New Strategist

Table 5.15 Income of Men under Age 30, 2007: Non-Hispanic White Men

(number and percent distribution of non-Hispanic white men aged 15 or older and under age 30 by income, 2007; median income by work status, and percent working year-round, full-time; men in thousands as of 2008)

	total	15 to 24	25 to 29
TOTAL NON-HISPANIC WHITE MEN	**79,100**	**13,018**	**6,286**
Without income	**5,483**	**3,677**	**291**
With income	**73,617**	**9,341**	**5,995**
Under $10,000	8,760	4,480	540
$10,000 to $19,999	10,470	1,969	795
$20,000 to $29,999	9,834	1,441	1,141
$30,000 to $39,999	9,518	765	1,125
$40,000 to $49,999	7,703	338	762
$50,000 to $59,999	6,323	144	656
$60,000 to $69,999	4,493	68	335
$70,000 to $79,999	3,717	49	208
$80,000 to $89,999	2,491	32	110
$90,000 to $99,999	1,871	5	97
$100,000 or more	8,438	50	227
Median income of men with income	$37,373	$10,683	$34,033
Median income of full-time workers	51,465	25,256	40,139
Percent working full-time	55.0%	22.5%	69.2%
TOTAL NON-HISPANIC WHITE MEN	**100.0%**	**100.0%**	**100.0%**
Without income	**6.9**	**28.2**	**4.6**
With income	**93.1**	**71.8**	**95.4**
Under $10,000	11.1	34.4	8.6
$10,000 to $19,999	13.2	15.1	12.6
$20,000 to $29,999	12.4	11.1	18.2
$30,000 to $39,999	12.0	5.9	17.9
$40,000 to $49,999	9.7	2.6	12.1
$50,000 to $59,999	8.0	1.1	10.4
$60,000 to $69,999	5.7	0.5	5.3
$70,000 to $79,999	4.7	0.4	3.3
$80,000 to $89,999	3.1	0.2	1.7
$90,000 to $99,999	2.4	0.0	1.5
$100,000 or more	10.7	0.4	3.6

Note: Non-Hispanic whites are those who identify themselves as being white alone and not Hispanic.
Source: Bureau of the Census, 2008 Current Population Survey Annual Social and Economic Supplement, Internet site http://www.census.gov/hhes/www/macro/032008/perinc/new01_000.htm; calculations by New Strategist

Incomes of Young Women Are Low

Incomes are low because few women under age 25 work full-time.

The median income of women aged 15 to 24 is even lower than that of their male counterparts, standing at just $8,959 in 2007. Behind the low figures for both men and women lies the fact that few in the age group work full-time. Only 17 percent of women under age 25 work full-time compared with 37 percent of all women aged 15 or older. Among women aged 15 to 24 who work full-time, median income was $22,652, well below the $36,167 median of all women who work full-time. Median income rises to $32,305 among full-time working women aged 25 to 29.

Among women under age 25, Asians are least likely to work full-time (14 percent) because they are most likely to attend college. The median income of Asian women under age 25 was just $8,853 in 2007. The median income of non-Hispanic white women in the age group is about the same ($9,061), although a larger share (17 percent) has a full-time job. Black women aged 15 to 24 have the lowest median income among racial and ethnic groups, just $8,079. Only 16 percent of black women under age 25 work full-time. Among women under age 25, Hispanics have the highest income, a median of $9,727 in 2007. Hispanic women do not retain this lead, however. By age 25 to 29, the median income of Hispanic women is lower than that of Asians, blacks, or non-Hispanics whites.

■ Young women are more likely to be in school than young men, many working part-time or not at all. Their incomes will rise as they gain the credentials to advance in the job market.

Among the youngest women, Hispanics have the highest incomes

(median income of women aged 15 to 24, by race and Hispanic origin, 2007)

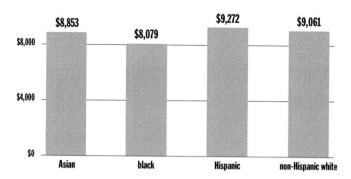

Table 5.16 Income of Women under Age 30, 2007: Total Women

(number and percent distribution of women aged 15 or older and under age 30 by income, 2007; median income by work status, and percent working year-round, full-time; women in thousands as of 2008)

	total	15 to 24	25 to 29
TOTAL WOMEN	**122,470**	**20,635**	**10,337**
Without income	**17,240**	**7,480**	**1,423**
With income	**105,230**	**13,155**	**8,914**
Under $10,000	26,931	7,012	1,591
$10,000 to $19,999	23,616	3,183	1,742
$20,000 to $29,999	16,710	1,615	1,921
$30,000 to $39,999	12,457	755	1,496
$40,000 to $49,999	8,573	339	963
$50,000 to $59,999	5,461	134	510
$60,000 to $69,999	3,589	56	297
$70,000 to $79,999	2,317	20	174
$80,000 to $89,999	1,371	10	55
$90,000 to $99,999	958	6	40
$100,000 or more	3,246	25	126
Median income of women with income	$20,922	$8,959	$25,500
Median income of full-time workers	36,167	22,652	32,305
Percent working full-time	37.3%	16.6%	51.6%
TOTAL WOMEN	**100.0%**	**100.0%**	**100.0%**
Without income	**14.1**	**36.2**	**13.8**
With income	**85.9**	**63.8**	**86.2**
Under $10,000	22.0	34.0	15.4
$10,000 to $19,999	19.3	15.4	16.9
$20,000 to $29,999	13.6	7.8	18.6
$30,000 to $39,999	10.2	3.7	14.5
$40,000 to $49,999	7.0	1.6	9.3
$50,000 to $59,999	4.5	0.6	4.9
$60,000 to $69,999	2.9	0.3	2.9
$70,000 to $79,999	1.9	0.1	1.7
$80,000 to $89,999	1.1	0.0	0.5
$90,000 to $99,999	0.8	0.0	0.4
$100,000 or more	2.7	0.1	1.2

Source: Bureau of the Census, 2008 Current Population Survey Annual Social and Economic Supplement, Internet site http://www.census.gov/hhes/www/macro/032008/perinc/new01_000.htm; calculations by New Strategist

Table 5.17 Income of Women under Age 30, 2007: Asian Women

(number and percent distribution of Asian women aged 15 or older and under age 30 by income, 2007; median income by work status, and percent working year-round, full-time; women in thousands as of 2008)

	total	15 to 24	25 to 29
TOTAL ASIAN WOMEN	**6,029**	**982**	**588**
Without income	**1,243**	**438**	**107**
With income	**4,786**	**544**	**481**
Under $10,000	1,217	292	92
$10,000 to $19,999	866	103	76
$20,000 to $29,999	632	69	66
$30,000 to $39,999	511	38	58
$40,000 to $49,999	426	21	77
$50,000 to $59,999	289	11	34
$60,000 to $69,999	212	4	20
$70,000 to $79,999	171	1	24
$80,000 to $89,999	102	0	7
$90,000 to $99,999	94	2	13
$100,000 or more	265	3	13
Median income of women with income	$24,095	$8,853	$30,807
Median income of full-time workers	41,254	25,463	40,465
Percent working full-time	40.4%	13.5%	51.2%
TOTAL ASIAN WOMEN	**100.0%**	**100.0%**	**100.0%**
Without income	**20.6**	**44.6**	**18.2**
With income	**79.4**	**55.4**	**81.8**
Under $10,000	20.2	29.7	15.6
$10,000 to $19,999	14.4	10.5	12.9
$20,000 to $29,999	10.5	7.0	11.2
$30,000 to $39,999	8.5	3.9	9.9
$40,000 to $49,999	7.1	2.1	13.1
$50,000 to $59,999	4.8	1.1	5.8
$60,000 to $69,999	3.5	0.4	3.4
$70,000 to $79,999	2.8	0.1	4.1
$80,000 to $89,999	1.7	0.0	1.2
$90,000 to $99,999	1.6	0.2	2.2
$100,000 or more	4.4	0.3	2.2

Note: Asians include those who identify themselves as being of the race alone and those who identify themselves as being of the race in combination with other races.
Source: Bureau of the Census, 2008 Current Population Survey Annual Social and Economic Supplement, Internet site http:// www.census.gov/hhes/www/macro/032008/perinc/new01_000.htm; calculations by New Strategist

Table 5.18 Income of Women under Age 30, 2007: Black Women

(number and percent distribution of black women aged 15 or older and under age 30 by income, 2007; median income by work status, and percent working year-round, full-time; women in thousands as of 2008)

	total	15 to 24	25 to 29
TOTAL BLACK WOMEN	**16,097**	**3,387**	**1,566**
Without income	**2,670**	**1,473**	**185**
With income	**13,427**	**1,914**	**1,381**
Under $10,000	3,628	1,099	292
$10,000 to $19,999	3,158	468	315
$20,000 to $29,999	2,295	203	320
$30,000 to $39,999	1,659	86	227
$40,000 to $49,999	1,016	16	93
$50,000 to $59,999	594	30	56
$60,000 to $69,999	435	6	38
$70,000 to $79,999	220	3	12
$80,000 to $89,999	139	2	7
$90,000 to $99,999	63	0	0
$100,000 or more	223	4	20
Median income of women with income	$19,712	$8,079	$22,234
Median income of full-time workers	31,672	20,867	29,237
Percent working full-time	41.2%	15.5%	52.9%
TOTAL BLACK WOMEN	**100.0%**	**100.0%**	**100.0%**
Without income	**16.6**	**43.5**	**11.8**
With income	**83.4**	**56.5**	**88.2**
Under $10,000	22.5	32.4	18.6
$10,000 to $19,999	19.6	13.8	20.1
$20,000 to $29,999	14.3	6.0	20.4
$30,000 to $39,999	10.3	2.5	14.5
$40,000 to $49,999	6.3	0.5	5.9
$50,000 to $59,999	3.7	0.9	3.6
$60,000 to $69,999	2.7	0.2	2.4
$70,000 to $79,999	1.4	0.1	0.8
$80,000 to $89,999	0.9	0.1	0.4
$90,000 to $99,999	0.4	0.0	0.0
$100,000 or more	1.4	0.1	1.3

Note: Blacks include those who identify themselves as being of the race alone and those who identify themselves as being of the race in combination with other races.
Source: Bureau of the Census, 2008 Current Population Survey Annual Social and Economic Supplement, Internet site http://www.census.gov/hhes/www/macro/032008/perinc/new01_000.htm; calculations by New Strategist

Table 5.19 Income of Women under Age 30, 2007: Hispanic Women

(number and percent distribution of Hispanic women aged 15 or older and under age 30 by income, 2007; median income by work status, and percent working year-round, full-time; women in thousands as of 2008)

	total	15 to 24	25 to 29
TOTAL HISPANIC WOMEN	**15,853**	**3,573**	**1,863**
Without income	**4,588**	**1,783**	**532**
With income	**11,265**	**1,790**	**1,331**
Under $10,000	3,397	910	305
$10,000 to $19,999	2,967	462	333
$20,000 to $29,999	1,973	286	316
$30,000 to $39,999	1,284	93	199
$40,000 to $49,999	675	24	77
$50,000 to $59,999	359	10	36
$60,000 to $69,999	202	1	26
$70,000 to $79,999	144	2	18
$80,000 to $89,999	66	0	3
$90,000 to $99,999	51	2	2
$100,000 or more	148	0	15
Median income of women with income	$16,748	$9,727	$20,619
Median income of full-time workers	27,154	21,284	26,695
Percent working full-time	34.2%	15.7%	41.5%
TOTAL HISPANIC WOMEN	**100.0%**	**100.0%**	**100.0%**
Without income	**16.6**	**43.5**	**11.8**
With income	**83.4**	**56.5**	**88.2**
Under $10,000	22.5	32.4	18.6
$10,000 to $19,999	19.6	13.8	20.1
$20,000 to $29,999	14.3	6.0	20.4
$30,000 to $39,999	10.3	2.5	14.5
$40,000 to $49,999	6.3	0.5	5.9
$50,000 to $59,999	3.7	0.9	3.6
$60,000 to $69,999	2.7	0.2	2.4
$70,000 to $79,999	1.4	0.1	0.8
$80,000 to $89,999	0.9	0.1	0.4
$90,000 to $99,999	0.4	0.0	0.0
$100,000 or more	1.4	0.1	1.3

Source: Bureau of the Census, 2008 Current Population Survey Annual Social and Economic Supplement, Internet site http://www.census.gov/hhes/www/macro/032008/perinc/new01_000.htm; calculations by New Strategist

Table 5.20 Income of Women under Age 30, 2007: Non-Hispanic White Women

(number and percent distribution of non-Hispanic white women aged 15 or older and under age 30 by income, 2007; median income by work status, and percent working year-round, full-time; women in thousands as of 2008)

	total	15 to 24	25 to 29
TOTAL NON-HISPANIC WHITE WOMEN	**83,534**	**12,537**	**6,258**
Without income	**8,632**	**3,727**	**601**
With income	**74,902**	**8,810**	**5,657**
Under $10,000	18,386	4,656	883
$10,000 to $19,999	16,472	2,134	997
$20,000 to $29,999	11,666	1,053	1,212
$30,000 to $39,999	8,904	529	1,010
$40,000 to $49,999	6,403	276	712
$50,000 to $59,999	4,185	81	381
$60,000 to $69,999	2,719	41	209
$70,000 to $79,999	1,769	15	117
$80,000 to $89,999	1,053	8	38
$90,000 to $99,999	746	2	24
$100,000 or more	2,596	18	76
Median income of women with income	$21,687	$9,061	$27,164
Median income of full-time workers	38,678	23,892	35,229
Percent working full-time	37.0%	17.3%	54.7%
TOTAL NON-HISPANIC WHITE WOMEN	**100.0%**	**100.0%**	**100.0%**
Without income	**16.6**	**43.5**	**11.8**
With income	**83.4**	**56.5**	**88.2**
Under $10,000	22.5	32.4	18.6
$10,000 to $19,999	19.6	13.8	20.1
$20,000 to $29,999	14.3	6.0	20.4
$30,000 to $39,999	10.3	2.5	14.5
$40,000 to $49,999	6.3	0.5	5.9
$50,000 to $59,999	3.7	0.9	3.6
$60,000 to $69,999	2.7	0.2	2.4
$70,000 to $79,999	1.4	0.1	0.8
$80,000 to $89,999	0.9	0.1	0.4
$90,000 to $99,999	0.4	0.0	0.0
$100,000 or more	1.4	0.1	1.3

Note: Non-Hispanic whites are only those who identify themselves as being white alone and not Hispanic.
Source: Bureau of the Census, 2008 Current Population Survey Annual Social and Economic Supplement, Internet site http://www.census.gov/hhes/www/macro/032008/perinc/new01_000.htm; calculations by New Strategist

Many Young Adults Are Poor

The Millennial generation accounts for almost one-third of the nation's poor.

Children and young adults are much more likely to be poor than middle-aged or older adults. While 12.5 percent of Americans were poor in 2007, the poverty rate among the Millennial generation (aged 13 to 30 in 2007) was a larger 15.2 percent. Millennials account for 31 percent of the nation's poor.

There is great variation in the poverty rate of Millennials by race and Hispanic origin. The figure ranges from a low of 10.6 percent among non-Hispanic whites to a high of 26.0 percent among blacks. Non-Hispanic whites account for a 42 percent minority of the Millennial poor, while Hispanics are 27 percent and blacks 26 percent.

■ Poverty rates for Millennials are above average because many live in female-headed families—the poorest household type. Until single parenthood becomes less common, poverty among the young will remain stubbornly high.

Among Millennials, non-Hispanic whites have the lowest poverty rate

(percent of people aged 13 to 30 who live below poverty level, by race and Hispanic origin, 2007)

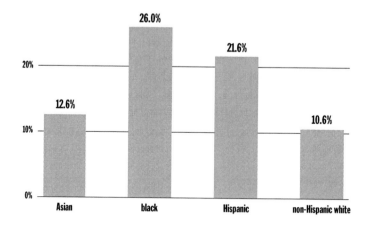

Table 5.21 People below Poverty Level by Age, Race, and Hispanic Origin, 2007

(number, percent, and percent distribution of people below poverty level by age, race, and Hispanic origin, 2007; people in thousands as of 2008)

	total	Asian	black	Hispanic	non-Hispanic white
NUMBER IN POVERTY					
Total people	**37,276**	**1,467**	**9,668**	**9,890**	**16,032**
Millennials (13 to 30)	11,389	462	2,979	3,044	4,822
Under age 18	13,325	431	4,178	4,483	4,256
Aged 18 to 24	4,902	186	1,184	1,104	2,399
Aged 25 to 29	2,681	134	651	762	1,104
Aged 30 or older	16,375	716	3,657	3,542	8,274
PERCENT IN POVERTY					
Total people	**12.5%**	**10.2%**	**24.4%**	**21.5%**	**8.2%**
Millennials (13 to 30)	15.2	12.6	26.0	21.6	10.6
Under age 18	18.0	11.9	33.8	28.7	10.1
Aged 18 to 24	17.3	14.0	27.3	22.0	13.7
Aged 25 to 29	12.7	11.7	22.1	17.8	8.8
Aged 30 or older	9.3	8.6	18.4	16.9	6.6
PERCENT DISTRIBUTION OF POOR BY AGE					
Total people	**100.0%**	**100.0%**	**100.0%**	**100.0%**	**100.0%**
Millennials (13 to 30)	30.6	31.5	30.8	30.8	30.1
Under age 18	35.7	29.4	43.2	45.3	26.5
Aged 18 to 24	13.2	12.7	12.2	11.2	15.0
Aged 25 to 29	7.2	9.1	6.7	7.7	6.9
Aged 30 or older	43.9	48.8	37.8	35.8	51.6
PERCENT DISTRIBUTION OF POOR BY RACE AND HISPANIC ORIGIN					
Total people	**100.0%**	**3.9%**	**25.9%**	**26.5%**	**43.0%**
Millennials (13 to 30)	100.0	4.1	26.2	26.7	42.3
Under age 18	100.0	3.2	31.4	33.6	31.9
Aged 18 to 24	100.0	3.8	24.2	22.5	48.9
Aged 25 to 29	100.0	5.0	24.3	28.4	41.2
Aged 30 or older	100.0	4.4	22.3	21.6	50.5

Note: Numbers do not add to total because Asians and blacks include those who identify themselves as being of the race alone and those who identify themselves as being of the race in combination with other races, because Hispanics may be of any race, and because not all races are shown. Non-Hispanic whites are only those who identify themselves as being white alone and not Hispanic.
Source: Bureau of the Census, 2008 Current Population Survey Annual Social and Economic Supplement, Internet site http://www.census.gov/hhes/www/macro/032008/pov/new34_100.htm; calculations by New Strategist

6

Labor Force

■ The percentage of men and women under age 30 (Millennials were aged 14 to 31 in 2008) who are in the labor force fell sharply between 2000 and 2008. The decline was particularly steep among teenagers.

■ Workers under age 30 account for a large share of the nation's unemployed. Among the 8.9 million unemployed workers in 2008, nearly 4 million (or 44 percent) were younger than age 30.

■ Nearly one-third of black men aged 18 to 19 were unemployed in 2005. In contrast, only 13 percent of Asian men in the age group were unemployed.

■ Workers under age 35 account for 75 percent of waiters and waitresses, 63 percent of food preparation workers, 63 percent of cashiers, and half of retail salespersons and customer service representatives.

■ Among the nation's 75 million workers who were paid hourly rates in 2008, only 2 million made minimum wage or less. Of those 2 million workers, nearly two out of three are under age 30.

■ Between 2006 and 2016, the Millennial generation will age into its thirties. The number of workers aged 25 to 34 will expand by 14 percent between 2006 and 2016—a gain of nearly 5 million.

Fewer Teenagers Have Jobs

Labor force participation rate has fallen sharply among young boys and girls.

The percentage of men and women under age 30 (Millennials were aged 14 to 31 in 2008) who are in the labor force fell sharply between 2000 and 2008. The decline was particularly steep among teenagers. In 2008, only 27 percent of boys aged 16 to 17 were in the labor force, down fully 14 percentage points from the 41 percent of 2000. Among their female counterparts, labor force participation fell from 41 to 29 percent during those years. The labor force participation rate has also declined substantially among men and women in their twenties.

The weak economy is one factor behind declining labor force participation among teens. Another factor is high school students' greater focus on academics and extracurricular activities as they position themselves for college.

■ With college costs rising, many teens are polishing their academic resumes and hoping for scholarships.

A shrinking share of teenagers is in the labor force

(percent of people aged 16 to 17 in the labor force, by sex, 2000 and 2008)

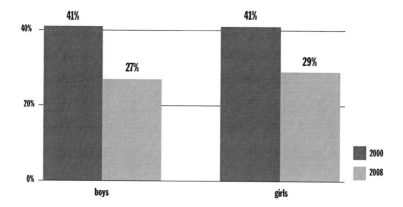

Table 6.1 Labor Force Participation Rate by Sex and Age, 2000 and 2008

(civilian labor force participation rate of people aged 16 or older, by sex and age, 2000 and 2008; percentage point change, 2000–2008)

	2008	2000	percentage point change
Men aged 16 or older	**73.0%**	**74.8%**	**−1.8**
Aged 16 to 17	26.8	40.9	−14.1
Aged 18 to 19	55.4	65.0	−9.6
Aged 20 to 24	78.7	82.6	−3.9
Aged 25 to 29	90.2	92.5	−2.3
Aged 30 to 34	92.9	94.2	−1.3
Aged 35 to 39	92.7	93.2	−0.5
Aged 40 to 44	91.8	92.1	−0.3
Aged 45 to 49	89.7	90.2	−0.5
Aged 50 to 54	86.2	86.8	−0.6
Aged 55 to 59	78.8	77.0	1.8
Aged 60 to 64	59.9	54.9	5.0
Aged 65 or older	21.5	17.7	3.8
Women aged 16 or older	**59.5**	**59.9**	**−0.4**
Aged 16 to 17	29.2	40.8	−11.6
Aged 18 to 19	53.0	61.3	−8.3
Aged 20 to 24	70.0	73.1	−3.1
Aged 25 to 29	75.9	76.7	−0.8
Aged 30 to 34	74.4	75.5	−1.1
Aged 35 to 39	75.2	75.7	−0.5
Aged 40 to 44	77.1	78.7	−1.6
Aged 45 to 49	77.2	79.1	−1.9
Aged 50 to 54	74.8	74.1	0.7
Aged 55 to 59	67.7	61.4	6.3
Aged 60 to 64	48.7	40.2	8.5
Aged 65 or older	13.3	9.4	3.9

Source: Bureau of Labor Statistics, Public Query Data Tool, Internet site http://www.bls.gov/data; and 2008 Current Population Survey, Internet site http://www.bls.gov/cps/tables.htm#empstat; calculations by New Strategist

Most Young Adults Have Jobs

More than 70 percent of 20-to-29-year-olds are in the labor force.

Young men join the labor force at a slower rate than they once did. Among men aged 18 to 19, only 55 percent have jobs because most are in college. The labor force participation rate of young men increases to 79 percent in the 20-to-24 age group, then rises to 90 percent among men aged 25 to 29.

The labor force participation rate of women under age 25 is almost identical to that of men. Among 18-to-19-year old women, 53 percent are in the labor force. The proportion increases to 70 percent among women aged 20 to 24. A substantial gap in participation rates emerges in the 25-to-29 age group. Fully 90 percent of men and a smaller 76 percent of women aged 25 to 29 are in the labor force.

Workers under age 30 account for a large share of the nation's unemployed. Among the 8.9 million unemployed workers in 2008, nearly 4 million (or 44 percent) were younger than age 30. The unemployment rate in the under-30 age group was 10 percent in 2008—much higher than the 5.8 percent national rate at the time. Unemployment was highest among 16-to-17-year-olds at 22 percent.

■ Young adults are much more likely than older workers to be unemployed because many are in entry-level positions and are the first to be let go during economic downturns.

Participation rates of men and women under age 25 are similar

(labor force participation rates of people under age 30, by sex, 2008)

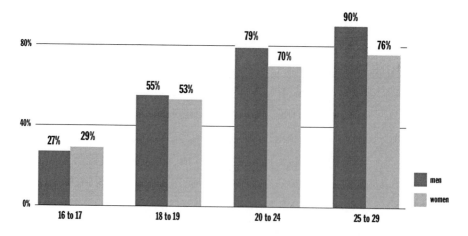

Table 6.2 Employment Status by Sex and Age, 2008

(number and percent of people aged 16 or older in the civilian labor force by sex and age, 2008; numbers in thousands)

	civilian noninstitutional population	civilian labor force			unemployed	
		total	percent of population	employed	number	percent of labor force
Total, aged 16 or older	**233,788**	**154,287**	**66.0%**	**145,362**	**8,924**	**5.8%**
Under age 30	58,299	39,325	67.5	35,373	3,952	10.0
Aged 16 to 17	9,133	2,552	27.9	1,989	563	22.1
Aged 18 to 19	7,942	4,306	54.2	3,584	722	16.8
Aged 20 to 24	20,409	15,174	74.4	13,629	1,545	10.2
Aged 25 to 29	20,815	17,293	83.1	16,171	1,122	6.5
Aged 30 to 34	19,179	16,039	83.6	15,212	827	5.2
Aged 35 to 44	41,699	35,061	84.1	33,457	1,604	4.6
Aged 45 to 54	43,960	36,003	81.9	34,529	1,473	4.1
Aged 55 to 64	33,491	21,615	64.5	20,812	803	3.7
Aged 65 or older	37,161	6,243	16.8	5,979	264	4.2
Men, aged 16 or older	**113,113**	**82,520**	**73.0**	**77,486**	**5,033**	**6.1**
Under age 30	29,360	20,969	71.4	18,655	2,314	11.0
Aged 16 to 17	4,625	1,238	26.8	926	312	25.2
Aged 18 to 19	4,035	2,235	55.4	1,810	425	19.0
Aged 20 to 24	10,249	8,065	78.7	7,145	920	11.4
Aged 25 to 29	10,451	9,431	90.2	8,774	657	7.0
Aged 30 to 34	9,548	8,871	92.9	8,409	462	5.2
Aged 35 to 44	20,567	18,972	92.2	18,097	875	4.6
Aged 45 to 54	21,512	18,928	88.0	18,124	804	4.2
Aged 55 to 64	16,123	11,345	70.4	10,919	425	3.8
Aged 65 or older	16,002	3,436	21.5	3,282	153	4.5
Women, aged 16 or older	**120,675**	**71,767**	**59.5**	**67,876**	**3,891**	**5.4**
Under age 30	28,938	18,356	63.4	16,718	1,639	8.9
Aged 16 to 17	4,508	1,314	29.2	1,063	251	19.1
Aged 18 to 19	3,907	2,071	53.0	1,774	297	14.3
Aged 20 to 24	10,160	7,109	70.0	6,484	625	8.8
Aged 25 to 29	10,363	7,862	75.9	7,397	466	5.9
Aged 30 to 34	9,631	7,168	74.4	6,803	365	5.1
Aged 35 to 44	21,132	16,089	76.1	15,360	730	4.5
Aged 45 to 54	22,448	17,075	76.1	16,406	669	3.9
Aged 55 to 64	17,367	10,270	59.1	9,893	377	3.7
Aged 65 or older	21,160	2,808	13.3	2,697	111	3.9

Source: Bureau of Labor Statistics, 2008 Current Population Survey, Internet site http://www.bls.gov/cps/tables.htm#empstat; calculations by New Strategist

Among Young Adults, Asians and Blacks Are Least Likely to Work

Young black men are most likely to be unemployed.

Among teenagers, labor force participation is higher for Hispanics and whites than for Asians or blacks. While 59 percent of Hispanic and white men aged 18 to 19 are in the labor force, the figure is just 43 percent among blacks and 37 percent among Asians. The pattern is the same for women in the age group, with whites and Hispanics being more likely to work than Asians or blacks. There are striking differences by race and ethnicity in the 20-to-24 age group as well. Among Asian men aged 20 to 24, only 62 percent are in the labor force. Among blacks, the figure is 71 percent. The labor force participation rates of white and Hispanic men aged 20 to 24 are a much higher 81 and 84 percent, respectively. Behind the lower labor force participation rate of young Asian men is their greater college attendance.

Teenagers and young adults have relatively high unemployment rates regardless of race or Hispanic origin, but young black men have a much higher unemployment rate than anyone else. Among black men aged 16 to 17, an enormous 44 percent were unemployed in 2008. This compares with an unemployment rate of 31 percent for Hispanics and 22 percent for whites.

■ Some black men have so much difficulty finding a job that they drop out of the labor force entirely.

Nearly one-third of black men aged 18 to 19 are unemployed

(percent of men aged 18 to 19 who are unemployed, by race and Hispanic origin, 2008)

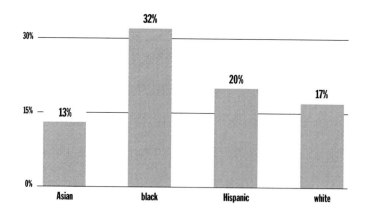

Table 6.3 Employment Status of Men by Race, Hispanic Origin, and Age, 2008

(number and percent of men aged 16 or older in the civilian labor force by race, Hispanic origin, and age, 2008; numbers in thousands)

	civilian noninstitutional population	civilian labor force			unemployed	
		total	percent of population	employed	number	percent of labor force
ASIAN MEN						
Total aged 16 or older	5,112	3,852	75.3%	3,692	160	4.1%
Aged 16 to 17	175	30	17.2	23	–	–
Aged 18 to 19	149	55	36.7	48	7	12.5
Aged 20 to 24	429	268	62.5	251	17	6.5
Aged 25 to 29	519	448	86.2	432	16	3.5
Aged 30 to 34	592	548	92.6	521	27	4.9
Aged 35 to 44	1,159	1,089	93.9	1,058	30	2.8
Aged 45 to 54	919	836	91.0	806	29	3.5
Aged 55 to 64	616	457	74.2	438	19	4.3
Aged 65 or older	553	120	21.8	114	6	5.1
BLACK MEN						
Total aged 16 or older	12,516	8,347	66.7	7,398	949	11.4
Aged 16 to 17	718	124	17.3	70	54	43.9
Aged 18 to 19	604	261	43.2	177	84	32.0
Aged 20 to 24	1,384	984	71.1	794	190	19.3
Aged 25 to 29	1,311	1,102	84.0	956	146	13.3
Aged 30 to 34	1,087	945	86.9	849	96	10.1
Aged 35 to 44	2,313	2,008	86.8	1,854	154	7.7
Aged 45 to 54	2,335	1,846	79.1	1,703	143	7.7
Aged 55 to 64	1,519	852	56.1	792	61	7.1
Aged 65 or older	1,245	225	18.1	204	21	9.5
HISPANIC MEN						
Total aged 16 or older	16,524	13,255	80.2	12,248	1,007	7.6
Aged 16 to 17	838	202	24.2	140	63	30.9
Aged 18 to 19	716	424	59.2	340	84	19.9
Aged 20 to 24	1,890	1,594	84.3	1,406	188	11.8
Aged 25 to 29	2,260	2,110	93.4	1,958	152	7.2
Aged 30 to 34	2,178	2,063	94.7	1,939	124	6.0
Aged 35 to 44	3,655	3,425	93.7	3,233	192	5.6
Aged 45 to 54	2,502	2,216	88.6	2,080	136	6.2
Aged 55 to 64	1,365	979	71.7	929	50	5.1
Aged 65 or older	1,121	243	21.7	224	19	7.8
WHITE MEN						
Total aged 16 or older	92,725	68,351	73.7	64,624	3,727	5.5
Aged 16 to 17	3,550	1,040	29.3	808	231	22.2
Aged 18 to 19	3,120	1,829	58.6	1,512	317	17.3
Aged 20 to 24	8,072	6,526	80.8	5,858	668	10.2
Aged 25 to 29	8,289	7,591	91.6	7,125	466	6.1
Aged 30 to 34	7,596	7,125	93.8	6,807	318	4.5
Aged 35 to 44	16,599	15,436	93.0	14,775	662	4.3
Aged 45 to 54	17,830	15,905	89.2	15,300	604	3.8
Aged 55 to 64	13,698	9,855	71.9	9,518	337	3.4
Aged 65 or older	13,972	3,046	21.8	2,922	124	4.1

Note: Race is shown only for those selecting that race group only. People who selected more than one race are not included. Hispanics may be of any race. "–" means sample is too small to make a reliable estimate.
Source: Bureau of Labor Statistics, 2008 Current Population Survey, Internet site http://www.bls.gov/cps/tables.htm#empstat; calculations by New Strategist

Table 6.4 Employment Status of Women by Race, Hispanic Origin, and Age, 2008

(number and percent of women aged 16 or older in the civilian labor force by race, Hispanic origin, and age, 2008; numbers in thousands)

	civilian noninstitutional population	total	percent of population	employed	unemployed number	percent of labor force
ASIAN WOMEN						
Total aged 16 or older	5,639	3,350	59.4%	3,225	125	3.7%
Aged 16 to 17	166	28	16.7	26	–	–
Aged 18 to 19	140	44	31.7	37	7	15.7
Aged 20 to 24	443	258	58.2	242	16	6.1
Aged 25 to 29	543	376	69.2	354	21	5.7
Aged 30 to 34	624	439	70.4	430	10	2.2
Aged 35 to 44	1,244	900	72.3	873	27	3.0
Aged 45 to 54	1,015	773	76.1	748	25	3.2
Aged 55 to 64	726	434	59.7	418	15	3.5
Aged 65 or older	738	99	13.4	97	2	2.2
BLACK WOMEN						
Total aged 16 or older	15,328	9,393	61.3	8,554	839	8.9
Aged 16 to 17	741	146	19.7	102	44	29.9
Aged 18 to 19	613	256	41.8	192	64	25.0
Aged 20 to 24	1,530	997	65.2	831	166	16.6
Aged 25 to 29	1,511	1,209	80.0	1,090	119	9.9
Aged 30 to 34	1,353	1,072	79.2	975	97	9.1
Aged 35 to 44	2,885	2,308	80.0	2,161	147	6.4
Aged 45 to 54	2,848	2,099	73.7	1,967	132	6.3
Aged 55 to 64	1,910	1,056	55.3	1,000	56	5.3
Aged 65 or older	1,937	251	13.0	236	15	5.8
HISPANIC WOMEN						
Total aged 16 or older	15,616	8,769	56.2	8,098	672	7.7
Aged 16 to 17	782	151	19.3	108	42	28.1
Aged 18 to 19	706	344	48.7	282	62	18.0
Aged 20 to 24	1,730	1,074	62.1	955	119	11.1
Aged 25 to 29	1,866	1,175	63.0	1,089	86	7.3
Aged 30 to 34	1,844	1,209	65.6	1,133	76	6.3
Aged 35 to 44	3,291	2,274	69.1	2,138	136	6.0
Aged 45 to 54	2,435	1,646	67.6	1,541	105	6.4
Aged 55 to 64	1,475	722	48.9	690	32	4.4
Aged 65 or older	1,488	174	11.7	161	13	7.7
WHITE WOMEN						
Total aged 16 or older	96,814	57,284	59.2	54,501	2,782	4.9
Aged 16 to 17	3,412	1,086	31.8	895	191	17.6
Aged 18 to 19	3,003	1,690	56.3	1,482	207	12.3
Aged 20 to 24	7,842	5,616	71.6	5,197	419	7.5
Aged 25 to 29	7,979	6,043	75.7	5,738	305	5.1
Aged 30 to 34	7,370	5,452	74.0	5,205	246	4.5
Aged 35 to 44	16,493	12,495	75.8	11,961	534	4.3
Aged 45 to 54	18,111	13,875	76.6	13,386	489	3.5
Aged 55 to 64	14,411	8,609	59.7	8,312	298	3.5
Aged 65 or older	18,193	2,417	13.3	2,325	92	3.8

Note: Race is shown only for those selecting that race group only. People who selected more than one race are not included. Hispanics may be of any race. "–" means sample is too small to make a reliable estimate.
Source: Bureau of Labor Statistics, 2008 Current Population Survey, Internet site http://www.bls.gov/cps/tables.htm#empstat; calculations by New Strategist

Most Couples under Age 30 Are Dual Earners

The husband is the sole support of only 31 percent of young couples.

Dual incomes are by far the norm among married couples. Both husband and wife are in the labor force in 55 percent of the nation's couples. In another 22 percent, the husband is the only worker. Not far behind are the 16 percent of couples in which neither spouse is in the labor force. The wife is the sole worker among 7 percent of couples.

Sixty-three percent of couples under age 30 are dual earners. The proportion is just 54 percent among couples under age 25, but leaps to 66 percent among those aged 25 to 29. The proportion peaks among couples aged 45 to 54 because their children are grown and wives are more likely to work. The dual-earner share falls to just 49 percent among couples aged 55 to 64 because many are retired.

■ The proportion of couples in which the husband is the sole earner is highest among the youngest adults because many wives are at home with newborns.

Dual earners dominate married couples under age 55

(percent of married couples in which both husband and wife are in the labor force, by age, 2008)

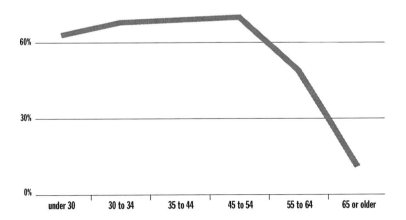

Table 6.5 Labor Force Status of Married-Couple Family Groups by Age, 2008

(number and percent distribution of married-couple family groups by age of reference person and labor force status of husband and wife, 2008; numbers in thousands)

	total	husband and wife in labor force	husband only in labor force	wife only in labor force	neither husband nor wife in labor force
Total married-couple family groups	**60,129**	**32,988**	**13,141**	**4,118**	**9,882**
Under age 30	5,379	3,378	1,679	198	122
Under age 25	1,417	763	543	60	49
Aged 25 to 29	3,962	2,615	1,136	138	73
Aged 30 to 34	5,408	3,680	1,490	138	99
Aged 35 to 44	13287	9232	3370	438	248
Aged 45 to 54	14,210	9,922	3,000	796	491
Aged 55 to 64	11,399	5,613	2,426	1,446	1,915
Aged 65 or older	10,446	1,163	1,176	1,102	7,007
PERCENT DISTRIBUTION					
Total married-couple family groups	**100.0%**	**54.9%**	**21.9%**	**6.8%**	**16.4%**
Under age 30	100.0	62.8	31.2	3.7	2.3
Under age 25	100.0	53.8	38.3	4.2	3.5
Aged 25 to 29	100.0	66.0	28.7	3.5	1.8
Aged 30 to 34	100.0	68.0	27.6	2.6	1.8
Aged 35 to 44	100.0	69.5	25.4	3.3	1.9
Aged 45 to 54	100.0	69.8	21.1	5.6	3.5
Aged 55 to 64	100.0	49.2	21.3	12.7	16.8
Aged 65 or older	100.0	11.1	11.3	10.5	67.1

Source: Bureau of the Census, America's Families and Living Arrangements: 2008, Internet site http://www.census.gov/population/www/socdemo/hh-fam/cps2008.html; calculations by New Strategist

The Youngest Workers Dominate Many Entry-Level Positions

They account for 63 percent of food preparation workers.

Among the 145 million employed Americans in 2008, just over 50 million—or 35 percent—were under age 35. In some occupations, however, workers under age 35 account for a disproportionate share. While workers under age 35 are only 21 percent of the nation's managers, they are 75 percent of waiters and waitresses.

More than one in four employed 16-to-19-year-olds work in a food preparation and serving occupation. The figure declines with age to 6 percent among workers aged 25 to 34. Another 24 percent of workers aged 16 to 19 are in sales occupations, a figure that falls to 10 percent among workers aged 25 to 34. Workers under age 35 account for 63 percent of cashiers, 49 percent of grounds maintenance workers, and 50 percent of retail salespersons and customer service representatives. Most young adults will move out of these entry-level positions as they earn educational credentials and gain job experience.

■ Young adults account for a large share of workers in occupations with a great deal of public contact.

Many occupations are dominated by young adults

(percent of workers under age 35, by occupation, 2008)

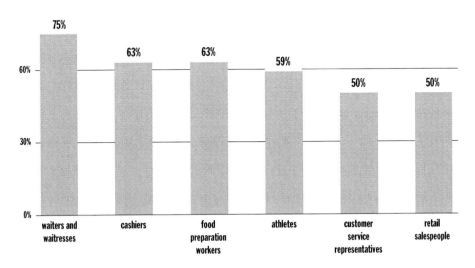

Table 6.6 Occupations of Workers under Age 35, 2008

(number of employed workers aged 16 or older, median age of workers, and number of workers under age 35, by occupation, 2008; numbers in thousands)

	total	median age	under age 35 total	16 to 19	20 to 24	25 to 34
TOTAL WORKERS	145,362	41.3	50,585	5,573	13,629	31,383
Management and professional occupations	**52,761**	**43.5**	**14,756**	**318**	**2,815**	**11,623**
Management, business and financial operations	22,059	44.8	5,140	53	825	4,262
Management	15,852	45.6	3,273	42	493	2,738
Business and financial operations	6,207	42.8	1,867	11	332	1,524
Professional and related occupations	30,702	42.5	9,615	264	1,990	7,361
Computer and mathematical	3,676	39.9	1,300	17	229	1,054
Architecture and engineering	2,931	43.1	844	11	180	653
Life, physical, and social sciences	1,307	41.4	455	8	95	352
Community and social services	2,293	44.1	684	16	139	529
Legal	1,671	44.7	412	4	64	344
Education, training, and library	8,605	42.8	2,725	99	598	2,028
Arts, design, entertainment, sports, and media	2,820	40.5	1,073	73	267	733
Health care practitioner and technician	7,399	43.3	2,124	37	419	1,668
Service occupations	**24,451**	**37.1**	**11,090**	**2,254**	**3,550**	**5,286**
Health care support	3,212	38.5	1,357	93	443	821
Protective service	3,047	40.6	1,059	105	250	704
Food preparation and serving	7,824	28.9	4,918	1,484	1,706	1,728
Building and grounds cleaning and maintenance	5,445	42.4	1,711	238	479	994
Personal care and service	4,923	39.0	2,044	334	671	1,039
Sales and office occupations	**35,544**	**40.6**	**13,370**	**2,028**	**4,163**	**7,179**
Sales and related occupations	16,295	39.5	6,539	1,314	1,971	3,254
Office and administrative support	19,249	41.4	6,832	714	2,193	3,925
Natural resources, construction, and maintenance occupations	**14,806**	**39.9**	**5,564**	**411**	**1,518**	**3,635**
Farming, fishing, and forestry	988	37.7	434	120	116	198
Construction and extraction	8,667	39.0	3,473	186	937	2,350
Installation, maintenance, and repair	5,152	41.7	1,657	105	465	1,087
Production, transportation, and material moving occupations	**17,800**	**41.9**	**5,806**	**563**	**1,583**	**3,660**
Production	8,973	42.3	2,786	187	732	1,867
Transportation and material moving	8,827	41.4	3,021	377	851	1,793

Source: Bureau of Labor Statistics, unpublished data from the 2008 Current Population Survey; calculations by New Strategist

Table 6.7 Distribution of Workers under Age 35 by Occupation, 2008

(percent distribution of employed people aged 16 or older and under age 35 by occupation, 2008)

	total	under age 35			
		total	16 to 19	20 to 24	25 to 34
TOTAL WORKERS	100.0%	100.0%	100.0%	100.0%	100.0%
Management and professional occupations	**36.3**	**29.2**	**5.7**	**20.7**	**37.0**
Management, business and financial operations	15.2	10.2	1.0	6.1	13.6
Management	10.9	6.5	0.8	3.6	8.7
Business and financial operations	4.3	3.7	0.2	2.4	4.9
Professional and related occupations	21.1	19.0	4.7	14.6	23.5
Computer and mathematical	2.5	2.6	0.3	1.7	3.4
Architecture and engineering	2.0	1.7	0.2	1.3	2.1
Life, physical, and social sciences	0.9	0.9	0.1	0.7	1.1
Community and social services	1.6	1.4	0.3	1.0	1.7
Legal	1.1	0.8	0.1	0.5	1.1
Education, training, and library	5.9	5.4	1.8	4.4	6.5
Arts, design, entertainment, sports, and media	1.9	2.1	1.3	2.0	2.3
Health care practitioner and technician	5.1	4.2	0.7	3.1	5.3
Service occupations	**16.8**	**21.9**	**40.4**	**26.0**	**16.8**
Health care support	2.2	2.7	1.7	3.3	2.6
Protective service	2.1	2.1	1.9	1.8	2.2
Food preparation and serving	5.4	9.7	26.6	12.5	5.5
Building and grounds cleaning and maintenance	3.7	3.4	4.3	3.5	3.2
Personal care and service	3.4	4.0	6.0	4.9	3.3
Sales and office occupations	**24.5**	**26.4**	**36.4**	**30.5**	**22.9**
Sales and related occupations	11.2	12.9	23.6	14.5	10.4
Office and administrative support	13.2	13.5	12.8	16.1	12.5
Natural resources, construction, maintenance occupations	**10.2**	**11.0**	**7.4**	**11.1**	**11.6**
Farming, fishing, and forestry	0.7	0.9	2.2	0.9	0.6
Construction and extraction	6.0	6.9	3.3	6.9	7.5
Installation, maintenance, and repair	3.5	3.3	1.9	3.4	3.5
Production, transportation, material-moving occupations	**12.2**	**11.5**	**10.1**	**11.6**	**11.7**
Production	6.2	5.5	3.4	5.4	5.9
Transportation and material moving	6.1	6.0	6.8	6.2	5.7

Source: Calculations by New Strategist based on Bureau of Labor Statistics, unpublished data from the 2008 Current Population Survey

Table 6.8 Share of Workers under Age 35 by Occupation, 2008

(percent distribution of total employed people aged 16 or older by occupation and age, 2008)

	total	under age 35			
		total	16 to 19	20 to 24	25 to 34
TOTAL WORKERS	**100.0%**	**34.8%**	**3.8%**	**9.4%**	**21.6%**
Management and professional occupations	**100.0**	**28.0**	**0.6**	**5.3**	**22.0**
Management, business and financial operations	100.0	23.3	0.2	3.7	19.3
Management	100.0	20.6	0.3	3.1	17.3
Business and financial operations	100.0	30.1	0.2	5.3	24.6
Professional and related occupations	100.0	31.3	0.9	6.5	24.0
Computer and mathematical	100.0	35.4	0.5	6.2	28.7
Architecture and engineering	100.0	28.8	0.4	6.1	22.3
Life, physical, and social sciences	100.0	34.8	0.6	7.3	26.9
Community and social services	100.0	29.8	0.7	6.1	23.1
Legal	100.0	24.7	0.2	3.8	20.6
Education, training, and library	100.0	31.7	1.2	6.9	23.6
Arts, design, entertainment, sports, and media	100.0	38.0	2.6	9.5	26.0
Health care practitioner and technician	100.0	28.7	0.5	5.7	22.5
Service occupations	**100.0**	**45.4**	**9.2**	**14.5**	**21.6**
Health care support	100.0	42.2	2.9	13.8	25.6
Protective service	100.0	34.8	3.4	8.2	23.1
Food preparation and serving	100.0	62.9	19.0	21.8	22.1
Building and grounds cleaning and maintenance	100.0	31.4	4.4	8.8	18.3
Personal care and service	100.0	41.5	6.8	13.6	21.1
Sales and office occupations	**100.0**	**37.6**	**5.7**	**11.7**	**20.2**
Sales and related occupations	100.0	40.1	8.1	12.1	20.0
Office and administrative support	100.0	35.5	3.7	11.4	20.4
Natural resources, construction, maintenance occupations	**100.0**	**37.6**	**2.8**	**10.3**	**24.6**
Farming, fishing, and forestry	100.0	43.9	12.1	11.7	20.0
Construction and extraction	100.0	40.1	2.1	10.8	27.1
Installation, maintenance, and repair	100.0	32.2	2.0	9.0	21.1
Production, transportation, material-moving occupations	**100.0**	**32.6**	**3.2**	**8.9**	**20.6**
Production	100.0	31.0	2.1	8.2	20.8
Transportation and material moving	100.0	34.2	4.3	9.6	20.3

Source: Calculations by New Strategist based on Bureau of Labor Statistics' unpublished data from the 2008 Current Population Survey

Table 6.9 Workers under Age 35 by Detailed Occupation, 2008

(number of employed workers aged 16 or older, median age, and number and percent under age 35, by selected detailed occupation, 2008; numbers in thousands)

	total workers	median age	total under 35		aged 16 to 19		aged 20 to 24		aged 25 to 34	
			number	percent of total	number	percent of total	number	percent of total	number	percent of total
TOTAL WORKERS	**145,362**	**41.3**	**50,585**	**34.8%**	**5,573**	**3.8%**	**13,629**	**9.4%**	**31,383**	**21.6%**
Chief executives	1,655	49.9	154	9.3	–	–	9	0.5	145	8.8
Legislators	23	54.5	2	8.7	–	–	0	0.0	2	8.7
Marketing and sales managers	922	41.5	256	27.8	1	0.1	35	3.8	220	23.9
Computer and information systems managers	475	42.5	105	22.1	0	0.0	7	1.5	98	20.6
Financial managers	1,168	42.9	316	27.1	2	0.2	36	3.1	278	23.8
Human resources managers	293	44.1	60	20.5	0	0.0	9	3.1	51	17.4
Farmers and ranchers	751	55.5	69	9.2	2	0.3	16	2.1	51	6.8
Construction managers	1,244	44.7	264	21.2	2	0.2	28	2.3	234	18.8
Education administrators	829	47.7	151	18.2	4	0.5	15	1.8	132	15.9
Food service managers	1,039	40.0	389	37.4	16	1.5	107	10.3	266	25.6
Medical and health services managers	561	46.8	90	16.0	1	0.2	7	1.2	82	14.6
Accountants and auditors	1,762	41.6	578	32.8	1	0.1	101	5.7	476	27.0
Computer scientists and systems analysts	837	41.0	274	32.7	4	0.5	59	7.0	211	25.2
Computer programmers	534	40.3	188	35.2	1	0.2	30	5.6	157	29.4
Computer software engineers	1,034	39.5	389	37.6	1	0.1	48	4.6	340	32.9
Architects	233	44.2	61	26.2	0	0.0	8	3.4	53	22.7
Civil engineers	346	42.9	110	31.8	1	0.3	16	4.6	93	26.9
Electrical engineers	350	44.7	83	23.7	1	0.3	13	3.7	69	19.7
Mechanical engineers	318	43.6	90	28.3	1	0.3	18	5.7	71	22.3
Medical scientists	132	39.7	46	34.8	–	–	7	5.3	39	29.5
Economists	19	47.3	3	15.8	–	–	1	5.3	2	10.5
Market researchers	134	38.8	57	42.5	–	–	13	9.7	44	32.8
Psychologists	176	48.9	38	21.6	–	–	4	2.3	34	19.3
Social workers	729	42.3	232	31.8	1	0.1	32	4.4	199	27.3
Clergy	441	51.3	78	17.7	0	0.0	14	3.2	64	14.5
Lawyers	1,014	45.8	216	21.3	2	0.2	3	0.3	211	20.8
Postsecondary teachers	1,218	43.7	385	31.6	4	0.3	98	8.0	283	23.2
Preschool and kindergarten teachers	685	39.2	265	38.7	11	1.6	67	9.8	187	27.3
Elementary and middle school teachers	2,958	42.6	933	31.5	3	0.1	151	5.1	779	26.3
Secondary school teachers	1,210	43.4	377	31.2	3	0.2	52	4.3	322	26.6
Librarians	197	51.2	33	16.8	1	0.5	13	6.6	19	9.6
Teacher assistants	1,020	43.1	302	29.6	31	3.0	104	10.2	167	16.4
Artists	213	46.2	57	26.8	2	0.9	11	5.2	44	20.7
Designers	834	40.8	315	37.8	8	1.0	79	9.5	228	27.3
Actors	30	32.6	15	50.0	1	3.3	6	20.0	8	26.7
Athletes, coaches, umpires	252	31.4	148	58.7	38	15.1	44	17.5	66	26.2
Musicians	186	44.0	55	29.6	3	1.6	16	8.6	36	19.4
Editors	171	40.9	62	36.3	2	1.2	12	7.0	48	28.1
Writers and authors	186	46.9	37	19.9	0	0.0	8	4.3	29	15.6
Dentists	152	48.2	28	18.4	–	–	1	0.7	27	17.8
Pharmacists	243	42.2	80	32.9	1	0.4	10	4.1	69	28.4

	total workers	median age	total under 35		aged 16 to 19		aged 20 to 24		aged 25 to 34	
			number	percent of total	number	percent of total	number	percent of total	number	percent of total
Physicians and surgeons	877	45.7	163	18.6%	1	0.1%	4	0.5%	158	18.0%
Registered nurses	2,778	45.0	688	24.8	1	0.0	113	4.1	574	20.7
Physical therapists	197	40.9	63	32.0	1	0.5	7	3.6	55	27.9
Emergency medical technicians and paramedics	138	32.8	78	56.5	4	2.9	24	17.4	50	36.2
Licensed practical nurses	566	43.7	162	28.6	3	0.5	39	6.9	120	21.2
Nursing, psychiatric, and home health aides	1,889	39.8	758	40.1	57	3.0	242	12.8	459	24.3
Firefighters	293	39.3	105	35.8	1	0.3	18	6.1	86	29.4
Police, sheriff's patrol officers	674	38.7	258	38.3	1	0.1	38	5.6	219	32.5
Security guards and gaming surveillance officers	867	42.0	318	36.7	24	2.8	124	14.3	170	19.6
Chefs and head cooks	351	37.3	155	44.2	9	2.6	36	10.3	110	31.3
Cooks	1,997	32.2	1,115	55.8	275	13.8	348	17.4	492	24.6
Food preparation workers	724	27.9	453	62.6	168	23.2	151	20.9	134	18.5
Waiters and waitresses	2,010	24.8	1,503	74.8	385	19.2	670	33.3	448	22.3
Janitors and building cleaners	2,125	45.5	569	26.8	91	4.3	170	8.0	308	14.5
Maids, housekeeping cleaners	1,434	43.6	361	25.2	38	2.6	89	6.2	234	16.3
Grounds maintenance workers	1,262	35.5	615	48.7	106	8.4	187	14.8	322	25.5
Hairdressers, hair stylists, and cosmetologists	773	39.0	304	39.3	15	1.9	93	12.0	196	25.4
Child care workers	1,314	36.3	613	46.7	146	11.1	210	16.0	257	19.6
Cashiers	3,031	27.1	1,913	63.1	771	25.4	644	21.2	498	16.4
Retail salespersons	3,416	34.9	1,709	50.0	396	11.6	657	19.2	656	19.2
Insurance sales agents	573	44.8	154	26.9	2	0.3	24	4.2	128	22.3
Securities, commodities, and financial services sales agents	388	40.0	145	37.4	1	0.3	31	8.0	113	29.1
Sales representatives, wholesale and manufacturing	1,343	42.8	376	28.0	13	1.0	71	5.3	292	21.7
Real estate brokers, sales agents	962	47.9	179	18.6	4	0.4	36	3.7	139	14.4
Bookkeeping, accounting, and auditing clerks	1,434	46.5	318	22.2	9	0.6	72	5.0	237	16.5
Customer service representatives	1,908	35.3	950	49.8	122	6.4	336	17.6	492	25.8
Receptionists, information clerks	1,413	37.2	666	47.1	102	7.2	263	18.6	301	21.3
Stock clerks and order fillers	1,481	33.0	773	52.2	180	12.2	293	19.8	300	20.3
Secretaries and administrative assistants	3,296	45.7	825	25.0	40	1.2	232	7.0	553	16.8
Misc. agricultural workers	723	34.1	372	51.5	114	15.8	100	13.8	158	21.9
Carpenters	1,562	39.4	624	39.9	30	1.9	152	9.7	442	28.3
Construction laborers	1,651	35.9	807	48.9	73	4.4	245	14.8	489	29.6
Automotive service technicians and mechanics	852	38.8	342	40.1	27	3.2	111	13.0	204	23.9
Miscellaneous assemblers and fabricators	1,050	40.8	366	34.9	25	2.4	101	9.6	240	22.9
Machinists	409	44.8	108	26.4	5	1.2	26	6.4	77	18.8
Aircraft pilots and flight engineers	141	43.6	32	22.7	1	0.7	3	2.1	28	19.9
Driver/sales workers and truck drivers	3,388	43.5	893	26.4	40	1.2	213	6.3	640	18.9
Laborers and freight, stock, and material movers	1,889	34.3	961	50.9	214	11.3	328	17.4	419	22.2

Note: "–" means sample is too small to make a reliable estimate.
Source: Bureau of Labor Statistics, unpublished tables from the 2008 Current Population Survey; calculations by New Strategist

The Youngest Workers Are Part-Timers

Among employed 20-to-24-year-olds, however, most work full-time.

Among people aged 16 or older in the civilian labor force, 12 percent of men and 24 percent of women work part-time. Among teenagers, however, part-time work predominates—66 percent of male and 76 percent of female workers aged 16 to 19 have part-time jobs. Many are high school students with after-school jobs or college students trying to earn tuition money.

Among 20-to-24-year-olds in the labor force, most work full-time. Women in the age group are more likely than their male counterparts to work part-time—36 percent of women and 26 percent of men have part-time jobs. Among workers in the broad 25-to-54 age group, the great majority of both men and women have full-time jobs.

Most workers with part-time jobs prefer to work part-time. But a substantial portion would like a full-time job. Among 16-to-19-year-olds with part-time jobs, from 8 to 12 percent would prefer full-time employment. Among 20-to-24-year-olds with part-time jobs, the figure is a higher 18 to 29 percent. Among men aged 25 to 54 with part-time jobs, fully 57 percent would prefer full-time work.

■ With college costs rising and family savings disappearing, part-time work will probably become more important in the educational plans of young adults.

Most working teens have part-time jobs

(percent of employed workers aged 16 to 24 who work part-time, by sex, 2008)

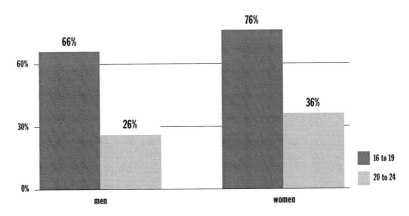

Table 6.10 Full-Time and Part-Time Workers by Age and Sex, 2008

(number and percent distribution of people aged 16 or older at work in nonagricultural industries by age, employment status, and sex, 2008; numbers in thousands)

	total			men			women		
	total	full-time	part-time	total	full-time	part-time	total	full-time	part-time
Total at work	**137,739**	**112,961**	**24,778**	**73,471**	**64,375**	**9,095**	**64,268**	**48,586**	**15,682**
Aged 16 to 19	5,252	1,526	3,727	2,556	875	1,681	2,696	650	2,046
Aged 20 to 24	13,091	9,058	4,033	6,866	5,067	1,798	6,225	3,990	2,235
Aged 25 to 54	94,577	82,960	11,617	50,972	47,468	3,504	43,605	35,492	8,112
Aged 55 or older	24,819	19,418	5,401	13,077	10,964	2,112	11,742	8,454	3,288

PERCENT DISTRIBUTION BY EMPLOYMENT STATUS

	total			men			women		
Total at work	**100.0%**	**82.0%**	**18.0%**	**100.0%**	**87.6%**	**12.4%**	**100.0%**	**75.6%**	**24.4%**
Aged 16 to 19	100.0	29.1	71.0	100.0	34.2	65.8	100.0	24.1	75.9
Aged 20 to 24	100.0	69.2	30.8	100.0	73.8	26.2	100.0	64.1	35.9
Aged 25 to 54	100.0	87.7	12.3	100.0	93.1	6.9	100.0	81.4	18.6
Aged 55 or older	100.0	78.2	21.8	100.0	83.8	16.2	100.0	72.0	28.0

PERCENT DISTRIBUTION BY AGE

	total			men			women		
Total at work	**100.0%**	**100.0%**	**100.0%**	**100.0%**	**100.0%**	**100.0%**	**100.0%**	**100.0%**	**100.0%**
Aged 16 to 19	3.8	1.4	15.0	3.5	1.4	18.5	4.2	1.3	13.0
Aged 20 to 24	9.5	8.0	16.3	9.3	7.9	19.8	9.7	8.2	14.3
Aged 25 to 54	68.7	73.4	46.9	69.4	73.7	38.5	67.8	73.0	51.7
Aged 55 or older	18.0	17.2	21.8	17.8	17.0	23.2	18.3	17.4	21.0

Note: Part-time work is less than 35 hours per week. Part-time workers exclude those who worked less than 35 hours in the previous week because of vacation, holidays, child care problems, weather issues, and other temporary, noneconomic reasons.
Source: Bureau of Labor Statistics, Current Population Survey, Internet site http://www.bls.gov/cps/tables.htm#empstat; calculations by New Strategist

Table 6.11 Part-Time Workers by Sex, Age, and Reason, 2008

(total number of people aged 16 or older who work in nonagricultural industries part-time, and number and percent working part-time for economic reasons, by sex and age, 2008; numbers in thousands)

	total	working part-time for economic reasons	
		number	share of total
Men working part-time	**9,095**	**3,162**	**34.8%**
Aged 16 to 19	1,681	209	12.4
Aged 20 to 24	1,798	526	29.3
Aged 25 to 54	3,504	2,014	57.5
Aged 55 or older	2,112	412	19.5
Women working part-time	**15,682**	**2,611**	**16.6**
Aged 16 to 19	2,046	173	8.5
Aged 20 to 24	2,235	412	18.4
Aged 25 to 54	8,112	1,637	20.2
Aged 55 or older	3,288	388	11.8

Note: Part-time work is less than 35 hours per week. Part-time workers exclude those who worked less than 35 hours in the previous week because of vacation, holidays, child care problems, weather issues, and other temporary, noneconomic reasons. "Economic reasons" means a worker's hours have been reduced or workers cannot find full-time employment.
Source: Bureau of Labor Statistics, Current Population Survey, Internet site http://www.bls.gov/cps/tables.htm#empstat; calculations by New Strategist

Few Millennials Are Self-Employed

Self-employment rises with age and experience.

Although many teens and young adults may dream of being their own boss, few are able to do so. Among the nation's 145 million employed workers, only 7 percent are self-employed. Among workers under age 25, the figure is only 1 to 2 percent. It rises to 5 percent among those aged 25 to 34.

As people age, self-employment increases, reaching 17 percent among workers aged 65 or older. Self-employment increases with age because it takes years of experience to gain marketable skills.

■ Self-employment is relatively uncommon in the United States because the cost of buying private health insurance is prohibitive.

Self-employment rises with age

(percent of workers who are self-employed, by age, 2008)

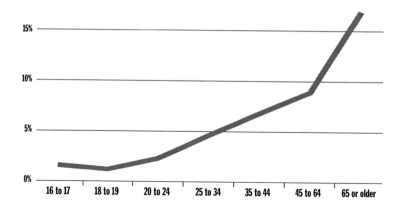

Table 6.12 Self-Employed Workers by Sex and Age, 2008

(number of employed workers aged 16 or older, number and percent who are self-employed, and percent distribution of self-employed, by age, 2008; numbers in thousands)

	total	self-employed number	self-employed percent	percent distribution of self-employed by age
Total workers aged 16 or older	**145,362**	**10,079**	**6.9%**	**100.0%**
Aged 16 to 17	1,989	31	1.6	0.3
Aged 18 to 19	3,584	42	1.2	0.4
Aged 20 to 24	13,629	313	2.3	3.1
Aged 25 to 34	31,383	1,447	4.6	14.4
Aged 35 to 44	33,457	2,286	6.8	22.7
Aged 45 to 64	55,341	4,952	8.9	49.1
Aged 65 or older	5,979	1,009	16.9	10.0
Total men aged 16 or older	**77,486**	**6,373**	**8.2**	**100.0**
Aged 16 to 17	926	22	2.4	0.3
Aged 18 to 19	1,810	29	1.6	0.5
Aged 20 to 24	7,145	214	3.0	3.4
Aged 25 to 34	17,183	921	5.4	14.5
Aged 35 to 44	18,097	1,407	7.8	22.1
Aged 45 to 64	29,043	3,110	10.7	48.8
Aged 65 or older	3,283	670	20.4	10.5
Total women aged 16 or older	**67,876**	**3,707**	**5.5**	**100.0**
Aged 16 to 17	1,063	10	0.9	0.3
Aged 18 to 19	1,774	13	0.7	0.4
Aged 20 to 24	6,484	95	1.5	2.6
Aged 25 to 34	14,200	525	3.7	14.2
Aged 35 to 44	15,360	879	5.7	23.7
Aged 45 to 64	26,298	1,842	7.0	49.7
Aged 65 or older	2,697	340	12.6	9.2

Source: Bureau of Labor Statistics, 2005 Current Population Survey, Internet site http://www.bls.gov/cps/home.htm; calculations by New Strategist

Few Young Adults Have Alternative Work Arrangements

But the young are more likely than average to be on-call workers.

According to a 2005 study by the Bureau of Labor Statistics, 15 million of the nation's 139 million employed workers (or 11 percent) have alternative work arrangements. Alternative workers are defined as independent contractors, on-call workers, temporary-help agency workers, and people who work for contract firms (such as lawn or janitorial service companies).

The most popular alternative work arrangement is independent contracting—which includes most of the self-employed and accounts for 7 percent of the workforce. Among the youngest workers, however, independent contracting is less common than on-call work. Among 20-to-24-year-olds, independent contracting and on-call work are equally common. Among 25-to-34-year-olds, independent contracting is more than twice as common as on-call work. The popularity of independent contracting rises with age, and the arrangement accounts for 10 percent of workers aged 45 or older.

■ Older workers have more skills and experience, which makes it easier for them to earn a living by self-employment.

Few young workers are independent contractors

(percent of employed workers who are independent contractors, by age, 2005)

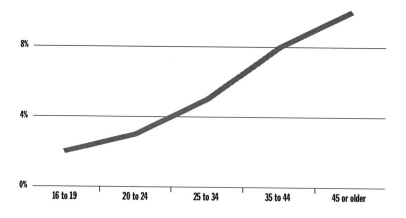

Table 6.13 Alternative Work Arrangements by Age, 2005

(number and percent distribution of employed people aged 16 or older by age and work arrangement, 2005; numbers in thousands)

			alternative workers				
	total employed	traditional arrangements	total	independent contractors	on-call workers	temporary-help agency workers	workers provided by contract firms
Total people	**138,952**	**123,843**	**14,826**	**10,342**	**2,454**	**1,217**	**813**
Aged 16 to 19	5,510	5,194	262	89	133	33	7
Aged 20 to 24	13,114	12,055	1,000	356	355	202	87
Aged 25 to 34	30,103	27,427	2,622	1,520	535	362	205
Aged 35 to 44	34,481	30,646	3,774	2,754	571	253	196
Aged 45 or older	55,744	48,521	7,168	5,623	859	368	318
PERCENT DISTRIBUTION BY ALTERNATIVE WORK STATUS							
Total people	**100.0%**	**89.1%**	**10.7%**	**7.4%**	**1.8%**	**0.9%**	**0.6%**
Aged 16 to 19	100.0	94.3	4.8	1.6	2.4	0.6	0.1
Aged 20 to 24	100.0	91.9	7.6	2.7	2.7	1.5	0.7
Aged 25 to 34	100.0	91.1	8.7	5.0	1.8	1.2	0.7
Aged 35 to 44	100.0	88.9	10.9	8.0	1.7	0.7	0.6
Aged 45 or older	100.0	87.0	12.9	10.1	1.5	0.7	0.6
PERCENT DISTRIBUTION BY AGE							
Total people	**100.0%**	**100.0%**	**100.0%**	**100.0%**	**100.0%**	**100.0%**	**100.0%**
Aged 16 to 19	4.0	4.2	1.8	0.9	5.4	2.7	0.9
Aged 20 to 24	9.4	9.7	6.7	3.4	14.5	16.6	10.7
Aged 25 to 34	21.7	22.1	17.7	14.7	21.8	29.7	25.2
Aged 35 to 44	24.8	24.7	25.5	26.6	23.3	20.8	24.1
Aged 45 or older	40.1	39.2	48.3	54.4	35.0	30.2	39.1

Note: Numbers may not add to total because "total employed" includes day laborers, an alternative arrangement not shown separately, and a small number of workers were both on call and provided by contract firms. Independent contractors are workers who obtain customers on their own to provide a product or service, and includes the self-employed. On-call workers are in a pool of workers who are called to work only as needed, such as substitute teachers and construction workers supplied by a union hiring hall. Temporary-help agency workers are those who said they are paid by a temporary-help agency. Workers provided by contract firms are those employed by a company that provides employees or their services under contract, such as security, landscaping, and computer programming.
Source: Bureau of Labor Statistics, Contingent and Alternative Employment Arrangements, February 2005, Internet site http:// www.bls.gov/news.release/conemp.t05.htm; calculations by New Strategist

Most Minimum-Wage Workers Are Teens and Young Adults

Nearly two of three are under age 30.

Among the nation's 75 million workers who were paid hourly rates in 2008, only 2 million (3 percent) made minimum wage or less, according to the Bureau of Labor Statistics. Of those 2 million workers, half are under age 25 and nearly two out of three (64 percent) are under age 30.

Twenty-four percent of minimum wage workers are aged 16 to 19, and another 26 percent are aged 20 to 24. Among workers paid hourly rates in the 16-to-19 age group, 11 percent earn minimum wage or less. In the 20-to-24 age group, 5 percent earn minimum wage or less.

■ Younger workers are most likely to earn minimum wage or less because many hold entry-level jobs.

Teens and young adults account for the majority of minimum wage workers

(percent distribution of workers who make minimum wage or less, by age, 2008)

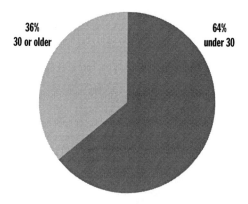

36%
30 or older

64%
under 30

Table 6.14 Workers Earning Minimum Wage by Age, 2008

(number, percent, and percent distribution of workers aged 16 or older paid hourly rates at or below minimum wage, by age, 2008; numbers in thousands)

	total paid hourly rates	at or below minimum wage		
		number	share of total	percent distribution
Total aged 16 or older	**75,305**	**2,226**	**3.0%**	**100.0%**
Under age 30	24,988	1,414	5.7	63.5
Aged 16 to 19	5,137	545	10.6	24.5
Aged 20 to 24	10,542	577	5.5	25.9
Aged 25 to 29	9,309	292	3.1	13.1
Aged 30 to 34	7,584	190	2.5	8.5
Aged 35 to 44	15,478	242	1.6	10.9
Aged 45 to 54	15,625	201	1.3	9.0
Aged 55 to 64	8,987	106	1.2	4.8
Aged 65 or older	2,642	72	2.7	3.2

Source: Bureau of Labor Statistics, Characteristics of Minimum Wage Workers, 2008, Internet site http://www.bls.gov/cps/minwage2008.htm; calculations by New Strategist

Few Millennials Are Represented by a Union

Men are more likely than women to be represented by a union.

Union representation has fallen sharply over the past few decades. In 2008, only 14 percent of employed wage and salary workers were represented by a union.

The percentage of workers represented by a union peaks in the 55-to-64 age group at 18 percent. Men are more likely than women to be represented by a union because men are more likely to work in manufacturing—the traditional stronghold of labor unions. In fact, the decline of labor unions is partly the result of the shift in jobs from manufacturing to services. Among workers under age 25, only 6 percent are represented by a union. Among workers aged 25 to 34, the figure is 12 percent.

■ Union representation may rise along with workers' concerns about job security and the cost of health care coverage.

Few workers are represented by a union

(percent of employed wage and salary workers who are represented by unions, by age, 2008)

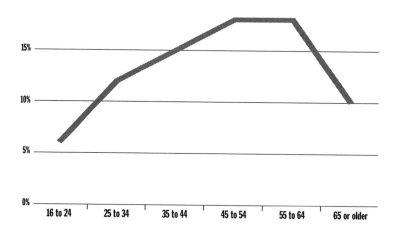

Table 6.15 Union Representation by Sex and Age, 2008

(number and percent of employed wage and salary workers aged 16 or older by union representation status, sex, and age, 2008; numbers in thousands)

	total employed	represented by unions	
		number	percent
Total aged 16 or older	**129,377**	**17,761**	**13.7%**
Aged 16 to 24	18,705	1,062	5.7
Aged 25 to 34	29,276	3,443	11.8
Aged 35 to 44	29,708	4,365	14.7
Aged 45 to 54	29,787	5,228	17.6
Aged 55 to 64	17,430	3,209	18.4
Aged 65 or older	4,471	454	10.2
Men aged 16 or older	**66,846**	**9,724**	**14.5**
Aged 16 to 24	9,537	617	6.5
Aged 25 to 34	15,780	1,909	12.1
Aged 35 to 44	15,653	2,491	15.9
Aged 45 to 54	14,988	2,812	18.8
Aged 55 to 64	8,657	1,682	19.4
Aged 65 or older	2,230	213	9.6
Women aged 16 or older	**62,532**	**8,036**	**12.9**
Aged 16 to 24	9,168	445	4.8
Aged 25 to 34	13,496	1,534	11.4
Aged 35 to 44	14,055	1,874	13.3
Aged 45 to 54	14,799	2,416	16.3
Aged 55 to 64	8,773	1,527	17.4
Aged 65 or older	2,241	241	10.7

Note: Workers represented by unions are either members of a labor union or similar employee association or workers who report no union affiliation but whose jobs are covered by a union or an employee association contract.
Source: Bureau of Labor Statistics, 2008 Current Population Survey, Internet site http://www.bls.gov/cps/tables.htm#empstat; calculations by New Strategist

The Millennial Generation Will Expand the Labor Force

The number of workers aged 25 to 34 will increase during the coming decade.

Between 2006 and 2016, the Millennial generation will age into its thirties (the oldest Millennials turn 39 in 2016). The number of workers aged 25 to 34 will expand by 14 percent between 2006 and 2016, a gain of nearly 5 million, according to the Bureau of Labor Statistics. At the same time, the number of workers aged 35 to 54 will decline as the small Generation X fills the age group.

The number of older workers is projected to soar during the coming decade as Boomers age into their late sixties. Between 2006 and 2016, the Bureau of Labor Statistics projects a 78 percent increase in the number of male workers and an even larger 91 percent increase in the number of female workers aged 65 or older.

■ As Boomers remain in the labor force well into old age, they may slow the movement of younger workers up the career ladder.

The number of workers aged 25 to 34 will increase, while the number aged 35 to 44 will decline

(projected percent change in number of workers, by age, 2006–16)

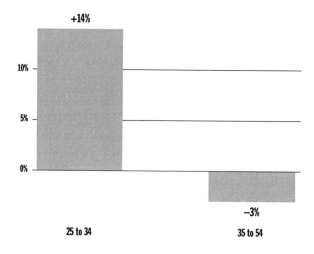

Table 6.16 Projections of the Labor Force by Sex and Age, 2006 and 2016

(number and percent of people aged 16 or older in the civilian labor force by sex and age, 2006 and 2016; percent change in number and percentage point change in participation rate, 2006–16; numbers in thousands)

	number			participation rate		
	2006	2016	percent change 2006–16	2006	2016	percentage point change 2006–16
TOTAL LABOR FORCE	**151,428**	**164,232**	**8.5%**	**66.2%**	**65.5%**	**–0.7**
Total men in labor force	**81,255**	**87,781**	**8.0**	**73.5**	**72.3**	**–1.2**
Aged 16 to 19	3,693	2,923	–20.9	43.7	36.8	–6.9
Aged 20 to 24	8,116	7,992	–1.5	79.6	76.4	–3.2
Aged 25 to 34	17,944	20,913	16.5	91.7	95.7	4.0
Aged 35 to 44	19,407	18,373	–5.3	92.1	91.7	–0.4
Aged 45 to 54	18,489	18,205	–1.5	88.1	86.6	–1.5
Aged 55 to 64	10,509	13,865	31.9	69.6	70.1	0.5
Aged 65 or older	3,096	5,511	78.0	20.3	27.1	6.8
Total women in labor force	**70,173**	**76,450**	**8.9**	**59.4**	**59.2**	**–0.2**
Aged 16 to 19	3,588	2,974	–17.1	43.7	38.3	–5.4
Aged 20 to 24	6,997	6,963	–0.5	69.5	67.2	–2.3
Aged 25 to 34	14,628	16,376	11.9	74.4	75.0	0.6
Aged 35 to 44	16,441	15,281	–7.1	75.9	75.1	–0.8
Aged 45 to 54	16,656	16,877	1.3	76.0	77.8	1.8
Aged 55 to 64	9,475	13,423	41.7	58.2	63.5	5.3
Aged 65 or older	2,388	4,556	90.8	11.7	17.5	5.8

Source: Bureau of Labor Statistics, Labor Force Projections to 2016: More Workers in Their Golden Years, Monthly Labor Review, November 2007, Internet site http://www.bls.gov/opub/mlr/2007/11/contents.htm; calculations by New Strategist

7

Living Arrangements

■ People younger than age 30 headed only 14 percent of the nation's 117 million households in 2008. (Millennials were aged 14 to 31 in that year.)

■ The living arrangements of young adults depend greatly on their race and Hispanic origin. Married couples account for 40 percent of households headed by Hispanics under age 30, but for only 14 percent of black households in the age group.

■ Fifty-one percent of Hispanic householders under age 30 have children under age 18 at home, as do 46 percent of their black counterparts. This compares with a smaller 31 percent of non-Hispanic whites and only 18 percent of Asians in the age group.

■ Many young-adult households include preschoolers. While 13 percent of all households include children under age 6, the proportion is 32 percent among householders under age 30.

■ Among the nation's 7 million cohabiting couples, 39 percent of the male partners and a larger 47 percent of the female partners are under age 30.

The Millennial Generation Heads Few Households

Only 14 percent of households are headed by people under age 30.

People younger than age 30 headed only 14 percent of the nation's 117 million households in 2008. (Millennials were aged 14 to 31 in that year.) Young adults are slow to establish their own households because many are in college and still financially dependent on their parents. In addition, the economic downturn has made it more difficult to find a job. Consequently, few young adults can afford to strike out on their own.

Households headed by young adults are extremely diverse. Married couples account for the 31 percent plurality of households headed by people under age 30. Nearly 24 percent are men and women who live alone, while another 17 percent are female-headed families. Eighteen percent of householders under age 30 live with nonrelatives, some with roommates and others with romantic partners. Nine percent of householders under age 30 are male-headed families, including 12 percent of households headed by people under age 25.

■ The diversity of young adults' living arrangements makes it difficult for marketers, politicians, and community organizations to reach them.

Households headed by young adults are diverse

(percent distribution of households headed by people under age 30, by type, 2008)

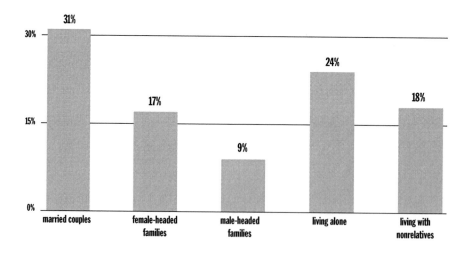

Table 7.1 Households Headed by People under Age 30 by Household Type, 2008: Total Households

(number and percent distribution of total households and households headed by people under age 30, by household type, 2008; numbers in thousands)

		aged 15 to 29		
	total	total	15 to 24	25 to 29
TOTAL HOUSEHOLDS	**116,783**	**15,954**	**6,554**	**9,400**
Family households	**77,873**	**9,228**	**3,359**	**5,869**
Married couples	58,370	4,977	1,224	3,753
Female householder, no spouse present	14,404	2,784	1,318	1,466
Male householder, no spouse present	5,100	1,467	817	650
Nonfamily households	**38,910**	**6,726**	**3,195**	**3,531**
Female householder	21,038	2,984	1,527	1,457
Living alone	18,297	1,727	805	922
Male householder	17,872	3,742	1,668	2,074
Living alone	13,870	2,089	844	1,245
Percent distribution by type				
TOTAL HOUSEHOLDS	**100.0%**	**100.0%**	**100.0%**	**100.0%**
Family households	**66.7**	**57.8**	**51.3**	**62.4**
Married couples	50.0	31.2	18.7	39.9
Female householder, no spouse present	12.3	17.5	20.1	15.6
Male householder, no spouse present	4.4	9.2	12.5	6.9
Nonfamily households	**33.3**	**42.2**	**48.7**	**37.6**
Female householder	18.0	18.7	23.3	15.5
Living alone	15.7	10.8	12.3	9.8
Male householder	15.3	23.5	25.5	22.1
Living alone	11.9	13.1	12.9	13.2
Percent distribution by age				
TOTAL HOUSEHOLDS	**100.0%**	**13.7%**	**5.6%**	**8.0%**
Family households	**100.0**	**11.9**	**4.3**	**7.5**
Married couples	100.0	8.5	2.1	6.4
Female householder, no spouse present	100.0	19.3	9.2	10.2
Male householder, no spouse present	100.0	28.8	16.0	12.7
Nonfamily households	**100.0**	**17.3**	**8.2**	**9.1**
Female householder	100.0	14.2	7.3	6.9
Living alone	100.0	9.4	4.4	5.0
Male householder	100.0	20.9	9.3	11.6
Living alone	100.0	15.1	6.1	9.0

Source: Bureau of the Census, 2008 Current Population Survey, Annual Social and Economic Supplement, Internet site http://www.census.gov/hhes/www/macro/032008/hhinc/new02_000.htm; calculations by New Strategist

Young-Adult Households Differ by Race and Hispanic Origin

A large share of the nation's young married couples are Hispanic.

Non-Hispanic whites account for the 62 percent majority of householders under age 30. But the figure varies greatly by type of household. Non-Hispanic whites account for 71 percent of nonfamily householders under age 30, but for only 39 percent of female-headed families in the age group. Among married couples under age 30, Hispanics head 22 percent, and blacks just 7 percent.

Female-headed families account for the 39 percent plurality of black households headed by young adults. In contrast only 11 percent of non-Hispanic white and 14 percent of Asian households under age 30 are female-headed families. Married couples account for the 40 percent plurality of households headed by Hispanic young adults, but for only 14 percent of black households in the age group.

■ Young adults have different wants and needs depending on their living arrangements.

Hispanic young adults are least likely to live alone

(percent of householders under age 30 who live alone, by race and Hispanic origin, 2008)

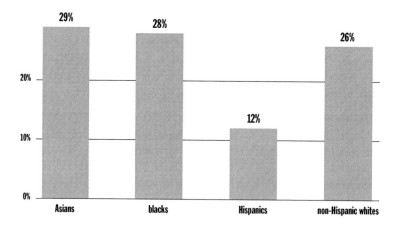

Table 7.2 Households Headed by People under Age 30 by Household Type, Race, and Hispanic Origin, 2008

(number and percent distribution of households headed by people under age 30, by household type, race, and Hispanic origin, 2008; numbers in thousands)

	total	Asian	black	Hispanic	non-Hispanic white
TOTAL HOUSEHOLDERS UNDER 30	**15,954**	**696**	**2,518**	**2,783**	**9,860**
Family households	**9,228**	**347**	**1,579**	**2,134**	**5,114**
Married couples	4,977	179	358	1,101	3,301
Female householder, no spouse present	2,784	96	971	616	1,094
Male householder, no spouse present	1,467	71	250	416	719
Nonfamily households	**6,726**	**348**	**940**	**649**	**4,745**
Female householder	2,984	170	514	235	2,055
Living alone	1,727	107	382	111	1,111
Male householder	3,742	179	427	415	2,691
Living alone	2,089	93	311	220	1,451
Percent distribution by race and Hispanic origin					
TOTAL HOUSEHOLDERS UNDER 30	**100.0%**	**4.4%**	**15.8%**	**17.4%**	**61.8%**
Family households	**100.0**	**3.8**	**17.1**	**23.1**	**55.4**
Married couples	100.0	3.6	7.2	22.1	66.3
Female householder, no spouse present	100.0	3.4	34.9	22.1	39.3
Male householder, no spouse present	100.0	4.8	17.0	28.4	49.0
Nonfamily households	**100.0**	**5.2**	**14.0**	**9.6**	**70.5**
Female householder	100.0	5.7	17.2	7.9	68.9
Living alone	100.0	6.2	22.1	6.4	64.3
Male householder	100.0	4.8	11.4	11.1	71.9
Living alone	100.0	4.5	14.9	10.5	69.5

Note: Numbers do not add to total because Asian and black include those who identify themselves as being of the race alone as well as those who identify themselves as being of the race in combination with other races and because Hispanics may be of any race. Non-Hispanic whites are those who identify themselves as being white alone and not Hispanic.
Source: Bureau of the Census, 2008 Current Population Survey, Annual Social and Economic Supplement, Internet site http:// www.census.gov/hhes/www/macro/032008/hhinc/new02_000.htm; calculations by New Strategist

Table 7.3 Households Headed by People under Age 30 by Household Type, 2008: Asian Households

(number and percent distribution of total households headed by Asians and households headed by Asians under age 30, by household type, 2008; numbers in thousands)

	total	aged 15 to 29 total	aged 15 to 29 15 to 24	aged 15 to 29 25 to 29
TOTAL ASIAN HOUSEHOLDS	4,715	696	248	448
Family households	3,451	347	122	225
Married couples	2,757	179	28	151
Female householder, no spouse present	452	96	49	47
Male householder, no spouse present	242	71	45	26
Nonfamily households	1,265	348	125	223
Female householder	662	170	69	101
Living alone	545	107	35	72
Male householder	602	179	57	122
Living alone	420	93	27	66
Percent distribution by type				
TOTAL ASIAN HOUSEHOLDS	100.0%	100.0%	100.0%	100.0%
Family households	73.2	49.9	49.2	50.2
Married couples	58.5	25.7	11.3	33.7
Female householder, no spouse present	9.6	13.8	19.8	10.5
Male householder, no spouse present	5.1	10.2	18.1	5.8
Nonfamily households	26.8	50.0	50.4	49.8
Female householder	14.0	24.4	27.8	22.5
Living alone	11.6	15.4	14.1	16.1
Male householder	12.8	25.7	23.0	27.2
Living alone	8.9	13.4	10.9	14.7
Percent distribution by age				
TOTAL ASIAN HOUSEHOLDS	100.0%	14.8%	5.3%	9.5%
Family households	100.0	10.1	3.5	6.5
Married couples	100.0	6.5	1.0	5.5
Female householder, no spouse present	100.0	21.2	10.8	10.4
Male householder, no spouse present	100.0	29.3	18.6	10.7
Nonfamily households	100.0	27.5	9.9	17.6
Female householder	100.0	25.7	10.4	15.3
Living alone	100.0	19.6	6.4	13.2
Male householder	100.0	29.7	9.5	20.3
Living alone	100.0	22.1	6.4	15.7

Note: Asians include those who identifyy themselves as being of the race alone and those who identify themselves as being of the race in combination with other races.
Source: Bureau of the Census, 2008 Current Population Survey, Annual Social and Economic Supplement, Internet site http://www.census.gov/hhes/www/macro/032008/hhinc/new02_000.htm; calculations by New Strategist

Table 7.4 Households Headed by People under Age 30 by Household Type, 2008: Black Households

(number and percent distribution of total households headed by blacks and households headed by blacks under age 30, by household type, 2008; numbers in thousands)

		aged 15 to 29		
	total	total	15 to 24	25 to 29
TOTAL BLACK HOUSEHOLDS	14,976	2,518	1,182	1,336
Family households	9,503	1,579	694	885
Married couples	4,461	358	98	260
Female householder, no spouse present	4,218	971	441	530
Male householder, no spouse present	824	250	155	95
Nonfamily households	5,474	940	488	452
Female householder	3,064	514	277	237
Living alone	2,748	382	196	186
Male householder	2,410	427	212	215
Living alone	2,012	311	140	171
Percent distribution by type				
TOTAL BLACK HOUSEHOLDS	100.0%	100.0%	100.0%	100.0%
Family households	63.5	62.7	58.7	66.2
Married couples	29.8	14.2	8.3	19.5
Female householder, no spouse present	28.2	38.6	37.3	39.7
Male householder, no spouse present	5.5	9.9	13.1	7.1
Nonfamily households	36.6	37.3	41.3	33.8
Female householder	20.5	20.4	23.4	17.7
Living alone	18.3	15.2	16.6	13.9
Male householder	16.1	17.0	17.9	16.1
Living alone	13.4	12.4	11.8	12.8
Percent distribution by age				
TOTAL BLACK HOUSEHOLDS	100.0%	16.8%	7.9%	8.9%
Family households	100.0	16.6	7.3	9.3
Married couples	100.0	8.0	2.2	5.8
Female householder, no spouse present	100.0	23.0	10.5	12.6
Male householder, no spouse present	100.0	30.3	18.8	11.5
Nonfamily households	100.0	17.2	8.9	8.3
Female householder	100.0	16.8	9.0	7.7
Living alone	100.0	13.9	7.1	6.8
Male householder	100.0	17.7	8.8	8.9
Living alone	100.0	15.5	7.0	8.5

Note: Blacks include those who identify themselves as being of the race alone and those who identify themselves as being of the race in combination with other races.
Source: Bureau of the Census, 2008 Current Population Survey, Annual Social and Economic Supplement, Internet site http:// www.census.gov/hhes/www/macro/032008/hhinc/new02_000.htm; calculations by New Strategist

Table 7.5 Households Headed by People under Age 30 by Household Type, 2008: Hispanic Households

(number and percent distribution of total households headed by Hispanics and households headed by Hispanics under age 30, by household type, 2008; numbers in thousands)

	total	aged 15 to 29 total	15 to 24	25 to 29
TOTAL HISPANIC HOUSEHOLDS	**13,339**	**2,783**	**1,182**	**1,601**
Family households	**10,394**	**2,134**	**886**	**1,248**
Married couples	6,888	1,101	331	770
Female householder, no spouse present	2,522	616	314	302
Male householder, no spouse present	983	416	241	175
Nonfamily households	**2,945**	**649**	**296**	**353**
Female householder	1,291	235	101	134
Living alone	1,065	111	46	65
Male householder	1,654	415	196	219
Living alone	1,138	220	96	124
Percent distribution by type				
TOTAL HISPANIC HOUSEHOLDS	**100.0%**	**100.0%**	**100.0%**	**100.0%**
Family households	**77.9**	**76.7**	**75.0**	**78.0**
Married couples	51.6	39.6	28.0	48.1
Female householder, no spouse present	18.9	22.1	26.6	18.9
Male householder, no spouse present	7.4	14.9	20.4	10.9
Nonfamily households	**22.1**	**23.3**	**25.0**	**22.0**
Female householder	9.7	8.4	8.5	8.4
Living alone	8.0	4.0	3.9	4.1
Male householder	12.4	14.9	16.6	13.7
Living alone	8.5	7.9	8.1	7.7
Percent distribution by age				
TOTAL HISPANIC HOUSEHOLDS	**100.0%**	**20.9%**	**8.9%**	**12.0%**
Family households	**100.0**	**20.5**	**8.5**	**12.0**
Married couples	100.0	16.0	4.8	11.2
Female householder, no spouse present	100.0	24.4	12.5	12.0
Male householder, no spouse present	100.0	42.3	24.5	17.8
Nonfamily households	**100.0**	**22.0**	**10.1**	**12.0**
Female householder	100.0	18.2	7.8	10.4
Living alone	100.0	10.4	4.3	6.1
Male householder	100.0	25.1	11.9	13.2
Living alone	100.0	19.3	8.4	10.9

Source: Bureau of the Census, 2008 Current Population Survey, Annual Social and Economic Supplement, Internet site http://www.census.gov/hhes/www/macro/032008/hhinc/new02_000.htm; calculations by New Strategist

Table 7.6 Households Headed by People under Age 30 by Household Type, 2008: Non-Hispanic White Households

(number and percent distribution of total households headed by non-Hispanic whites and households headed by non-Hispanic whites under age 30, by household type, 2008; numbers in thousands)

	total	aged 15 to 29		
		total	15 to 24	25 to 29
TOTAL NON-HISPANIC WHITE HOUSEHOLDS	**82,765**	**9,860**	**3,918**	**5,942**
Family households	**53,902**	**5,114**	**1,642**	**3,472**
Married couples	43,739	3,301	748	2,553
Female householder, no spouse present	7,171	1,094	514	580
Male householder, no spouse present	2,991	719	379	340
Nonfamily households	**28,863**	**4,745**	**2,276**	**2,469**
Female householder	15,844	2,055	1,078	977
Living alone	13,771	1,111	519	592
Male householder	13,019	2,691	1,198	1,493
Living alone	10,151	1,451	581	870
Percent distribution by type				
TOTAL NON-HISPANIC WHITE HOUSEHOLDS	**100.0%**	**100.0%**	**100.0%**	**100.0%**
Family households	**65.1**	**51.9**	**41.9**	**58.4**
Married couples	52.8	33.5	19.1	43.0
Female householder, no spouse present	8.7	11.1	13.1	9.8
Male householder, no spouse present	3.6	7.3	9.7	5.7
Nonfamily households	**34.9**	**48.1**	**58.1**	**41.6**
Female householder	19.1	20.8	27.5	16.4
Living alone	16.6	11.3	13.2	10.0
Male householder	15.7	27.3	30.6	25.1
Living alone	12.3	14.7	14.8	14.6
Percent distribution by age				
TOTAL NON-HISPANIC WHITE HOUSEHOLDS	**100.0%**	**11.9%**	**4.7%**	**7.2%**
Family households	**100.0**	**9.5**	**3.0**	**6.4**
Married couples	100.0	7.5	1.7	5.8
Female householder, no spouse present	100.0	15.3	7.2	8.1
Male householder, no spouse present	100.0	24.0	12.7	11.4
Nonfamily households	**100.0**	**16.4**	**7.9**	**8.6**
Female householder	100.0	13.0	6.8	6.2
Living alone	100.0	8.1	3.8	4.3
Male householder	100.0	20.7	9.2	11.5
Living alone	100.0	14.3	5.7	8.6

Note: Non-Hispanic whites are those who identify themselves as being white alone and not Hispanic.
Source: Bureau of the Census, 2008 Current Population Survey, Annual Social and Economic Supplement, Internet site http:// www.census.gov/hhes/www/macro/032008/hhinc/new02_000.htm; calculations by New Strategist

Households of Young Adults Are of Average Size

Between two and three people live in Millennial households.

Households headed by people aged 20 to 29 (the Millennial generation was aged 14 to 31 in 2008) are home to an average of 2.42 to 2.62 people—close to the national average of 2.56 people. The few households headed by people under age 20 are somewhat larger, at 3.01 people.

Household size grows as householders age through their thirties. It peaks among householders aged 35 to 39—at 3.31 people—because this age group is most likely to have at least one child at home. As householders age into their forties and fifties, the nest empties and household size shrinks.

■ As young adults marry and have children, the nest becomes increasingly crowded.

Among householders in their twenties, average household size is less than three

(average household size by age of householder, 2008)

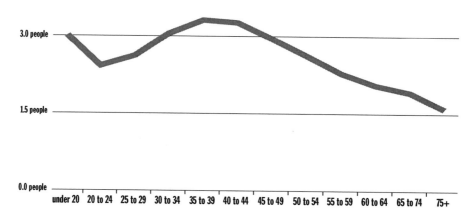

Table 7.7 Average Size of Household by Age of Householder, 2008

(number of households, average number of people per household, and average number of people under age 18 per household, by age of householder, 2008; number of households in thousands)

	number	average number of people	average number of people under age 18
Total households	**116,783**	**2.56**	**0.64**
Under age 20	862	3.01	0.84
Aged 20 to 24	5,691	2.42	0.51
Aged 25 to 29	9,400	2.62	0.80
Aged 30 to 34	9,825	3.05	1.25
Aged 35 to 39	10,900	3.31	1.43
Aged 40 to 44	11,548	3.26	1.25
Aged 45 to 49	12,685	2.95	0.81
Aged 50 to 54	11,851	2.62	0.44
Aged 55 to 59	10,813	2.28	0.23
Aged 60 to 64	9,096	2.05	0.14
Aged 65 to 74	12,284	1.91	0.09
Aged 75 or older	11,829	1.59	0.04

Source: Bureau of the Census, Current Population Survey Annual Social and Economic Supplement, America's Families and Living Arrangements: 2008, detailed tables, Internet site http://www.census.gov/population/www/socdemo/hh-fam/cps2008.html

A Minority of Young-Adult Households include Children

Most Hispanic householders under age 30 have children at home, however.

Among all households headed by people under age 30, only 36 percent include children. The figure is a higher 64 percent for married-couple householders in the age group, and an even higher 78 percent for female-headed families.

The percentage of households that include children varies greatly by race and Hispanic origin. Fifty-one percent of Hispanic householders under age 30 have children at home, as do 46 percent of their black counterparts. This compares with a smaller 31 percent of non-Hispanic whites and only 18 percent of Asians in the age group.

■ The lifestyles of young adults are diverse, ranging from students with class schedules to parents with family and work schedules.

Few households headed by Asians under age 30 include children

(percent of householders under age 30 with children under age 18 at home, by race and Hispanic origin, 2008)

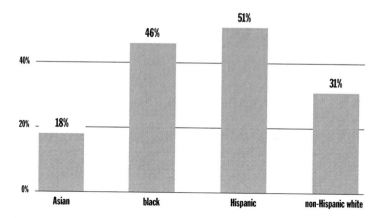

Table 7.8 Households by Type, Age of Householder, and Presence of Children, 2008: Total Households

(total number of households and number and percent with own children under age 18 at home, by household type and age of householder, 2008; numbers in thousands)

	total	with own children under age 18	
		number	percent
TOTAL HOUSEHOLDS	**116,783**	**35,709**	**30.6%**
Under age 30	15,954	5,801	36.4
Aged 15 to 24	6,554	1,779	27.1
Aged 25 to 29	9,400	4,022	42.8
Aged 30 to 34	9,825	5,820	59.2
Aged 35 to 44	22,448	14,195	63.2
Aged 45 or older	68,558	9,893	14.4
Married couples	**58,370**	**25,173**	**43.1**
Under age 30	4,977	3,161	63.5
Aged 15 to 24	1,224	711	58.1
Aged 25 to 29	3,753	2,450	65.3
Aged 30 to 34	5,240	4,005	76.4
Aged 35 to 44	12,989	10,453	80.5
Aged 45 or older	35,164	7,553	21.5
Female family householder, no spouse present	**14,404**	**8,374**	**58.1**
Under age 30	2,784	2,167	77.8
Aged 15 to 24	1,318	894	67.8
Aged 25 to 29	1,466	1,273	86.8
Aged 30 to 34	1,599	1,480	92.6
Aged 35 to 44	3,551	3,007	84.7
Aged 45 or older	6,471	1,720	26.6
Male family householder, no spouse present	**5,100**	**2,162**	**42.4**
Under age 30	1,467	473	32.2
Aged 15 to 24	817	174	21.3
Aged 25 to 29	650	299	46.0
Aged 30 to 34	546	334	61.2
Aged 35 to 44	1,061	736	69.4
Aged 45 or older	2,027	620	30.6

Source: Bureau of the Census, Current Population Survey Annual Social and Economic Supplement, America's Families and Living Arrangements: 2008, detailed tables, Internet site http://www.census.gov/population/www/socdemo/hh-fam/cps2008 .html; calculations by New Strategist

Table 7.9 Households by Type, Age of Householder, and Presence of Children, 2008: Asian Households

(total number of Asian households and number and percent with own children under age 18 at home, by household type and age of householder, 2008; numbers in thousands)

	total	with own children under age 18	
		number	percent
TOTAL ASIAN HOUSEHOLDS	**4,715**	**1,743**	**37.0%**
Under age 30	696	123	17.7
Aged 15 to 24	248	20	8.1
Aged 25 to 29	448	103	23.0
Aged 30 to 34	620	297	47.9
Aged 35 to 44	1,148	741	64.5
Aged 45 or older	2,252	581	25.8
Married couples	**2,757**	**1,482**	**53.8**
Under age 30	179	78	43.6
Aged 15 to 24	28	8	28.6
Aged 25 to 29	151	70	46.4
Aged 30 to 34	368	257	69.8
Aged 35 to 44	760	626	82.4
Aged 45 or older	1,449	519	35.8
Female family householder, no spouse present	**452**	**202**	**44.7**
Under age 30	96	39	40.6
Aged 15 to 24	49	9	–
Aged 25 to 29	47	30	63.8
Aged 30 to 34	50	35	70.0
Aged 35 to 44	110	82	74.5
Aged 45 or older	196	48	24.5
Male family householder, no spouse present	**242**	**60**	**24.8**
Under age 30	71	7	9.9
Aged 15 to 24	45	3	6.7
Aged 25 to 29	26	4	15.4
Aged 30 to 34	29	5	17.2
Aged 35 to 44	68	33	48.5
Aged 45 or older	73	15	20.5

Note: Asians include those who identify themselves as being of the race alone and those who identify themselves as being of the race in combination with other races.
Source: Bureau of the Census, Current Population Survey Annual Social and Economic Supplement, America's Families and Living Arrangements: 2008, detailed tables, Internet site http://www.census.gov/population/www/socdemo/hh-fam/cps2008 .html; calculations by New Strategist

Table 7.10 Households by Type, Age of Householder, and Presence of Children, 2008: Black Households

(total number of black households and number and percent with own children under age 18 at home, by household type and age of householder, 2008; numbers in thousands)

| | total | with own children under age 18 | |
		number	percent
TOTAL BLACK HOUSEHOLDS	**14,976**	**5,078**	**33.9%**
Under age 30	2,518	1,158	46.0
Aged 15 to 24	1,182	434	36.7
Aged 25 to 29	1,336	724	54.2
Aged 30 to 34	1,421	882	62.1
Aged 35 to 44	3,202	1,861	58.1
Aged 45 or older	7,835	1,178	15.0
Married couples	**4,461**	**2,070**	**46.4**
Under age 30	358	246	68.7
Aged 15 to 24	98	59	60.2
Aged 25 to 29	260	187	71.9
Aged 30 to 34	370	298	80.5
Aged 35 to 44	1,126	863	76.6
Aged 45 or older	2,607	664	25.5
Female family householder, no spouse present	**4,218**	**2,694**	**63.9**
Under age 30	971	840	86.5
Aged 15 to 24	441	348	78.9
Aged 25 to 29	530	492	92.8
Aged 30 to 34	559	530	94.8
Aged 35 to 44	1,078	890	82.6
Aged 45 or older	1,609	434	27.0
Male family householder, no spouse present	**824**	**314**	**38.1**
Under age 30	250	72	28.8
Aged 15 to 24	155	27	17.4
Aged 25 to 29	95	45	47.4
Aged 30 to 34	96	54	56.3
Aged 35 to 44	176	108	61.4
Aged 45 or older	303	79	26.1

Note: Blacks include those who identify themselves as being of the race alone and those who identify themselves as being of the race in combination with other races.
Source: Bureau of the Census, Current Population Survey Annual Social and Economic Supplement, America's Families and Living Arrangements: 2008, detailed tables, Internet site http://www.census.gov/population/www/socdemo/hh-fam/cps2008 .html; calculations by New Strategist

Table 7.11 Households by Type, Age of Householder, and Presence of Children, 2008: Hispanic Households

(total number of Hispanic households and number and percent with own children under age 18 at home, by household type and age of householder, 2008; numbers in thousands)

	total	with own children under age 18	
		number	percent
TOTAL HISPANIC HOUSEHOLDS	**13,339**	**6,431**	**48.2%**
Under age 30	2,783	1,425	51.2
Aged 15 to 24	1,182	482	40.8
Aged 25 to 29	1,601	943	58.9
Aged 30 to 34	1,800	1,272	70.7
Aged 35 to 44	3,385	2,447	72.3
Aged 45 or older	5,371	1,288	24.0
Married couples	**6,888**	**4,425**	**64.2**
Under age 30	1,081	864	79.9
Aged 15 to 24	331	242	73.1
Aged 25 to 29	770	622	80.8
Aged 30 to 34	1,024	874	85.4
Aged 35 to 44	1,989	1,730	87.0
Aged 45 or older	2,775	959	34.6
Female family householder, no spouse present	**2,522**	**1,642**	**65.1**
Under age 30	616	454	73.7
Aged 15 to 24	314	201	64.0
Aged 25 to 29	302	253	83.8
Aged 30 to 34	329	314	95.4
Aged 35 to 44	706	610	86.4
Aged 45 or older	872	265	30.4
Male family householder, no spouse present	**983**	**365**	**37.1**
Under age 30	416	108	26.0
Aged 15 to 24	241	39	16.2
Aged 25 to 29	175	69	39.4
Aged 30 to 34	156	85	54.5
Aged 35 to 44	180	108	60.0
Aged 45 or older	231	64	27.7

Source: Bureau of the Census, Current Population Survey Annual Social and Economic Supplement, America's Families and Living Arrangements: 2008, detailed tables, Internet site http://www.census.gov/population/www/socdemo/hh-fam/cps2008 .html; calculations by New Strategist

Table 7.12 Households by Type, Age of Householder, and Presence of Children, 2008: Non-Hispanic White Households

(total number of non-Hispanic white households and number and percent with own children under age 18 at home, by household type and age of householder, 2008; numbers in thousands)

	total	with own children under age 18	
		number	percent
TOTAL NON-HISPANIC WHITE HOUSEHOLDS	**82,765**	**22,221**	**26.8%**
Under age 30	9,860	3,066	31.1
Aged 15 to 24	3918	842	21.5
Aged 25 to 29	5,942	2224	37.4
Aged 30 to 34	5,937	3,329	56.1
Aged 35 to 44	14,529	9,048	62.3
Aged 45 or older	52,440	6,778	12.9
Married couples	**43,739**	**16,998**	**38.9**
Under age 30	3,301	1,954	59.2
Aged 15 to 24	748	392	52.4
Aged 25 to 29	2,553	1,562	61.2
Aged 30 to 34	3,431	2,535	73.9
Aged 35 to 44	8,996	7,143	79.4
Aged 45 or older	28,011	5,366	19.2
Female family householder, no spouse present	**7,171**	**3,830**	**53.4**
Under age 30	1,094	834	76.2
Aged 15 to 24	514	344	66.9
Aged 25 to 29	580	490	84.5
Aged 30 to 34	665	609	91.6
Aged 35 to 44	1,658	1,425	85.9
Aged 45 or older	3,753	962	25.6
Male family householder, no spouse present	**2,991**	**1,393**	**46.6**
Under age 30	719	278	38.7
Aged 15 to 24	379	107	28.2
Aged 25 to 29	340	171	50.3
Aged 30 to 34	264	185	70.1
Aged 35 to 44	625	479	76.6
Aged 45 or older	1,382	450	32.6

Note: Non-Hispanic whites are those who identify themselves as being white alone and not Hispanic.
Source: Bureau of the Census, Current Population Survey Annual Social and Economic Supplement, America's Families and Living Arrangements: 2008, detailed tables, Internet site http://www.census.gov/population/www/socdemo/hh-fam/cps2008 .html; calculations by New Strategist

One-Third of Young-Adult Households include Preschoolers

The proportion with toddlers is well above average.

The majority of young adults go to college after high school, postponing marriage and family until their mid-twenties. Consequently, a 36 percent minority of householders under age 30 has children at home.

But young-adult households are more likely to include preschoolers than the average household. While 13 percent of all households include children under age 6, the proportion is 32 percent among householders under age 30. Similarly, while only 8 percent of all households include children under age 3, the figure is a much higher 23 percent among young adults. Ten percent of householders under age 30 have infants at home.

■ While most young adults postpone childbearing, others establish independent households because they have children.

Young-adult households are more likely than average to include preschoolers

(percent of total households and households headed by people under age 30 that include children under age 6, 2008)

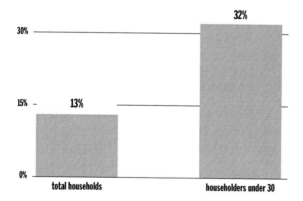

Table 7.13 Households by Presence and Age of Children and Age of Householder, 2008

(number and percent distribution of households by presence and age of own children at home, by age of children and age of householder, 2008; numbers in thousands)

	total	under age 30 total	15 to 19	20 to 24	25 to 29	30 to 34	35 or older
Total households	**116,783**	**15,954**	**862**	**5,691**	**9,400**	**9,825**	**91,006**
With children of any age	46,995	5,802	132	1,647	4,023	5,841	35,351
Under age 25	41,647	5,802	132	1,647	4,023	5,841	30,003
Under age 18	35,709	5,801	132	1,647	4,022	5,820	24,089
Under age 12	26,125	5,755	132	1,644	3,979	5,496	14,874
Under age 6	15,733	5,136	131	1,571	3,434	3,948	6,650
Under age 3	9,192	3,721	102	1,281	2,338	2,505	2,966
Under age 1	3,401	1,557	63	560	934	918	926
Aged 12 to 17	16,907	260	0	7	253	1,486	15,159

PERCENT DISTRIBUTION BY AGE OF CHILD

	total						
Total households	**100.0%**	**100.0%**	**100.0%**	**100.0%**	**100.0%**	**100.0%**	**100.0%**
With children of any age	40.2	36.4	15.3	28.9	42.8	59.5	38.8
Under age 25	35.7	36.4	15.3	28.9	42.8	59.5	33.0
Under age 18	30.6	36.4	15.3	28.9	42.8	59.2	26.5
Under age 12	22.4	36.1	15.3	28.9	42.3	55.9	16.3
Under age 6	13.5	32.2	15.2	27.6	36.5	40.2	7.3
Under age 3	7.9	23.3	11.8	22.5	24.9	25.5	3.3
Under age 1	2.9	9.8	7.3	9.8	9.9	9.3	1.0
Aged 12 to 17	14.5	1.6	0.0	0.1	2.7	15.1	16.7

PERCENT DISTRIBUTION BY AGE OF HOUSEHOLDER

	total						
Total households	**100.0%**	**13.7%**	**0.7%**	**4.9%**	**8.0%**	**8.4%**	**77.9%**
With children of any age	100.0	12.3	0.3	3.5	8.6	12.4	75.2
Under age 25	100.0	13.9	0.3	4.0	9.7	14.0	72.0
Under age 18	100.0	16.2	0.4	4.6	11.3	16.3	67.5
Under age 12	100.0	22.0	0.5	6.3	15.2	21.0	56.9
Under age 6	100.0	32.6	0.8	10.0	21.8	25.1	42.3
Under age 3	100.0	40.5	1.1	13.9	25.4	27.3	32.3
Under age 1	100.0	45.8	1.9	16.5	27.5	27.0	27.2
Aged 12 to 17	100.0	1.5	0.0	0.0	1.5	8.8	89.7

Source: Bureau of the Census, Current Population Survey Annual Social and Economic Supplement, America's Families and Living Arrangements: 2008, detailed tables, Internet site http://www.census.gov/population/www/socdemo/hh-fam/cps2008 .html; calculations by New Strategist

Young Married Parents Are Most Likely to Have Only One Child

A substantial 18 percent have three or more, however.

Among married couples under age 30 with children, the 48 percent plurality has only one child. Another 34 percent have two, 12 percent have three, and 5 percent have four or more.

The numbers are similar among families headed by females under age 30. Their male counterparts are far more likely to have only one child (69 percent), and few have three or more (4 percent).

■ The percentage of married parents with three or more children in the household reaches 27 percent in the 30-to-34 age group.

Among married couples under age 30, 48 percent have just one child

(percent of married couples under age 30 with children under age 18 at home, by number of children, 2008)

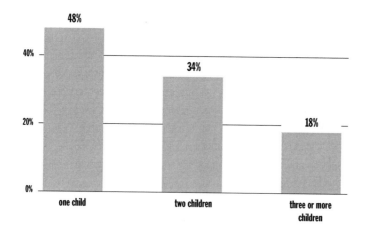

Table 7.14 Married Couples with Children by Number of Children and Age of Householder, 2008

(number and percent distribution of married couples with own children under age 18 at home, by number of children and age of householder, 2008; numbers in thousands)

	total	under age 30 total	15 to 19	20 to 24	25 to 29	30 to 34	35 or older
Married couples with children under 18	**25,173**	**3,161**	**35**	**676**	**2,450**	**4,005**	**18,006**
One	9,733	1,526	27	404	1,095	1,255	6,951
Two	9,886	1,076	6	207	863	1,673	7,136
Three	3,953	392	2	57	333	762	2,799
Four or more	1,602	168	0	8	160	315	1,117

PERCENT DISTRIBUTION BY NUMBER OF CHILDREN

	total	under age 30 total	15 to 19	20 to 24	25 to 29	30 to 34	35 or older
Married couples with children under 18	**100.0%**	**100.0%**	**100.0%**	**100.0%**	**100.0%**	**100.0%**	**100.0%**
One	38.7	48.3	77.1	59.8	44.7	31.3	38.6
Two	39.3	34.0	17.1	30.6	35.2	41.8	39.6
Three	15.7	12.4	5.7	8.4	13.6	19.0	15.5
Four or more	6.4	5.3	0.0	1.2	6.5	7.9	6.2

Source: Bureau of the Census, Current Population Survey Annual Social and Economic Supplement, America's Families and Living Arrangements: 2008, detailed tables, Internet site http://www.census.gov/population/www/socdemo/hh-fam/cps2008 .html; calculations by New Strategist

Table 7.15 Female-headed Families with Children by Number of Children and Age of Householder, 2008

(number and percent distribution of female-headed families with own children under age 18 at home, by number of children and age of householder, 2008; numbers in thousands)

	total	under age 30 total	15 to 19	20 to 24	25 to 29	30 to 34	35 or older
Female-headed families wiith children under 18	**8,374**	**2,167**	**90**	**804**	**1,273**	**1,480**	**4,727**
One	4,104	1,066	71	487	508	511	2,527
Two	2,675	681	19	227	435	488	1,506
Three	1,107	290	0	75	215	320	496
Four or more	487	130	0	15	115	161	196

PERCENT DISTRIBUTION

	total	under age 30 total	15 to 19	20 to 24	25 to 29	30 to 34	35 or older
Female-headed families with children under 18	**100.0%**	**100.0%**	**100.0%**	**100.0%**	**100.0%**	**100.0%**	**100.0%**
One	49.0	49.2	78.9	60.6	39.9	34.5	53.5
Two	31.9	31.4	21.1	28.2	34.2	33.0	31.9
Three	13.2	13.4	0.0	9.3	16.9	21.6	10.5
Four or more	5.8	6.0	0.0	1.9	9.0	10.9	4.1

Source: Bureau of the Census, Current Population Survey Annual Social and Economic Supplement, America's Families and Living Arrangements: 2008, detailed tables, Internet site http://www.census.gov/population/www/socdemo/hh-fam/cps2008 .html; calculations by New Strategist

Table 7.16 Male-headed Families with Children by Number of Children and Age of Householder, 2008

(number and percent distribution of male-headed families with own children under age 18 at home, by number of children and age of householder, 2008; numbers in thousands)

	total	under age 30 total	15 to 19	20 to 24	25 to 29	30 to 34	35 or older
Male-headed families with children under 18	**2,162**	**473**	**7**	**167**	**299**	**334**	**1,356**
One	1,323	327	7	142	178	172	823
Two	597	126	0	21	105	108	363
Three	174	18	0	4	14	41	114
Four or more	68	3	0	0	3	13	52

PERCENT DISTRIBUTION

	total	under age 30 total	15 to 19	20 to 24	25 to 29	30 to 34	35 or older
Male-headed families with children under 18	**100.0%**	**100.0%**	**100.0%**	**100.0%**	**100.0%**	**100.0%**	**100.0%**
One	61.2	69.1	100.0	85.0	59.5	51.5	60.7
Two	27.6	26.6	0.0	12.6	35.1	32.3	26.8
Three	8.0	3.8	0.0	2.4	4.7	12.3	8.4
Four or more	3.1	0.6	0.0	0.0	1.0	3.9	3.8

Source: Bureau of the Census, Current Population Survey Annual Social and Economic Supplement, America's Families and Living Arrangements: 2008, detailed tables, Internet site http://www.census.gov/population/www/socdemo/hh-fam/cps2008 .html; calculations by New Strategist

Most Young Men Live with Their Parents

Few head their own households.

Among people under age 30, 51 percent of men and 45 percent of women live with their parents. These figures include college students living in dormitories because they are considered dependents. Not surprisingly, the proportion of young adults who live with their parents falls with age—more slowly for men than for women. Among men aged 20 to 24, 48 percent still live with their parents, a figure that drops to 20 percent in the 25-to-29 age group. Among women aged 20 to 24, 39 percent live with their parents, as do 14 percent of those aged 25 to 29.

It is much more common for young adults to live with nonrelatives, than to live with a spouse. Twenty-two percent of men aged 20 to 24 live with a nonrelative and only 9 percent live with a spouse. Among women in the age group, 21 percent live with nonrelatives and 15 percent with a spouse. Among the nation's 7 million cohabiting couples, 39 percent of the male partners and a larger 47 percent of the female partners are under age 30.

■ With more young adults pursuing a college degree, the dependency of childhood has stretched well into the twenties.

Many young adults live with parents

(percent of people aged 15 to 29 who live with their parents, by sex and age, 2008)

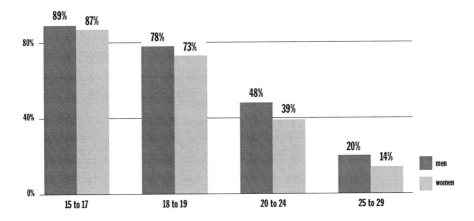

Table 7.17 Living Arrangements of Men under Age 30, 2008

(number and percent distribution of men aged 15 to 29 by living arrangement and age, 2008; numbers in thousands)

			aged 15 to 29		
	total	15 to 17	18 to 19	20 to 24	25 to 29
Total men under age 30	**31,905**	**6,816**	**3,998**	**10,380**	**10,711**
Child of householder	16,256	6,059	3,129	4,937	2,131
Married householder or spouse	4,405	4	27	904	3,470
Living alone	2,090	2	60	783	1,245
Living with nonrelatives	5,109	150	312	2,246	2,401
Other living arrangement	9,154	751	782	3,756	3,865
PERCENT DISTRIBUTION					
Total men under age 30	**100.0%**	**100.0%**	**100.0%**	**100.0%**	**100.0%**
Child of householder	51.0	88.9	78.3	47.6	19.9
Married householder or spouse	13.8	0.1	0.7	8.7	32.4
Living alone	6.6	0.0	1.5	7.5	11.6
Living with nonrelatives	16.0	2.2	7.8	21.6	22.4
Other living arrangement	28.7	11.0	19.6	36.2	36.1

Source: Bureau of the Census, Current Population Survey Annual Social and Economic Supplement, America's Families and Living Arrangements: 2008, detailed tables, Internet site http://www.census.gov/population/www/socdemo/hh-fam/cps2008 .html; calculations by New Strategist

Table 7.18 Living Arrangements of Women under Age 30, 2008

(number and percent distribution of women aged 15 to 29 by living arrangement and age, 2008; numbers in thousands)

			aged 15 to 29		
	total	15 to 17	18 to 19	20 to 24	25 to 29
Total women under age 30	**30,937**	**6,628**	**3,856**	**10,127**	**10,326**
Child of householder	13,963	5,794	2,830	3,906	1,433
Married householder or spouse	6,119	14	96	1,568	4,441
Living alone	1,727	0	81	724	922
Living with nonrelatives	4,333	170	375	2144	1644
Other living arrangement	9,128	820	849	3,929	3,530
PERCENT DISTRIBUTION					
Total women under age 30	**100.0%**	**100.0%**	**100.0%**	**100.0%**	**100.0%**
Child of householder	45.1	87.4	73.4	38.6	13.9
Married householder or spouse	19.8	0.2	2.5	15.5	43.0
Living alone	5.6	0.0	2.1	7.1	8.9
Living with nonrelatives	14.0	2.6	9.7	21.2	15.9
Other living arrangement	29.5	12.4	22.0	38.8	34.2

Source: Bureau of the Census, Current Population Survey Annual Social and Economic Supplement, America's Families and Living Arrangements: 2008, detailed tables, Internet site http://www.census.gov/population/www/socdemo/hh-fam/cps2008 .html; calculations by New Strategist

Table 7.19 Opposite-Sex Unmarried Couples by Age, 2008

(number and percent distribution of opposite-sex unmarried couples by age of male and female partner, 2008; numbers in thousands)

	number	percent distribution
TOTAL COUPLES	**6,799**	**100.0%**
Age of male partner		
Under age 30	2,622	38.6
Under age 25	1,184	17.4
Aged 25 to 29	1,438	21.2
Aged 30 to 34	992	14.6
Aged 35 to 39	733	10.8
Aged 40 to 44	665	9.8
Aged 45 to 49	534	7.9
Aged 50 to 54	466	6.9
Aged 55 to 64	541	8.0
Aged 65 or older	246	3.6
Age of female partner		
Under age 30	3,176	46.7
Under age 25	1,834	27.0
Aged 25 to 29	1,342	19.7
Aged 30 to 34	793	11.7
Aged 35 to 39	655	9.6
Aged 40 to 44	582	8.6
Aged 45 to 49	592	8.7
Aged 50 to 54	407	6.0
Aged 55 to 64	404	5.9
Aged 65 or older	189	2.8

Source: Bureau of the Census, Current Population Survey Annual Social and Economic Supplement, America's Families and Living Arrangements: 2008, detailed tables, Internet site http://www.census.gov/population/www/socdemo/hh-fam/cps2008 .html; calculations by New Strategis

Among Young Adults, the Married Are a Minority

Most women are single until their late twenties, men until their early thirties.

The majority of men and women under age 30 have never married. Among men aged 20 to 24, fully 87 percent are single. The figure is 79 percent among their female counterparts. The percentage of women who have never married drops sharply in the 25-to-29 age group, to just 45 percent. But the 59 percent majority of men aged 25 to 29 are still single. The proportion of men who have married surpasses 50 percent in the 30-to-34 age group.

Marital patterns do not vary much by race and Hispanic origin. The percentage of women who have never married falls below 50 percent in the 25-to-29 age group for Asians, Hispanics, and non-Hispanic whites. Among black women and all men regardless of race or Hispanic origin, the proportion of those who have never married does not fall below 50 percent until they are in their thirties or older.

■ The great diversity in the living arrangements of young adults is the consequence of postponed marriages.

Most women have married by age 29, while most men are still single

(percent of people aged 25 to 29 who have never married, by sex, 2008)

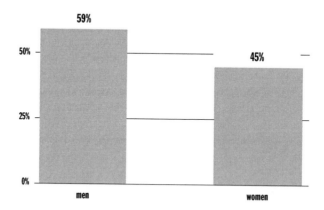

Table 7.20 Marital Status by Sex and Age, 2008: Total People

(number and percent distribution of people aged 15 or older by sex, age, and current marital status, 2008; numbers in thousands)

	total	never married	married spouse present	married spouse absent	separated	divorced	widowed
NUMBER							
Total men	**115,599**	**38,685**	**60,129**	**1,944**	**2,144**	**9,782**	**2,916**
Under age 30	31,905	25,986	4,738	371	375	407	27
Aged 15 to 17	6,816	6,716	8	32	47	10	3
Aged 18 to 19	3,998	3,907	42	12	34	1	–
Aged 20 to 24	10,380	9,064	1,027	103	99	78	9
Aged 25 to 29	10,711	6,299	3,661	222	195	318	15
Aged 30 or older	83,695	12,699	55,391	1,573	1,769	9,377	2,889
Total women	**122,394**	**32,794**	**60,129**	**1,470**	**3,039**	**13,564**	**11,398**
Under age 30	30,937	22,839	6,520	299	563	646	73
Aged 15 to 17	6,628	6,496	22	48	47	14	3
Aged 18 to 19	3,856	3,658	124	29	28	14	3
Aged 20 to 24	10,127	7,990	1,721	87	170	139	20
Aged 25 to 29	10,326	4,695	4,653	135	318	479	47
Aged 30 or older	91,457	9,956	53,610	1,172	2,476	12,918	11,324
PERCENT DISTRIBUTION							
Total men	**100.0%**	**33.5%**	**52.0%**	**1.7%**	**1.9%**	**8.5%**	**2.5%**
Under age 30	100.0	81.4	14.9	1.2	1.2	1.3	0.1
Aged 15 to 17	100.0	98.5	0.1	0.5	0.7	0.1	0.0
Aged 18 to 19	100.0	97.7	1.1	0.3	0.9	0.0	–
Aged 20 to 24	100.0	87.3	9.9	1.0	1.0	0.8	0.1
Aged 25 to 29	100.0	58.8	34.2	2.1	1.8	3.0	0.1
Aged 30 or older	100.0	15.2	66.2	1.9	2.1	11.2	3.5
Total women	**100.0**	**26.8**	**49.1**	**1.2**	**2.5**	**11.1**	**9.3**
Under age 30	100.0	73.8	21.1	1.0	1.8	2.1	0.2
Aged 15 to 17	100.0	98.0	0.3	0.7	0.7	0.2	0.0
Aged 18 to 19	100.0	94.9	3.2	0.8	0.7	0.4	0.1
Aged 20 to 24	100.0	78.9	17.0	0.9	1.7	1.4	0.2
Aged 25 to 29	100.0	45.5	45.1	1.3	3.1	4.6	0.5
Aged 30 or older	100.0	10.9	58.6	1.3	2.7	14.1	12.4

Note: "–" means number is less than 500 or sample is too small to make a reliable estimate.
Source: Bureau of the Census, Current Population Survey Annual Social and Economic Supplement, America's Families and Living Arrangements: 2008, detailed tables, Internet site http://www.census.gov/population/www/socdemo/hh-fam/cps2008 .html; calculations by New Strategist

Table 7.21 Marital Status by Sex and Age, 2008: Asians

(number and percent distribution of Asians aged 15 or older by sex, age, and current marital status, 2008; numbers in thousands)

	total	never married	married spouse present	married spouse absent	separated	divorced	widowed
NUMBER							
Total Asian men	**5,408**	**1,922**	**2,968**	**202**	**79**	**155**	**83**
Under age 30	1,526	1,303	177	28	10	8	1
Aged 15 to 17	301	299	–	–	–	–	1
Aged 18 to 19	182	182	–	–	–	–	–
Aged 20 to 24	481	452	21	5	2	2	–
Aged 25 to 29	562	370	156	23	8	6	–
Aged 30 or older	3,880	618	2,791	173	70	145	82
Total Asian women	**6,022**	**1,596**	**3,413**	**158**	**105**	**325**	**424**
Under age 30	1,563	1,136	348	36	24	16	4
Aged 15 to 17	319	313	–	5	1	–	–
Aged 18 to 19	170	164	4	2	–	–	–
Aged 20 to 24	489	407	71	8	3	–	1
Aged 25 to 29	585	252	273	21	20	16	3
Aged 30 or older	4,458	460	3,066	121	82	312	420
PERCENT DISTRIBUTION							
Total Asian men	**100.0%**	**35.5%**	**54.9%**	**3.7%**	**1.5%**	**2.9%**	**1.5%**
Under age 30	100.0	85.4	11.6	1.8	0.7	0.5	0.1
Aged 15 to 17	100.0	99.3	–	–	–	–	0.3
Aged 18 to 19	100.0	100.0	–	–	–	–	–
Aged 20 to 24	100.0	94.0	4.4	1.0	0.4	0.4	–
Aged 25 to 29	100.0	65.8	27.8	4.1	1.4	1.1	–
Aged 30 or older	100.0	15.9	71.9	4.5	1.8	3.7	2.1
Total Asian women	**100.0**	**26.5**	**56.7**	**2.6**	**1.7**	**5.4**	**7.0**
Under age 30	100.0	72.7	22.3	2.3	1.5	1.0	0.3
Aged 15 to 17	100.0	98.1	–	1.6	0.3	–	–
Aged 18 to 19	100.0	96.5	2.4	1.2	–	–	–
Aged 20 to 24	100.0	83.2	14.5	1.6	0.6	–	0.2
Aged 25 to 29	100.0	43.1	46.7	3.6	3.4	2.7	0.5
Aged 30 or older	100.0	10.3	68.8	2.7	1.8	7.0	9.4

Note: Asians include those who identify themselves as being of the race alone and those who identify themselves as being of the race in combination with other races. "–" means number is less than 500 or sample is too small to make a reliable estimate.
Source: Bureau of the Census, Current Population Survey Annual Social and Economic Supplement, America's Families and Living Arrangements: 2008, detailed tables, Internet site http://www.census.gov/population/www/socdemo/hh-fam/cps2008 .html; calculations by New Strategist

Table 7.22 Marital Status by Sex and Age, 2008: Blacks

(number and percent distribution of blacks aged 15 or older by sex, age, and current marital status, 2008; numbers in thousands)

| | | | married | | | | |
	total	never married	spouse present	spouse absent	separated	divorced	widowed
NUMBER							
Total black men	**13,360**	**6,412**	**4,636**	**241**	**517**	**1,219**	**335**
Under age 30	4,612	4,107	321	46	82	53	–
Aged 15 to 17	1,140	1,118	–	10	11	1	–
Aged 18 to 19	630	611	8	5	5	–	–
Aged 20 to 24	1,461	1,350	76	5	26	3	–
Aged 25 to 29	1,381	1,028	237	26	40	49	–
Aged 30 or older	8,747	2,305	4,314	196	435	1,166	335
Total black women	**16,094**	**7,136**	**4,439**	**261**	**820**	**2,034**	**1,404**
Under age 30	4,952	4,238	467	40	99	96	12
Aged 15 to 17	1,143	1,120	2	8	7	4	1
Aged 18 to 19	650	631	12	1	3	2	–
Aged 20 to 24	1,594	1,422	108	13	29	20	3
Aged 25 to 29	1,565	1,065	344	18	60	70	8
Aged 30 or older	11,144	2,898	3,973	221	721	1,939	1,392
PERCENT DISTRIBUTION							
Total black men	**100.0%**	**48.0%**	**34.7%**	**1.8%**	**3.9%**	**9.1%**	**2.5%**
Under age 30	100.0	89.1	7.0	1.0	1.8	1.1	–
Aged 15 to 17	100.0	98.1	–	0.9	1.0	0.1	–
Aged 18 to 19	100.0	97.0	1.3	0.8	0.8	–	–
Aged 20 to 24	100.0	92.4	5.2	0.3	1.8	0.2	–
Aged 25 to 29	100.0	74.4	17.2	1.9	2.9	3.5	–
Aged 30 or older	100.0	26.4	49.3	2.2	5.0	13.3	3.8
Total black women	**100.0**	**44.3**	**27.6**	**1.6**	**5.1**	**12.6**	**8.7**
Under age 30	100.0	85.6	9.4	0.8	2.0	1.9	0.2
Aged 15 to 17	100.0	98.0	0.2	0.7	0.6	0.3	0.1
Aged 18 to 19	100.0	97.1	1.8	0.2	0.5	0.3	–
Aged 20 to 24	100.0	89.2	6.8	0.8	1.8	1.3	0.2
Aged 25 to 29	100.0	68.1	22.0	1.2	3.8	4.5	0.5
Aged 30 or older	100.0	26.0	35.7	2.0	6.5	17.4	12.5

Note: Blacks include those who identify themselves as being of the race alone and those who identify themselves as being of the race in combination with other races. "–" means number is less than 500 or sample is too small to make a reliable estimate.
Source: Bureau of the Census, Current Population Survey Annual Social and Economic Supplement, America's Families and Living Arrangements: 2008, detailed tables, Internet site http://www.census.gov/population/www/socdemo/hh-fam/cps2008 .html; calculations by New Strategist

Table 7.23 Marital Status by Sex and Age, 2008: Hispanics

(number and percent distribution of Hispanics aged 15 or older by sex, age, and current marital status, 2008; numbers in thousands)

	total	never married	married spouse present	married spouse absent	separated	divorced	widowed
NUMBER							
Total Hispanic men	**16,832**	**6,955**	**7,445**	**820**	**438**	**945**	**228**
Under age 30	6,254	4,762	1,176	185	89	34	10
Aged 15 to 17	1,213	1,186	4	11	9	1	1
Aged 18 to 19	730	699	14	5	13	–	–
Aged 20 to 24	1,899	1,502	308	61	20	6	2
Aged 25 to 29	2,412	1,375	850	108	47	27	7
Aged 30 or older	10,578	2,193	6,270	635	350	911	217
Total Hispanic women	**15,845**	**5,066**	**7,557**	**288**	**709**	**1,385**	**839**
Under age 30	5,435	3,644	1,490	71	119	100	11
Aged 15 to 17	1,191	1,156	10	8	13	3	1
Aged 18 to 19	664	592	57	6	9	–	–
Aged 20 to 24	1,717	1,185	456	22	28	21	5
Aged 25 to 29	1,863	711	967	35	69	76	5
Aged 30 or older	10,410	1,423	6,067	217	590	1,284	828
PERCENT DISTRIBUTION							
Total Hispanic men	**100.0%**	**41.3%**	**44.2%**	**4.9%**	**2.6%**	**5.6%**	**1.4%**
Under age 30	100.0	76.1	18.8	3.0	1.4	0.5	0.2
Aged 15 to 17	100.0	97.8	0.3	0.9	0.7	0.1	0.1
Aged 18 to 19	100.0	95.8	1.9	0.7	1.8	–	–
Aged 20 to 24	100.0	79.1	16.2	3.2	1.1	0.3	0.1
Aged 25 to 29	100.0	57.0	35.2	4.5	1.9	1.1	0.3
Aged 30 or older	100.0	20.7	59.3	6.0	3.3	8.6	2.1
Total Hispanic women	**100.0**	**32.0**	**47.7**	**1.8**	**4.5**	**8.7**	**5.3**
Under age 30	100.0	67.0	27.4	1.3	2.2	1.8	0.2
Aged 15 to 17	100.0	97.1	0.8	0.7	1.1	0.3	0.1
Aged 18 to 19	100.0	89.2	8.6	0.9	1.4	–	–
Aged 20 to 24	100.0	69.0	26.6	1.3	1.6	1.2	0.3
Aged 25 to 29	100.0	38.2	51.9	1.9	3.7	4.1	0.3
Aged 30 or older	100.0	13.7	58.3	2.1	5.7	12.3	8.0

Note: "–" means number is less than 500 or sample is too small to make a reliable estimate.
Source: Bureau of the Census, Current Population Survey Annual Social and Economic Supplement, America's Families and Living Arrangements: 2008, detailed tables, Internet site http://www.census.gov/population/www/socdemo/hh-fam/cps2008 .html; calculations by New Strategist

Table 7.24 Marital Status by Sex and Age, 2008: Non-Hispanic Whites

(number and percent distribution of non-Hispanic whites aged 15 or older by sex, age, and current marital status, 2008; numbers in thousands)

	total	never married	married spouse present	married spouse absent	separated	divorced	widowed
NUMBER							
Total non-Hispanic white men	**79,043**	**23,142**	**44,570**	**681**	**1,099**	**7,309**	**2,242**
Under age 30	19,290	15,632	3,028	113	193	307	16
Aged 15 to 17	4,113	4,065	4	12	24	8	1
Aged 18 to 19	2,419	2,377	20	4	17	1	–
Aged 20 to 24	6,478	5,713	608	32	51	67	7
Aged 25 to 29	6,280	3,477	2,396	65	101	231	8
Aged 30 or older	59,753	7,511	41,542	568	906	7,002	2,226
Total non-Hispanic white women	**83,479**	**18,794**	**44,246**	**757**	**1,401**	**9,642**	**8,639**
Under age 30	18,773	13,660	4,177	147	320	423	46
Aged 15 to 17	3,917	3,847	9	27	25	6	2
Aged 18 to 19	2,357	2,258	50	19	16	12	3
Aged 20 to 24	6,248	4,918	1,072	43	108	96	11
Aged 25 to 29	6,251	2,637	3,046	58	171	309	30
Aged 30 or older	64,707	5,136	40,070	611	1,082	9,218	8,592
PERCENT DISTRIBUTION							
Total non-Hispanic white men	**100.0%**	**29.3%**	**56.4%**	**0.9%**	**1.4%**	**9.2%**	**2.8%**
Under age 30	100.0	81.0	15.7	0.6	1.0	1.6	0.1
Aged 15 to 17	100.0	98.8	0.1	0.3	0.6	0.2	0.0
Aged 18 to 19	100.0	98.3	0.8	0.2	0.7	0.0	–
Aged 20 to 24	100.0	88.2	9.4	0.5	0.8	1.0	0.1
Aged 25 to 29	100.0	55.4	38.2	1.0	1.6	3.7	0.1
Aged 30 or older	100.0	12.6	69.5	1.0	1.5	11.7	3.7
Total non-Hispanic white women	**100.0**	**22.5**	**53.0**	**0.9**	**1.7**	**11.6**	**10.3**
Under age 30	100.0	72.8	22.3	0.8	1.7	2.3	0.2
Aged 15 to 17	100.0	98.2	0.2	0.7	0.6	0.2	0.1
Aged 18 to 19	100.0	95.8	2.1	0.8	0.7	0.5	0.1
Aged 20 to 24	100.0	78.7	17.2	0.7	1.7	1.5	0.2
Aged 25 to 29	100.0	42.2	48.7	0.9	2.7	4.9	0.5
Aged 30 or older	100.0	7.9	61.9	0.9	1.7	14.2	13.3

Note: Non-Hispanic whites are only those who identify themselves as being white alone and not Hispanic.
Source: Bureau of the Census, Current Population Survey Annual Social and Economic Supplement, America's Families and Living Arrangements: 2008, detailed tables, Internet site http://www.census.gov/population/www/socdemo/hh-fam/cps2008 .html; calculations by New Strategist

8

Population

■ The Millennial generation numbers nearly 76 million, a figure that includes everyone born between 1977 and 1994 (aged 14 to 31 in 2008). Millennials account for 25 percent of the total population—just slightly behind the Boomer share.

■ Millennials are much more diverse than middle-aged or older people. Non-Hispanic whites account for 72 percent of Boomers, for example, but for only 60 percent of Millennials.

■ Millennials account for a large share of immigrants. Twenty-nine percent of immigrants admitted to the United States in 2008 were aged 15 to 29.

■ Hispanics outnumber blacks in the 15-to-29 age group. But there is great variation by region. Hispanic Millennials outnumber black Millennials by a substantial margin only in the West.

■ Millennials account for only 22 percent of the population of Maine. They account for 30 percent of the population of Utah.

Millennials Are the Second-Largest Generation

They have reinvigorated the youth market.

The Millennial generation numbers nearly 76 million, a figure that includes everyone born between 1977 and 1994 (aged 14 to 31 in 2008). Millennials account for just under 25 percent of the total population, making them the second-largest generation. Boomers, the parents of many Millennials, are in first place. They numbered just over 76 million in 2008 and accounted for slightly more than 25 percent of the population.

Between 2000 and 2008, Millennials entirely filled the 20-to-29 age group. During those years, the number of 20-to-29-year-olds grew 10 to 11 percent, faster than the 8 percent gain for the overall population as Millennials replaced the small Generation X in the age group. Between 2008 and 2025, Millennials will enter their thirties and forties. The generation will increase in size to almost 83 million because of immigration. In 2025, Millennials will outnumber Boomers by 17 million. By then, they may be outnumbered by the generation that follows them—the iGeneration. The oldest members of the iGeneration were born in 1995. By 2025, the iGeneration and younger Americans will account for 40 percent of the population.

■ Millennials have brought renewed attention to the youth market not only because of their numbers, but also because their Boomer parents demanded it.

Millennials are almost as big a generation as Boomers

(percent distribution of the population by generation, 2008)

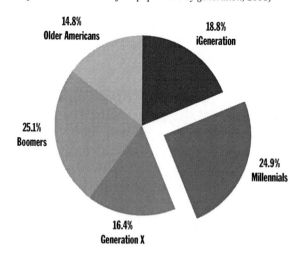

14.8%
Older Americans

18.8%
iGeneration

25.1%
Boomers

24.9%
Millennials

16.4%
Generation X

Table 8.1 Population by Age and Generation, 2008

(number and percent distribution of people by age and generation, 2008; numbers in thousands)

	number	percent distribution
Total people	**304,060**	**100.0%**
Under age 5	21,006	6.9
Aged 5 to 9	20,065	6.6
Aged 10 to 14	20,055	6.6
Aged 15 to 29	63,907	21.0
Aged 15 to 19	21,514	7.1
Aged 20 to 24	21,059	6.9
Aged 25 to 29	21,334	7.0
Aged 30 to 34	19,598	6.4
Aged 35 to 39	20,994	6.9
Aged 40 to 44	21,507	7.1
Aged 45 to 49	22,880	7.5
Aged 50 to 54	21,492	7.1
Aged 55 to 59	18,583	6.1
Aged 60 to 64	15,103	5.0
Aged 65 to 69	11,349	3.7
Aged 70 to 74	8,774	2.9
Aged 75 to 79	7,275	2.4
Aged 80 to 84	5,750	1.9
Aged 85 or older	5,722	1.9
Total people	**304,060**	**100.0**
iGeneration (under age 14)	57,115	18.8
Millennial (aged 14 to 31)	75,757	24.9
Generation X (aged 32 to 43)	49,958	16.4
Baby Boom (aged 44 to 62)	76,319	25.1
Older Americans (aged 63 or older)	44,911	14.8

Source: Bureau of the Census, Population Estimates, Internet site http://www.census.gov/popest/national/asrh/ NC-EST2008-sa.html; calculations by New Strategist

Table 8.2 Population by Age and Sex, 2008

(number of people by age and sex, and sex ratio by age, 2008; numbers in thousands)

	total	female	male	sex ratio
Total people	**304,060**	**154,135**	**149,925**	**97**
Under age 5	21,006	10,258	10,748	105
Aged 5 to 9	20,065	9,806	10,259	105
Aged 10 to 14	20,055	9,792	10,262	105
Aged 15 to 29	63,907	31,093	32,814	106
Aged 15 to 19	21,514	10,487	11,027	105
Aged 20 to 24	21,059	10,214	10,845	106
Aged 25 to 29	21,334	10,393	10,941	105
Aged 30 to 34	19,598	9,639	9,959	103
Aged 35 to 39	20,994	10,425	10,569	101
Aged 40 to 44	21,507	10,762	10,746	100
Aged 45 to 49	22,880	11,566	11,314	98
Aged 50 to 54	21,492	10,954	10,539	96
Aged 55 to 59	18,583	9,569	9,015	94
Aged 60 to 64	15,103	7,867	7,236	92
Aged 65 to 69	11,349	6,042	5,306	88
Aged 70 to 74	8,774	4,816	3,959	82
Aged 75 to 79	7,275	4,178	3,097	74
Aged 80 to 84	5,750	3,510	2,239	64
Aged 85 or older	5,722	3,858	1,864	48

Note: The sex ratio is the number of males per 100 females.
Source: Bureau of the Census, Population Estimates, Internet site http://www.census.gov/popest/national/asrh/ NC-EST2008-sa.html; calculations by New Strategist

Table 8.3 Population by Age, 2000 and 2008

(number of people by age, 2000 and 2008; percent change, 2000–08)

	2008	2000	percent change 2000–08
Total people	**304,060**	**281,422**	**8.0%**
Under age 5	21,006	19,176	9.5
Aged 5 to 9	20,065	20,550	–2.4
Aged 10 to 14	20,055	20,528	–2.3
Aged 15 to 19	21,514	20,220	6.4
Aged 20 to 24	21,059	18,964	11.0
Aged 25 to 29	21,334	19,381	10.1
Aged 30 to 34	19,598	20,510	–4.4
Aged 35 to 39	20,994	22,707	–7.5
Aged 40 to 44	21,507	22,442	–4.2
Aged 45 to 49	22,880	20,092	13.9
Aged 50 to 54	21,492	17,586	22.2
Aged 55 to 59	18,583	13,469	38.0
Aged 60 to 64	15,103	10,805	39.8
Aged 65 to 69	11,349	9,534	19.0
Aged 70 to 74	8,774	8,857	–0.9
Aged 75 to 79	7,275	7,416	–1.9
Aged 80 to 84	5,750	4,945	16.3
Aged 85 or older	5,722	4,240	35.0
Aged 18 to 24	29,757	27,143	9.6
Aged 18 or older	230,118	209,128	10.0
Aged 65 or older	38,870	34,992	11.1

*Source: Bureau of the Census, National Population Estimates, Internet site http://www.census.gov/popest/national/asrh/
NC-EST2008-asrh.html; calculations by New Strategist*

Table 8.4 Population by Age, 2008 to 2025

(number of people by age, 2008 to 2025; percent change for selected years; numbers in thousands)

	2008	2010	2015	2025	percent change 2008–10	2008–15	2008–25
Total people	**304,060**	**310,233**	**325,540**	**357,452**	**2.0%**	**7.1%**	**17.6%**
Under age 5	21,006	21,100	22,076	23,484	0.4	5.1	11.8
Aged 5 to 9	20,065	20,886	21,707	23,548	4.1	8.2	17.4
Aged 10 to 14	20,055	20,395	21,658	23,677	1.7	8.0	18.1
Aged 15 to 19	21,514	21,770	21,209	23,545	1.2	–1.4	9.4
Aged 20 to 24	21,059	21,779	22,342	23,168	3.4	6.1	10.0
Aged 25 to 29	21,334	21,418	22,400	22,417	0.4	5.0	5.1
Aged 30 to 34	19,598	20,400	22,099	23,699	4.1	12.8	20.9
Aged 35 to 39	20,994	20,267	20,841	23,645	–3.5	–0.7	12.6
Aged 40 to 44	21,507	21,010	20,460	22,851	–2.3	–4.9	6.2
Aged 45 to 49	22,880	22,596	21,001	21,154	–1.2	–8.2	–7.5
Aged 50 to 54	21,492	22,109	22,367	20,404	2.9	4.1	–5.1
Aged 55 to 59	18,583	19,517	21,682	20,575	5.0	16.7	10.7
Aged 60 to 64	15,103	16,758	18,861	21,377	11.0	24.9	41.5
Aged 65 to 69	11,349	12,261	15,812	19,957	8.0	39.3	75.9
Aged 70 to 74	8,774	9,202	11,155	16,399	4.9	27.1	86.9
Aged 75 to 79	7,275	7,282	7,901	12,598	0.1	8.6	73.2
Aged 80 to 84	5,750	5,733	5,676	7,715	–0.3	–1.3	34.2
Aged 85 or older	5,722	5,751	6,292	7,239	0.5	10.0	26.5

Source: Bureau of the Census, 2008 National Population Projections, Internet site http://www.census.gov/population/www/ projections/2008projections.html; calculations by New Strategist

Table 8.5 Population by Generation, 2008 to 2025

(number and percent distribution of people by generation, 2008 to 2025; numbers in thousands)

	number	percent distribution
2008		
Total people	**304,060**	**100.0%**
iGeneration (under age 14)	57,115	18.8
Millennial (aged 14 to 31)	75,757	24.9
Generation X (aged 32 to 43)	49,958	16.4
Baby Boom (aged 44 to 62)	76,319	25.1
Older Americans (aged 63 or older)	44,911	14.8
2010		
Total people	**310,233**	**100.0**
iGeneration (under age 16)	66,594	21.5
Millennial (aged 16 to 33)	77,248	24.9
Generation X (aged 34 to 45)	49,651	16.0
Baby Boom (aged 46 to 64)	76,511	24.7
Older Americans (aged 65 or older)	40,229	13.0
2015		
Total people	**325,540**	**100.0**
iGeneration (under age 21)	91,002	28.0
Millennial (aged 21 to 38)	79,357	24.4
Generation X (aged 39 to 50)	49,872	15.3
Baby Boom (aged 51 to 69)	74,284	22.8
Older Americans (aged 70 or older)	31,025	9.5
2025		
Total people	**357,452**	**100.0**
iGeneration (under age 31)	144,444	40.4
Millennial (aged 31 to 48)	82,736	23.1
Generation X (aged 49 to 60)	49,278	13.8
Baby Boom (aged 61 to 79)	66,041	18.5
Older Americans (aged 80 or older)	14,953	4.2

Source: Bureau of the Census, 2008 National Population Projections, Internet site http://www.census.gov/population/www/projections/2008projections.html; calculations by New Strategist"

The Nation's Children and Young Adults Are Diverse

Hispanics outnumber blacks among Millennials.

America's children and young adults are much more diverse than middle-aged or older people. While non-Hispanic whites account for 66 percent of all Americans, their share is a smaller 60 percent among Millennials, aged 14 to 31 in 2008. Among the iGeneration (children under age 14), non-Hispanic whites account for only 55 percent of the population.

Hispanics account for a larger share of the Millennial generation than blacks—19 percent are Hispanic and 16 percent are black. In the iGeneration, Hispanics outnumber blacks by an even larger margin—23 to 17 percent. Among Asians, Hispanics, and blacks, Millennials are the largest generation, outnumbering Boomers. Among non-Hispanic whites, Boomers outnumber Millennials.

■ Racial and ethnic differences between young and old may divide the nation in the years ahead as older non-Hispanic whites attempt to govern young Hispanics, blacks, and Asians.

Minorities account for a large share of children and young adults

(minority share of population by generation, 2008)

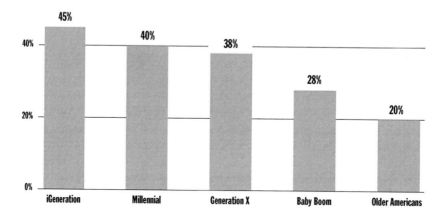

Table 8.6 Population by Age, Race, and Hispanic Origin, 2008

(number and percent distribution of people by age, race, and Hispanic origin, 2008; numbers in thousands)

	total	Asian	black	Hispanic	non-Hispanic white
Total people	**304,060**	**15,480**	**41,127**	**46,944**	**199,491**
Under age 5	21,006	1,242	3,573	5,288	11,065
Aged 5 to 9	20,065	1,107	3,298	4,464	11,222
Aged 10 to 14	20,055	1,033	3,363	3,989	11,660
Aged 15 to 29	63,907	3,251	10,140	11,654	38,592
Aged 15 to 19	21,514	1,018	3,667	3,850	12,903
Aged 20 to 24	21,059	1,027	3,307	3,663	12,949
Aged 25 to 29	21,334	1,206	3,166	4,141	12,740
Aged 30 to 34	19,598	1,334	2,724	4,041	11,456
Aged 35 to 39	20,994	1,404	2,823	3,730	12,981
Aged 40 to 44	21,507	1,210	2,847	3,279	14,085
Aged 45 to 49	22,880	1,107	2,882	2,795	15,964
Aged 50 to 54	21,492	986	2,563	2,187	15,615
Aged 55 to 59	18,583	829	2,068	1,650	13,907
Aged 60 to 64	15,103	612	1,471	1,204	11,706
Aged 65 to 69	11,349	443	1,075	853	8,899
Aged 70 to 74	8,774	339	829	653	6,899
Aged 75 to 79	7,275	255	614	496	5,871
Aged 80 to 84	5,750	176	438	346	4,763
Aged 85 or older	5,722	154	419	313	4,807

PERCENT DISTRIBUTION BY RACE AND HISPANIC ORIGIN

	total	Asian	black	Hispanic	non-Hispanic white
Total people	**100.0%**	**5.1%**	**13.5%**	**15.4%**	**65.6%**
Under age 5	100.0	5.9	17.0	25.2	52.7
Aged 5 to 9	100.0	5.5	16.4	22.2	55.9
Aged 10 to 14	100.0	5.1	16.8	19.9	58.1
Aged 15 to 29	100.0	5.1	15.9	18.2	60.4
Aged 15 to 19	100.0	4.7	17.0	17.9	60.0
Aged 20 to 24	100.0	4.9	15.7	17.4	61.5
Aged 25 to 29	100.0	5.7	14.8	19.4	59.7
Aged 30 to 34	100.0	6.8	13.9	20.6	58.5
Aged 35 to 39	100.0	6.7	13.4	17.8	61.8
Aged 40 to 44	100.0	5.6	13.2	15.2	65.5
Aged 45 to 49	100.0	4.8	12.6	12.2	69.8
Aged 50 to 54	100.0	4.6	11.9	10.2	72.7
Aged 55 to 59	100.0	4.5	11.1	8.9	74.8
Aged 60 to 64	100.0	4.1	9.7	8.0	77.5
Aged 65 to 69	100.0	3.9	9.5	7.5	78.4
Aged 70 to 74	100.0	3.9	9.5	7.4	78.6
Aged 75 to 79	100.0	3.5	8.4	6.8	80.7
Aged 80 to 84	100.0	3.1	7.6	6.0	82.8
Aged 85 or older	100.0	2.7	7.3	5.5	84.0

Note: Numbers do not add to total because Asians and blacks include those who identified themselves as being of the race alone and those who identified themselves as being of the race in combination with other races, and because Hispanics may be of any race. Non-Hispanic whites include those who identified themselves as being white alone and not Hispanic.
Source: Bureau of the Census, Population Estimates, Internet site http://www.census.gov/popest/national/asrh/NC-EST2008-sa.html; calculations by New Strategist

Table 8.7 Population by Generation, Race, and Hispanic Origin, 2008

(number and percent distribution of people by generation, race, and Hispanic origin, 2008; numbers in thousands)

	total	Asian	black	Hispanic	non-Hispanic white
Total people	**304,060**	**15,480**	**41,127**	**46,944**	**199,491**
iGeneration (under age 14)	57,115	3,174	9,562	12,944	31,615
Millennial (aged 14 to 31)	75,757	3,991	11,902	14,068	45,506
Generation X (aged 32 to 43)	49,958	3,172	6,735	8,778	31,123
Baby Boom (aged 44 to 62)	76,319	3,531	8,965	8,011	55,326
Older Americans (aged 63 or older)	44,911	1,612	3,964	3,143	35,920

PERCENT DISTRIBUTION BY RACE AND HISPANIC ORIGIN

Total people	**100.0%**	**5.1%**	**13.5%**	**15.4%**	**65.6%**
iGeneration (under age 14)	100.0	5.6	16.7	22.7	55.4
Millennial (aged 14 to 31)	100.0	5.3	15.7	18.6	60.1
Generation X (aged 32 to 43)	100.0	6.3	13.5	17.6	62.3
Baby Boom (aged 44 to 62)	100.0	4.6	11.7	10.5	72.5
Older Americans (aged 63 or older)	100.0	3.6	8.8	7.0	80.0

PERCENT DISTRIBUTION BY GENERATION

Total people	**100.0%**	**100.0%**	**100.0%**	**100.0%**	**100.0%**
iGeneration (under age 14)	18.8	20.5	23.2	27.6	15.8
Millennial (aged 14 to 31)	24.9	25.8	28.9	30.0	22.8
Generation X (aged 32 to 43)	16.4	20.5	16.4	18.7	15.6
Baby Boom (aged 44 to 62)	25.1	22.8	21.8	17.1	27.7
Older Americans (aged 63 or older)	14.8	10.4	9.6	6.7	18.0

Note: Numbers do not add to total because Asians and blacks include those who identified themselves as being of the race alone and those who identified themselves as being of the race in combination with other races, and because Hispanics may be of any race. Non-Hispanic whites are those who identified themselves as being white alone and not Hispanic.
Source: Bureau of the Census, Population Estimates, Internet site http://www.census.gov/popest/national/asrh/ NC-EST2008-sa.html; calculations by New Strategist

Most Millennials Live in Their State of Birth

Among 25-to-34-year-olds, one in five is foreign-born.

According to the 2007 American Community Survey, 63 percent of people aged 18 to 24 and 52 percent of those aged 25 to 34 (Millennials were aged 13 to 30 in that year) were born in their current state of residence. The figure among 18-to-24-year-olds is larger than average because many have not yet moved away from home. The rate among 25-to-34-year-olds is about the same as among older U.S. residents. About one in four 18-to-34-year-olds was born in the United States, but in a different state. Twelve percent of 18-to-24-year-olds and a much larger 20 percent of 25-to-34-year-olds were born in another country.

Among the foreign-born in the broad 18-to-44 age group, from 58 to 62 percent were born in Latin America—including 36 to 41 percent who were born in Mexico. From 21 to 25 percent of 18-to-44-year-olds were born in Asia, and only 8 percent are from Europe.

■ The foreign-born population adds to the multicultural mix, which is becoming a significant factor in American business and politics.

Most of the foreign-born in the 25-to-44 age group are from Latin America

(percent distribution of the foreign-born aged 25 to 44 by region of birth, 2008)

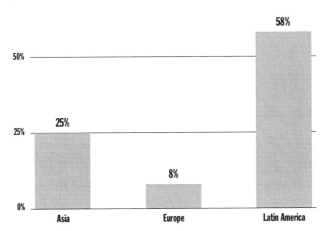

Table 8.8 Population by Age and Place of Birth, 2007

(number and percent distribution of people by age and place of birth, 2007; numbers in thousands)

	total	born in the United States — in state of current residence	outside state of current residence	citizen born outside United states	foreign-born
Total people	**301,621**	**177,509**	**82,253**	**3,799**	**38,060**
Under age 18	73,908	59,667	10,643	625	2,973
Aged 18 to 24	29,821	18,880	7,062	395	3,484
Aged 25 to 34	39,987	20,889	10,532	611	7,955
Aged 35 to 44	43,410	21,083	13,067	692	8,569
Aged 45 to 54	43,925	22,275	14,527	669	6,455
Aged 55 or older	70,570	34,715	26,422	808	8,624
PERCENT DISTRIBUTION BY PLACE OF BIRTH					
Total people	**100.0%**	**58.9%**	**27.3%**	**1.3%**	**12.6%**
Under age 18	100.0	80.7	14.4	0.8	4.0
Aged 18 to 24	100.0	63.3	23.7	1.3	11.7
Aged 25 to 34	100.0	52.2	26.3	1.5	19.9
Aged 35 to 44	100.0	48.6	30.1	1.6	19.7
Aged 45 to 54	100.0	50.7	33.1	1.5	14.7
Aged 55 or older	100.0	49.2	37.4	1.1	12.2
PERCENT DISTRIBUTION BY AGE					
Total people	**100.0%**	**100.0%**	**100.0%**	**100.0%**	**100.0%**
Under age 18	24.5	33.6	12.9	16.4	7.8
Aged 18 to 24	9.9	10.6	8.6	10.4	9.2
Aged 25 to 34	13.3	11.8	12.8	16.1	20.9
Aged 35 to 44	14.4	11.9	15.9	18.2	22.5
Aged 45 to 54	14.6	12.5	17.7	17.6	17.0
Aged 55 or older	23.4	19.6	32.1	21.3	22.7

Source: Bureau of the Census, 2007 American Community Survey, Internet site http://factfinder.census.gov/home/saff/main .html?_lang=en; calculations by New Strategist

Table 8.9 Foreign-Born Population by Age and World Region of Birth, 2007

(number and percent distribution of foreign-born by age and world region of birth, 2007; numbers in thousands)

	total	Asia	Europe	Latin America total	Mexico
Total people	**38,060**	**9,941**	**4,996**	**19,891**	**11,425**
Under age 5	299	89	35	139	80
Aged 5 to 17	2,673	606	295	1,512	994
Aged 18 to 24	3,484	726	285	2,168	1,417
Aged 25 to 44	16,524	4,205	1,384	9,607	5,941
Aged 45 to 54	6,455	1,869	809	3,202	1,611
Aged 55 or older	8,624	2,445	2,183	3,282	1,371
Median age (years)	40.2	42.0	50.8	37.4	35.1

PERCENT DISTRIBUTION OF FOREIGN-BORN BY REGION OF BIRTH

	total	Asia	Europe	Latin America total	Mexico
Total people	**100.0%**	**26.1%**	**13.1%**	**52.3%**	**30.0%**
Under age 5	100.0	29.9	11.7	46.6	26.7
Aged 5 to 17	100.0	22.7	11.0	56.6	37.2
Aged 18 to 24	100.0	20.8	8.2	62.2	40.7
Aged 25 to 44	100.0	25.4	8.4	58.1	36.0
Aged 45 to 54	100.0	29.0	12.5	49.6	25.0
Aged 55 to 64	100.0	28.4	25.3	38.1	15.9

PERCENT DISTRIBUTION BY AGE

	total	Asia	Europe	Latin America total	Mexico
Total people	**100.0%**	**100.0%**	**100.0%**	**100.0%**	**100.0%**
Under age 5	0.8	0.9	0.7	0.7	0.7
Aged 5 to 17	7.0	6.1	5.9	7.6	8.7
Aged 18 to 24	9.2	7.3	5.7	10.9	12.4
Aged 25 to 44	43.4	42.3	27.7	48.3	52.0
Aged 45 to 54	17.0	18.8	16.2	16.1	14.1
Aged 55 or older	22.7	24.6	43.7	16.5	12.0

Note: Numbers do not add to total because "other" is not shown.
Source: Bureau of the Census, 2007 American Community Survey, Internet site http://factfinder.census.gov/home/saff/main
.html?_lang=en; calculations by New Strategist

Millennials Are a Large Share of Immigrants

More than one-fourth of immigrants admitted in 2008 were Millennials.

In 2008, more than 1 million immigrants were admitted to the United States, and 320,000 of them were aged 15 to 29 (Millennials were aged 14 to 31 in that year). Many immigrants to the United States are young adults looking for job opportunities.

The 15-to-29 age group accounted for 29 percent of total immigrants admitted to the United States in 2008. By five-year age group, 30-to-34-year-olds account for the largest share of immigrants—13 percent in 2008.

■ Immigrants are adding to the diversity of the young adult population.

Many immigrants are young adults

(percent distribution of immigrants admitted in 2008, by age)

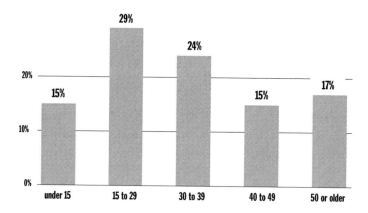

Table 8.10 Newly Arrived Immigrants by Age, 2008

(number and percent distribution of immigrants admitted in 2008, by age)

	number	percent distribution
Total immigrants	**1,107,126**	**100.0%**
Under age 1	8,280	0.7
Aged 1 to 4	29,998	2.7
Aged 5 to 9	52,993	4.8
Aged 10 to 14	74,608	6.7
Aged 15 to 29	320,445	28.9
Aged 15 to 19	94,697	8.6
Aged 20 to 24	104,332	9.4
Aged 25 to 29	121,416	11.0
Aged 30 to 34	140,132	12.7
Aged 35 to 39	124,341	11.2
Aged 40 to 44	92,627	8.4
Aged 45 to 49	69,868	6.3
Aged 50 to 54	53,848	4.9
Aged 55 to 59	43,789	4.0
Aged 60 to 64	35,586	3.2
Aged 65 or older	60,604	5.5

Note: Immigrants are those granted legal permanent residence in the United States. They either arrive in the United States with immigrant visas issued abroad or adjust their status in the United States from temporary to permanent residence. Numbers may not sum to total because "age not stated" is not shown.
Source: Department of Homeland Security, 2008 Yearbook of Immigration Statistics, Internet site http://www.uscis.gov/graphics/shared/statistics/yearbook/index.htm

Many Working-Age Adults Do Not Speak English at Home

Most are Spanish speakers, and most have trouble speaking English.

Fifty-five million residents of the United States speak a language other than English at home, according to the Census Bureau's 2007 American Community Survey—20 percent of the population aged 5 or older. The 62 percent majority of those who do not speak English at home are Spanish speakers.

Among working-age adults (aged 18 to 64), 21 percent do not speak English at home, and 62 percent of those who do not speak English at home are Spanish speakers. Among the Spanish speakers, 53 percent say they speak English less than "very well."

■ The language barrier is a problem for many working-age adults.

Most adults who speak Spanish at home cannot speak English very well

(percent of people aged 18 to 64 who speak a language other than English at home who speak English less than "very well," by language spoken at home, 2007)

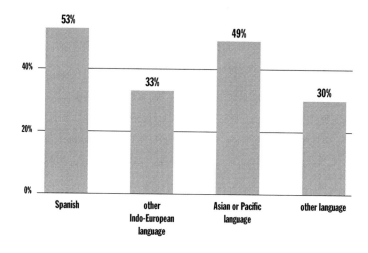

Table 8.11 Language Spoken at Home by People Aged 18 to 64, 2007

(number and percent distribution of people aged 5 or older and aged 18 to 64 who speak a language other than English at home by language spoken at home and ability to speak English very well, by age, 2007; numbers in thousands)

	total		aged 18 to 64	
	number	percent distribution	number	percent distribution
Total, aged 5 or older	**280,950**	**100.0%**	**189,873**	**100.0%**
Speak only English at home	225,506	80.3	150,635	79.3
Speak a language other than English at home	55,444	19.7	39,238	20.7
Speak English less than very well	24,469	8.7	18,624	9.8
Total who speak a language other than English at home	**55,444**	**100.0**	**39,238**	**100.0**
Speak Spanish at home	34,547	62.3	24,333	62.0
Speak other Indo-European language at home	10,321	18.6	7,034	17.9
Speak Asian or Pacific Island language at home	8,316	15.0	6,202	15.8
Speak other language at home	2,260	4.1	1,669	4.3
Speak Spanish at home	34,547	100.0	24,333	100.0
Speak English less than very well	16,368	47.4	12,791	52.6
Speak other Indo-European language at home	10,321	100.0	7,034	100.0
Speak English less than very well	3,384	32.8	2,291	32.6
Speak Asian or Pacific Island language at home	8,316	100.0	6,202	100.0
Speak English less than very well	4,042	48.6	3,034	48.9
Speak other language at home	2,260	100.0	1,669	100.0
Speak English less than very well	676	29.9	508	30.4

Source: Bureau of the Census, 2007 American Community Survey, Internet site http://factfinder.census.gov/servlet/ DatasetMainPageServlet?_program=ACS&_submenuId=&_lang=en&_ts=; calculations by New Strategist

The Largest Share of Millennials Lives in the South

Millennials account for 30 percent of Utah's population.

The South is home to the largest share of the population, and consequently to the largest share of Millennials. Thirty-seven percent of Millennials live in the South, according to Census Bureau estimates for 2008. There, they account for 25 percent of the population.

Among all 15-to-29-year-olds in 2008 (Millennials were aged 14 to 31 in that year), Hispanics outnumbered blacks. But there is great variation by region. Hispanic Millennials outnumber black Millennials by a substantial margin only in the West. In that region, 33 percent of 15-to-29-year-olds are Hispanic and only 5 percent are black. In the Midwest and South, black Millennials outnumber Hispanic Millennials. In the Northeast, the numbers are about even.

Millennials account for only 22 percent of the population of Maine. They account for 30 percent of the population of Utah. Boomers outnumber Millennials in most states, but in some states—including Texas and California—Millennials outnumber Boomers.

■ Millennials will outnumber Boomers in a growing number of states as the Boomer population ages.

The Northeast is home to just 17 percent of Millennials

(percent distribution of the Millennial generation by region, 2008)

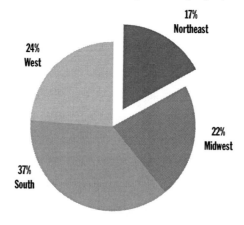

17% Northeast

24% West

22% Midwest

37% South

Table 8.12 Population by Age and Region, 2008

(number and percent distribution of people by age and region, 2008; numbers in thousands)

	total	Northeast	Midwest	South	West
Total people	**304,060**	**54,925**	**66,561**	**111,719**	**70,855**
Under age 15	61,126	10,116	13,236	22,900	14,874
Aged 15 to 29	63,907	11,114	13,961	23,334	15,498
Aged 15 to 19	21,514	3,899	4,769	7,749	5,097
Aged 20 to 24	21,059	3,739	4,619	7,627	5,074
Aged 25 to 29	21,334	3,477	4,573	7,957	5,327
Aged 30 to 34	19,598	3,354	4,126	7,261	4,857
Aged 35 or older	159,429	30,340	35,239	58,225	35,625
PERCENT DISTRIBUTION BY AGE					
Total people	**100.0%**	**100.0%**	**100.0%**	**100.0%**	**100.0%**
Under age 15	20.1	18.4	19.9	20.5	21.0
Aged 15 to 29	21.0	20.2	21.0	20.9	21.9
Aged 15 to 19	7.1	7.1	7.2	6.9	7.2
Aged 20 to 24	6.9	6.8	6.9	6.8	7.2
Aged 25 to 29	7.0	6.3	6.9	7.1	7.5
Aged 30 to 34	6.4	6.1	6.2	6.5	6.9
Aged 35 or older	52.4	55.2	52.9	52.1	50.3
PERCENT DISTRIBUTION BY REGION					
Total people	**100.0%**	**18.1%**	**21.9%**	**36.7%**	**23.3%**
Under age 15	100.0	16.5	21.7	37.5	24.3
Aged 15 to 29	100.0	17.4	21.8	36.5	24.3
Aged 15 to 19	100.0	18.1	22.2	36.0	23.7
Aged 20 to 24	100.0	17.8	21.9	36.2	24.1
Aged 25 to 29	100.0	16.3	21.4	37.3	25.0
Aged 30 to 34	100.0	17.1	21.1	37.0	24.8
Aged 35 or older	100.0	19.0	22.1	36.5	22.3

Source: Bureau of the Census, State Population Estimates, Internet site http://www.census.gov/popest/states/asrh/; calculations by New Strategist

Table 8.13 Population by Generation and Region, 2008

(number and percent distribution of people by generation and region, 2008; numbers in thousands)

	total	Northeast	Midwest	South	West
Total people	**304,060**	**54,925**	**66,561**	**111,719**	**70,855**
iGeneration (under age 14)	57,115	9,422	12,350	21,429	13,914
Millennial (aged 14 to 31)	75,757	13,150	16,497	27,709	18,401
Generation X (aged 32 to 43)	49,958	9,063	10,583	18,408	11,905
Baby Boom (aged 44 to 62)	76,319	14,522	17,078	27,612	17,106
Older Americans (aged 63 or older)	44,911	8,768	10,054	16,560	9,529

PERCENT DISTRIBUTION BY GENERATION

	total	Northeast	Midwest	South	West
Total people	**100.0%**	**100.0%**	**100.0%**	**100.0%**	**100.0%**
iGeneration (under age 14)	18.8	17.2	18.6	19.2	19.6
Millennial (aged 14 to 31)	24.9	23.9	24.8	24.8	26.0
Generation X (aged 32 to 43)	16.4	16.5	15.9	16.5	16.8
Baby Boom (aged 44 to 62)	25.1	26.4	25.7	24.7	24.1
Older Americans (aged 63 or older)	14.8	16.0	15.1	14.8	13.4

PERCENT DISTRIBUTION BY REGION

	total	Northeast	Midwest	South	West
Total people	**100.0%**	**18.1%**	**21.9%**	**36.7%**	**23.3%**
iGeneration (under age 14)	100.0	16.5	21.6	37.5	24.4
Millennial (aged 14 to 31)	100.0	17.4	21.8	36.6	24.3
Generation X (aged 32 to 43)	100.0	18.1	21.2	36.8	23.8
Baby Boom (aged 44 to 62)	100.0	19.0	22.4	36.2	22.4
Older Americans (aged 63 or older)	100.0	19.5	22.4	36.9	21.2

Source: Bureau of the Census, State Population Estimates, Internet site http://www.census.gov/popest/states/asrh/; calculations by New Strategist

Table 8.14 Millennial Generation by Region, Race, and Hispanic Origin, 2007

(number and percent distribution of people aged 15 to 29 by region, race, and Hispanic origin, 2007; numbers in thousands)

	total 15 to 29	Asian	black	Hispanic	non-Hispanic white
United States	**63,455**	**2,768**	**9,030**	**11,624**	**38,291**
Northeast	11,013	594	1,502	1,571	7,177
Midwest	13,919	369	1,629	1,077	10,524
South	23,141	563	5,099	3,946	13,038
West	15,382	1,242	799	5,030	7,552
PERCENT DISTRIBUTION BY RACE AND HISPANIC ORIGIN					
United States	**100.0%**	**4.4%**	**14.2%**	**18.3%**	**60.3%**
Northeast	100.0	5.4	13.6	14.3	65.2
Midwest	100.0	2.7	11.7	7.7	75.6
South	100.0	2.4	22.0	17.1	56.3
West	100.0	8.1	5.2	32.7	49.1
PERCENT DISTRIBUTION BY REGION					
United States	**100.0%**	**100.0%**	**100.0%**	**100.0%**	**100.0%**
Northeast	17.4	21.5	16.6	13.5	18.7
Midwest	21.9	13.3	18.0	9.3	27.5
South	36.5	20.3	56.5	33.9	34.0
West	24.2	44.9	8.8	43.3	19.7

Note: Numbers do not add to total because Asians and blacks are only those who identified themselves as being of the race alone and because Hispanics may be of any race. Non-Hispanic whites are those who identified themselves as being white alone and not Hispanic.
Source: Bureau of the Census, 2007 American Community Survey, Internet site http://factfinder.census.gov/home/saff/main .html?_lang=en; calculations by New Strategist

Table 8.15 State Populations By Age, 2008

(total number of people and number aged 15 to 29 by state, 2008; numbers in thousands)

| | total population | aged 15 to 29 | | | |
		total	15 to 19	20 to 24	25 to 29
United States	**304,060**	**63,907**	**21,514**	**21,059**	**21,334**
Alabama	4,662	968	328	319	321
Alaska	686	164	51	55	57
Arizona	6,500	1,364	444	431	488
Arkansas	2,855	586	197	186	202
California	36,757	8,201	2,769	2,718	2,714
Colorado	4,939	1,053	324	341	388
Connecticut	3,501	679	250	224	205
Delaware	873	177	62	59	56
District of Columbia	592	155	41	54	61
Florida	18,328	3,510	1,159	1,149	1,202
Georgia	9,686	2,057	688	653	716
Hawaii	1,288	270	81	92	97
Idaho	1,524	330	111	104	115
Illinois	12,902	2,778	940	919	920
Indiana	6,377	1,323	452	427	445
Iowa	3,003	627	217	215	195
Kansas	2,802	608	200	211	197
Kentucky	4,269	865	283	273	310
Louisiana	4,411	994	329	336	329
Maine	1,316	242	88	78	76
Maryland	5,634	1,164	407	377	380
Massachusetts	6,498	1,353	460	465	428
Michigan	10,003	2,068	740	679	650
Minnesota	5,220	1,094	367	360	368
Mississippi	2,939	643	224	214	205
Missouri	5,912	1,233	413	399	421
Montana	967	202	67	69	66
Nebraska	1,783	386	129	133	124
Nevada	2,600	520	165	155	200
New Hampshire	1,316	253	93	83	78
New Jersey	8,683	1,653	590	540	522
New Mexico	1,984	433	144	144	144
New York	19,490	4,112	1,403	1,400	1,309
North Carolina	9,222	1,876	629	627	620
North Dakota	641	154	48	60	46
Ohio	11,486	2,346	809	763	775
Oklahoma	3,642	796	252	270	274
Oregon	3,790	768	248	243	278
Pennsylvania	12,448	2,473	890	829	754
Rhode Island	1,051	224	80	77	67
South Carolina	4,480	927	321	304	302

	total population	aged 15 to 29			
		total	15 to 19	20 to 24	25 to 29
South Dakota	804	172	57	60	55
Tennessee	6,215	1,247	413	392	442
Texas	24,327	5,392	1,765	1,759	1,868
Utah	2,736	707	213	243	251
Vermont	621	124	45	42	37
Virginia	7,769	1,632	536	545	551
Washington	6,549	1,370	442	441	488
West Virginia	1,814	346	117	110	119
Wisconsin	5,628	1,171	398	393	380
Wyoming	533	116	37	39	40

Source: Bureau of the Census, State Population Estimates, Internet site http://www.census.gov/popest/states/asrh/; calculations by New Strategist

Table 8.16 Distribution of State Populations by Age, 2008

(percent distribution of people aged 15 to 29 by state and age, 2008; numbers in thousands)

	total population	aged 15 to 29			
		total	15 to 19	20 to 24	25 to 29
United States	**100.0%**	**21.0%**	**7.1%**	**6.9%**	**7.0%**
Alabama	100.0	20.8	7.0	6.8	6.9
Alaska	100.0	23.9	7.5	8.0	8.4
Arizona	100.0	21.0	6.8	6.6	7.5
Arkansas	100.0	20.5	6.9	6.5	7.1
California	100.0	22.3	7.5	7.4	7.4
Colorado	100.0	21.3	6.6	6.9	7.9
Connecticut	100.0	19.4	7.1	6.4	5.9
Delaware	100.0	20.2	7.1	6.7	6.4
District of Columbia	100.0	26.2	6.9	9.1	10.2
Florida	100.0	19.1	6.3	6.3	6.6
Georgia	100.0	21.2	7.1	6.7	7.4
Hawaii	100.0	21.0	6.3	7.1	7.5
Idaho	100.0	21.7	7.3	6.8	7.5
Illinois	100.0	21.5	7.3	7.1	7.1
Indiana	100.0	20.7	7.1	6.7	7.0
Iowa	100.0	20.9	7.2	7.2	6.5
Kansas	100.0	21.7	7.1	7.5	7.0
Kentucky	100.0	20.3	6.6	6.4	7.3
Louisiana	100.0	22.5	7.5	7.6	7.5
Maine	100.0	18.4	6.7	6.0	5.8
Maryland	100.0	20.7	7.2	6.7	6.7
Massachusetts	100.0	20.8	7.1	7.2	6.6
Michigan	100.0	20.7	7.4	6.8	6.5
Minnesota	100.0	21.0	7.0	6.9	7.0
Mississippi	100.0	21.9	7.6	7.3	7.0
Missouri	100.0	20.9	7.0	6.8	7.1
Montana	100.0	20.9	6.9	7.1	6.8
Nebraska	100.0	21.7	7.2	7.5	7.0
Nevada	100.0	20.0	6.3	5.9	7.7
New Hampshire	100.0	19.2	7.0	6.3	5.9
New Jersey	100.0	19.0	6.8	6.2	6.0
New Mexico	100.0	21.8	7.3	7.3	7.3
New York	100.0	21.1	7.2	7.2	6.7
North Carolina	100.0	20.3	6.8	6.8	6.7
North Dakota	100.0	24.0	7.5	9.4	7.1
Ohio	100.0	20.4	7.0	6.6	6.7
Oklahoma	100.0	21.9	6.9	7.4	7.5
Oregon	100.0	20.3	6.5	6.4	7.3
Pennsylvania	100.0	19.9	7.2	6.7	6.1
Rhode Island	100.0	21.3	7.6	7.4	6.4
South Carolina	100.0	20.7	7.2	6.8	6.8

	total population	aged 15 to 29			
		total	15 to 19	20 to 24	25 to 29
South Dakota	100.0%	21.4%	7.1%	7.4%	6.8%
Tennessee	100.0	20.1	6.6	6.3	7.1
Texas	100.0	22.2	7.3	7.2	7.7
Utah	100.0	25.8	7.8	8.9	9.2
Vermont	100.0	20.0	7.3	6.8	5.9
Virginia	100.0	21.0	6.9	7.0	7.1
Washington	100.0	20.9	6.7	6.7	7.5
West Virginia	100.0	19.1	6.4	6.1	6.5
Wisconsin	100.0	20.8	7.1	7.0	6.8
Wyoming	100.0	21.8	7.0	7.3	7.5

Source: Bureau of the Census, State Population Estimates, Internet site http://www.census.gov/popest/states/asrh/; calculations by New Strategist

Table 8.17 State Populations by Generation, 2008

(number of people by state and generation, 2008; numbers in thousands)

	total population	iGeneration (under 14)	Millennial (14 to 31)	Generation X (32 to 43)	Baby Boom (44 to 62)	Older Americans (63 or older)
United States	**304,060**	**57,115**	**75,757**	**49,958**	**76,319**	**44,911**
Alabama	4,662	864	1,145	732	1,180	741
Alaska	686	138	192	113	181	62
Arizona	6,500	1,344	1,631	1,053	1,484	988
Arkansas	2,855	545	695	443	703	469
California	36,757	7,224	9,724	6,342	8,706	4,760
Colorado	4,939	946	1,258	863	1,266	606
Connecticut	3,501	617	806	577	949	552
Delaware	873	159	209	140	224	141
District of Columbia	592	87	180	106	137	82
Florida	18,328	3,087	4,164	2,887	4,597	3,593
Georgia	9,686	1,993	2,459	1,719	2,353	1,162
Hawaii	1,288	222	319	208	321	218
Idaho	1,524	323	391	233	364	212
Illinois	12,902	2,458	3,300	2,148	3,180	1,816
Indiana	6,377	1,225	1,574	1,028	1,610	940
Iowa	3,003	548	735	447	767	505
Kansas	2,802	545	714	426	696	421
Kentucky	4,269	779	1,031	699	1,104	656
Louisiana	4,411	855	1,160	669	1,100	627
Maine	1,316	206	287	207	385	231
Maryland	5,634	1,026	1,378	950	1,486	793
Massachusetts	6,498	1,088	1,595	1,093	1,717	1,006
Michigan	10,003	1,810	2,442	1,598	2,641	1,511
Minnesota	5,220	967	1,294	842	1,366	751
Mississippi	2,939	593	756	449	710	429
Missouri	5,912	1,092	1,455	924	1,513	927
Montana	967	168	235	137	268	159
Nebraska	1,783	348	453	267	441	275
Nevada	2,600	525	631	457	637	351
New Hampshire	1,316	220	299	218	379	200
New Jersey	8,683	1,572	1,985	1,502	2,296	1,327
New Mexico	1,984	391	509	298	487	300
New York	19,490	3,360	4,857	3,257	5,013	3,004
North Carolina	9,222	1,752	2,241	1,577	2,320	1,333
North Dakota	641	110	176	88	162	107
Ohio	11,486	2,088	2,774	1,810	3,008	1,806
Oklahoma	3,642	706	934	547	890	565
Oregon	3,790	668	918	614	1,002	589
Pennsylvania	12,448	2,091	2,913	1,943	3,324	2,177
Rhode Island	1,051	173	262	170	276	169
South Carolina	4,480	822	1,096	717	1,147	697

	total population	iGeneration (under 14)	Millennial (14 to 31)	Generation X (32 to 43)	Baby Boom (44 to 62)	Older Americans (63 or older)
South Dakota	804	153	201	114	204	132
Tennessee	6,215	1,143	1,489	1,028	1,600	954
Texas	24,327	5,307	6,426	4,130	5,575	2,890
Utah	2,736	680	828	413	530	286
Vermont	621	96	145	96	183	102
Virginia	7,769	1,413	1,935	1,332	1,990	1,099
Washington	6,549	1,185	1,630	1,096	1,718	921
West Virginia	1,814	296	412	283	496	328
Wisconsin	5,628	1,005	1,379	891	1,490	863
Wyoming	533	99	136	78	143	77

Source: Bureau of the Census, State Population Estimates, Internet site http://www.census.gov/popest/states/asrh/; calculations by New Strategist

Table 8.18 Distribution of State Populations by Generation, 2008

(percent distribution of people by state and generation, 2008)

	total population	iGeneration (under 14)	Millennial (14 to 31)	Generation X (32 to 43)	Baby Boom (44 to 62)	Older Americans (63 or older)
United States	**100.0%**	**18.8%**	**24.9%**	**16.4%**	**25.1%**	**14.8%**
Alabama	100.0	18.5	24.6	15.7	25.3	15.9
Alaska	100.0	20.1	28.0	16.5	26.3	9.1
Arizona	100.0	20.7	25.1	16.2	22.8	15.2
Arkansas	100.0	19.1	24.4	15.5	24.6	16.4
California	100.0	19.7	26.5	17.3	23.7	12.9
Colorado	100.0	19.2	25.5	17.5	25.6	12.3
Connecticut	100.0	17.6	23.0	16.5	27.1	15.8
Delaware	100.0	18.2	23.9	16.1	25.6	16.1
District of Columbia	100.0	14.7	30.4	17.8	23.1	13.9
Florida	100.0	16.8	22.7	15.8	25.1	19.6
Georgia	100.0	20.6	25.4	17.7	24.3	12.0
Hawaii	100.0	17.2	24.8	16.1	25.0	16.9
Idaho	100.0	21.2	25.7	15.3	23.9	13.9
Illinois	100.0	19.0	25.6	16.6	24.7	14.1
Indiana	100.0	19.2	24.7	16.1	25.3	14.7
Iowa	100.0	18.3	24.5	14.9	25.5	16.8
Kansas	100.0	19.5	25.5	15.2	24.8	15.0
Kentucky	100.0	18.2	24.1	16.4	25.9	15.4
Louisiana	100.0	19.4	26.3	15.2	24.9	14.2
Maine	100.0	15.6	21.8	15.7	29.3	17.6
Maryland	100.0	18.2	24.5	16.9	26.4	14.1
Massachusetts	100.0	16.7	24.5	16.8	26.4	15.5
Michigan	100.0	18.1	24.4	16.0	26.4	15.1
Minnesota	100.0	18.5	24.8	16.1	26.2	14.4
Mississippi	100.0	20.2	25.7	15.3	24.2	14.6
Missouri	100.0	18.5	24.6	15.6	25.6	15.7
Montana	100.0	17.3	24.3	14.1	27.7	16.5
Nebraska	100.0	19.5	25.4	15.0	24.7	15.4
Nevada	100.0	20.2	24.2	17.6	24.5	13.5
New Hampshire	100.0	16.7	22.7	16.5	28.8	15.2
New Jersey	100.0	18.1	22.9	17.3	26.4	15.3
New Mexico	100.0	19.7	25.6	15.0	24.5	15.1
New York	100.0	17.2	24.9	16.7	25.7	15.4
North Carolina	100.0	19.0	24.3	17.1	25.2	14.5
North Dakota	100.0	17.1	27.4	13.7	25.2	16.6
Ohio	100.0	18.2	24.1	15.8	26.2	15.7
Oklahoma	100.0	19.4	25.6	15.0	24.4	15.5
Oregon	100.0	17.6	24.2	16.2	26.4	15.5
Pennsylvania	100.0	16.8	23.4	15.6	26.7	17.5
Rhode Island	100.0	16.5	25.0	16.2	26.3	16.1
South Carolina	100.0	18.4	24.5	16.0	25.6	15.6

	total population	iGeneration (under 14)	Millennial (14 to 31)	Generation X (32 to 43)	Baby Boom (44 to 62)	Older Americans (63 or older)
South Dakota	100.0%	19.1%	25.0%	14.1%	25.3%	16.5%
Tennessee	100.0	18.4	24.0	16.5	25.7	15.4
Texas	100.0	21.8	26.4	17.0	22.9	11.9
Utah	100.0	24.9	30.2	15.1	19.4	10.4
Vermont	100.0	15.4	23.4	15.5	29.4	16.4
Virginia	100.0	18.2	24.9	17.1	25.6	14.1
Washington	100.0	18.1	24.9	16.7	26.2	14.1
West Virginia	100.0	16.3	22.7	15.6	27.3	18.1
Wisconsin	100.0	17.9	24.5	15.8	26.5	15.3
Wyoming	100.0	18.7	25.5	14.7	26.8	14.4

Source: Bureau of the Census, State Population Estimates, Internet site http://www.census.gov/popest/states/asrh/; calculations by New Strategist

9

Spending

■ Households headed by people under age 30 spent 7 percent more in 2007 than they did in 2000, a slightly smaller increase than the 8 percent gain for the average household.

■ The average spending of households headed by young adults is well below average. Householders under age 30 spent $37,007 in 2007, just 75 percent as much as the average household.

■ Householders under age 30 spent 18 percent less on new and used cars and trucks in 2007 than they did in 2000. But they spent 31 percent more on audio and visual equipment and services—a category that includes big-screen TVs.

■ Many members of the Millennial generation are adults living at home with their parents. Married couples with grown children (aged 18 or older) at home are the most affluent household type, spending an average of $70,822 in 2007.

Millennial Spending Has Grown More Slowly than Average

Their spending on mortgage interest climbed sharply however.

Households headed by people under age 30 (the oldest Millennials turned 30 in 2007) boosted their spending by 7 percent between 2000 and 2007, after adjusting for inflation. This increase is slightly lower than the 8 percent gain for the average household during those years. Households headed by Millennials spent an average of $37,007 in 2007.

Householders under age 30 cut their spending on many items between 2000 and 2007. Among the biggest declines were new and used cars and trucks, footwear, and gifts for people in other households. Spending on furniture also declined. Householders under age 30 boosted their spending on a variety of items as well, including food away from home, alcoholic beverages, and health insurance. The average householder under 30 paid 40 percent more in mortgage interest in 2007 than in 2000 as homeownership rates increased.

Many householders under age 30 are in college, but their spending on education remained flat between 2000 and 2007 even in the face of rising tuition costs. Despite their pursuit of higher education, young adults are not big on reading. Their spending on reading material fell 40 percent between 2000 and 2007—a troubling trend for the print media.

■ Householders under age 30 are a diverse mix of single parents, people living alone, and friends living together. Their spending patterns reflect this diversity.

Young adults are spending more on some items

(percent change in spending by householders under age 30, 2000 to 2007; in 2007 dollars)

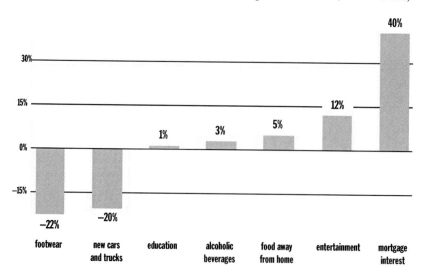

Table 9.1 Average Spending of Total Households, 2000 and 2007

(average annual spending of consumer units, 2000 and 2007; percent change, 2000–07; in 2007 dollars)

	2007	2000	percent change 2000–07
Number of consumer units (in 000s)	120,171	109,367	9.9%
Average annual spending	$49,638	$45,809	8.4
FOOD	6,133	6,211	−1.2
Food at home	3,465	3,638	−4.7
Cereals and bakery products	460	545	−15.7
Cereals and cereal products	143	188	−23.9
Bakery products	317	358	−11.4
Meats, poultry, fish, and eggs	777	957	−18.8
Beef	216	287	−24.6
Pork	150	201	−25.4
Other meats	104	122	−14.5
Poultry	142	175	−18.7
Fish and seafood	122	132	−7.9
Eggs	43	41	5.0
Dairy products	387	391	−1.1
Fresh milk and cream	154	158	−2.4
Other dairy products	234	232	0.7
Fruits and vegetables	600	627	−4.4
Fresh fruits	202	196	2.9
Fresh vegetables	190	191	−0.8
Processed fruits	112	138	−19.1
Processed vegetables	96	101	−5.1
Other food at home	1,241	1,116	11.2
Sugar and other sweets	124	141	−12.0
Fats and oils	91	100	−8.9
Miscellaneous foods	650	526	23.5
Nonalcoholic beverages	333	301	10.6
Food prepared by household on trips	43	48	−10.7
Food away from home	2,668	2,573	3.7
ALCOHOLIC BEVERAGES	457	448	2.0
HOUSING	16,920	14,833	14.1
Shelter	10,023	8,566	17.0
Owned dwellings	6,730	5,541	21.5
Mortgage interest and charges	3,890	3,178	22.4
Property taxes	1,709	1,371	24.6
Maintenance, repairs, insurance, other expenses	1,131	993	13.9
Rented dwellings	2,602	2,449	6.2
Other lodging	691	576	20.1

	2007	2000	percent change 2000–07
Utilities, fuels, public services	**$3,477**	**$2,997**	**16.0%**
Natural gas	480	370	29.9
Electricity	1,303	1,097	18.8
Fuel oil and other fuels	151	117	29.3
Telephone services	1,110	1,056	5.1
Water and other public services	434	356	21.8
Household services	**984**	**824**	**19.5**
Personal services	415	393	5.7
Other household services	569	431	32.0
Housekeeping supplies	**639**	**580**	**10.1**
Laundry and cleaning supplies	140	158	−11.2
Other household products	347	272	27.5
Postage and stationery	152	152	0.2
Household furnishings and equipment	**1,797**	**1,865**	**−3.7**
Household textiles	133	128	4.2
Furniture	446	471	−5.3
Floor coverings	46	53	−13.2
Major appliances	231	228	1.5
Small appliances, miscellaneous housewares	101	105	−3.6
Miscellaneous household equipment	840	880	−4.6
APPAREL AND SERVICES	**1,881**	**2,235**	**−15.8**
Men and boys	**435**	**530**	**−17.9**
Men, aged 16 or older	351	414	−15.3
Boys, aged 2 to 15	84	116	−27.3
Women and girls	**749**	**873**	**−14.2**
Women, aged 16 or older	627	731	−14.2
Girls, aged 2 to 15	122	142	−14.1
Children under age 2	**93**	**99**	**−5.8**
Footwear	**327**	**413**	**−20.8**
Other apparel products and services	**276**	**320**	**−13.8**
TRANSPORTATION	**8,758**	**8,931**	**−1.9**
Vehicle purchases	**3,244**	**4,116**	**−21.2**
Cars and trucks, new	1,572	1,933	−18.7
Cars and trucks, used	1,567	2,131	−26.5
Other vehicles	105	52	102.8
Gasoline and motor oil	**2,384**	**1,554**	**53.4**
Other vehicle expenses	**2,592**	**2,746**	**−5.6**
Vehicle finance charges	305	395	−22.8
Maintenance and repairs	738	751	−1.8
Vehicle insurance	1,071	937	14.3
Vehicle rental, leases, licenses, other charges	478	663	−28.0
Public transportation	**538**	**514**	**4.6**

	2007	2000	percent change 2000–07
HEALTH CARE	**$2,853**	**$2,488**	**14.7%**
Health insurance	1,545	1,184	30.5
Medical services	709	684	3.7
Drugs	481	501	–4.0
Medical supplies	118	119	–1.0
ENTERTAINMENT	**2,698**	**2,243**	**20.3**
Fees and admissions	658	620	6.1
Audio and visual equipment and services	987	749	31.8
Pets, toys, hobbies, and playground equipment	560	402	39.2
Other entertainment supplies, services	493	473	4.2
PERSONAL CARE PRODUCTS, SERVICES	**588**	**679**	**–13.4**
READING	**118**	**176**	**–32.9**
EDUCATION	**945**	**761**	**24.2**
TOBACCO PRODUCTS, SMOKING SUPPLIES	**323**	**384**	**–15.9**
MISCELLANEOUS	**808**	**934**	**–13.5**
CASH CONTRIBUTIONS	**1,821**	**1,435**	**26.9**
PERSONAL INSURANCE AND PENSIONS	**5,336**	**4,052**	**31.7**
Life and other personal insurance	309	480	–35.7
Pensions and Social Security	5,027	–	–
PERSONAL TAXES	**2,233**	**3,753**	**–40.5**
Federal income taxes	1,569	2,901	–45.9
State and local income taxes	468	677	–30.8
Other taxes	196	176	11.5
GIFTS FOR PEOPLE IN OTHER HOUSEHOLDS	**1,198**	**1,304**	**–8.1**

Note: The Bureau of Labor Statistics uses consumer unit rather than household as the sampling unit in the Consumer Expenditure Survey. For the definition of consumer unit, see the glossary. Spending on gifts is also included in the preceding product and service categories. Average spending is rounded to the nearest dollar, but the percent change calculation is based on unrounded figures. "–" means comparable data are not available.
Source: Bureau of Labor Statistics, 2000 and 2007 Consumer Expenditure Survey, Internet site http://www.bls.gov/cex/; calculations by New Strategist

Table 9.2 Average Spending of Householders under Age 30, 2000 and 2007

(average annual spending of consumer units headed by people under age 30, 2000 and 2007; percent change, 2000–07; in 2007 dollars)

	2007	2000	percent change 2000–07
Number of consumer units (in 000s)	18,150	16,787	8.1%
Average annual spending	$37,007	$34,663	6.8
FOOD	5,024	4,839	3.8
Food at home	2,687	2,624	2.4
Cereals and bakery products	341	379	−10.1
Cereals and cereal products	115	147	−21.7
Bakery products	226	232	−2.7
Meats, poultry, fish, and eggs	582	675	−13.8
Beef	164	210	−21.7
Pork	102	131	−22.3
Other meats	80	88	−9.0
Poultry	116	136	−14.7
Fish and seafood	84	83	1.1
Eggs	35	29	21.1
Dairy products	292	281	4.1
Fresh milk and cream	125	119	4.9
Other dairy products	167	161	3.5
Fruits and vegetables	422	424	−0.4
Fresh fruits	134	126	6.0
Fresh vegetables	128	130	−1.6
Processed fruits	90	98	−7.7
Processed vegetables	70	70	0.2
Other food at home	1,051	866	21.4
Sugar and other sweets	85	102	−16.9
Fats and oils	63	67	−6.6
Miscellaneous foods	601	435	38.3
Nonalcoholic beverages	280	234	19.9
Food prepared by household on trips	22	28	−20.6
Food away from home	2,336	2,216	5.4
ALCOHOLIC BEVERAGES	513	498	2.9
HOUSING	12,545	11,233	11.7
Shelter	7,909	6,944	13.9
Owned dwellings	2,961	2,095	41.3
Mortgage interest and charges	2,028	1,447	40.1
Property taxes	564	402	40.2
Maintenance, repairs, insurance, other expenses	369	246	50.2
Rented dwellings	4,739	4,526	4.7
Other lodging	209	323	−35.2

	2007	2000	percent change 2000–07
Utilities, fuels, public services	$2,312	$2,052	12.7%
Natural gas	253	203	24.3
Electricity	873	734	18.9
Fuel oil and other fuels	49	45	10.0
Telephone services	896	892	0.4
Water and other public services	240	177	35.6
Household services	**669**	**539**	**24.0**
Personal services	407	396	2.7
Other household services	262	142	84.4
Housekeeping supplies	**389**	**382**	**1.9**
Laundry and cleaning supplies	104	104	0.4
Other household products	201	175	15.1
Postage and stationery	84	104	−18.9
Household furnishings and equipment	**1,267**	**1,317**	**−3.8**
Household textiles	94	94	0.1
Furniture	357	405	−11.8
Floor coverings	21	22	−3.1
Major appliances	151	144	4.5
Small appliances, miscellaneous housewares	72	77	−6.6
Miscellaneous household equipment	572	574	−0.4
APPAREL AND SERVICES	**1,788**	**1,931**	**−7.4**
Men and boys	**414**	**461**	**−10.2**
Men, aged 16 or older	360	385	−6.6
Boys, aged 2 to 15	54	76	−28.8
Women and girls	**607**	**618**	**−1.7**
Women, aged 16 or older	543	549	−1.1
Girls, aged 2 to 15	64	69	−6.7
Children under age 2	**178**	**164**	**8.7**
Footwear	**321**	**409**	**−21.6**
Other apparel products and services	**268**	**281**	**−4.5**
TRANSPORTATION	**7,449**	**7,864**	**−5.3**
Vehicle purchases	**3,216**	**3,933**	**−18.2**
Cars and trucks, new	1,225	1,538	−20.3
Cars and trucks, used	1,863	2,306	−19.2
Other vehicles	129	89	44.8
Gasoline and motor oil	**2,057**	**1,318**	**56.0**
Other vehicle expenses	**1,826**	**2,241**	**−18.5**
Vehicle finance charges	292	397	−26.5
Maintenance and repairs	529	624	−15.2
Vehicle insurance	665	698	−4.8
Vehicle rental, leases, licenses, other charges	339	521	−35.0
Public transportation	**350**	**373**	**−6.2**

	2007	2000	percent change 2000–07
HEALTH CARE	**$1,147**	**$957**	**19.8%**
Health insurance	602	470	28.2
Medical services	366	287	27.7
Drugs	135	147	–8.1
Medical supplies	44	53	–16.9
ENTERTAINMENT	**1,837**	**1,645**	**11.7**
Fees and admissions	349	384	–9.1
Audio and visual equipment and services	872	666	31.0
Pets, toys, hobbies, and playground equipment	332	285	16.3
Other entertainment supplies, services	283	311	–8.9
PERSONAL CARE PRODUCTS, SERVICES	**412**	**537**	**–23.3**
READING	**59**	**98**	**–39.5**
EDUCATION	**1,170**	**1,158**	**1.0**
TOBACCO PRODUCTS, SMOKING SUPPLIES	**304**	**328**	**–7.2**
MISCELLANEOUS	**507**	**579**	**–12.5**
CASH CONTRIBUTIONS	**698**	**419**	**66.6**
PERSONAL INSURANCE AND PENSIONS	**3,554**	**2,577**	**37.9**
Life and other personal insurance	77	136	–43.4
Pensions and Social Security	3,477	–	–
PERSONAL TAXES	**1,028**	**2,073**	**–50.4**
Federal income taxes	684	1,597	–57.2
State and local income taxes	299	447	–33.1
Other taxes	45	30	49.5
GIFTS FOR PEOPLE IN OTHER HOUSEHOLDS	**474**	**768**	**–38.3**

Note: The Bureau of Labor Statistics uses consumer unit rather than household as the sampling unit in the Consumer Expenditure Survey. For the definition of consumer unit, see the glossary. Spending on gifts is also included in the preceding product and service categories. Average spending is rounded to the nearest dollar, but the percent change calculation is based on unrounded figures. "–" means comparable data are not available.
Source: Bureau of Labor Statistics, 2000 and 2007 Consumer Expenditure Survey, Internet site http://www.bls.gov/cex/; calculations by New Strategist

Young Adults Spend Less than Average on Most Things

Householders under age 30 spend just 75 percent as much as the average household.

The incomes of householders under age 30 are well below average, and so is their spending. On some things, however, Millennials (the oldest Millennials turned 30 in 2007) spend more. They spend 12 percent more than the average household on alcoholic beverages and 82 percent more on rent. Because many young householders are parents, they spend 91 percent more than the average household on clothes for children under age 2. They spend 19 percent more on used cars and trucks. Millennial householders spend 24 percent more than average on education. Many are students paying for college at least partly out of their own pocket.

On most items, Millennials spend far less than the average household. They spend 12 percent less than the average household on food away from home (with an index of 88). They spend 56 percent less than average on owned dwellings because most are renters. They spend 60 percent less than average on health care since most are in good health and have few medical needs. Their spending on reading material is just half the average.

■ As Millennial householders age, their spending will rise along with their income.

The youngest householders are big spenders on alcohol, rent, and education

(indexed spending by householders under age 30 on selected items, 2007)

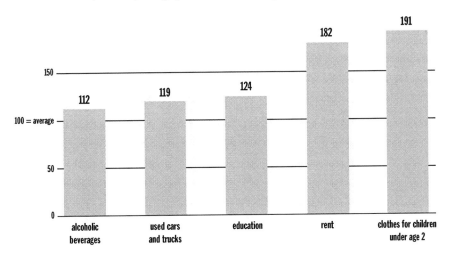

Table 9.3 Average, Indexed, and Market Share of Spending by Householders under Age 30, 2007

(average annual spending of total consumer units and average annual, indexed, and market share of spending by consumer units headed by people under age 30, 2007)

	total consumer units	consumer units headed by people under age 30		
		average spending	indexed spending	market share
Number of consumer units (in 000s)	120,171	18,150	–	15.1%
Average annual spending	$49,638	$37,007	75	11.3
FOOD	**6,133**	**5,024**	**82**	**12.4**
Food at home	**3,465**	**2,687**	**78**	**11.7**
Cereals and bakery products	460	341	74	11.2
Cereals and cereal products	143	115	80	12.1
Bakery products	317	226	71	10.8
Meats, poultry, fish, and eggs	777	582	75	11.3
Beef	216	164	76	11.5
Pork	150	102	68	10.3
Other meats	104	80	77	11.6
Poultry	142	116	82	12.3
Fish and seafood	122	84	69	10.4
Eggs	43	35	81	12.3
Dairy products	387	292	75	11.4
Fresh milk and cream	154	125	81	12.3
Other dairy products	234	167	71	10.8
Fruits and vegetables	600	422	70	10.6
Fresh fruits	202	134	66	10.0
Fresh vegetables	190	128	67	10.2
Processed fruits	112	90	80	12.1
Processed vegetables	96	70	73	11.0
Other food at home	1,241	1,051	85	12.8
Sugar and other sweets	124	85	69	10.4
Fats and oils	91	63	69	10.5
Miscellaneous foods	650	601	92	14.0
Nonalcoholic beverages	333	280	84	12.7
Food prepared by household on trips	43	22	51	7.7
Food away from home	**2,668**	**2,336**	**88**	**13.2**
ALCOHOLIC BEVERAGES	**457**	**513**	**112**	**17.0**
HOUSING	**16,920**	**12,545**	**74**	**11.2**
Shelter	**10,023**	**7,909**	**79**	**11.9**
Owned dwellings	6,730	2,961	44	6.6
Mortgage interest and charges	3,890	2,028	52	7.9
Property taxes	1,709	564	33	5.0
Maintenance, repairs, insurance, other expenses	1,131	369	33	4.9
Rented dwellings	2,602	4,739	182	27.5
Other lodging	691	209	30	4.6

	total consumer units	consumer units headed by people under age 30		
		average spending	indexed spending	market share
Utilities, fuels, public services	**$3,477**	**$2,312**	**66**	**10.0%**
Natural gas	480	253	53	8.0
Electricity	1,303	873	67	10.1
Fuel oil and other fuels	151	49	32	4.9
Telephone services	1,110	896	81	12.2
Water and other public services	434	240	55	8.4
Household services	**984**	**669**	**68**	**10.3**
Personal services	415	407	98	14.8
Other household services	569	262	46	7.0
Housekeeping supplies	**639**	**389**	**61**	**9.2**
Laundry and cleaning supplies	140	104	74	11.2
Other household products	347	201	58	8.7
Postage and stationery	152	84	55	8.3
Householf furnishings and equipment	**1,797**	**1,267**	**71**	**10.6**
Household textiles	133	94	71	10.7
Furniture	446	357	80	12.1
Floor coverings	46	21	46	6.9
Major appliances	231	151	65	9.9
Small appliances, miscellaneous housewares	101	72	71	10.8
Miscellaneous household equipment	840	572	68	10.3
APPAREL AND SERVICES	**1,881**	**1,788**	**95**	**14.4**
Men and boys	**435**	**414**	**95**	**14.4**
Men, aged 16 or older	351	360	103	15.5
Boys, aged 2 to 15	84	54	64	9.7
Women and girls	**749**	**607**	**81**	**12.2**
Women, aged 16 or older	627	543	87	13.1
Girls, aged 2 to 15	122	64	52	7.9
Children under age 2	**93**	**178**	**191**	**28.9**
Footwear	**327**	**321**	**98**	**14.8**
Other apparel products and services	**276**	**268**	**97**	**14.7**
TRANSPORTATION	**8,758**	**7,449**	**85**	**12.8**
Vehicle purchases	**3,244**	**3,216**	**99**	**15.0**
Cars and trucks, new	1,572	1,225	78	11.8
Cars and trucks, used	1,567	1,863	119	18.0
Other vehicles	105	129	123	18.6
Gasoline and motor oil	**2,384**	**2,057**	**86**	**13.0**
Other vehicle expenses	**2,592**	**1,826**	**70**	**10.6**
Vehicle finance charges	305	292	96	14.5
Maintenance and repairs	738	529	72	10.8
Vehicle insurance	1,071	665	62	9.4
Vehicle rental, leases, licenses, other charges	478	339	71	10.7
Public transportation	**538**	**350**	**65**	**9.8**

	total consumer units	consumer units headed by people under age 30		
		average spending	indexed spending	market share
HEALTH CARE	$2,853	$1,147	40	6.1%
Health insurance	1,545	602	39	5.9
Medical services	709	366	52	7.8
Drugs	481	135	28	4.2
Medical supplies	118	44	37	5.6
ENTERTAINMENT	2,698	1,837	68	10.3
Fees and admissions	658	349	53	8.0
Audio and visual equipment and services	987	872	88	13.3
Pets, toys, hobbies, and playground equipment	560	332	59	9.0
Other entertainment supplies, services	493	283	57	8.7
PERSONAL CARE PRODUCTS, SERVICES	588	412	70	10.6
READING	118	59	50	7.6
EDUCATION	945	1,170	124	18.7
TOBACCO PRODUCTS, SMOKING SUPPLIES	323	304	94	14.2
MISCELLANEOUS	808	507	63	9.5
CASH CONTRIBUTIONS	1,821	698	38	5.8
PERSONAL INSURANCE AND PENSIONS	5,336	3,554	67	10.1
Life and other personal insurance	309	77	25	3.8
Pensions and Social Security	5,027	3,477	69	10.4
PERSONAL TAXES	2,233	1,028	46	7.0
Federal income taxes	1,569	684	44	6.6
State and local income taxes	468	299	64	9.6
Other taxes	196	45	23	3.5
GIFTS FOR PEOPLE IN OTHER HOUSEHOLDS	1,198	474	40	6.0

Note: The Bureau of Labor Statistics uses consumer unit rather than household as the sampling unit in the Consumer Expenditure Survey. For the definition of consumer unit, see the glossary. Spending on gifts is also included in the preceding product and service categories; "–" means not applicable.
Source: Bureau of Labor Statistics, 2007 Consumer Expenditure Survey, Internet site http://www.bls.gov/cex/; calculations by New Strategist

Couples with Adult Children at Home Are Spending More

Education and health insurance are among the biggest gainers.

Many members of the Millennial generation are adults living at home with their parents. Married couples with grown children (aged 18 or older) at home are the most affluent household type because these households have the most earners—2.5 versus 1.7 earners in the average household. Couples with adult children at home spent an average of $70,822 in 2007, which is 8 percent more than they spent in 2000 after adjusting for inflation.

Married couples with adult children at home are spending less on many items. They cut their grocery (food at home) spending by 1.1 percent between 2000 and 2007, and their spending on alcoholic beverages fell 1.5 percent. But they spent 6 percent more on food away from home (mostly restaurant meals). Spending on owned homes increased 17 percent, but spending on home furnishings and equipment fell by a sharp 20 percent. Spending on entertainment increased 18 percent, but spending on apparel slumped by 11 percent. This household type spent 27 percent more on out-of-pocket health insurance costs in 2007 than in 2000.

Many couples with adult children at home have at least one child in college. Their spending on education rose 21 percent between 2000 and 2007, after adjusting for inflation.

■ Many couples with adult children at home are trying to save for college expenses, tempering their discretionary purchases.

Couples with adult children at home are spending more on education

(percent change in spending by married couples with children aged 18 or older at home, 2000 and 2007; in 2007 dollars)

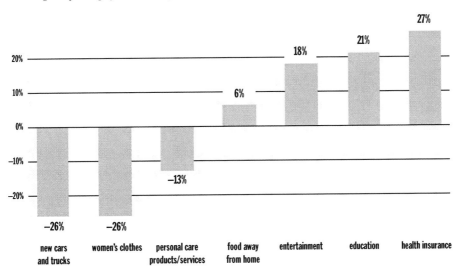

Table 9.4 Average Spending of Married Couples with Oldest Child Aged 18 or Older, 2000 and 2007

(average annual spending of married-couple consumer units with oldest child aged 18 or older at home, 2000 and 2007; percent change, 2000–07; in 2007 dollars)

	2007	2000	percent change 2000–07
Number of consumer units (in 000s)	8,854	8,090	9.4%
Average annual spending	$70,822	$65,682	7.8
FOOD	**9,623**	**9,462**	**1.7**
Food at home	**5,626**	**5,688**	**−1.1**
Cereals and bakery products	750	902	−16.8
Cereals and cereal products	221	302	−26.9
Bakery products	529	598	−11.6
Meats, poultry, fish, and eggs	1,337	1,530	−12.6
Beef	353	471	−25.0
Pork	249	323	−22.8
Other meats	193	205	−5.7
Poultry	269	277	−2.9
Fish and seafood	207	188	10.2
Eggs	66	67	−2.1
Dairy products	582	608	−4.3
Fresh milk and cream	216	248	−12.9
Other dairy products	366	360	1.7
Fruits and vegetables	914	928	−1.5
Fresh fruits	297	290	2.3
Fresh vegetables	299	276	8.4
Processed fruits	177	196	−9.8
Processed vegetables	142	166	−14.5
Other food at home	2,043	1,719	18.8
Sugar and other sweets	201	243	−17.4
Fats and oils	155	163	−4.6
Miscellaneous foods	1,041	756	37.7
Nonalcoholic beverages	595	497	19.6
Food prepared by household on trips	51	60	−15.3
Food away from home	**3,997**	**3,774**	**5.9**
ALCOHOLIC BEVERAGES	**566**	**574**	**−1.5**
HOUSING	**20,596**	**18,708**	**10.1**
Shelter	**11,696**	**10,332**	**13.2**
Owned dwellings	9,466	8,119	16.6
Mortgage interest and charges	5,422	4,742	14.3
Property taxes	2,500	2,070	20.8
Maintenance, repairs, insurance, other expenses	1,544	1,308	18.1
Rented dwellings	1,195	1,196	−0.1
Other lodging	1,035	1,017	1.7

	2007	2000	percent change 2000–07
Utilities, fuels, public services	**$4,891**	**$4,095**	**19.4%**
Natural gas	697	503	38.5
Electricity	1,800	1,538	17.1
Fuel oil and other fuels	165	157	5.4
Telephone services	1,622	1,364	18.9
Water and other public services	606	533	13.6
Household services	**943**	**643**	**46.7**
Personal services	249	129	93.3
Other household services	694	514	35.0
Housekeeping supplies	**861**	**879**	**−2.0**
Laundry and cleaning supplies	207	241	−14.0
Other household products	472	425	11.0
Postage and stationery	181	213	−15.1
Household furnishings and equipment	**2,206**	**2,759**	**−20.0**
Household textiles	160	196	−18.5
Furniture	477	583	−18.1
Floor coverings	44	130	−66.2
Major appliances	305	412	−25.9
Small appliances, miscellaneous housewares	148	149	−0.9
Miscellaneous household equipment	1,072	1,290	−16.9
APPAREL AND SERVICES	**2,876**	**3,249**	**−11.5**
Men and boys	**743**	**875**	**−15.1**
Men, aged 16 or older	667	747	−10.7
Boys, aged 2 to 15	76	129	−41.0
Women and girls	**1,062**	**1,433**	**−25.9**
Women, aged 16 or older	959	1,299	−26.2
Girls, aged 2 to 15	104	134	−22.2
Children under age 2	**66**	**76**	**−13.0**
Footwear	**519**	**466**	**11.4**
Other apparel products and services	**485**	**399**	**21.7**
TRANSPORTATION	**13,651**	**14,639**	**−6.8**
Vehicle purchases	**5,190**	**6,883**	**−24.6**
Cars and trucks, new	2,293	3,081	−25.6
Cars and trucks, used	2,753	3,756	−26.7
Other vehicles	144	46	214.7
Gasoline and motor oil	**3,797**	**2,519**	**50.7**
Other vehicle expenses	**4,076**	**4,567**	**−10.8**
Vehicle finance charges	472	669	−29.5
Maintenance and repairs	1,202	1,190	1.0
Vehicle insurance	1,620	1,695	−4.4
Vehicle rental, leases, licenses, other charges	782	1,013	−22.8
Public transportation	**588**	**672**	**−12.5**

	2007	2000	percent change 2000–07
HEALTH CARE	**$3,737**	**$3,228**	**15.8%**
Health insurance	1,993	1,569	27.0
Medical services	925	881	4.9
Drugs	628	613	2.5
Medical supplies	190	166	14.3
ENTERTAINMENT	**3,682**	**3,114**	**18.2**
Fees and admissions	863	852	1.2
Audio and visual equipment and services	1,376	993	38.5
Pets, toys, hobbies, and playground equipment	775	509	52.2
Other entertainment supplies, services	669	757	−11.7
PERSONAL CARE PRODUCTS, SERVICES	**881**	**1,017**	**−13.4**
READING	**149**	**218**	**−31.6**
EDUCATION	**2,587**	**2,130**	**21.5**
TOBACCO PRODUCTS, SMOKING SUPPLIES	**346**	**548**	**−36.8**
MISCELLANEOUS	**1,011**	**1,095**	**−7.6**
CASH CONTRIBUTIONS	**2,194**	**1,650**	**33.0**
PERSONAL INSURANCE AND PENSIONS	**8,923**	**6,053**	**47.4**
Life and other personal insurance	585	845	−30.8
Pensions and Social Security	8,339	–	–
PERSONAL TAXES	**3,100**	**4,961**	**−37.5**
Federal income taxes	2,135	3,926	−45.6
State and local income taxes	657	816	−19.5
Other taxes	307	218	40.9
GIFTS FOR PEOPLE IN OTHER HOUSEHOLDS	**1,426**	**2,081**	**−31.5**

Note: The Bureau of Labor Statistics uses consumer unit rather than household as the sampling unit in the Consumer Expenditure Survey. For the definition of consumer unit, see the glossary. Spending on gifts is also included in the preceding product and service categories. "–" means comparable data are not available.
Source: Bureau of Labor Statistics, 2000 and 2007 Consumer Expenditure Survey, Internet site http://www.bls.gov/cex/; calculations by New Strategist

Table 9.5 Average, Indexed, and Market Share of Spending by Married Couples with Oldest Child Aged 18 or Older, 2007

(average annual spending of total consumer units and average annual, indexed, and market share of spending by married-couple consumer units with children aged 18 or older at home, 2007)

	total consumer units	consumer units headed by married couples with children aged 18 or older at home		
		average spending	indexed spending	market share
Number of consumer units (in 000s)	120,171	8,854	–	7.4%
Average annual spending	$49,638	$70,822	110	10.5
FOOD	6,133	9,623	122	11.6
Food away from home	3,465	5,626	126	12.0
Cereals and bakery products	460	750	126	12.0
Cereals and cereal products	143	221	121	11.4
Bakery products	317	529	128	12.3
Meats, poultry, fish, and eggs	777	1,337	136	12.7
Beef	216	353	127	12.0
Pork	150	249	131	12.2
Other meats	104	193	147	13.7
Poultry	142	269	148	14.0
Fish and seafood	122	207	136	12.5
Eggs	43	66	125	11.3
Dairy products	387	582	114	11.1
Fresh milk and cream	154	216	109	10.3
Other dairy products	234	366	117	11.5
Fruits and vegetables	600	914	117	11.2
Fresh fruits	202	297	112	10.8
Fresh vegetables	190	299	118	11.6
Processed fruits	112	177	125	11.6
Processed vegetables	96	142	118	10.9
Other food at home	1,241	2,043	129	12.1
Sugar and other sweets	124	201	126	11.9
Fats and oils	91	155	129	12.5
Miscellaneous foods	650	1,041	126	11.8
Nonalcoholic beverages	333	595	142	13.2
Food prepared by household on trips	43	51	82	8.7
Food away from home	2,668	3,997	116	11.0
ALCOHOLIC BEVERAGES	457	566	112	9.1
HOUSING	16,920	20,596	98	9.0
Shelter	10,023	11,696	97	8.6
Owned dwellings	6,730	9,466	101	10.4
Mortgage interest and charges	3,890	5,422	99	10.3
Property taxes	1,709	2,500	106	10.8
Maintenance, repairs, insurance, other expenses	1,131	1,544	102	10.1
Rented dwellings	2,602	1,195	72	3.4
Other lodging	691	1,035	101	11.0

	total consumer units	consumer units headed by married couples with children aged 18 or older at home		
		average spending	indexed spending	market share
Utilities, fuels, public services	**$3,477**	**$4,891**	**116**	**10.4%**
Natural gas	480	697	119	10.7
Electricity	1,303	1,800	113	10.2
Fuel oil and other fuels	151	165	90	8.1
Telephone services	1,110	1,622	123	10.8
Water and other public services	434	606	111	10.3
Household services	**984**	**943**	**70**	**7.1**
Personal services	415	249	41	4.4
Other household services	569	694	94	9.0
Housekeeping supplies	**639**	**861**	**99**	**9.9**
Laundry and cleaning supplies	140	207	117	10.9
Other household products	347	472	94	10.0
Postage and stationery	152	181	94	8.8
Household furnishings and equipment	**1,797**	**2,206**	**91**	**9.0**
Household textiles	133	160	90	8.9
Furniture	446	477	77	7.9
Floor coverings	46	44	68	7.0
Major appliances	231	305	96	9.7
Small appliances, miscellaneous housewares	101	148	116	10.8
Miscellaneous household equipment	840	1,072	96	9.4
APPAREL AND SERVICES	**1,881**	**2,876**	**121**	**11.3**
Men and boys	**435**	**743**	**137**	**12.6**
Men, aged 16 or older	351	667	157	14.0
Boys, aged 2 to 15	84	76	64	6.7
Women and girls	**749**	**1,062**	**113**	**10.4**
Women, aged 16 or older	627	959	124	11.3
Girls, aged 2 to 15	122	104	62	6.3
Children under age 2	**93**	**66**	**51**	**5.2**
Footwear	**327**	**519**	**125**	**11.7**
Other apparel products and services	**276**	**485**	**143**	**12.9**
TRANSPORTATION	**8,758**	**13,651**	**118**	**11.5**
Vehicle purchases	**3,244**	**5,190**	**117**	**11.8**
Cars and trucks, new	1,572	2,293	102	10.7
Cars and trucks, used	1,567	2,753	136	12.9
Other vehicles	105	144	91	10.1
Gasoline and motor oil	**2,384**	**3,797**	**122**	**11.7**
Other vehicle expenses	**2,592**	**4,076**	**122**	**11.6**
Vehicle finance charges	305	472	111	11.4
Maintenance and repairs	738	1,202	128	12.0
Vehicle insurance	1,071	1,620	124	11.1
Vehicle rental, leases, licenses, other charges	478	782	119	12.1
Public transportation	**538**	**588**	**81**	**8.1**

	total consumer units	consumer units headed by married couples with children aged 18 or older at home		
		average spending	indexed spending	market share
HEALTH CARE	$2,853	$3,737	97	9.7%
Health insurance	1,545	1,993	96	9.5
Medical services	709	925	93	9.6
Drugs	481	628	98	9.6
Medical supplies	118	190	115	11.9
ENTERTAINMENT	2,698	3,682	103	10.1
Fees and admissions	658	863	90	9.7
Audio and visual equipment and services	987	1,376	114	10.3
Pets, toys, hobbies, and playground equipment	560	775	106	10.2
Other entertainment supplies, services	493	669	98	10.0
PERSONAL CARE PRODUCTS, SERVICES	588	881	119	11.0
READING	118	149	101	9.3
EDUCATION	945	2,587	207	20.2
TOBACCO PRODUCTS, SMOKING SUPPLIES	323	346	107	7.9
MISCELLANEOUS	808	1,011	103	9.2
CASH CONTRIBUTIONS	1,821	2,194	89	8.9
PERSONAL INSURANCE AND PENSIONS	5,336	8,923	120	12.3
Life and other personal insurance	309	585	126	13.9
Pensions and Social Security	5,027	8,339	119	12.2
PERSONAL TAXES	2,233	3,100	101	10.2
Federal income taxes	1,569	2,135	99	10.0
State and local income taxes	468	657	102	10.3
Other taxes	196	307	111	11.5
GIFTS FOR PEOPLE IN OTHER HOUSEHOLDS	1,198	1,426	90	8.8

Note: The Bureau of Labor Statistics uses consumer unit rather than household as the sampling unit in the Consumer Expenditure Survey. For the definition of consumer unit, see the glossary. Spending on gifts is also included in the preceding product and service categories. "–" means not applicable.
Source: Bureau of Labor Statistics, 2000 and 2007 Consumer Expenditure Survey, Internet site http://www.bls.gov/cex/; calculations by New Strategist

Time Use

■ People aged 15 to 19 have 4.56 hours of leisure time per day—an amount of leisure that they will not experience again until they are aged 65 or older.

■ People aged 25 to 34 spend more time at work on an average day (4.62 hours) than they do at leisure (3.73), a situation that will continue until they reach the 55-to-64-age group.

■ Women aged 25 to 34 spend more than twice as much time as the average woman caring for household children.

■ Men aged 25 to 34 spend only 0.32 hours per day doing housework, much less than the 0.86 hours per day the average woman in the age group spends doing housework.

Adults Aged 20 to 24 Spend More Time at Work than at Play

Teenagers have much more leisure time than young adults.

Time use varies sharply by age, with teenagers aged 15 to 19 having much more leisure time than adults in their twenties and thirties. People aged 15 to 19 have 4.56 hours of leisure time per day—an amount of leisure that they will not experience again until they are aged 65 or older. On an average day, teenagers spend much more time in leisure activities than they do at work (1.54 hours) or in school (2.87 hours)

In the 20-to-24 age group, time at work expands to 4.15 hours per day, and leisure time shrinks to 4.12 hours. People aged 25 to 34 spend more time at work on an average day (4.62 hours) than they do at leisure (3.73), a situation that will continue for many years—until they reach the 55-to-64-age group.

■ Women aged 25 to 34 spend more than twice as much time as the average woman caring for household children.

Time at work expands sharply as people enter their twenties

(average number of hours per day spent working, by age, 2007)

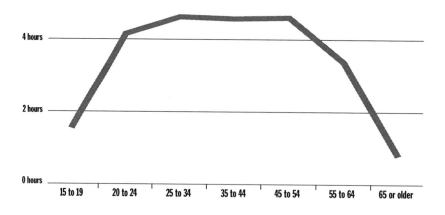

Table 10.1 Detailed Time Use of People Aged 15 to 19, 2007

(hours per day spent in primary activities by total people aged 15 or older and people aged 15 to 19, and index of age group to total, 2007)

	hours per day for total people	hours per day for people aged 15 to 19	index, 15 to 19 to total
TOTAL, ALL ACTIVITIES	24.00	24.00	100
Personal care activities	9.31	10.25	110
Sleeping	8.57	9.44	110
Grooming	0.67	0.80	119
Health-related self-care	0.07	0.01	14
Household activities	1.87	0.74	40
Housework	0.64	0.27	42
Food preparation and cleanup	0.52	0.10	19
Lawn, garden, and houseplants	0.21	0.03	14
Animals and pets	0.09	0.06	67
Vehicles	0.04	0.03	75
Household management	0.22	0.20	91
Household and personal mail and messages (except email)	0.02	0.01	50
Household and personal email and messages	0.05	0.11	220
Caring for and helping household members	0.45	0.08	18
Caring for and helping household children	0.38	0.06	16
Caring for household adults	0.03	–	–
Helping household adults	0.01	0.01	100
Caring for and helping people in other households	0.14	0.10	71
Caring for and helping children in other households	0.06	0.05	83
Caring for adults in other households	0.01	–	–
Helping adults in other households	0.06	0.05	83
Working and work-related activities	3.53	1.54	44
Working	3.47	1.44	41
Educational activities	0.40	2.87	718
Attending class	0.26	2.15	827
Homework and research	0.14	0.65	464
Consumer purchases	0.39	0.28	72
Shopping (store, telephone, Internet)	0.39	0.28	72
Grocery shopping	0.10	0.04	40
Shopping (except groceries, food, and gas)	0.27	0.22	81
Professional and personal care services	0.09	0.05	56
Medical and care services	0.05	0.02	40
Eating and drinking	1.11	0.88	79
Socializing, relaxing, and leisure	4.52	4.56	101
Socializing and communicating	0.64	0.81	127
Attending or hosting social events	0.09	0.15	167
Relaxing and leisure	3.70	3.45	93
Television and movies	2.62	2.14	82
Playing games	0.19	0.46	242
Computer use for leisure (except games)	0.14	0.32	229
Reading for personal interest	0.35	0.14	40
Arts and entertainment (other than sports)	0.09	0.14	156
Attending movies	0.03	0.10	333

	hours per day for total people	hours per day for people aged 15 to 19	index, 15 to 19 to total
Sports, exercise, and recreation	0.35	0.76	217
Participating in sports, exercise, and recreation	0.32	0.68	213
Attending sporting or recreational events	0.03	0.08	267
Religious and spiritual activities	0.15	0.10	67
Volunteer activities	0.16	0.16	100
Telephone calls	0.11	0.24	218
Traveling	1.23	1.23	100

Note: Primary activities are those respondents identified as their main activity. Other activities done simultaneously are not included. Travel related to activities is reported separately. Numbers do not sum to total because not all activities are shown. The index is calculated by dividing time spent by age group by time spent by average person and multiplying by 100. "–" means sample is too small to make a reliable estimate.

Source: Bureau of Labor Statistics, unpublished tables from the 2007 American Time Use Survey, Internet site http://www.bls.gov/tus/home.htm

Table 10.2 Detailed Time Use of Men Aged 15 to 19, 2007

(hours per day spent in primary activities by total men aged 15 or older and men aged 15 to 19, and index of age group to total, 2007)

	hours per day for total men	hours per day for men aged 15 to 19	index, 15 to 19 to total
TOTAL, ALL ACTIVITIES	**24.00**	**24.00**	**100**
Personal care activities	**9.12**	**10.00**	**110**
Sleeping	8.52	9.35	110
Grooming	0.54	0.63	117
Health-related self-care	0.05	0.02	40
Household activities	**1.45**	**0.62**	**43**
Housework	0.29	0.15	52
Food preparation and cleanup	0.28	0.07	25
Lawn, garden, and houseplants	0.30	0.06	20
Animals and pets	0.09	0.06	67
Vehicles	0.07	0.06	86
Household management	0.19	0.16	84
Household and personal mail and messages (except email)	0.02	–	–
Household and personal email and messages	0.05	0.10	200
Caring for and helping household members	**0.27**	**0.04**	**15**
Caring for and helping household children	0.22	0.03	14
Caring for household adults	0.02	–	–
Helping household adults	0.01	0.01	100
Caring for and helping people in other households	**0.11**	**0.10**	**91**
Caring for and helping children in other households	0.04	0.03	75
Caring for adults in other households	0.01	–	–
Helping adults in other households	0.06	0.07	117
Working and work-related activities	**4.16**	**1.66**	**40**
Working	4.09	1.58	39
Educational activities	**0.38**	**2.91**	**766**
Attending class	0.26	2.17	835
Homework and research	0.12	0.67	558
Consumer purchases	**0.31**	**0.21**	**68**
Shopping (store, telephone, Internet)	0.31	0.20	65
Grocery shopping	0.07	0.02	29
Shopping (except groceries, food, and gas)	0.21	0.17	81
Professional and personal care services	**0.06**	**0.03**	**50**
Medical and care services	0.04	0.02	50
Eating and drinking	**1.14**	**0.87**	**76**
Socializing, relaxing, and leisure	**4.77**	**4.79**	**100**
Socializing and communicating	0.59	0.65	110
Attending or hosting social events	0.08	0.12	150
Relaxing and leisure	4.02	3.87	96
Television and movies	2.88	2.23	77
Playing games	0.24	0.72	300
Computer use for leisure (except games)	0.17	0.37	218
Reading for personal interest	0.28	0.09	32
Arts and entertainment (other than sports)	0.09	0.15	167
Attending movies	0.03	0.11	367

	hours per day for total men	hours per day for men aged 15 to 19	index, 15 to 19 to total
Sports, exercise, and recreation	**0.45**	**1.03**	**229**
Participating in sports, exercise, and recreation	0.42	0.94	224
Attending sporting or recreational events	0.03	0.09	300
Religious and spiritual activities	**0.11**	**0.12**	**109**
Volunteer activities	**0.13**	**0.12**	**92**
Telephone calls	**0.06**	**0.20**	**333**
Traveling	**1.28**	**1.18**	**92**

Note: Primary activities are those respondents identified as their main activity. Other activities done simultaneously are not included. Travel related to activities is reported separately. Numbers do not sum to total because not all activities are shown. The index is calculated by dividing time spent by age group by time spent by average man and multiplying by 100. "–" means sample is too small to make a reliable estimate.
Source: Bureau of Labor Statistics, unpublished tables from the 2007 American Time Use Survey, Internet site http://www.bls .gov/tus/home.htm

Table 10.3 Detailed Time Use of Women Aged 15 to 19, 2007

(hours per day spent in primary activities by total women aged 15 or older and women aged 15 to 19, and index of age group to total, 2007)

	hours per day for total women	hours per day for women aged 15 to 19	index, 15 to 19 to total
TOTAL, ALL ACTIVITIES	**24.00**	**24.00**	**100**
Personal care activities	**9.50**	**10.51**	**111**
Sleeping	8.63	9.54	111
Grooming	0.79	0.97	123
Health-related self-care	0.08	–	–
Household activities	**2.27**	**0.86**	**38**
Housework	0.97	0.40	41
Food preparation and cleanup	0.74	0.13	18
Lawn, garden, and houseplants	0.12	0.01	8
Animals and pets	0.10	0.05	50
Vehicles	0.01	0.01	100
Household management	0.24	0.24	100
Household and personal mail and messages (except email)	0.03	0.11	367
Household and personal email and messages	0.05	0.01	20
Caring for and helping household members	**0.62**	**0.12**	**19**
Caring for and helping household children	0.52	0.11	21
Caring for household adults	0.03	–	–
Helping household adults	0.01	0.01	100
Caring for and helping people in other households	**0.16**	**0.10**	**63**
Caring for and helping children in other households	0.09	0.07	78
Caring for adults in other households	0.02	–	–
Helping adults in other households	0.05	0.03	60
Working and work-related activities	**2.93**	**1.42**	**48**
Working	2.89	1.29	45
Educational activities	**0.42**	**2.84**	**676**
Attending class	0.25	2.13	852
Homework and research	0.15	0.63	420
Consumer purchases	**0.48**	**0.36**	**75**
Shopping (store, telephone, Internet)	0.48	0.36	75
Grocery shopping	0.12	0.07	58
Shopping (except groceries, food, and gas)	0.33	0.27	82
Professional and personal care services	**0.12**	**0.07**	**58**
Medical and care services	0.06	0.01	17
Eating and drinking	**1.09**	**0.89**	**82**
Socializing, relaxing, and leisure	**4.29**	**4.32**	**101**
Socializing and communicating	0.69	0.97	141
Attending or hosting social events	0.10	0.18	180
Relaxing and leisure	3.40	3.01	89
Television and movies	2.38	2.05	86
Playing games	0.14	0.20	143
Computer use for leisure (except games)	0.11	0.28	255
Reading for personal interest	0.42	0.20	48
Arts and entertainment (other than sports)	0.10	0.13	130
Attending movies	0.03	0.10	333

	hours per day for total women	hours per day for women aged 15 to 19	index, 15 to 19 to total
Sports, exercise, and recreation	**0.25**	**0.47**	**188**
Participating in sports, exercise, and recreation	0.22	0.41	186
Attending sporting or recreational events	0.03	0.06	200
Religious and spiritual activities	**0.18**	**0.12**	67
Volunteer activities	**0.18**	**0.20**	**111**
Telephone calls	**0.15**	**0.29**	**193**
Traveling	**1.18**	**1.28**	**108**

Note: Primary activities are those respondents identified as their main activity. Other activities done simultaneously are not included. Travel related to activities is reported separately. Numbers do not sum to total because not all activities are shown. The index is calculated by dividing time spent by age group by time spent by average woman and multiplying by 100. "–" means sample is too small to make a reliable estimate.

Source: Bureau of Labor Statistics, unpublished tables from the 2007 American Time Use Survey, Internet site http://www.bls.gov/tus/home.htm

Table 10.4 Detailed Time Use of People Aged 20 to 24, 2007

(hours per day spent in primary activities by total people aged 15 or older and people aged 20 to 24, and index of age group to total, 2007)

	hours per day for total people	hours per day for people aged 20 to 24	index, 20 to 24 to total
TOTAL, ALL ACTIVITIES	**24.00**	**24.00**	**100**
Personal care activities	**9.31**	**9.52**	**102**
Sleeping	8.57	8.77	102
Grooming	0.67	0.74	110
Health-related self-care	0.07	0.01	14
Household activities	**1.87**	**1.07**	**57**
Housework	0.64	0.37	58
Food preparation and cleanup	0.52	0.27	52
Lawn, garden, and houseplants	0.21	0.10	48
Animals and pets	0.09	0.06	67
Vehicles	0.04	0.04	100
Household management	0.22	0.14	64
Household and personal mail and messages (except email)	0.02	–	–
Household and personal email and messages	0.05	0.05	100
Caring for and helping household members	**0.45**	**0.35**	**78**
Caring for and helping household children	0.38	0.33	87
Caring for household adults	0.03	0.01	33
Helping household adults	0.01	–	–
Caring for and helping people in other households	**0.14**	**0.13**	**93**
Caring for and helping children in other households	0.06	0.03	50
Caring for adults in other households	0.01	0.01	100
Helping adults in other households	0.06	0.08	133
Working and work-related activities	**3.53**	**4.15**	**118**
Working	3.47	4.04	116
Educational activities	**0.40**	**0.82**	**205**
Attending class	0.26	0.35	135
Homework and research	0.14	0.46	329
Consumer purchases	**0.39**	**0.39**	**100**
Shopping (store, telephone, Internet)	0.39	0.39	100
Grocery shopping	0.10	0.09	90
Shopping (except groceries, food, and gas)	0.27	0.02	7
Professional and personal care services	**0.09**	**0.08**	**89**
Medical and care services	0.05	0.06	120
Eating and drinking	**1.11**	**1.04**	**94**
Socializing, relaxing, and leisure	**4.52**	**4.12**	**91**
Socializing and communicating	0.64	0.74	116
Attending or hosting social events	0.09	0.10	111
Relaxing and leisure	3.70	3.16	85
Television and movies	2.62	2.26	86
Playing games	0.19	0.31	163
Computer use for leisure (except games)	0.14	0.17	121
Reading for personal interest	0.35	0.13	37
Arts and entertainment (other than sports)	0.09	0.13	144
Attending movies	0.03	0.06	200

	hours per day for total people	hours per day for people aged 20 to 24	index, 20 to 24 to total
Sports, exercise, and recreation	**0.35**	**0.50**	**143**
Participating in sports, exercise, and recreation	0.32	0.46	144
Attending sporting or recreational events	0.03	0.04	133
Religious and spiritual activities	**0.15**	**0.07**	**47**
Volunteer activities	**0.16**	**0.12**	**75**
Telephone calls	**0.11**	**0.07**	**64**
Traveling	**1.23**	**1.34**	**109**

Note: Primary activities are those respondents identified as their main activity. Other activities done simultaneously are not included. Travel related to activities is reported separately. Numbers do not sum to total because not all activities are shown. The index is calculated by dividing time spent by age group by time spent by average person and multiplying by 100. "–" means sample is too small to make a reliable estimate.
Source: Bureau of Labor Statistics, unpublished tables from the 2007 American Time Use Survey, Internet site http://www.bls .gov/tus/home.htm

Table 10.5 Detailed Time Use of Men Aged 20 to 24, 2007

(hours per day spent in primary activities by total men aged 15 or older and men aged 20 to 24, and index of age group to total, 2007)

	hours per day for total men	hours per day for men aged 20 to 24	index, 20 to 24 to total
TOTAL, ALL ACTIVITIES	24.00	24.00	100
Personal care activities	**9.12**	**9.30**	**102**
Sleeping	8.52	8.69	102
Grooming	0.54	0.61	113
Health-related self-care	0.05	–	–
Household activities	**1.45**	**0.94**	**65**
Housework	0.29	0.26	90
Food preparation and cleanup	0.28	0.19	68
Lawn, garden, and houseplants	0.30	0.17	57
Animals and pets	0.09	0.04	44
Vehicles	0.07	0.07	100
Household management	0.19	0.09	47
Household and personal mail and messages (except email)	0.02	–	–
Household and personal email and messages	0.05	0.03	60
Caring for and helping household members	**0.27**	**0.14**	**52**
Caring for and helping household children	0.22	0.11	50
Caring for household adults	0.02	0.01	50
Helping household adults	0.01	–	–
Caring for and helping people in other households	**0.11**	**0.14**	**127**
Caring for and helping children in other households	0.04	0.03	75
Caring for adults in other households	0.01	0.02	200
Helping adults in other households	0.06	0.09	150
Working and work-related activities	**4.16**	**4.34**	**104**
Working	4.09	4.19	102
Educational activities	**0.38**	**0.62**	**163**
Attending class	0.26	0.35	135
Homework and research	0.12	0.25	208
Consumer purchases	**0.31**	**0.27**	**87**
Shopping (store, telephone, Internet)	0.31	0.27	87
Grocery shopping	0.07	0.06	86
Shopping (except groceries, food, and gas)	0.21	0.01	5
Professional and personal care services	**0.06**	**0.10**	**167**
Medical and care services	0.04	0.07	175
Eating and drinking	**1.14**	**1.01**	**89**
Socializing, relaxing, and leisure	**4.77**	**4.49**	**94**
Socializing and communicating	0.59	0.61	103
Attending or hosting social events	0.08	0.07	88
Relaxing and leisure	4.02	3.67	91
Television and movies	2.88	2.48	86
Playing games	0.24	0.54	225
Computer use for leisure (except games)	0.17	0.22	129
Reading for personal interest	0.28	0.11	39
Arts and entertainment (other than sports)	0.09	0.14	156
Attending movies	0.03	0.05	167

	hours per day for total men	hours per day for men aged 20 to 24	index, 20 to 24 to total
Sports, exercise, and recreation	**0.45**	**0.70**	**156**
Participating in sports, exercise, and recreation	0.42	0.66	157
Attending sporting or recreational events	0.03	0.04	133
Religious and spiritual activities	**0.11**	**0.07**	**64**
Volunteer activities	**0.13**	**0.07**	**54**
Telephone calls	**0.06**	**0.05**	**83**
Traveling	**1.28**	**1.50**	**117**

Note: Primary activities are those respondents identified as their main activity. Other activities done simultaneously are not included. Travel related to activities is reported separately. Numbers do not sum to total because not all activities are shown. The index is calculated by dividing time spent by age group by time spent by average man and multiplying by 100. "–" means sample is too small to make a reliable estimate.
Source: Bureau of Labor Statistics, unpublished tables from the 2007 American Time Use Survey, Internet site http://www.bls .gov/tus/home.htm

Table 10.6 Detailed Time Use of Women Aged 20 to 24, 2007

(hours per day spent in primary activities by total women aged 15 or older and women aged 20 to 24, and index of age group to total, 2007)

	hours per day for total women	hours per day for women aged 20 to 24	index, 20 to 24 to total
TOTAL, ALL ACTIVITIES	24.00	24.00	100
Personal care activities	9.50	9.74	103
Sleeping	8.63	8.85	103
Grooming	0.79	0.88	111
Health-related self-care	0.08	0.01	13
Household activities	2.27	1.20	53
Housework	0.97	0.48	49
Food preparation and cleanup	0.74	0.35	47
Lawn, garden, and houseplants	0.12	0.04	33
Animals and pets	0.10	0.08	80
Vehicles	0.01	0.01	100
Household management	0.24	0.18	75
Household and personal mail and messages (except email)	0.03	–	–
Household and personal email and messages	0.05	0.06	120
Caring for and helping household members	0.62	0.57	92
Caring for and helping household children	0.52	0.55	106
Caring for household adults	0.03	–	–
Helping household adults	0.01	–	–
Caring for and helping people in other households	0.16	0.11	69
Caring for and helping children in other households	0.09	0.03	33
Caring for adults in other households	0.02	0.01	50
Helping adults in other households	0.05	0.08	160
Working and work-related activities	2.93	3.95	135
Working	2.89	3.89	135
Educational activities	0.42	1.03	245
Attending class	0.25	0.36	144
Homework and research	0.15	0.66	440
Consumer purchases	0.48	0.51	106
Shopping (store, telephone, Internet)	0.48	0.51	106
Grocery shopping	0.12	0.11	92
Shopping (except groceries, food, and gas)	0.33	0.37	112
Professional and personal care services	0.12	0.07	58
Medical and care services	0.06	0.04	67
Eating and drinking	1.09	1.08	99
Socializing, relaxing, and leisure	4.29	3.75	87
Socializing and communicating	0.69	0.87	126
Attending or hosting social events	0.10	0.13	130
Relaxing and leisure	3.40	2.63	77
Television and movies	2.38	2.04	86
Playing games	0.14	0.09	64
Computer use for leisure (except games)	0.11	0.12	109
Reading for personal interest	0.42	0.15	36
Arts and entertainment (other than sports)	0.10	0.11	110
Attending movies	0.03	0.07	233

	hours per day for total women	hours per day for women aged 20 to 24	index, 20 to 24 to total
Sports, exercise, and recreation	0.25	0.30	120
Participating in sports, exercise, and recreation	0.22	0.26	118
Attending sporting or recreational events	0.03	0.04	133
Religious and spiritual activities	0.18	0.08	44
Volunteer activities	0.18	0.17	94
Telephone calls	0.15	0.10	67
Traveling	1.18	1.19	101

Note: Primary activities are those respondents identified as their main activity. Other activities done simultaneously are not included. Travel related to activities is reported separately. Numbers do not sum to total because not all activities are shown. The index is calculated by dividing time spent by age group by time spent by average woman and multiplying by 100. "–" means sample is too small to make a reliable estimate.

Source: Bureau of Labor Statistics, unpublished tables from the 2007 American Time Use Survey, Internet site http://www.bls .gov/tus/home.htm

Table 10.7 Detailed Time Use of People Aged 25 to 34, 2007

(hours per day spent in primary activities by total people aged 15 or older and people aged 25 to 34, and index of age group to total, 2007)

	hours per day for total people	hours per day for people aged 25 to 34	index, 25 to 34 to total
TOTAL, ALL ACTIVITIES	**24.00**	**24.00**	**100**
Personal care activities	**9.31**	**9.27**	**100**
Sleeping	8.57	8.57	100
Grooming	0.67	0.65	97
Health-related self-care	0.07	0.04	57
Household activities	**1.87**	**1.60**	**86**
Housework	0.64	0.59	92
Food preparation and cleanup	0.52	0.50	96
Lawn, garden, and houseplants	0.21	0.11	52
Animals and pets	0.09	0.07	78
Vehicles	0.04	0.04	100
Household management	0.22	0.16	73
Household and personal mail and messages (except email)	0.02	0.01	50
Household and personal email and messages	0.05	0.04	80
Caring for and helping household members	**0.45**	**0.99**	**220**
Caring for and helping household children	0.38	0.90	237
Caring for household adults	0.03	0.01	33
Helping household adults	0.01	0.01	100
Caring for and helping people in other households	**0.14**	**0.09**	**64**
Caring for and helping children in other households	0.06	0.04	67
Caring for adults in other households	0.01	–	–
Helping adults in other households	0.06	0.04	67
Working and work-related activities	**3.53**	**4.62**	**131**
Working	3.47	4.56	131
Educational activities	**0.40**	**0.18**	**45**
Attending class	0.26	0.07	27
Homework and research	0.14	0.11	79
Consumer purchases	**0.39**	**0.38**	**97**
Shopping (store, telephone, Internet)	0.39	0.38	97
Grocery shopping	0.10	0.09	90
Shopping (except groceries, food, and gas)	0.27	0.26	96
Professional and personal care services	**0.09**	**0.07**	**78**
Medical and care services	0.05	0.03	60
Eating and drinking	**1.11**	**1.06**	**95**
Socializing, relaxing, and leisure	**4.52**	**3.73**	**83**
Socializing and communicating	0.64	0.64	100
Attending or hosting social events	0.09	0.09	100
Relaxing and leisure	3.70	2.89	78
Television and movies	2.62	2.22	85
Playing games	0.19	0.18	95
Computer use for leisure (except games)	0.14	0.11	79
Reading for personal interest	0.35	0.13	37
Arts and entertainment (other than sports)	0.09	0.09	100
Attending movies	0.03	0.04	133

	hours per day for total people	hours per day for people aged 25 to 34	index, 25 to 34 to total
Sports, exercise, and recreation	0.35	0.29	83
Participating in sports, exercise, and recreation	0.32	0.26	81
Attending sporting or recreational events	0.03	0.03	100
Religious and spiritual activities	0.15	0.11	73
Volunteer activities	0.16	0.10	63
Telephone calls	0.11	0.08	73
Traveling	1.23	1.30	106

Note: Primary activities are those respondents identified as their main activity. Other activities done simultaneously are not included. Travel related to activities is reported separately. Numbers do not sum to total because not all activities are shown. The index is calculated by dividing time spent by age group by time spent by average person and multiplying by 100. "–" means sample is too small to make a reliable estimate.

Source: Bureau of Labor Statistics, unpublished tables from the 2007 American Time Use Survey, Internet site http://www.bls.gov/tus/home.htm

Table 10.8 Detailed Time Use of Men Aged 25 to 34, 2007

(hours per day spent in primary activities by total men aged 15 or older and men aged 25 to 34, and index of age group to total, 2007)

	hours per day for total men	hours per day for men aged 25 to 34	index, 25 to 34 to total
TOTAL, ALL ACTIVITIES	**24.00**	**24.00**	**100**
Personal care activities	**9.12**	**9.03**	**99**
Sleeping	8.52	8.45	99
Grooming	0.54	0.53	98
Health-related self-care	0.05	0.04	80
Household activities	**1.45**	**1.24**	**86**
Housework	0.29	0.32	110
Food preparation and cleanup	0.28	0.26	93
Lawn, garden, and houseplants	0.30	0.17	57
Animals and pets	0.09	0.08	89
Vehicles	0.07	0.08	114
Household management	0.19	0.13	68
Household and personal mail and messages (except email)	0.02	–	–
Household and personal email and messages	0.05	0.02	40
Caring for and helping household members	**0.27**	**0.50**	**185**
Caring for and helping household children	0.22	0.44	200
Caring for household adults	0.02	0.01	50
Helping household adults	0.01	0.01	100
Caring for and helping people in other households	**0.11**	**0.09**	**82**
Caring for and helping children in other households	0.04	0.04	100
Caring for adults in other households	0.01	–	–
Helping adults in other households	0.06	0.05	83
Working and work-related activities	**4.16**	**5.54**	**133**
Working	4.09	5.50	134
Educational activities	**0.38**	**0.12**	**32**
Attending class	0.26	0.04	15
Homework and research	0.12	0.08	67
Consumer purchases	**0.31**	**0.31**	**100**
Shopping (store, telephone, Internet)	0.31	0.31	100
Grocery shopping	0.07	0.07	100
Shopping (except groceries, food, and gas)	0.21	0.22	105
Professional and personal care services	**0.06**	**0.03**	**50**
Medical and care services	0.04	0.01	25
Eating and drinking	**1.14**	**1.06**	**93**
Socializing, relaxing, and leisure	**4.77**	**4.07**	**85**
Socializing and communicating	0.59	0.59	100
Attending or hosting social events	0.08	0.10	125
Relaxing and leisure	4.02	3.29	82
Television and movies	2.88	2.56	89
Playing games	0.24	0.21	88
Computer use for leisure (except games)	0.17	0.13	76
Reading for personal interest	0.28	0.10	36
Arts and entertainment (other than sports)	0.09	0.09	100
Attending movies	0.03	0.04	133

	hours per day for total men	hours per day for men aged 25 to 34	index, 25 to 34 to total
Sports, exercise, and recreation	**0.45**	**0.33**	**73**
Participating in sports, exercise, and recreation	0.42	0.31	74
Attending sporting or recreational events	0.03	0.03	100
Religious and spiritual activities	**0.11**	**0.07**	**64**
Volunteer activities	**0.13**	**0.11**	**85**
Telephone calls	**0.06**	**0.06**	**100**
Traveling	**1.28**	**1.31**	**102**

Note: Primary activities are those respondents identified as their main activity. Other activities done simultaneously are not included. Travel related to activities is reported separately. Numbers do not sum to total because not all activities are shown. The index is calculated by dividing time spent by age group by time spent by average man and multiplying by 100. "–" means sample is too small to make a reliable estimate.

Source: Bureau of Labor Statistics, unpublished tables from the 2007 American Time Use Survey, Internet site http://www.bls.gov/tus/home.htm

Table 10.9 Detailed Time Use of Women Aged 25 to 34, 2007

(hours per day spent in primary activities by total women aged 15 or older and women aged 25 to 34, and index of age group to total, 2007)

	hours per day for total women	hours per day for women aged 25 to 34	index, 25 to 34 to total
TOTAL, ALL ACTIVITIES	**24.00**	**24.00**	**100**
Personal care activities	**9.50**	**9.51**	**100**
Sleeping	8.63	8.69	101
Grooming	0.79	0.76	96
Health-related self-care	0.08	0.04	50
Household activities	**2.27**	**1.96**	**86**
Housework	0.97	0.86	89
Food preparation and cleanup	0.74	0.75	101
Lawn, garden, and houseplants	0.12	0.05	42
Animals and pets	0.10	0.06	60
Vehicles	0.01	0.01	100
Household management	0.24	0.18	75
Household and personal mail and messages (except email)	0.03	0.02	67
Household and personal email and messages	0.05	0.05	100
Caring for and helping household members	**0.62**	**1.49**	**240**
Caring for and helping household children	0.52	1.37	263
Caring for household adults	0.03	–	–
Helping household adults	0.01	–	–
Caring for and helping people in other households	**0.16**	**0.09**	**56**
Caring for and helping children in other households	0.09	0.04	44
Caring for adults in other households	0.02	0.01	50
Helping adults in other households	0.05	0.03	60
Working and work-related activities	**2.93**	**3.69**	**126**
Working	2.89	3.63	126
Educational activities	**0.42**	**0.25**	**60**
Attending class	0.25	0.10	40
Homework and research	0.15	0.13	87
Consumer purchases	**0.48**	**0.45**	**94**
Shopping (store, telephone, Internet)	0.48	0.45	94
Grocery shopping	0.12	0.11	92
Shopping (except groceries, food, and gas)	0.33	0.30	91
Professional and personal care services	**0.12**	**0.10**	**83**
Medical and care services	0.06	0.05	83
Eating and drinking	**1.09**	**1.06**	**97**
Socializing, relaxing, and leisure	**4.29**	**3.38**	**79**
Socializing and communicating	0.69	0.69	100
Attending or hosting social events	0.10	0.09	90
Relaxing and leisure	3.40	2.49	73
Television and movies	2.38	1.88	79
Playing games	0.14	0.15	107
Computer use for leisure (except games)	0.11	0.10	91
Reading for personal interest	0.42	0.15	36
Arts and entertainment (other than sports)	0.10	0.10	100
Attending movies	0.03	0.04	133

	hours per day for total women	hours per day for women aged 25 to 34	index, 25 to 34 to total
Sports, exercise, and recreation	0.25	0.24	96
Participating in sports, exercise, and recreation	0.22	0.21	95
Attending sporting or recreational events	0.03	0.03	100
Religious and spiritual activities	0.18	0.15	83
Volunteer activities	0.18	0.10	56
Telephone calls	0.15	0.11	73
Traveling	1.18	1.29	109

Note: Primary activities are those respondents identified as their main activity. Other activities done simultaneously are not included. Travel related to activities is reported separately. Numbers do not sum to total because not all activities are shown. The index is calculated by dividing time spent by age group by time spent by average woman and multiplying by 100. "–" means sample is too small to make a reliable estimate.

Source: Bureau of Labor Statistics, unpublished tables from the 2007 American Time Use Survey, Internet site http://www.bls.gov/tus/home.htm

11

Wealth

■ Householders under age 35 (the oldest Millennials turned 30 in 2007) saw their median net worth plummet to just $11,800, down 24 percent between 2004 and 2007 after adjusting for inflation.

■ Only 39 percent of householders under age 35 owned stock in 2007, down from 41 percent in 2004. They saw the median value of their stock drop 20 percent during those years.

■ The value of nonfinancial assets owned by householders under age 35 took a 13 percent dive between 2004 and 2007, settling at a modest $30,900.

■ The percentage of householders under age 35 with debt grew almost 4 percentage points between 2004 and 2007. In 2007, 83.5 percent of the youngest householders were in debt, many with college loans.

■ Few Millennials are offered a workplace retirement plan, and even fewer participate. Among workers aged 21 to 24, only 19 percent participate in an employer's retirement plan. Among those aged 25 to 34 the figure is 39 percent.

Net Worth of Youngest Householders Fell Steeply

The growing burden of student loans is one reason for the decline.

Net worth is one of the most important measures of wealth. It is the amount that remains after a household's debts are subtracted from its assets. During this decade's housing bubble, housing values rose faster than mortgage debt. Consequently, net worth grew substantially—up 18 percent for the average household between 2004 and 2007, after adjusting for inflation. The gain did not last, however. The Federal Reserve Board estimates that by October 2008, median net worth for the average household had fallen to $99,000—3 percent less than in 2004.

Householders under age 35 (the oldest Millennials turned 30 in 2007) saw their median net worth plummet to $11,800 in 2007—24 percent below the level of 2004 after adjusting for inflation. Behind the decline in the net worth of the youngest householders was the growing share with debt, in part because so many young adults now have student loans.

■ In today's financial climate, householders under age 35 will have to struggle to grow their net worth.

Net worth of householders under age 35 fell between 2004 and 2007

(percent change in net worth of households by age of householder, 2004 to 2007; in 2007 dollars)

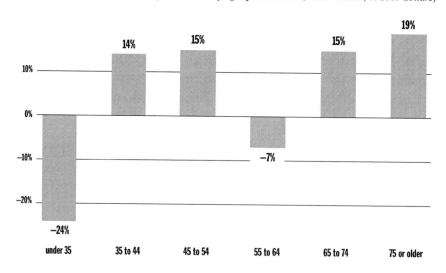

Table 11.1 Net Worth of Households by Age of Householder, 2004 to 2007

(median net worth of households by age of householder, 2004 to 2007; percent change, 2004–07; in 2007 dollars)

	2007	2004	percent change 2004–07
Total households	**$120,300**	**$102,200**	**17.7%**
Under age 35	11,800	15,600	–24.4
Aged 35 to 44	86,600	76,200	13.6
Aged 45 to 54	182,500	158,900	14.9
Aged 55 to 64	253,700	273,100	–7.1
Aged 65 to 74	239,400	208,800	14.7
Aged 75 or older	213,500	179,100	19.2

Source: Federal Reserve Board, Changes in U.S. Family Finances from 2004 to 2007: Evidence from the Survey of Consumer Finances, Federal Reserve Bulletin, February 2009, Internet site http://www.federalreserve.gov/pubs/oss/oss2/2007/scf2007home.html; calculations by New Strategist

Most Millennials Do Not Own Stock

Among those with stock, median value fell between 2004 and 2007.

Between 2004 and 2007, the value of the financial assets of the average American household rose 14 percent after adjusting for inflation—to a median of $28,800, according to the Federal Reserve Board's Survey of Consumer Finances. The median value of the financial assets owned by householders under age 35 grew at a faster clip—up 19 percent during those years to $6,800.

Only 39 percent of householders under age 35 owned stock in 2007, down from 41 percent in 2004. Householders under age 35 saw the median value of their stock drop by a substantial 20 percent during those years.

Over half of all households (53 percent) owned a retirement account in 2007. Not surprisingly, among householders under age 35 the figure is a lower 42 percent. Among those with retirement accounts, the median value was just $10,000 in 2007.

■ The value of financial assets owned by householders in every age group has plunged since these figures were collected by the Survey of Consumer Finances.

Millennials have few financial assets

(median value of financial assets of households, by age of householder, 2007)

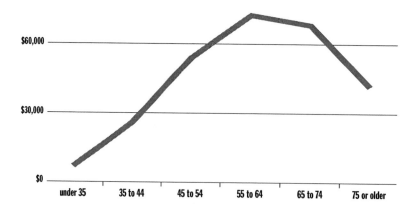

Table 11.2 Financial Assets of Households by Age of Householder, 2004 and 2007

(percentage of households owning financial assets and median value of assets for owners, by age of householder, 2004 and 2007; percentage point change in ownership and percent change in value of asset, 2004–07; in 2007 dollars)

	2007	2004	percentage point change
PERCENT OWNING ANY FINANCIAL ASSET			
Total households	**93.9%**	**93.8%**	**0.1**
Under age 35	89.2	90.1	−0.9
Aged 35 to 44	93.1	93.6	−0.5
Aged 45 to 54	93.3	93.6	−0.3
Aged 55 to 64	97.8	95.2	2.6
Aged 65 to 74	96.1	96.5	−0.4
Aged 75 or older	97.4	97.6	−0.2

	2007	2004	percent change
MEDIAN VALUE OF FINANCIAL ASSETS			
Total households	**$28,800**	**$25,300**	**13.8%**
Under age 35	6,800	5,700	19.3
Aged 35 to 44	25,800	20,900	23.4
Aged 45 to 54	54,000	42,400	27.4
Aged 55 to 64	72,400	85,700	−15.5
Aged 65 to 74	68,100	39,600	72.0
Aged 75 or older	41,500	42,600	−2.6

Source: Federal Reserve Board, Changes in U.S. Family Finances from 2004 to 2007: Evidence from the Survey of Consumer Finances, Federal Reserve Bulletin, February 2009, Internet site http://www.federalreserve.gov/pubs/oss/oss2/2007/scf2007home.html; calculations by New Strategist

Table 11.3 Financial Assets of Households by Type of Asset and Age of Householder, 2007

(percentage of households owning financial assets, and median value of asset for owners, by type of asset and age of householder, 2007)

	total	under 35	35 to 44	45 to 54	55 to 64	65 to 74	75 or older
PERCENT OWNING ASSET							
Any financial asset	**93.9%**	**89.2%**	**93.1%**	**93.3%**	**97.8%**	**96.1%**	**97.4%**
Transaction accounts	92.1	87.3	91.2	91.7	96.4	94.6	95.3
Certificates of deposit	16.1	6.7	9.0	14.3	20.5	24.2	37.0
Savings bonds	14.9	13.7	16.8	19.0	16.2	10.3	7.9
Bonds	1.6	–	0.7	1.1	2.1	4.2	3.5
Stocks	17.9	13.7	17.0	18.6	21.3	19.1	30.2
Pooled investment funds	11.4	5.3	11.6	12.6	14.3	14.6	13.2
Retirement accounts	52.6	41.6	57.5	64.7	60.9	51.7	30.0
Cash value life insurance	23.0	11.4	17.5	22.3	35.2	34.3	27.6
Other managed assets	5.8	–	2.2	5.1	7.7	13.2	14.0
Other financial assets	9.3	10.0	9.6	10.5	9.2	9.4	5.3
MEDIAN VALUE OF ASSET							
Any financial asset	**$28,800**	**$6,800**	**$25,800**	**$54,000**	**$72,400**	**$68,100**	**$41,500**
Transaction accounts	4,000	2,400	3,400	5,000	5,200	7,700	6,100
Certificates of deposit	20,000	5,000	5,000	15,000	23,000	23,200	30,000
Savings bonds	1,000	700	1,000	1,000	1,900	1,000	20,000
Bonds	80,000	–	9,700	200,000	90,800	50,000	100,000
Stocks	17,000	3,000	15,000	18,500	24,000	38,000	40,000
Pooled investment funds	56,000	18,000	22,500	50,000	112,000	86,000	75,000
Retirement accounts	45,000	10,000	36,000	67,000	98,000	77,000	35,000
Cash value life insurance	8,000	2,800	8,300	10,000	10,000	10,000	5,000
Other managed assets	70,000	–	24,000	45,000	59,000	70,000	100,000
Other financial assets	6,000	1,500	8,000	6,000	20,000	10,000	15,000

Note: "–" means sample is too small to make a reliable estimate.
Source: Federal Reserve Board, Changes in U.S. Family Finances from 2004 to 2007: Evidence from the Survey of Consumer Finances, Federal Reserve Bulletin, February 2009, Internet site http://www.federalreserve.gov/pubs/oss/oss2/2007/scf2007home.html; calculations by New Strategist

Table 11.4 Stock Ownership of Households by Age of Householder, 2004 and 2007

(percentage of households owning stock directly or indirectly, median value of stock for owners, and share of total household financial assets accounted for by stock holdings, by age of householder, 2004 and 2007; percent and percentage point change, 2004–07; in 2007 dollars)

	2007	2004	percentage point change
PERCENT OWNING STOCK			
Total households	**51.1%**	**50.2%**	**0.9**
Under age 35	38.6	40.8	–2.2
Aged 35 to 44	53.5	54.5	–1.0
Aged 45 to 54	60.4	56.5	3.9
Aged 55 to 64	58.9	62.8	–3.9
Aged 65 to 74	52.1	46.9	5.2
Aged 75 or older	40.1	34.8	5.3

	2007	2004	percent change
MEDIAN VALUE OF STOCK			
Total households	**$35,000**	**$35,700**	**–2.0%**
Under age 35	7,000	8,800	–20.5
Aged 35 to 44	26,000	22,000	18.2
Aged 45 to 54	45,000	54,900	–18.0
Aged 55 to 64	78,000	78,000	0.0
Aged 65 to 74	57,000	76,900	–25.9
Aged 75 or older	41,000	94,300	–56.5

	2007	2004	percentage point change
STOCK AS SHARE OF FINANCIAL ASSETS			
Total households	**53.3%**	**51.3%**	**2.0**
Under age 35	44.3	40.3	4.0
Aged 35 to 44	53.7	53.5	0.2
Aged 45 to 54	53.0	53.8	–0.8
Aged 55 to 64	55.0	55.0	0.0
Aged 65 to 74	55.3	51.5	3.8
Aged 75 or older	48.1	39.3	8.8

Source: Federal Reserve Board, Changes in U.S. Family Finances from 2004 to 2007: Evidence from the Survey of Consumer Finances, Federal Reserve Bulletin, February 2009, Internet site http://www.federalreserve.gov/pubs/oss/oss2/2007/scf2007home.html; calculations by New Strategist

Value of Nonfinancial Assets of Millennials Declined

Their homeownership rate retreated between 2004 and 2007.

The median value of nonfinancial assets owned by the average American household stood at $177,400 in 2007—9 percent more than in 2004, after adjusting for inflation. The value of nonfinancial assets owned by householders under age 35, however, took a 13 percent dive during those years. In 2007, the median value of the nonfinancial assets owned by householders in the age group stood at a modest $30,900.

Because housing equity accounts for the largest share of nonfinancial assets, the relatively low—and declining—homeownership rate of the age group wiped out any gains in the category. Only 41 percent of householders under age 35 owned a home in 2007, down 1 percentage point in three years. Among homeowners under age 35, median home value rose 18 percent in the same time span, after adjusting for inflation, to $175,000. There is little doubt that the bursting housing bubble and the financial tsunami of 2008–09 have reversed, or at least seriously slowed, the trend since then.

■ The drop in housing values since 2007 has greatly reduced household net worth.

Nonfinancial assets of Millennials are well below average

(median value of nonfinancial assets of households by age of householder, 2007)

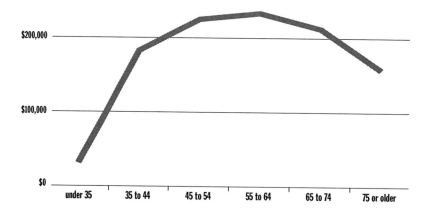

Table 11.5 Nonfinancial Assets of Households by Age of Householder, 2004 and 2007

(percentage of households owning nonfinancial assets and median value of assets for owners, by age of house-holder, 2004 and 2007; percentage point change in ownership and percent change in value of asset, 2004–07; in 2007 dollars)

	2007	2004	percentage point change
PERCENT OWNING ANY NONFINANCIAL ASSET			
Total households	**92.0%**	**92.5%**	**−0.5**
Under age 35	88.2	88.6	−0.4
Aged 35 to 44	91.3	93.0	−1.7
Aged 45 to 54	95.0	94.7	0.3
Aged 55 to 64	95.6	92.6	3.0
Aged 65 to 74	94.5	95.6	−1.1
Aged 75 or older	87.3	92.5	−5.2

	2007	2004	percent change
MEDIAN VALUE OF NONFINANCIAL ASSETS			
Total households	**$177,400**	**$162,300**	**9.3%**
Under age 35	30,900	35,500	−13.0
Aged 35 to 44	182,600	166,200	9.9
Aged 45 to 54	224,900	202,600	11.0
Aged 55 to 64	233,100	248,600	−6.2
Aged 65 to 74	212,200	177,000	19.9
Aged 75 or older	157,100	150,600	4.3

Source: Federal Reserve Board, Changes in U.S. Family Finances from 2004 to 2007: Evidence from the Survey of Consumer Finances, Federal Reserve Bulletin, February 2009, Internet site http://www.federalreserve.gov/pubs/oss/oss2/2007/scf2007home.html; calculations by New Strategist

Table 11.6 Nonfinancial Assets of Households by Type of Asset and Age of Householder, 2007

(percentage of households owning nonfinancial assets, and median value of asset for owners, by type of asset and age of householder, 2007)

	total	under 35	35 to 44	45 to 54	55 to 64	65 to 74	75 or older
PERCENT OWNING ASSET							
Any nonfinancial asset	**92.0%**	**88.2%**	**91.3%**	**95.0%**	**95.6%**	**94.5%**	**87.3%**
Vehicles	87.0	85.4	87.5	90.3	92.2	90.6	71.5
Primary residence	68.6	40.7	66.1	77.3	81.0	85.5	77.0
Other residential property	13.7	5.6	12.0	15.7	20.9	18.9	13.4
Equity in nonresidential property	8.1	3.2	7.5	9.5	11.5	12.3	6.8
Business equity	12.0	6.8	16.0	15.2	16.3	10.1	3.8
Other nonfinancial assets	7.2	5.9	5.5	8.7	8.5	9.1	5.8
MEDIAN VALUE OF ASSET							
Total nonfinancial assets	**$177,400**	**$30,900**	**$182,600**	**$224,900**	**$233,100**	**$212,200**	**$157,100**
Vehicles	15,500	13,300	17,400	18,700	17,400	14,600	9,400
Primary residence	200,000	175,000	205,000	230,000	210,000	200,000	150,000
Other residential property	146,000	85,000	150,000	150,000	157,000	150,000	100,000
Equity in nonresidential property	75,000	50,000	50,000	80,000	90,000	75,000	110,000
Business equity	100,500	59,900	86,000	100,000	116,300	415,000	250,000
Other nonfinancial assets	14,000	8,000	10,000	15,000	20,000	20,000	25,000

Source: Federal Reserve Board, Changes in U.S. Family Finances from 2004 to 2007: Evidence from the Survey of Consumer Finances, Federal Reserve Bulletin, February 2009, Internet site http://www.federalreserve.gov/pubs/oss/oss2/2007/ scf2007home.html; calculations by New Strategist

Table 11.7 Household Ownership of Primary Residence by Age of Householder, 2004 and 2007

(percentage of households owning their primary residence, median value of asset for owners, and median value of home-secured debt for owners, by age of householder, 2004 and 2007; percentage point change in ownership and percent change in value of asset, 2004–07; in 2007 dollars)

	2007	2004	percentage point change
PERCENT OWNING PRIMARY RESIDENCE			
Total households	**68.6%**	**69.1%**	**–0.5**
Under age 35	40.7	41.6	–0.9
Aged 35 to 44	66.1	68.3	–2.2
Aged 45 to 54	77.3	77.3	0.0
Aged 55 to 64	81.0	79.1	1.9
Aged 65 to 74	85.5	81.3	4.2
Aged 75 or older	77.0	85.2	–8.2

	2007	2004	percent change
MEDIAN VALUE OF PRIMARY RESIDENCE			
Total households	**$200,000**	**$175,700**	**13.8%**
Under age 35	175,000	148,300	18.0
Aged 35 to 44	205,000	175,700	16.7
Aged 45 to 54	230,000	186,700	23.2
Aged 55 to 64	210,000	218,700	–4.0
Aged 65 to 74	200,000	164,700	21.4
Aged 75 or older	150,000	137,300	9.2

	2007	2004	percent change
MEDIAN VALUE OF HOME-SECURED DEBT			
Total households	**$100,000**	**$95,600**	**4.6%**
Under age 35	78,000	68,600	13.7
Aged 35 to 44	101,600	82,400	23.3
Aged 45 to 54	82,000	95,600	–14.2
Aged 55 to 64	130,000	119,500	8.8
Aged 65 to 74	125,000	109,800	13.8
Aged 75 or older	50,000	42,800	16.8

Source: Federal Reserve Board, Changes in U.S. Family Finances from 2004 to 2007: Evidence from the Survey of Consumer Finances, Federal Reserve Bulletin, February 2009, Internet site http://www.federalreserve.gov/pubs/oss/oss2/2007/ scf2007home.html; calculations by New Strategist

A Growing Share of Millennials Are in Debt

Their median amount of debt changed little, however.

The median debt of the average American household grew 11 percent between 2004 and 2007 after adjusting for inflation—to $67,300. Among householders under age 35, however, median debt shrank a slight 2 percent during those years, to $36,200. The percentage of householders under age 35 with debt, on the other hand, grew almost 4 percentage points between 2004 and 2007, to 83.5 percent.

Home-secured debt accounts for the largest share of debt by far. Forty-nine percent of households have debt secured by their primary residence, and they owe a median of $107,000. The relatively few homeowners under age 35, who have had little time to pay off their mortgage, owe a median of $135,000 for their home. Only 48 percent of householders under age 35 carry a credit card balance; they owed a median of just $1,800 on credit cards in 2007. More important are installment loans, which include education debt and car loans. Sixty-five percent of householders under age 35 have such a loan—the largest share in any age group—and they owe a median of $15,000.

■ Many Millennials will find it difficult to pay off their student debt because jobs are scarce.

Millennials owe relatively little compared with other age groups

(median amount of debt owed by households, by age of householder, 2007)

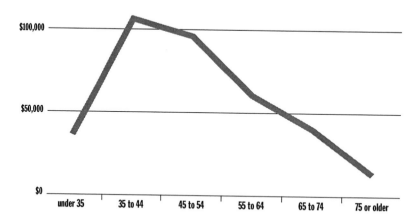

Table 11.8 Debt of Households by Age of Householder, 2004 and 2007

(percentage of households with debt and median amount of debt for debtors, by age of householder, 2004 and 2007; percentage point change in households with debt and percent change in amount of debt, 2004–07; in 2007 dollars)

	2007	2004	percentage point change
PERCENT WITH DEBT			
Total households	**77.0%**	**76.4%**	**0.6**
Under age 35	83.5	79.8	3.7
Aged 35 to 44	86.2	88.6	–2.4
Aged 45 to 54	86.8	88.4	–1.6
Aged 55 to 64	81.8	76.3	5.5
Aged 65 to 74	65.5	58.8	6.7
Aged 75 or older	31.4	40.3	–8.9

	2007	2004	percent change
MEDIAN AMOUNT OF DEBT			
Total households	**$67,300**	**$60,700**	**10.9%**
Under age 35	36,200	36,900	–1.9
Aged 35 to 44	106,200	95,800	10.9
Aged 45 to 54	95,900	91,400	4.9
Aged 55 to 64	60,300	52,700	14.4
Aged 65 to 74	40,100	27,500	45.8
Aged 75 or older	13,000	16,900	–23.1

Source: Federal Reserve Board, Changes in U.S. Family Finances from 2004 to 2007: Evidence from the Survey of Consumer Finances, Federal Reserve Bulletin, February 2009, Internet site http://www.federalreserve.gov/pubs/oss/oss2/2007/scf2007home.html; calculations by New Strategist

Table 11.9 Debt of Households by Type of Debt and Age of Householder, 2007

(percentage of households with debt, and median value of debt for those with debt, by type of debt and age of householder, 2007)

	total	under 35	35 to 44	45 to 54	55 to 64	65 to 74	75 or older
PERCENT WITH DEBT							
Any debt	77.0%	83.5%	86.2%	86.8%	81.8%	65.5%	31.4%
Secured by residential property							
Primary residence	48.7	37.3	59.5	65.5	55.3	42.9	13.9
Other	5.5	3.3	6.5	8.0	7.8	5.0	0.6
Lines of credit not secured by residential property	1.7	2.1	2.2	1.9	1.2	1.5	–
Installment loans	46.9	65.2	56.2	51.9	44.6	26.1	7.0
Credit card balances	46.1	48.5	51.7	53.6	49.9	37.0	18.8
Other debt	6.8	5.9	7.5	9.8	8.7	4.4	1.3
MEDIAN AMOUNT OF DEBT							
Any debt	$67,300	$36,200	$106,200	$95,900	$60,300	$40,100	$13,000
Secured by residential property							
Primary residence	107,000	135,300	128,000	110,000	85,000	69,000	40,000
Other	100,000	78,000	101,600	82,000	130,000	125,000	50,000
Lines of credit not secured by residential property	3,800	1,000	4,600	6,000	10,000	30,000	–
Installment loans	13,000	15,000	13,500	12,900	10,900	10,300	8,000
Credit card balances	3,000	1,800	3,500	3,600	3,600	3,000	800
Other debt	5,000	4,500	5,000	4,500	6,000	5,000	4,500

Note: "–" means sample is too small to make a reliable estimate.
Source: Federal Reserve Board, Changes in U.S. Family Finances from 2004 to 2007: Evidence from the Survey of Consumer Finances, Federal Reserve Bulletin, February 2009, Internet site http://www.federalreserve.gov/pubs/oss/oss2/2007/scf2007home.html; calculations by New Strategist

Few Millennials Participate in a Workplace Retirement Plan

Only half of 25-to-34-year-old workers are even offered a plan by their employers.

Fifty-two percent of American workers were offered an employer-sponsored retirement plan in 2007, but only 41.5 percent took advantage of the opportunity, according to an analysis by the Employee Benefit Research Institute (EBRI). Retirement plan participation peaks among older workers at just over 50 percent. Among workers aged 21 to 24, only 19 percent participate in an employer's retirement plan, although twice as many are eligible to do so. Among those aged 25 to 34, participation is a higher 39 percent (51 percent are eligible).

Another EBRI study shows that only 35 percent of workers aged 25 to 34, and just 11 percent of those aged 21 to 24, own an IRA or participate in a 401(k)-type retirement plan. Among those aged 25 to 34 who participate in 401(k)-type plans, just one in 20 made the maximum contribution.

Even at their youthful age, many young adults worry about retirement. Only 18 percent of workers aged 25 to 34 are "very confident" they will have enough money to live comfortably throughout retirement, according to EBRI's Retirement Confidence Survey. Nevertheless, 31 percent think they will be able to retire before age 65.

■ The substitution of defined-contribution for defined-benefit pension plans puts the burden of retirement savings on workers rather than employers.

Few Millennials participate in an employer-sponsored retirement plan

(percent of workers who are offered and participate in an employer-sponsored retirement plan, by age, 2004)

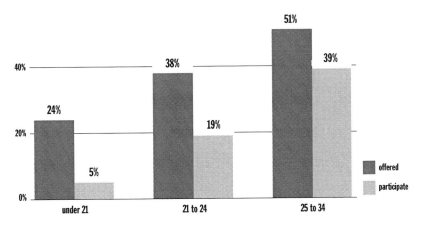

Table 11.10 Retirement Plan Coverage by Age, 2007

(total number of workers, percent whose employer offers a retirement plan, and percent participating in plan, by type of employment and age of worker, 2007; numbers in thousands)

	number of workers	percent with an employer who sponsors a retirement plan	percent participating in employer's retirement plan
Total workers	**158,099**	**51.8%**	**41.5%**
Under age 21	10,450	24.0	4.9
Aged 21 to 24	12,695	38.5	19.3
Aged 25 to 34	33,485	51.1	38.7
Aged 35 to 44	35,299	55.8	47.5
Aged 45 to 54	36,139	59.3	52.6
Aged 55 to 64	22,782	59.2	52.0
Aged 65 or older	7,249	39.1	28.7
PRIVATE WAGE AND SALARY WORKERS AGED 21 TO 64			
Total workers	**110,148**	**52.7**	**42.0**
Aged 21 to 24	11,397	37.3	17.9
Aged 25 to 34	27,816	48.9	35.7
Aged 35 to 44	27,788	54.5	45.3
Aged 45 to 54	27,068	58.1	50.7
Aged 55 to 64	16,079	57.7	49.9
PUBLIC WAGE AND SALARY WORKERS AGED 21 TO 64			
Total workers	**21,106**	**83.3**	**75.4**
Aged 21 to 24	1,035	58.5	38.9
Aged 25 to 34	4,250	80.1	69.5
Aged 35 to 44	5,183	84.3	77.7
Aged 45 to 54	6,179	85.7	79.9
Aged 55 to 64	4,459	87.9	80.7

Source: Employee Benefit Research Institute, Employment-Based Retirement Plan Participation: Geographic Differences and Trends, 2007, Issue Brief 322, October 2008, Internet site http://www.ebri.org/publications/ib/index.cfm?fa=ibDisp&content_ id=3989

Table 11.11 Ownership of IRAs and 401(k)s by Age, 2005

(percentage of workers aged 21 to 64 owning IRAs and/or participating in a 401(k)-type plan, by age, 2005)

	IRA and/or 401(k)-type plan	IRA only	401(k)-type plan only	both IRA and 401(k)-type plan	neither IRA nor 401(k)-type plan
Total workers	**43.8%**	**10.7%**	**20.9%**	**12.2%**	**56.2%**
Aged 21 to 24	11.4	2.1	8.3	1.0	88.6
Aged 25 to 34	35.4	6.6	20.4	8.4	64.6
Aged 35 to 44	47.4	10.2	24.4	12.8	52.6
Aged 45 to 54	51.2	12.4	22.7	16.1	48.8
Aged 55 to 64	52.1	18.5	18.2	15.4	47.9

Source: Employee Benefit Research Institute, Ownership of Individual Retirement Accounts (IRAs) and 401(k)-Type Plans, by Craig Copeland, Notes, Vol. 29, No. 5, May 2008, Internet site http://www.ebri.org/publications/notes/index.cfm?fa=main&doc_type=2

Table 11.12 Participation in IRAs and 401(k)s by Age, 2005

(percent of workers aged 21 to 64 owning an IRA or participating in 401(k)-type plan, percent making a contribution to the IRA, and mean amount contributed and percent making maximum contribution among contributors, by age, 2005)

	has IRA in own name	made tax-deductible contribution to IRA	among IRA contributors mean contribution	among IRA contributors percent making maximum contribution
Total workers	**22.9%**	**6.2%**	**$2,540**	**26.8%**
Aged 21 to 24	3.2	0.6	1,149	0.0
Aged 25 to 34	15.0	4.3	2,089	20.5
Aged 35 to 44	23.0	6.4	2,497	31.3
Aged 45 to 54	28.5	7.4	2,527	25.0
Aged 55 to 64	33.9	9.2	2,943	29.3

	percent participating in 401(k)	among 401(k) contributors mean contribution	among 401(k) contributors percent making maximum contribution
Total workers	**33.1%**	**$4,274**	**8.9%**
Aged 21 to 24	9.3	1,597	0.0
Aged 25 to 34	28.8	3,353	5.0
Aged 35 to 44	37.2	4,226	8.4
Aged 45 to 54	38.8	1,695	10.3
Aged 55 to 64	33.5	4,993	13.2

Source: Employee Benefit Research Institute, Ownership of Individual Retirement Accounts (IRAs) and 401(k)-Type Plans, by Craig Copeland, Notes, Vol. 29, No. 5, May 2008, Internet site http://www.ebri.org/publications/notes/index.cfm?fa=main&doc_type=2

Table 11.13 Retirement Planning by Age, 2009

(percentage of workers aged 25 or older responding by age, 2009)

	total	25 to 34	35 to 44	45 to 54	55 or older
Very confident in having enough money to live comfortably throughout retirement	13%	18%	12%	10%	13%
Very confident in having enough money to take care of medical expenses in retirement	13	16	13	11	14
Worker and/or spouse have saved for retirement	75	66	78	78	79
Worker and/or spouse are currently saving for retirement	65	57	68	68	66
Contribute to a workplace retirement savings plan	64	52	72	65	64
Expected retirement age					
Before age 60	9	17	8	9	1
Aged 60 to 64	17	14	16	17	22
Aged 65	23	29	29	18	15
Aged 66 or older	31	22	33	35	34
Never retire	10	9	6	13	11
Don't know/refused	7	8	3	6	12
Total savings and investments (not including value of primary residence)					
Less than $25,000	53	73	53	43	36
$25,000 to $49,999	11	12	8	11	13
$50,000 to $99,999	12	9	14	14	10
$100,000 to $249,999	12	5	16	15	15
$250,000 or more	12	2	9	17	26

Source: Employee Benefit Research Institute, Retirement Confidence Surveys, Internet site http://www.ebri.org/surveys/rcs/2009/

Table 11.14 Changes in Retirement Confidence by Age, 1999 and 2009

(percentage of workers aged 25 or older responding by age, 1999 and 2009)

	total	25 to 34	35 to 44	45 to 54	55 or older
Very confident in having enough money to live comfortably throughout retirement					
2009	13%	18%	12%	10%	13%
1999	22	27	20	21	18
Very confident in having enough money to take care of medical expenses in retirement					
2009	13	16	13	11	14
1999	16	16	15	13	22
Say they are doing a good job of preparing financially for retirement					
2009	20	23	21	18	16
1999	23	22	22	24	29

Source: Employee Benefit Research Institute, Retirement Confidence Surveys, Internet site http://www.ebri.org/surveys/rcs/2009/

Special Supplement

The iGeneration

Americans Born 1995 to the Present

12

Education

■ Most young children today are in school. The percentage of 3-to-4-year-olds enrolled in nursery school or kindergarten has grown substantially over the decades, from 38 percent in 1987 to 55 percent in 2007.

■ Ten states have minority majorities in their public schools: Hawaii (81 percent minority), California (70 percent), New Mexico (69 percent), Texas (64 percent), Nevada (56 percent), Arizona (55 percent), Mississippi (54 percent), Maryland (52 percent), Georgia (52 percent), and Florida (52 percent).

■ Only 25 percent of students in the nation's private schools are minority compared with 44 percent of students in public schools.

■ Most of today's parents are actively involved in their children's education. The parents of 89 percent of the nation's elementary and secondary school children say they attended a PTA or general school meeting during the past year.

■ Complaints about the nation's schools are commonplace, but in fact the parents of most children in kindergarten through 12th grade are "very satisfied" with various aspects of their child's school.

Most Young Children Attend School

The percentage of 3- and 4-year-olds enrolled in school rises with mother's education.

Most young children today are in school. The percentage of 3-to-4-year-olds enrolled in nursery school or kindergarten has grown substantially over the decades, from 38 percent in 1987 to the 55 percent majority in 2007.

A mother's labor force status has a surprisingly small effect on nursery school or kindergarten enrollment. Among 3-to-4-year-olds whose mother works full-time, 59 percent were enrolled in school in 2007. Among those whose mother is not in the labor force, 50 percent were in school. A mother's educational attainment is a more important factor in the school enrollment of young children. Among 3-to-4-year-olds whose mother has a bachelor's degree, two-thirds are in nursery school or kindergarten compared with a much smaller 41 percent of children whose mother did not graduate from high school.

■ Enrolling children in preschool has become the norm, especially for working women and college graduates.

The school enrollment of young children has grown substantially

(percent of 3-to-4-year-olds enrolled in nursery school or kindergarten, 1987 and 2007)

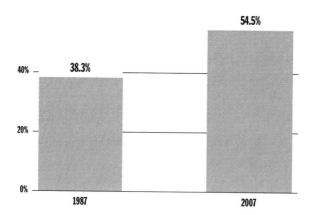

Table 12.1 Three- and Four-Year-Olds Enrolled in School, 1980 to 2007

(percentage of three- and four-year-olds enrolled in nursery school or kindergarten, 1980 to 2007)

Year	Percentage
2007	54.5%
2006	55.7
2005	53.6
2004	54.0
2003	55.1
2002	54.5
2001	52.2
2000	52.1
1999	54.2
1998	52.1
1997	52.6
1996	48.3
1995	48.7
1994	47.3
1993	40.1
1992	39.7
1991	40.5
1990	44.4
1989	39.1
1988	38.2
1987	38.3
1986	39.0
1985	38.9
1984	36.3
1983	37.6
1982	36.4
1981	36.0
1980	36.7

Source: Bureau of the Census, School Enrollment, Historical Tables, Internet site http://www.census.gov/population/www/socdemo/school.html

Table 12.2 School Enrollment Status of Children Aged 3 to 6 by Labor Force Status of Mother, 2007

(number and percent distribution of children aged 3 to 6 by labor force status of mother and school enrollment status, by age of child, 2007; numbers in thousands)

			enrolled		
	total	not enrolled	nursery school	kindergarten	elementary school
Aged 3 to 4	**8,234**	**3,743**	**4,008**	**483**	**0**
Mother employed full-time	3,221	1,318	1,724	179	0
Mother employed part-time	1,327	549	720	57	0
Mother unemployed	286	153	111	22	0
Mother not in the labor force	2,802	1,402	1,224	176	0
Aged 5	**4,091**	**311**	**561**	**3,004**	**215**
Mother employed full-time	1,688	112	224	1,281	72
Mother employed part-time	571	22	86	443	20
Mother unemployed	157	16	15	104	23
Mother not in the labor force	1,379	125	205	962	87
Aged 6	**4,140**	**128**	**59**	**576**	**3,376**
Mother employed full-time	1,796	41	41	222	1,492
Mother employed part-time	646	14	3	104	525
Mother unemployed	110	1	3	5	100
Mother not in the labor force	1,262	58	9	215	980

PERCENT DISTRIBUTION BY SCHOOL ENROLLMENT STATUS

Aged 3 to 4	**100.0%**	**45.5%**	**48.7%**	**5.9%**	**0.0%**
Mother employed full-time	100.0	40.9	53.5	5.6	0.0
Mother employed part-time	100.0	41.4	54.3	4.3	0.0
Mother unemployed	100.0	53.5	38.8	7.7	0.0
Mother not in the labor force	100.0	50.0	43.7	6.3	0.0
Aged 5	**100.0**	**7.6**	**13.7**	**73.4**	**5.3**
Mother employed full-time	100.0	6.6	13.3	75.9	4.3
Mother employed part-time	100.0	3.9	15.1	77.6	3.5
Mother unemployed	100.0	10.2	9.6	66.2	14.6
Mother not in the labor force	100.0	9.1	14.9	69.8	6.3
Aged 6	**100.0**	**3.1**	**1.4**	**13.9**	**81.5**
Mother employed full-time	100.0	2.3	2.3	12.4	83.1
Mother employed part-time	100.0	2.2	0.5	16.1	81.3
Mother unemployed	100.0	0.9	2.7	4.5	90.9
Mother not in the labor force	100.0	4.6	0.7	17.0	77.7

Note: Numbers do not add to age totals because "children not living with mother" is not shown.
Source: Bureau of the Census, School Enrollment—Social and Economic Characteristics of Students: October 2007, Internet site http://www.census.gov/population/www/socdemo/school/cps2007.html; calculations by New Strategist

Table 12.3 School Enrollment Status of Children Aged 3 to 6 by Education of Mother, 2007

(number and percent distribution of children aged 3 to 6 by educational attainment of mother and school enrollment status, by age of child, 2007; numbers in thousands)

			enrolled		
	total	not enrolled	nursery school	kindergarten	elementary school
Aged 3 to 4	**8,234**	**3,743**	**4,008**	**483**	**0**
Not a high school graduate	1,063	628	348	87	0
High school graduate	2,119	1,115	856	148	0
Some college or associate's degree	2,111	898	1,135	78	0
Bachelor's degree or more	2,344	782	1,439	123	0
Aged 5	**4,091**	**311**	**561**	**3,004**	**215**
Not a high school graduate	626	81	87	418	39
High school graduate	948	68	110	720	50
Some college or associate's degree	1,132	71	168	828	64
Bachelor's degree or more	1,090	54	164	823	49
Aged 6	**4,140**	**128**	**59**	**576**	**3,376**
Not a high school graduate	477	27	7	66	377
High school graduate	1,049	35	14	137	864
Some college or associate's degree	1,107	30	11	166	900
Bachelor's degree or more	1,180	22	24	178	956

PERCENT DISTRIBUTION BY SCHOOL ENROLLMENT STATUS

Aged 3 to 4	**100.0%**	**45.5%**	**48.7%**	**5.9%**	**0.0%**
Not a high school graduate	100.0	59.1	32.7	8.2	0.0
High school graduate	100.0	52.6	40.4	7.0	0.0
Some college or associate's degree	100.0	42.5	53.8	3.7	0.0
Bachelor's degree or more	100.0	33.4	61.4	5.2	0.0
Aged 5	**100.0**	**7.6**	**13.7**	**73.4**	**5.3**
Not a high school graduate	100.0	12.9	13.9	66.8	6.2
High school graduate	100.0	7.2	11.6	75.9	5.3
Some college or associate's degree	100.0	6.3	14.8	73.1	5.7
Bachelor's degree or more	100.0	5.0	15.0	75.5	4.5
Aged 6	**100.0**	**3.1**	**1.4**	**13.9**	**81.5**
Not a high school graduate	100.0	5.7	1.5	13.8	79.0
High school graduate	100.0	3.3	1.3	13.1	82.4
Some college or associate's degree	100.0	2.7	1.0	15.0	81.3
Bachelor's degree or more	100.0	1.9	2.0	15.1	81.0

Note: Numbers do not add to age totals because "children not living with mother" is not shown.
Source: Bureau of the Census, School Enrollment—Social and Economic Characteristics of Students: October 2007, Internet site http://www.census.gov/population/www/socdemo/school/cps2007.html; calculations by New Strategist

Diversity in Public Schools Is on the Rise

In 10 states minority students are the majority.

School attendance has become common even among preschoolers. Among children aged 5, fully 92 percent attended school in 2007. The figure was 68 percent among children aged 4 and a substantial 41 percent among 3-year-olds.

With Asians, blacks, and Hispanics accounting for a growing percentage of children, the minority share of public school students is rising—although it varies considerably by state. The figure ranges from a low of 5 percent in Maine and Vermont to a high of 95 percent in the District of Columbia. Ten states have minority majorities in their public schools: Hawaii (81 percent minority), California (70 percent), New Mexico (69 percent), Texas (64 percent), Nevada (56 percent), Arizona (55 percent), Mississippi (54 percent), Maryland (52 percent), Georgia (52 percent), and Florida (52 percent).

Only 25 percent of students in the nation's private schools are minority compared with 44 percent of students in public schools. The 82 percent majority of private school pupils attend a religiously affiliated institution. Private schools in the South capture one-third of the market.

■ Private school enrollment may decline as the economic downturn forces more parents to send their children to public school.

Minorities account for a smaller share of private school students

(percent of students who are American Indian, Asian, black, or Hispanic, by control of school, 2005–06)

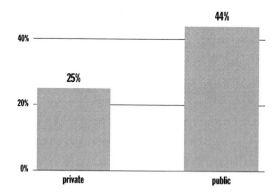

Table 12.4 School Enrollment by Age, 2007

(total people, number aged 3 to 18, and number and percent enrolled in school, by age, 2007; numbers in thousands)

		enrolled	
	total	number	percent
Total people	**285,410**	**75,967**	**26.6%**
Aged 3 to 18	65,553	59,203	90.3
Aged 3	4,142	1,717	41.5
Aged 4	4,092	2,774	67.8
Aged 5	4,091	3,780	92.4
Aged 6	4,140	4,012	96.9
Aged 7	3,967	3,875	97.7
Aged 8	3,904	3,830	98.1
Aged 9	3,875	3,815	98.5
Aged 10	4,028	3,953	98.1
Aged 11	3,903	3,866	99.1
Aged 12	4,308	4,234	98.3
Aged 13	4,004	3,958	98.9
Aged 14	4,086	4,020	98.4
Aged 15	4,155	4,116	99.1
Aged 16	4,339	4,169	96.1
Aged 17	4,363	4,035	92.5
Aged 18	4,156	3,049	73.4
Aged 19 or older	219,857	16,764	7.6

Source: Bureau of the Census, School Enrollment—Social and Economic Characteristics of Students: October 2007, Internet site http://www.census.gov/population/www/socdemo/school/cps2007.html; calculations by New Strategist

Table 12.5 Enrollment in Nursery School through High School, 2007

(number and percent distribution of people attending nursery school through high school, fall 2007; numbers in thousands)

	number	percent distribution
TOTAL, NURSERY SCHOOL THROUGH 12TH GRADE	58,010	100.0%
Nursery school	4,628	8.0
Kindergarten	4,132	7.1
Elementary and middle, total	32,169	55.5
1st grade	4,174	7.2
2nd grade	3,920	6.8
3rd grade	3,991	6.9
4th grade	4,011	6.9
5th grade	3,837	6.6
6th grade	4,184	7.2
7th grade	4,101	7.1
8th grade	3,951	6.8
High school, total	17,081	29.4
9th grade	4,291	7.4
10th grade	4,259	7.3
11th grade	4,080	7.0
12th grade	4,451	7.7

Source: Bureau of the Census, School Enrollment—Social and Economic Characteristics of Students: October 2007, Internet site http://www.census.gov/population/www/socdemo/school/cps2007.html; calculations by New Strategist

Table 12.6 Enrollment in Public Elementary and Secondary School by State, Race, and Hispanic Origin, 2006

(percent distribution of students enrolled in public elementary and secondary school by state, race, and Hispanic origin, 2006)

	total	minority students					non-Hispanic white
		total	American Indian	Asian	black	Hispanic	
Total public school children	**100.0%**	**43.5%**	**1.2%**	**4.7%**	**17.1%**	**20.5%**	**56.5%**
Alabama	100.0	41.0	0.8	1.1	35.9	3.2	59.1
Alaska	100.0	42.6	26.6	7.0	4.6	4.4	57.4
Arizona	100.0	54.6	5.6	2.6	5.4	41.0	45.4
Arkansas	100.0	32.4	0.7	1.5	22.7	7.5	67.6
California	100.0	69.8	0.8	11.7	7.8	49.5	30.2
Colorado	100.0	38.1	1.2	3.3	6.0	27.6	61.9
Connecticut	100.0	34.0	0.4	3.7	13.9	16.0	66.0
Delaware	100.0	46.2	0.4	3.0	33.0	9.8	53.9
District of Columbia	100.0	95.0	0.1	1.6	83.4	9.9	5.0
Florida	100.0	51.6	0.3	2.4	23.9	25.0	48.4
Georgia	100.0	51.7	0.1	2.9	39.2	9.5	48.2
Hawaii	100.0	80.5	0.6	73.0	2.4	4.5	19.6
Idaho	100.0	17.7	1.6	1.6	1.1	13.4	82.3
Illinois	100.0	44.1	0.2	3.9	20.3	19.7	55.9
Indiana	100.0	20.5	0.3	1.3	12.6	6.3	79.5
Iowa	100.0	14.1	0.6	2.0	5.3	6.2	85.9
Kansas	100.0	26.1	1.7	2.5	8.9	13.0	73.9
Kentucky	100.0	14.2	0.1	1.0	10.7	2.4	85.8
Louisiana	100.0	50.0	0.8	1.4	45.4	2.4	50.1
Maine	100.0	5.4	0.7	1.4	2.3	1.0	94.6
Maryland	100.0	52.2	0.4	5.4	38.1	8.3	47.8
Massachusetts	100.0	27.2	0.3	4.9	8.4	13.6	72.9
Michigan	100.0	28.0	0.9	2.4	20.2	4.5	71.8
Minnesota	100.0	22.8	2.1	5.9	9.1	5.7	77.2
Mississippi	100.0	53.5	0.2	0.8	50.8	1.7	46.5
Missouri	100.0	23.6	0.4	1.7	18.1	3.4	76.3
Montana	100.0	16.1	11.4	1.2	1.0	2.5	83.9
Nebraska	100.0	23.5	1.7	1.9	7.7	12.2	76.5
Nevada	100.0	55.7	1.6	7.6	11.1	35.4	44.4
New Hampshire	100.0	7.0	0.3	2.0	1.8	2.9	92.9
New Jersey	100.0	44.3	0.2	7.9	17.4	18.8	55.7
New Mexico	100.0	69.4	10.9	1.3	2.6	54.6	30.6
New York	100.0	48.0	0.5	7.2	19.7	20.6	52.1
North Carolina	100.0	42.6	1.5	2.3	29.2	9.6	57.5
North Dakota	100.0	13.2	8.6	1.0	1.8	1.8	86.8
Ohio	100.0	21.2	0.1	1.4	17.1	2.6	78.8
Oklahoma	100.0	41.4	19.3	1.8	10.8	9.5	58.6
Oregon	100.0	26.8	2.2	4.8	3.1	16.7	73.2

| | total | minority students | | | | | non-Hispanic white |
		total	American Indian	Asian	black	Hispanic	
Pennsylvania	100.0%	25.5%	0.2%	2.6%	15.9%	6.8%	74.6%
Rhode Island	100.0	30.6	0.7	3.1	8.8	18.0	69.5
South Carolina	100.0	46.1	0.3	1.4	39.8	4.6	53.9
South Dakota	100.0	15.4	10.6	1.0	1.7	2.1	84.5
Tennessee	100.0	30.9	0.2	1.5	24.8	4.4	69.1
Texas	100.0	64.3	0.3	3.3	14.4	46.3	35.7
Utah	100.0	19.2	1.5	3.1	1.4	13.2	80.8
Vermont	100.0	4.6	0.4	1.6	1.6	1.0	95.3
Virginia	100.0	40.7	0.3	5.4	26.7	8.3	59.3
Washington	100.0	31.0	2.6	8.4	5.7	14.3	68.9
West Virginia	100.0	6.7	0.1	0.7	5.1	0.8	93.3
Wisconsin	100.0	22.8	1.5	3.6	10.5	7.2	77.3
Wyoming	100.0	15.5	3.5	1.1	1.5	9.4	84.5

Source: National Center for Education Statistics, Digest of Education Statistics: 2008, Internet site http://nces.ed.gov/programs/digest/d07/tables/dt07_040.asp

Table 12.7 Enrollment in Private Elementary and Secondary Schools, 2005

(total number and percent distribution of students enrolled in private elementary and secondary schools by school characteristic, race, and Hispanic origin, 2005; numbers in thousands)

	total			minority				
	number	percent distribution	non-Hispanic white	total	American Indian	Asian	black	Hispanic
TOTAL STUDENTS	5,058	100.0%	75.4%	24.6%	0.7%	5.1%	9.5%	9.2%
Affiliation								
Roman Catholic	2,246	44.4	74.1	25.9	0.7	4.7	7.9	12.6
Other religions	1,885	37.3	77.8	22.2	0.5	4.5	10.8	6.3
Nonsectarian	927	18.3	73.7	26.3	1.0	7.4	10.8	7.0
School level								
Elementary	2,551	50.4	73.7	26.3	0.7	5.2	9.7	10.7
Secondary	859	17.0	75.4	24.6	0.7	5.2	8.3	10.5
Combined	1,647	32.6	78.2	21.8	0.7	4.9	9.8	6.4
Enrollment								
Fewer than 50	236	4.7	71.5	28.5	1.1	3.8	15.1	8.5
50 to 149	763	15.1	71.3	28.7	1.0	4.5	14.2	9.0
150 to 299	1,322	26.1	70.6	29.4	0.6	5.5	11.7	11.6
300 to 499	1,090	21.5	78.2	21.8	0.6	4.9	7.8	8.5
500 to 749	805	15.9	80.0	20.0	0.7	5.2	5.8	8.3
750 or more	842	16.7	80.0	20.0	0.5	5.7	6.1	7.7
Region								
Northeast	1,203	23.8	75.5	24.5	0.4	4.3	11.6	8.2
Midwest	1,233	24.4	84.0	16.0	0.7	2.4	8.0	4.8
South	1,626	32.2	76.2	23.8	0.4	3.2	11.3	8.8
West	995	19.7	63.5	36.5	1.4	12.5	6.0	16.6
Locale								
City	2,142	42.4	68.5	31.5	0.5	6.3	12.8	11.9
Suburban	1,949	38.5	77.4	22.6	0.6	4.8	8.5	8.7
Town	365	7.2	88.2	11.8	0.8	2.6	3.2	5.3
Rural	601	11.9	86.2	13.8	1.6	3.3	5.1	3.8

Note: Race categories exclude persons of Hispanic ethnicity.
Source: National Center for Education Statistics, The Condition of Education 2008, Trends in Private School Enrollments, Internet site http://nces.ed.gov/programs/coe/2008/section1/indicator04.asp

Parents Are Involved in Their Children's Education

In the past year, most have attended a school meeting, a parent–teacher conference, and a school or class event

Most of today's parents are actively involved in their children's education. The parents of 89 percent of the nation's elementary and secondary school children say they attended a PTA or general school meeting during the past year, according to a survey by the National Center for Education Statistics. Seventy-eight percent attended a parent–teacher conference, 74 percent attended a class event, and 46 percent volunteered.

Participation in a child's education typically rises with the educational attainment of the parent. The percentage of children whose parents attended a class event, for example, climbs from 48 percent among parents who did not graduate from high school to more than 80 percent among parents with at least a bachelor's degree. Surprisingly, however, the most educated parents are least likely to check their children's homework. Among students with homework, only 81 percent of parents with a graduate degree make sure their child has done his homework compared with 94 percent of parents without a high school diploma.

■ Poor parents are more likely than the nonpoor to make sure their child has done his homework.

Educated parents are most likely to attend their children's class events

(percent of children whose parents attended a class event in the past year, by educational attainment of parent, 2006–07)

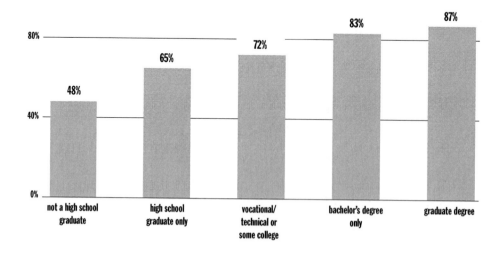

Table 12.8 Parental Involvement in School Activities, 2006–07

(total number and percent of elementary and secondary school children whose parents reported participation in school activities, by selected characteristics of child and parent, 2006–07)

	total		parent attended a PTA or general school meeting	parent attended a parent–teacher conference	parent attended a school or class event	parent volunteered at school	parent participated in school fundraising
	number	percent					
TOTAL CHILDREN	51,600	100%	89%	78%	74%	46%	65%
Race and Hispanic origin of child							
Asian, non-Hispanic	1,566	100	90	80	72	46	62
Black, non-Hispanic	7,837	100	87	77	65	35	58
Hispanic	9,767	100	87	80	65	32	51
White, non-Hispanic	29,832	100	91	78	80	54	72
Educational attainment of parent							
Not a high school graduate	3,504	100	75	70	48	20	34
High school graduate	11,070	100	84	74	65	33	55
Vocational/technical or some college	14,844	100	89	77	72	42	67
Bachelor's degree	11,353	100	94	81	83	56	72
Graduate degree	10,829	100	95	82	87	64	77
School type							
Public, assigned	37,168	100	89	76	72	42	63
Public, chosen	7,951	100	88	81	74	45	62
Private, religious	4,560	100	96	96	86	73	85
Private, nonreligious	1,438	100	97	90	86	68	72
Student's grade level							
Kindergarten through 2nd grade	11,516	100	93	90	78	63	72
3rd through 5th grade	11,519	100	94	92	83	57	71
6th through 8th grade	12,058	100	91	76	72	38	63
9th through 12th grade	16,503	100	83	61	68	34	57
Poverty status							
Poor	10,012	100	81	77	56	26	45
Not poor	41,587	100	91	78	79	51	70

Source: National Center for Education Statistics, Parent and Family Involvement in Education, 2006–07 School Year, from the National Household Education Surveys Program of 2007, August 2008, Internet site http://nces.ed.gov/pubsearch/pubsinfo .asp?pubid=2008050; calculations by New Strategist

Table 12.9 Parental Involvement in Child's Homework, 2006–07

(total number and percent of elementary and secondary school children whose parents reported involvement with child's homework, by selected characteristics of child and parent, 2006–07)

| | total | | | student does homework outside of school | |
	number	percent	total	place in home set aside for homework	adult in household checks that homework is done
TOTAL CHILDREN	51,600	100%	94%	89%	85%
Race and Hispanic origin of child					
Asian, non-Hispanic	1,566	100	96	93	83
Black, non-Hispanic	7,837	100	94	94	94
Hispanic	9,767	100	94	84	91
White, non-Hispanic	29,832	100	95	89	82
Educational attainment of parent					
Not a high school graduate	3,504	100	90	83	94
High school graduate	11,070	100	93	89	89
Vocational/technical or some college	14,844	100	94	90	86
Bachelor's degree	11,353	100	96	87	83
Graduate degree	10,829	100	96	90	81
School type					
Public, assigned	37,168	100	94	89	86
Public, chosen	7,951	100	95	90	88
Private, religious	4,560	100	97	86	79
Private, nonreligious	1,438	100	90	85	84
Student's grade level					
Kindergarten through 2nd grade	11,516	100	93	84	100
3rd through 5th grade	11,519	100	97	89	97
6th through 8th grade	12,058	100	95	91	88
9th through 12th grade	16,503	100	93	91	65
Poverty status					
Poor	10,012	100	93	87	93
Not poor	41,587	100	95	89	84

Source: National Center for Education Statistics, Parent and Family Involvement in Education, 2006–07 School Year, from the National Household Education Surveys Program of 2007, August 2008, Internet site http://nces.ed.gov/pubsearch/pubsinfo .asp?pubid=2008050; calculations by New Strategist

Most Parents Are Satisfied with Their Child's School

Most are also satisfied with their child's teachers and the amount of homework.

Complaints about the nation's schools are commonplace, but in fact the parents of most children in kindergarten through 12th grade are very satisfied with various aspects of their child's school. Fifty-nine percent of school children have parents who claim to be "very satisfied" with their child's school. The percentage "very satisfied" with the teachers is an even higher 64 percent. Similar proportions are very satisfied with their school's academic standards and discipline. Seventy-five percent say the amount of homework assigned to their child is about right.

The biggest difference in satisfaction levels is by type of school and grade level. Typically, private school parents are happier than public school parents, and the parents of younger children are happier than the parents of children in middle or high school. Nevertheless, the majority of parents, regardless of type of school or grade level, say they are very satisfied with their child's school.

■ Although most parents are very satisfied with their child's school, a substantial minority is not. Unhappy parents are driving the push for school reform.

Blacks are least likely to be very satisfied with their child's school

(percent of children in kindergarten through 12th grade whose parents are "very satisfied" with their child's school, by race and Hispanic origin, 2006–07)

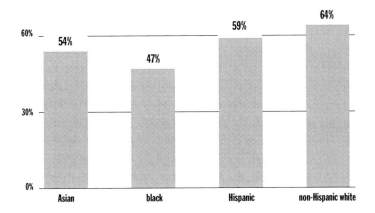

Table 12.10 Parental Satisfaction with School, 2006–07

(total number, percent distribution, and percent of elementary and secondary school children whose parents report satisfaction with school characteristics and amount of homework, by selected characteristics of child and parent, 2006–07)

| | total | | parent reports being "very satisfied" | | | | | amount of homework assigned is "about right" |
	number	percent	with the school	with teachers student had this year	with academic standards of the school	with order and discipline at the school	with the way school staff interacts with parents	
TOTAL CHILDREN	**51,600**	**100%**	**59%**	**64%**	**63%**	**62%**	**55%**	**75%**
Race and Hispanic origin of child								
Asian, non-Hispanic	1,566	100	54	59	56	57	50	67
Black, non-Hispanic	7,837	100	47	57	55	54	49	66
Hispanic	9,767	100	59	65	60	63	59	78
White, non-Hispanic	29,832	100	64	66	66	65	57	77
Educational attainment of parent								
Not a high school graduate	3,504	100	54	62	56	60	55	79
High school graduate	11,070	100	54	59	56	58	51	74
Vocational/technical or some college	14,844	100	55	61	59	57	53	73
Bachelor's degree	11,353	100	64	67	67	65	57	76
Graduate degree	10,829	100	68	70	71	70	62	76
School type								
Public, assigned	37,168	100	55	61	58	58	51	74
Public, chosen	7,951	100	63	68	67	63	59	72
Private, religious	4,560	100	81	79	84	83	77	80
Private, nonreligious	1,438	100	82	78	84	83	76	88
Student's grade level								
Kindergarten through 2nd grade	11,516	100	69	78	69	72	67	80
3rd through 5th grade	11,519	100	65	69	67	66	63	79
6th through 8th grade	12,058	100	55	58	60	59	51	71
9th through 12th grade	16,503	100	52	54	57	54	46	72
Poverty status								
Poor	10,012	100	56	64	59	57	56	73
Not poor	41,587	100	60	64	63	63	55	75

Source: National Center for Education Statistics, Parent and Family Involvement in Education, 2006–07 School Year, from the National Household Education Surveys Program of 2007, August 2008, Internet site http://nces.ed.gov/pubsearch/pubsinfo .asp?pubid=2008050; calculations by New Strategist

Health

■ The 56 percent majority of children under age 18 are in "excellent" health, according to their parents. Only about 2 percent of parents rate their child's health as only "fair" or "poor."

■ A government study of high school students found 15 percent of girls to be overweight. A larger 35 percent of girls thought they were overweight, and 60 percent were trying to lose weight.

■ Among boys, the 57 percent majority of 11th graders has had sexual intercourse. The figure rises to 63 percent among boys in 12th grade. The statistics are similar for girls.

■ In a government survey of high school students, 45 percent say they used alcohol in the past month, including the majority of boys in 11th grade and the majority of both boys and girls in 12th grade.

■ Among all Americans, 15 percent lacked health insurance in 2007. The figure was a a smaller 11 percent among children.

■ Nine million children (12 percent) have taken prescription medications regularly for at least three months during the past year.

■ Among children aged 1 to 14, accidents are by far the leading cause of death.

Most Children Are in Excellent Health

Fewer than one in five is overweight.

The 56 percent majority of children under age 18 are in "excellent" health, according to their parents. Only about 2 percent of parents rate their child's health as only "fair" or "poor."

Although most adults struggle with weight problems, among children ranging in age from 6 to 19, only 16 to 17 percent are overweight, according to government studies. In a separate government study of high school students, 15 percent of girls and 16 percent of boys were found to be overweight. A larger 35 percent of girls and 24 percent of boys thought they were overweight, however. Thirty percent of boys and 60 percent of girls were trying to lose weight.

Weight problems lie ahead for today's children, in part because fewer are taking part in physical activities. The percentage of children who participate in a variety of sports has plunged over the past decade, according to the National Sporting Goods Association. The percentage of 7-to-11-year-olds who rode a bicycle more than once in the past year fell from 51 to 36 percent between 1998 and 2007. Only 34 percent of high school students meet recommended levels of physical activity.

■ Although most teenage girls are weight conscious, those concerns are unlikely to prevent them from becoming overweight as young adults.

Many girls think they are overweight

(percent of girls in 9th to 12th grade who are overweight, percent who think they are overweight, and percent trying to lose weight, 2007)

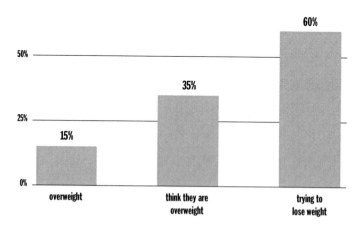

Table 13.1 Health Status of Children under Age 18, 2007

(parent-reported health status of people under age 18, by age, 2007)

	total	excellent	very good	good	fair/poor
Total children	**100.0%**	**55.7%**	**26.9%**	**15.6%**	**1.8%**
Under age 5	100.0	57.7	25.3	15.5	1.5
Aged 5 to 11	100.0	57.0	27.1	14.2	1.7
Aged 12 to 17	100.0	52.6	28.1	17.4	2.0

Source: National Center for Health Statistics, Summary Health Statistics for U.S. Children: National Health Interview Survey, 2007, Series 10, No. 239, 2008, Internet site http://www.cdc.gov/nchs/nhis.htm

Table 13.2 Overweight Children, 2003–06

(percent of children aged 6 to 19 who are overweight, by sex, race, Hispanic origin, and age, 2003–06)

	6 to 11	12 to 19
TOTAL CHILDREN	**17.0%**	**17.6%**
Total boys	**18.0**	**18.2**
Black, non-Hispanic	18.6	18.5
Mexican	27.5	22.1
White, non-Hispanic	15.5	17.3
Total girls	**15.8**	**16.8**
Black, non-Hispanic	24.0	27.7
Mexican	19.7	19.9
White, non-Hispanic	14.4	14.5

Note: Overweight is defined as a body mass index at or above the sex- and age-specific 95th percentile body mass index cutoff points from the 2000 Centers for Disease Control growth charts.
Source: National Center for Health Statistics, Health, United States, 2008, Internet site http://www.cdc.gov/nchs/hus.htm

Table 13.3 Weight Problems and Dieting Behavior of 9th to 12th Graders by Sex, 2007

(percent of 9th to 12th graders by weight status and dieting behavior, by sex and grade, 2007)

	total	9th grade	10th grade	11th grade	12th grade
BOYS					
Overweight*	16.4%	17.0%	17.7%	15.9%	14.9%
Described themselves as overweight	24.2	24.3	24.8	25.8	21.6
Were trying to lose weight	30.4	31.0	31.6	30.1	28.7
Ate less food, fewer calories, or foods low in fat to lose weight or to avoid gaining weight in past 30 days	28.3	27.3	29.1	29.8	27.4
Exercised to lose weight or to avoid gaining weight in past 30 days	55.0	58.7	54.2	54.9	51.1
Went without eating for at least 24 hours to lose weight or to avoid gaining weight in past 30 days	7.3	6.5	6.5	8.1	8.0
Took diet pills, powders, or liquids without a doctor's advice to lose weight or avoid gaining weight in past 30 days	4.2	2.9	3.8	5.0	5.7
Vomited or took a laxative to lose weight or to avoid gaining weight in past 30 days	2.2	2.1	1.8	2.1	2.6
GIRLS					
Overweight*	15.1	18.3	14.2	14.2	13.1
Described themselves as overweight	34.5	33.6	33.8	36.2	34.9
Were trying to lose weight	60.3	58.6	50.2	61.3	61.6
Ate less food, fewer calories, or foods low in fat to lose weight or to avoid gaining weight in past 30 days	53.2	50.5	53.0	54.0	56.4
Exercised to lose weight or to avoid gaining weight in past 30 days	67.0	70.6	67.7	65.0	63.7
Went without eating for at least 24 hours to lose weight or to avoid gaining weight in past 30 days	16.3	16.8	19.1	14.8	13.6
Took diet pills, powders, or liquids without a doctor's advice to lose weight or avoid gaining weight in past 30 days	7.5	6.1	6.9	7.4	10.2
Vomited or took a laxative to lose weight or to avoid gaining weight in past 30 days	6.4	5.5	7.6	5.7	6.6

* Students who were overweight were at or above the 95th percentile for body mass index, by age and sex, based on reference data.

Source: Centers for Disease Control and Prevention, Youth Risk Behavior Surveillance—United States, 2007, Mortality and Morbidity Weekly Report, Vol. 57/SS-4, June 6, 2008, Internet site http://www.cdc.gov/HealthyYouth/yrbs/index.htm

Table 13.4 Sports Participation of Children Aged 7 to 17, 1998 and 2007

(number and percent of people aged 7 to 17 participating in selected sports at least once during past year, by age, 1998 and 2007; percent change in number and percentage point change in participation rate; numbers in thousands)

	2007		1998		percent change in number	percentage point change in participation rate
	number	percent	number	percent		
AGED 7 TO 11						
Total children	**19,410**	**100.0%**	**19,873**	**100.0%**	**−2.3%**	−
Baseball	3,975	20.5	4,714	23.7	−15.7	−3.2
Basketball	4,923	25.4	6,273	31.6	−21.5	−6.2
Bicycle riding	7,046	36.3	10,055	50.6	−29.9	−14.3
Bowling	5,091	26.2	4,865	24.5	4.6	1.7
Fishing	2,894	14.9	4,627	23.3	−37.5	−8.4
Football (tackle)	1,442	7.4	1,211	6.1	19.1	1.3
Golf	654	3.4	1,264	6.4	−48.3	−3.0
Ice hockey	252	1.3	365	1.8	−31.0	−0.5
In-line skating	3,013	15.5	9,052	45.5	−66.7	−30.0
Mountain biking (off road)	640	3.3	1,040	5.2	−38.5	−1.9
Skateboarding	3,156	16.3	2,309	11.6	36.7	4.6
Skiing (alpine)	533	2.7	548	2.8	−2.7	0.0
Snowboarding	782	4.0	487	2.5	60.6	1.6
Soccer	5,041	26.0	5,489	27.6	−8.2	−1.6
Softball	1,155	6.0	3,040	15.3	−62.0	−9.3
Tennis	1,446	7.4	1,204	6.1	20.1	1.4
Volleyball	1,189	6.1	1,551	7.8	−23.3	−1.7
AGED 12 TO 17						
Total children	**25,341**	**100.0**	**23,241**	**100.0**	**9.0**	−
Baseball	2,909	11.5	4,307	18.5	−32.5	−7.1
Basketball	6,952	27.4	8,246	35.5	−15.7	−8.0
Bicycle riding	6,518	25.7	7,844	33.8	−16.9	−8.0
Bowling	6,813	26.9	6,055	26.1	12.5	0.8
Fishing	3,107	12.3	4,086	17.6	−24.0	−5.3
Football (tackle)	3,906	15.4	3,014	13.0	29.6	2.4
Golf	1,441	5.7	2,432	10.5	−40.7	−4.8
Ice hockey	419	1.7	593	2.6	−29.3	−0.9
In-line skating	3,384	13.4	6,892	29.7	−50.9	−16.3
Mountain biking (off road)	942	3.7	1,224	5.3	−23.0	−1.5
Skateboarding	4,171	16.5	2,253	9.7	85.1	6.8
Skiing (alpine)	821	3.2	1,262	5.4	−34.9	−2.2
Snowboarding	1,352	5.3	1,477	6.4	−8.5	−1.0
Soccer	3,332	13.1	3,936	16.9	−15.3	−3.8
Softball	1,795	7.1	3,263	14.0	−45.0	−7.0
Tennis	1,883	7.4	2,011	8.7	−6.4	−1.2
Volleyball	3,041	12.0	3,807	16.4	−20.1	−4.4

Note: "−" means not applicable.
Source: National Sporting Goods Association, Internet site http://www.nsga.org

Table 13.5 Participation of High School Students in Physical Education Classes, Team Sports, and Physical Activity, 2007

(percent of 9th through 12th graders who attended a physical education class at least one day a week, participated in at least one sports team, or met the recommended level of physical activity, by sex and grade, 2007)

	attended PE class	played on sports team in past year	met recommended level of physical activity
TOTAL HIGH SCHOOL STUDENTS	**53.6%**	**56.3%**	**34.7%**
Boys	**57.7**	**62.1**	**43.7**
9th grade	68.3	63.4	44.4
10th grade	62.3	64.7	45.1
11th grade	51.4	63.0	45.2
12th grade	44.6	56.2	38.7
Girls	**49.4**	**50.4**	**25.6**
9th grade	65.1	54.7	31.5
10th grade	51.2	50.8	24.4
11th grade	38.8	52.5	24.6
12th grade	38.5	41.9	20.6

Note: "Recommended level of physical activity" is any kind of physical activity that increased their heart rate and made them breathe hard for at least 60 minutes per day on five or more days during the past week.
Source: Centers for Disease Control and Prevention, Youth Risk Behavior Surveillance—United States, 2007, Mortality and Morbidity Weekly Report, Vol. 57/SS-4, June 6, 2008, Internet site http://www.cdc.gov/HealthyYouth/yrbs/index.htm

The Majority of 11th and 12th Graders Have Had Sex

Most sexually active teens use birth control.

Among boys, the 57 percent majority of 11th graders have had sexual intercourse. The figure rises to 63 percent among boys in 12th grade. The statistics are similar for girls—54 percent of 11th graders and 66 percent of 12th graders have had sexual intercourse. A smaller share of teens is currently sexually active—meaning they have had sexual intercourse in the past three months.

Among sexually active teens, most used birth control the last time they had sex. Among sexually active boys, 69 percent say they used a condom and 13 percent say their partner was on the pill. Among sexually active girls, 55 percent say their partner used a condom and 19 percent say they were taking the pill.

■ When teenagers are sexually active, the prevention of pregnancy and sexually transmitted diseases is of prime concern to parents and schools.

Girls and boys are almost equally sexually active

(percent of 9th to 12th graders who have had sexual intercourse, by sex, 2007)

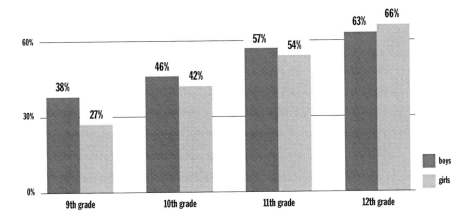

Table 13.6 Sexual Behavior of 9th to 12th Graders by Sex, 2007

(percent of 9th to 12th graders engaging in selected sexual activities, by sex and grade, 2007)

	total	9th grade	10th grade	11th grade	12th grade
BOYS					
Ever had sexual intercourse	49.8%	38.1%	45.6%	57.3%	62.8%
Currently sexually active*	34.3	22.2	29.4	42.0	48.3
First sexual intercourse before age 13	10.1	13.5	9.1	9.9	6.7
Four or more sex partners during lifetime	17.9	11.9	16.7	20.6	24.7
Condom use during last sexual intercourse	68.5	75.8	73.2	69.3	59.6
Birth control pill use before last sexual intercourse	13.1	8.3	9.5	11.0	20.8
GIRLS					
Ever had sexual intercourse	45.9	27.4	41.9	53.6	66.2
Currently sexually active*	35.6	18.0	31.8	41.5	56.7
First sexual intercourse before age 13	4.0	4.9	4.7	3.4	2.4
Four or more sex partners during lifetime	11.8	5.5	10.2	13.1	20.1
Condom use during last sexual intercourse	54.9	61.0	59.5	55.1	49.9
Birth control pill use before last sexual intercourse	18.7	9.2	13.7	18.9	25.6

* Sexual intercourse during the three months preceding the survey.
Source: Centers for Disease Control and Prevention, Youth Risk Behavior Surveillance—United States, 2007, Mortality and Morbidity Weekly Report, Vol. 57/SS-4, June 6, 2008, Internet site http://www.cdc.gov/HealthyYouth/yrbs/index.htm

Many Teens Smoke Cigarettes

Ten percent of 12-to-17-year-olds have smoked a cigarette in the past month.

Cigarette smoking has been declining in the population as a whole, but among teenagers it remains stubbornly high. Overall, 24 percent of people aged 12 or older smoked a cigarette in the past month, according to a 2007 survey. The proportion of teenagers who have ever smoked rises steadily with age to 23 percent among 17-year-olds.

In another government survey of high school students, 20 percent report having smoked a cigarette in the past month. The figure peaks at 26 to 27 percent among boys and girls in 12th grade.

■ Most teens have tried a cigarette by 11th grade and some will make smoking a lifelong habit.

Cigarette smoking doubles between ages 15 and 17

(percent of people aged 12 to 17 who have smoked a cigarette in the past month, by age, 2007)

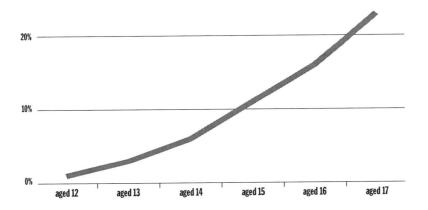

Table 13.7 Cigarette Smoking among People Aged 12 to 17, 2007

(percent of people aged 12 or older and people aged 12 to 17 reporting any, past year, and past month use of cigarettes, 2007)

	ever smoked	smoked in past year	smoked in past month
Total people aged 12 or older	**65.3%**	**28.5%**	**24.2%**
Total people aged 12 to 17	**23.7**	**15.7**	**9.8**
Aged 12	5.1	2.6	0.9
Aged 13	10.7	5.5	2.7
Aged 14	17.5	11.2	6.0
Aged 15	26.8	17.6	10.7
Aged 16	37.2	24.7	15.5
Aged 17	42.9	31.4	22.5

Source: SAMHSA, Office of Applied Studies, National Survey on Drug Use and Health, 2007, Internet site http://www.oas.samhsa.gov/nsduh/2k7nsduh/2k7Results.pdf

Table 13.8 Cigarette Use by 9th to 12th Graders, 2007

(percent of 9th to 12th graders who have ever tried cigarette smoking or who have smoked cigarettes in the past 30 days, by sex, 2007)

	lifetime cigarette use	past month cigarette use
TOTAL HIGH SCHOOL STUDENTS	**50.3%**	**20.0%**
Boys	**51.8**	**21.3**
9th grade	46.0	16.2
10th grade	48.8	20.0
11th grade	55.4	23.4
12th grade	60.1	27.4
Girls	**48.8**	**18.7**
9th grade	39.2	12.3
10th grade	48.7	19.1
11th grade	51.4	19.6
12th grade	58.5	25.5

Source: Centers for Disease Control and Prevention, Youth Risk Behavior Surveillance—United States, 2007, Mortality and Morbidity Weekly Report, Vol. 57/SS-4, June 6, 2008, Internet site http://www.cdc.gov/HealthyYouth/yrbs/index.htm

Most Teens Do Not Wait for Legal Drinking Age

The majority of 19- and 20-year-olds have had an alcoholic beverage in the past month.

More than half of Americans aged 12 or older have had an alcoholic beverage in the past month. The figure climbs above 50 percent among 19-year-olds although the legal drinking age is 21.

Many teens and young adults take part in binge drinking, meaning they have had five or more drinks on one occasion in the past month. Among people aged 19 and 20, more than one in 10 participated in heavy drinking during the past month—meaning they binged at least five times during the past month.

In another survey of high school students, 45 percent say they used alcohol in the past month. The figure rises with grade level to the majority of boys in 11th grade and the majority of both boys and girls in 12th grade.

■ Heavy drinking is a bigger problem than drug use among teenagers.

Many teens drink alcohol

(percent of people aged 16 to 20 who have consumed alcoholic beverages in the past month, by age, 2007)

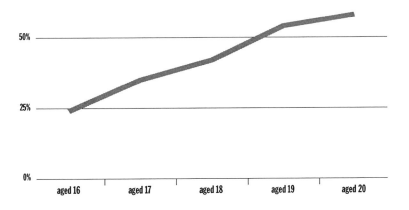

Table 13.9 Alcohol Use by People Aged 12 to 20, 2007

(percent of people aged 12 or older and people aged 12 to 20 who drank alcoholic beverages during the past month, by level of alcohol use, 2007)

	drank at any time during past month	binge drinking during past month	heavy drinking during past month
Total people aged 12 or older	**51.1%**	**23.3%**	**6.9%**
Aged 12	2.2	0.9	0.1
Aged 13	4.7	2.0	0.1
Aged 14	10.0	4.5	0.4
Aged 15	19.0	10.9	2.4
Aged 16	23.8	15.1	3.8
Aged 17	34.6	23.9	7.1
Aged 18	41.8	28.9	9.6
Aged 19	53.7	38.8	14.1
Aged 20	57.8	40.3	15.8

Note: Binge drinking is defined as having five or more drinks on the same occasion on at least one day in the 30 days prior to the survey. Heavy drinking is having five or more drinks on the same occasion on each of five or more days in 30 days prior to the survey.
Source: SAMHSA, Office of Applied Studies, National Survey on Drug Use and Health, 2007, Internet site http://www.oas .samhsa.gov/nsduh/2k7nsduh/2k7Results.pdf

Table 13.10 Alcohol Use by 9th to 12th Graders, 2007

(percent of 9th to 12th graders who have ever drunk alcohol or who have drunk alcohol in the past 30 days, by sex, 2007)

	lifetime alcohol use	past month alcohol use
TOTAL HIGH SCHOOL STUDENTS	**75.0%**	**44.7%**
Boys	**74.3**	**44.7**
9th grade	65.0	34.3
10th grade	74.9	41.4
11th grade	79.7	51.5
12th grade	80.2	55.6
Girls	**75.7**	**44.6**
9th grade	66.1	37.2
10th grade	74.6	42.3
11th grade	79.1	46.5
12th grade	85.2	54.2

Source: Centers for Disease Control and Prevention, Youth Risk Behavior Surveillance—United States, 2007, Mortality and Morbidity Weekly Report, Vol. 57/SS-4, June 6, 2008, Internet site http://www.cdc.gov/HealthyYouth/yrbs/index.htm

Drug Use Is Prevalent among Teens

More than one in four 12-to-17-year-olds have ever used an illicit drug.

Among Americans aged 12 or older, only 8 percent used an illicit drug in the past month. Teens and young adults are much more likely to be current drug users than the average person. Among 17-year-olds, 17 percent have used an illicit drug in the past month.

Marijuana is the most commonly used illicit drug. Among all 12-to-17-year olds, 7 percent have used marijuana in the past month. The figure rises to more than 10 percent among 16- and 17-year-olds.

In a survey of high school students, 38 percent say they have used marijuana in their lifetime and 20 percent have used it in the past month. The proportion who have used marijuana in the past month rises with grade level to 28 percent of senior boys and 23 percent of senior girls.

■ Drinking is a bigger problem among teens than drug use.

More than 10 percent of 15-to-17-year-olds have used an illicit drug in the past month

(percent of people aged 12 to 17 who have used an illicit drug in the past month, by age, 2007)

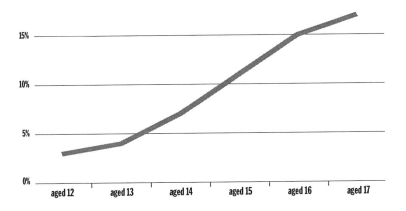

Table 13.11 Illicit Drug Use by People Aged 12 to 17, 2007

(percent of people aged 12 to 17 who ever used any illicit drug, who used an illicit drug in the past year, and who used an illicit drug in the past month, 2007)

	ever used	used in past year	used in past month
Total people aged 12 or older	**46.1%**	**14.4%**	**8.0%**
Total people aged 12 to 17	**26.2**	**18.7**	**9.5**
Aged 12	9.9	5.4	2.7
Aged 13	16.4	10.2	4.0
Aged 14	21.4	14.7	6.7
Aged 15	29.0	21.4	11.0
Aged 16	37.6	28.6	14.8
Aged 17	41.5	30.8	17.4

Note: Illicit drugs include marijuana, hashish, cocaine (including crack), heroin, hallucinogens, inhalants, or any prescription-type psychotherapeutic used nonmedically.
Source: SAMHSA, Office of Applied Studies, National Survey on Drug Use and Health, 2007, Internet site http://www.oas .samhsa.gov/nsduh/2k7nsduh/2k7Results.pdf

Table 13.12 Marijuana Use by People Aged 12 to 17, 2007

(percent of people aged 12 or older and people aged 12 to 17 who ever used marijuana, who used marijuana in the past year, and who used marijuana in the past month, 2007)

	ever used	used in past year	used in past month
Total people aged 12 or older	**40.6%**	**10.1%**	**5.8%**
Total people aged 12 to 17	**16.2**	**12.5**	**6.7**
Aged 12	1.3	1.0	0.6
Aged 13	4.1	2.9	1.3
Aged 14	9.9	7.8	3.7
Aged 15	17.9	14.4	7.6
Aged 16	27.5	21.8	11.4
Aged 17	34.9	25.8	14.9

Source: SAMHSA, Office of Applied Studies, National Survey on Drug Use and Health, 2007, Internet site http://oas.samhsa .gov/NSDUH/2k7NSDUH/tabs/Sect1peTabs1to46.htm#Tab1.1A

Table 13.13 Marijuana Use by 9th to 12th Graders, 2007

(percent of 9th to 12th graders who have ever used marijuana or who have used marijuana in the past 30 days, by sex, 2007)

	lifetime marijuana use	past month marijuana use
TOTAL HIGH SCHOOL STUDENTS	**38.1%**	**19.7%**
Boys	**41.6**	**22.4**
9th grade	33.0	16.9
10th grade	39.2	22.0
11th grade	48.3	25.2
12th grade	49.9	27.8
Girls	**34.5**	**17.0**
9th grade	21.7	12.5
10th grade	34.5	16.5
11th grade	36.6	17.5
12th grade	48.3	22.6

Source: Centers for Disease Control and Prevention, Youth Risk Behavior Surveillance—United States, 2007, Mortality and Morbidity Weekly Report, Vol. 57/SS-4, June 6, 2008, Internet site http://www.cdc.gov/HealthyYouth/yrbs/index.htm

Most Children Are Covered by Health Insurance

More than 8 million children do not have health insurance, however.

Among all Americans, 46 million lacked health insurance in 2007—or 15 percent of the population. The figure is a smaller 11 percent among children.

Hispanic children are most likely to be without health insurance. The 20 percent of Hispanic children who are not insured account for 39 percent of all uninsured children—a larger share than the 38 percent accounted for by non-Hispanic whites. More than one-third of foreign-born children who are not citizens do not have health insurance.

Eighty-five percent of children had health expenses in 2006, with a median cost of $462. Private insurance covered 51 percent of the cost, Medicaid (the government health insurance program for the poor) paid another 24 percent of those costs, and parents paid 21 percent of the cost out-of-pocket. Most parents are satisfied with the health care their children receive. Two out of three parents rated their child's last health care visit a 9 or 10 on a scale of 0 (worst) to 10 (best).

■ Providing health insurance coverage to all children is a thorny policy problem because many children without health insurance are in the country illegally.

Hispanic children are most likely to be without health insurance

(percent of children without health insurance, by race and Hispanic origin, 2007)

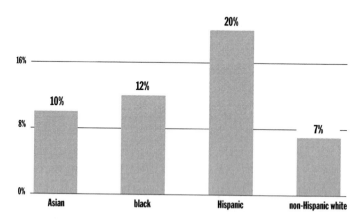

Table 13.14 Health Insurance Coverage of Children, 2007

(number and percent distribution of children under age 18 by age, race, Hispanic origin, and health insurance coverage status, 2007; numbers in thousands)

| | | covered by private or government health insurance | | | | | | | | |
| | | private insurance | | | government | | | | | |
	total	total	total	group health	direct purchase	total	Medicaid	Medicare	military	not covered
Number										
TOTAL CHILDREN UNDER 18	74,403	66,254	47,750	44,252	3,930	23,041	20,899	518	2,101	8,149
Under age 3	12,652	11,283	7,243	6,845	582	4,837	4,438	143	381	1,369
Aged 3 to 5	12,292	11,043	7,550	7,126	572	4,240	3,925	92	317	1,249
Aged 6 to 11	23,820	21,355	15,567	14,621	1,309	7,243	6,604	138	631	2,465
Aged 12 to 17	25,639	22,573	17,391	15,661	1,467	6,721	5,932	145	773	3,066
RACE AND HISPANIC ORIGIN										
Total children under age 18	74,403	66,254	47,750	44,252	3,930	23,041	20,899	518	2,101	8,149
Asian	3,620	3,249	2,625	2,421	293	782	657	27	114	371
Black	12,500	11,029	6,073	5,684	396	5,965	5,528	196	397	1,471
Hispanic	15,741	12,585	6,364	5,961	489	6,954	6,688	126	233	3,156
White, non-Hispanic	42,165	39,086	32,404	29,924	2,717	9,273	7,994	161	1,329	3,079
Percent distribution										
TOTAL CHILDREN UNDER 18	100.0%	89.0%	64.2%	59.5%	5.3%	31.0%	28.1%	0.7%	2.8%	11.0%
Under age 3	100.0	89.2	57.2	54.1	4.6	38.2	35.1	1.1	3.0	10.8
Aged 3 to 5	100.0	89.8	61.4	58.0	4.7	34.5	31.9	0.7	2.6	10.2
Aged 6 to 11	100.0	89.7	65.4	61.4	5.5	30.4	27.7	0.6	2.6	10.3
Aged 12 to 17	100.0	88.0	67.8	61.1	5.7	26.2	23.1	0.6	3.0	12.0
RACE AND HISPANIC ORIGIN										
Total children under age 18	100.0	89.0	64.2	59.5	5.3	31.0	28.1	0.7	2.8	11.0
Asian	100.0	89.8	72.5	66.9	8.1	21.6	18.1	0.7	3.1	10.2
Black	100.0	88.2	48.6	45.5	3.2	47.7	44.2	1.6	3.2	11.8
Hispanic	100.0	80.0	40.4	37.9	3.1	44.2	42.5	0.8	1.5	20.0
White, non-Hispanic	100.0	92.7	76.9	71.0	6.4	22.0	19.0	0.4	3.2	7.3

Note: Asians and blacks include those who identify themselves as being of the race alone and those who identify themselves as being of the race in combination with other races. Hispanics may be of any race. Non-Hispanic whites are only those who identify themselves as being white alone and not Hispanic. Numbers may not add to total because children may be covered by more than one type of health insurance.

Source: Bureau of the Census, Health Insurance Coverage: 2007, Internet site http://pubdb3.census.gov/macro/032008/health/toc.htm; calculations by New Strategist

Table 13.15 Children under Age 18 without Health Insurance, 2007

(number and percent distribution of children under age 18 without health insurance by selected characteristics, 2007; numbers in thousands)

| | children without health insurance | | |
	number	percent	percent distribution
TOTAL CHILDREN UNDER 18	**8,149**	**11.0%**	**100.0%**
Age			
Under age 3	1,369	10.8	16.8
Aged 3 to 5	1,249	10.2	15.3
Aged 6 to 11	2,465	10.3	30.2
Aged 12 to 17	3,066	12.0	37.6
Race and Hispanic origin			
Asian	371	10.2	4.6
Black	1,471	11.8	18.1
Hispanic	3,156	20.0	38.7
White, non-Hispanic	3,079	7.3	37.8
Region			
Northeast	1,024	8.2	12.6
Midwest	1,148	7.1	14.1
South	3,997	14.4	49.0
West	1,980	11.0	24.3
Family income			
Under $25,000	2,483	16.5	30.5
$25,000 to $49,999	2,703	16.2	33.2
$50,000 to $74,999	1,361	10.0	16.7
$75,000 or more	1,327	4.8	16.3
Family type			
Married couple	4,652	9.1	57.1
Female householder, no spouse present	2,445	13.8	30.0
Male householder, no spouse present	777	17.8	9.5
Nativity			
Native-born	7,236	10.1	88.8
Foreign-born	913	30.9	11.2
Naturalized citizen	84	15.4	1.0
Not a citizen	829	34.4	10.2

Note: Asians and blacks include those who identify themselves as being of the race alone and those who identify themselves as being of the race in combination with other races. Hispanics may be of any race. Non-Hispanic whites are only those who identify themselves as being white alone and not Hispanic.
Source: Bureau of the Census, Health Insurance Coverage: 2007, Internet site http://pubdb3.census.gov/macro/032008/health/toc.htm; calculations by New Strategist

Table 13.16 Spending on Health Care for Children, 2006

(percent of children under age 18 with health care expense, median expense per child, total expenses, and percent distribution of total expenses by source of payment, by age, 2006)

	total (thousands)	percent with expense	median expense per person	total expenses	
				amount (millions)	percent distribution
Total children	**74,106**	**85.4%**	**$462**	**$98,789**	**100.0%**
Under age 1	4,076	90.2	460	12,909	13.1
Aged 1 to 5	20,366	88.9	408	21,995	22.3
Aged 6 to 11	23,978	85.1	415	23,149	23.4
Aged 12 to 17	25,686	82.3	570	40,737	41.2

		percent distribution by source of payment			
	total	out of pocket	private insurance	Medicaid	other
Total children	**100.0%**	**20.5%**	**50.7%**	**23.7%**	**4.6%**
Under age 1	100.0	4.9	45.1	40.4	8.7
Aged 1 to 5	100.0	13.1	52.2	29.0	5.5
Aged 6 to 11	100.0	22.0	52.3	21.7	3.4
Aged 12 to 17	100.0	28.5	50.9	16.7	3.5

Note: "Other" insurance includes Department of Veterans Affairs (except Tricare), American Indian Health Service, state and local clinics, worker's compensation, homeowner's and automobile insurance, etc.
Source: Agency for Healthcare Research and Quality, Medical Expenditure Panel Survey, 2006, Internet site http://www.meps .ahrq.gov/mepsweb/data_stats/quick_tables_results.jsp?component=1&subcomponent=0&tableSeries=1&year=-1&SearchMet hod=1&Action=Search; calculations by New Strategist

Table 13.17 Parents' Rating of Health Care Received by Children at Doctor's Office or Clinic, 2006

(number of children under age 18 visiting a doctor or health care clinic in past 12 months, and percent distribution by rating given by parents for health care received by children on a scale from 0 (worst) to 10 (best), 2006; children in thousands)

	with health care visit		rating		
	number	percent	9 to 10	7 to 8	0 to 6
Total children	**55,656**	**100.0%**	**67.6%**	**27.2%**	**4.9%**
Under age 1	2,565	100.0	67.4	27.6	5.1
Aged 1 to 5	17,730	100.0	68.7	26.9	4.1
Aged 6 to 11	17,452	100.0	67.5	26.9	5.2
Aged 12 to 17	17,910	100.0	66.8	27.6	5.3

Source: Agency for Healthcare Research and Quality, Medical Expenditure Panel Survey, 2006, Internet site http://www.meps .ahrq.gov/mepsweb/data_stats/quick_tables_results.jsp?component=1&subcomponent=0&tableSeries=3&year=-1&SearchMet hod=1&Action=Search; calculations by New Strategist

Asthma and Allergies Affect Many Children

Boys are more likely than girls to have learning disabilities.

Asthma is a growing problem among children. Thirteen percent of the nation's 74 million children under age 18 have been diagnosed with asthma. Boys are more likely than girls to have been diagnosed with asthma (15 versus 11 percent), and blacks are more likely than other racial or ethnic groups (20 percent versus 11 to 13 percent for Asians, Hispanics, and non-Hispanic whites). Children in single-parent families headed by women are more likely to have asthma than those from two-parent families (18 versus 12 percent).

More than 4 million children (7.5 percent) have been diagnosed with a learning disability, and almost the same number has attention deficit hyperactivity disorder. Boys, who are far more likely than girls to have these conditions, account for 66 percent of those with learning disabilities and 71 percent of those with attention deficit hyperactivity disorder.

Many children use prescription medications. Nine million children have taken prescription medications regularly for at least three months during the past year. That's a substantial 12 percent of the nation's children. Among 12-to-17-year-olds, the figure is an even higher 17 percent.

■ Prescription drug use is becoming common among the nation's children.

Boys are more likely than girls to have attention deficit hyperactivity disorder

(percent of people under age 18 diagnosed with attention deficit hyperactivity disorder, by sex, 2007)

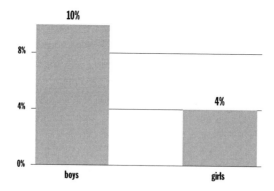

Table 13.18 Health Conditions among Children by Selected Characteristics, 2007

(number of people under age 18 with selected health conditions, by selected characteristics and type of condition, 2007; numbers in thousands)

| | | | | experienced in past 12 months | | | | ever told had* | prescription medication taken regularly at least 3 months |
	total children	diagnosed with asthma	still have asthma	hay fever	respiratory allergies	other allergies	learning disability	attention deficit hyperactivity disorder	
TOTAL CHILDREN	73,728	9,605	6,703	7,438	7,068	8,678	4,624	4,452	9,049
Sex									
Female	36,042	4,055	3,043	3,476	3,026	4,386	1,590	1,291	4,117
Male	37,686	5,550	3,660	3,962	4,042	4,292	3,034	3,161	4,932
Age									
Aged 0 to 4	20,579	1,636	1,395	915	1,323	2,880	179	170	1,535
Aged 5 to 11	27,932	3,702	2,445	2,888	2,863	3,227	1,867	1,644	3,281
Aged 12 to 17	25,216	4,267	2,862	3,635	2,882	2,571	2,577	2,637	4,234
Race and Hispanic origin									
Asian	2,937	362	217	227	207	299	90	57	236
Black	11,429	2,253	1,769	754	848	1,577	740	718	1,413
Hispanic	15,350	1,937	1,422	1,163	1,020	1,476	817	495	1,273
Non-Hispanic white	41,811	4,591	3,030	5,084	4,675	4,920	2,823	2,948	5,847
Family structure									
Mother and father	52,294	6,029	4,051	5,510	4,905	5,913	2,835	2,597	5,880
Mother, no father	16,935	2,977	2,207	1,499	1,703	2,223	1,430	1,507	2,581
Father, no mother	2,282	280	179	157	203	259	128	122	214
Neither mother nor father	2,216	320	265	272	258	283	231	225	375
Parent's education									
Less than high school diploma	9,038	1,253	894	549	640	637	474	470	750
High school diploma or GED	16,005	1,966	1,401	1,163	1,090	1,668	1,142	1,125	1,659
More than high school	45,877	6,034	4,113	5,430	5,057	6,083	2,732	2,594	6,213
Household income									
Less than $35,000	22,058	3,472	2,529	1,689	1,853	2,541	1,700	1,572	2,924
$35,000 to $49,999	9,732	1,147	723	924	868	1,016	473	563	1,054
$50,000 to $74,999	12,702	1,665	1,231	1,214	1,290	1,668	979	800	1,461
$75,000 to $99,999	9,142	916	559	1,224	989	1,043	565	558	1,114
$100,000 or more	13,641	1,699	1,167	1,756	1,621	1,715	583	682	1,973

* *Ever told by a school representative or health professional. Data exclude children under age 3.*
Note: *"Mother and father" can include biological, adoptive, step, in-law, or foster relationships. Legal guardians are classified as "neither mother nor father." "Parent's education" is the education level of the parent with the higher level of education. Race/Hispanic origin, education, and income categories do not sum to total because not all races are shown and those not reporting education or income are not shown. "Other allergies" include food or digestive allergies, eczema, and other skin allergies.*
Source: *National Center for Health Statistics, Summary Health Statistics for U.S. Children: National Health Interview Survey, 2007, Series 10, No. 239, 2008, Internet site http://www.cdc.gov/nchs/nhis.htm*

Table 13.19 Distribution of Health Conditions by Selected Characteristics of Children, 2007

(percent distribution of people under age 18 with health condition by selected characteristics, 2007)

	total children	diagnosed with asthma	still have asthma	hay fever	respiratory allergies	other allergies	learning disability	attention deficit hyperactivity disorder	prescription medication taken regularly at least 3 months
				experienced in past 12 months				**ever told had***	
TOTAL CHILDREN	100.0%	100.0%	100.0%	100.0%	100.0%	100.0%	100.0%	100.0%	100.0%
Sex									
Female	48.9	42.2	45.4	46.7	42.8	50.5	34.4	29.0	45.5
Male	51.1	57.8	54.6	53.3	57.2	49.5	65.6	71.0	54.5
Age									
Aged 0 to 4	27.9	17.0	20.8	12.3	18.7	33.2	3.9	3.8	17.0
Aged 5 to 11	37.9	38.5	36.5	38.8	40.5	37.2	40.4	36.9	36.3
Aged 12 to 17	34.2	44.4	42.7	48.9	40.8	29.6	55.7	59.2	46.8
Race and Hispanic origin									
Asian	4.0	3.8	3.2	3.1	2.9	3.4	1.9	1.3	2.6
Black	15.5	23.5	26.4	10.1	12.0	18.2	16.0	16.1	15.6
Hispanic	20.8	20.2	21.2	15.6	14.4	17.0	17.7	11.1	14.1
Non-Hispanic white	56.7	47.8	45.2	68.4	66.1	56.7	61.1	66.2	64.6
Family structure									
Mother and father	70.9	62.8	60.4	74.1	69.4	68.1	61.3	58.3	65.0
Mother, no father	23.0	31.0	32.9	20.2	24.1	25.6	30.9	33.8	28.5
Father, no mother	3.1	2.9	2.7	2.1	2.9	3.0	2.8	2.7	2.4
Neither mother nor father	3.0	3.3	4.0	3.7	3.7	3.3	5.0	5.1	4.1
Parent's education									
Less than high school diploma	12.3	13.0	13.3	7.4	9.1	7.3	10.3	10.6	8.3
High school diploma or GED	21.7	20.5	20.9	15.6	15.4	19.2	24.7	25.3	18.3
More than high school	62.2	62.8	61.4	73.0	71.5	70.1	59.1	58.3	68.7
Household income									
Less than $35,000	29.9	36.1	37.7	22.7	26.2	29.3	36.8	35.3	32.3
$35,000 to $49,999	13.2	11.9	10.8	12.4	12.3	11.7	10.2	12.6	11.6
$50,000 to $74,999	17.2	17.3	18.4	16.3	18.3	19.2	21.2	18.0	16.1
$75,000 to $99,999	12.4	9.5	8.3	16.5	14.0	12.0	12.2	12.5	12.3
$100,000 or more	18.5	17.7	17.4	23.6	22.9	19.8	12.6	15.3	21.8

* *Ever told by a school representative or health professional. Data exclude children under age 3.*
Note: *"Mother and father" can include biological, adoptive, step, in-law, or foster relationships. Legal guardians are classified as "neither mother nor father." "Parent's education" is the education level of the parent with the higher level of education. Race/Hispanic origin, education, and income categories do not sum to total because not all races are shown and those not reporting education or income are not shown. "Other allergies" include food or digestive allergies, eczema, and other skin allergies.*
Source: *National Center for Health Statistics, Summary Health Statistics for U.S. Children: National Health Interview Survey, 2007, Series 10, No. 239, 2008, Internet site http://www.cdc.gov/nchs/nhis.htm; calculations by New Strategist*

Table 13.20 Percent of Children with Health Conditions by Selected Characteristics, 2007

(percent of people under age 18 with selected health conditions, by type of condition and selected characteristics, 2007)

	total children	diagnosed with asthma	still have asthma	hay fever	respiratory allergies	other allergies	learning disability	attention deficit hyperactivity disorder	prescription medication taken regularly at least 3 months
				experienced in past 12 months				ever told had*	
TOTAL CHILDREN	**100.0%**	**13.1%**	**9.1%**	**10.1%**	**9.6%**	**11.8%**	**7.5%**	**7.2%**	**12.3%**
Sex									
Female	100.0	11.3	8.5	9.7	8.4	12.1	5.3	4.3	11.4
Male	100.0	14.8	9.8	10.6	10.8	11.4	9.7	10.0	13.2
Age									
Aged 0 to 4	100.0	8.0	6.8	4.5	6.4	14.0	2.1	2.0	7.5
Aged 5 to 11	100.0	13.3	8.8	10.4	10.3	11.6	6.7	5.9	11.8
Aged 12 to 17	100.0	17.0	11.4	14.4	11.4	10.2	10.2	10.5	16.8
Race and Hispanic origin									
Asian	100.0	12.4	7.5	8.0	7.0	10.0	3.7	2.5	8.2
Black	100.0	19.8	15.6	6.6	7.4	13.9	7.7	7.4	12.4
Hispanic	100.0	12.9	9.4	7.8	6.8	9.6	6.7	4.1	8.6
Non-Hispanic white	100.0	10.8	7.1	12.0	11.1	11.8	7.9	8.2	13.8
Family structure									
Mother and father	100.0	11.7	7.8	10.7	9.5	11.3	6.6	6.0	11.4
Mother, no father	100.0	17.6	13.0	8.8	10.1	13.1	10.0	10.5	15.3
Father, no mother	100.0	11.2	7.5	5.8	7.9	13.5	5.8	5.4	8.9
Neither mother nor father	100.0	14.6	12.2	12.5	12.3	13.7	10.9	10.7	16.7
Parent's education									
Less than high school diploma	100.0	14.4	9.9	6.2	7.0	6.9	6.9	6.5	8.1
High school diploma or GED	100.0	12.3	8.8	7.2	6.9	10.5	8.5	8.3	10.4
More than high school	100.0	13.2	9.0	11.9	11.1	13.2	7.1	6.8	13.6
Household income									
Less than $35,000	100.0	16.2	11.7	8.1	8.6	11.3	10.0	9.2	13.6
$35,000 to $49,999	100.0	12.0	7.6	9.6	9.0	10.5	5.8	7.0	11.0
$50,000 to $74,999	100.0	13.0	9.6	9.6	10.1	13.1	9.1	7.4	11.4
$75,000 to $99,999	100.0	9.7	6.0	13.0	10.7	11.7	7.1	6.9	11.9
$100,000 or more	100.0	11.8	8.2	12.2	11.5	12.8	4.6	5.4	13.8

* *Ever told by a school representative or health professional. Data exclude children under age 3.*
Note: *"Mother and father" can include biological, adoptive, step, in-law, or foster relationships. Legal guardians are classified as "neither mother nor father." "Parent's education" is the education level of the parent with the higher level of education. "Other allergies" include food or digestive allergies, eczema, and other skin allergies.*
Source: *National Center for Health Statistics, Summary Health Statistics for U.S. Children: National Health Interview Survey, 2007, Series 10, No. 239, 2008, Internet site http://www.cdc.gov/nchs/nhis.htm*

Many Children Use Alternative Medicine

Children with the most educated parents are most likely to use alternative medicine.

Among the nation's children under age 18, a substantial 12 percent have used alternative or complementary medicine in the past year, according to a government study. Among children whose parents use alternative medicine, the figure is twice as high, at 24 percent.

The most popular types of alternative medicine used by children are nonvitamin, nonmineral natural products (3.9 percent), chiropractic and osteopathic care (2.8 percent), deep breathing exercises (2.2 percent), and yoga (2.1 percent). The children most likely to use alternative medicine are in two-parent families, have the most educated parents, and have multiple health conditions. The more doctor visits a child has had in the past year, the more likely he or she is to use alternative medicine.

■ Many of the children who use alternative medicine have health problems for which their parents are struggling to find a cure.

Children's use of alternative medicine rises with a parent's educational level

(percent of children under age 18 who used alternative medicine in the past year, by parent's education, 2007)

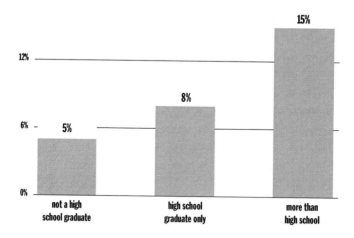

Table 13.21 Use of Alternative and Complementary Medicine by Children, 2007

(number and percent of children under age 18 who used complementary or alternative medicine in the past 12 months, 2007; numbers in thousands)

	children under age 18	
	number	percent
Any use	**8,720**	**11.8%**
Alternative medical systems		
Acupuncture	150	0.2
Homeopathic treatment	907	1.3
Biologically based therapies		
Nonvitamin, nonmineral natural products	2,850	3.9
Diet-based therapies	565	0.8
Vegetarian diet	367	0.5
Atkins diet	88	0.1
South Beach diet	128	0.2
Manipulative and body-based therapies		
Chiropractic or osteopathic manipulation	2,020	2.8
Massage	743	1.0
Movement therapies	299	0.4
Pilates	245	0.3
Mind–body therapies		
Meditation	725	1.0
Guided imagery	293	0.4
Progressive relaxation	329	0.5
Deep breathing exercises	1,558	2.2
Yoga	1,505	2.1
Tai chi	113	0.2
Energy healing therapy/Reiki	161	0.2

Source: National Center for Health Statistics, Complementary and Alternative Medicine Use Among Adults and Children: United States, 2007, National Health Statistics Report, No. 12, 2008, Internet site http://nccam.nih.gov/news/camstats/2007/index.htm

Table 13.22 Characteristics of Children Who Use Complementary and Alternative Medicine, 2007

(percent of people under age 18 who used complementary or alternative medicine (CAM) in the past 12 months, by selected characteristics, 2007)

	any	biologically based therapies	mind–body therapies	alternative medical systems	manipulative and body-based therapies
Total children	**11.8%**	**4.7%**	**4.3%**	**2.6%**	**3.7%**
Children whose parent uses CAM	23.9	10.3	9.8	4.2	7.5
Sex					
Female	12.6	4.6	4.9	2.8	4.2
Male	11.0	4.8	3.8	2.4	3.2
Age					
Aged 0 to 4	7.6	3.2	1.9	2.9	2.1
Aged 5 to 11	10.7	4.3	3.9	2.5	2.8
Aged 12 to 17	16.4	6.3	6.8	2.5	5.9
Race and Hispanic origin					
Black	5.9	1.7	3.0	1.4	0.8
Hispanic	7.9	2.8	2.8	2.5	1.9
White	12.8	5.2	4.4	2.8	4.4
Family structure					
Mother and father	12.7	5.2	4.3	2.7	4.2
Mother, no father	9.6	3.3	4.8	2.2	2.5
Parent's education					
Not a high school graduate	4.8	1.7	1.9	1.5	1.3
High school graduate or GED	8.0	2.8	2.3	1.7	2.5
More than high school	14.7	6.1	5.6	3.2	4.6
Number of health conditions					
No conditions	4.0	1.3	1.1	1.9	1.4
One to two conditions	8.5	2.9	3.2	1.5	2.3
Three to five conditions	14.1	6.0	4.8	2.9	4.2
Six or more conditions	23.8	8.8	10.2	5.6	5.4
Number of visits to doctor in past 12 months					
No visits	7.7	4.9	2.5	2.6	1.9
One visit	7.8	3.6	2.1	1.6	1.9
Two to three visits	11.1	3.4	4.5	2.6	3.1
Four to nine visits	15.0	6.0	5.0	2.5	5.6
10 or more visits	28.4	12.0	12.9	6.3	10.0
Delayed conventional care because of worry about costs					
Yes	16.9	7.3	6.6	5.0	6.2
No	11.6	4.6	4.2	2.6	3.6

Definitions: Biologically based therapies include chelation therapy, nonvitamin, nonmineral, natural products, and diet-based therapies. Mind–body therapies include biofeedback; meditation; guided imagery; progressive relxation; deep breathing exercises; hypnosis; yoga; tai chi; and qi gong. Alternative medical systems include acupuncture; ayurveda; homeopathic treatment; naturopathy; and traditional healers. Manipulative body-based therapies include chiropractic or osteopathic manipulation; massage; and movement therapies.
Note: Blacks and whites are those who identify themselves as being of the race alone. Hispanics may be of any race.
Source: National Center for Health Statistics, Complementary and Alternative Medicine Use Among Adults and Children: United States, 2007, National Health Statistics Report, No. 12, 2008, Internet site http://nccam.nih.gov/news/camstats/2007/index.htm

Among Children, Accidents Are the Leading Cause of Death

Homicide is an important cause of death as well.

Once past infancy, children under age 15 are more likely to die in an accident than from any other cause—which means a large portion of deaths in the age group are preventable. Among infants, congenital malformations are the leading cause of death.

In the 1-to-4 age group, accidents account for 35 percent of deaths, while congenital malformations rank second. Disturbingly, homicide is the fourth leading cause of death in the age group. Among 5-to-14-year-olds, accidents are the leading cause of death followed by cancer, congenital malformations, and homicide. Suicide ranks fifth as a cause of death among 5-to-14-year-olds.

■ As medical science has tamed the ailments that once killed many infants and children, accidents have become a more important cause of death.

Accidents are by far the leading cause of death among children aged 1 to 14

(percent of deaths due to the four leading causes of death among children, by age, 2006)

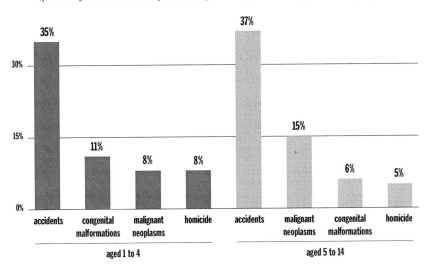

Table 13.23 Leading Causes of Death for Infants, 2005

(number and percent distribution of deaths accounted for by the 10 leading causes of death for children under age 1, 2005)

	number	percent distribution
All causes	**28,440**	**100.0%**
1. Congenital malformations, deformations, and chromosomal abnormalities	5,552	19.5
2. Disorders related to short gestation and low birth weight	4,714	16.6
3. Sudden infant death syndrome	2,230	7.8
4. Newborn affected by maternal complications of pregnancy	1,776	6.2
5. Newborn affected by complications of placenta, cord, and membranes	1,110	3.9
6. Accidents (unintentional injuries) (5)	1,083	3.8
7. Respiratory distress of newborn	860	3.0
8. Bacterial sepsis of newborn	834	2.9
9. Neonatal hemorrhage	665	2.3
10. Necrotizing enterocolitis of newborn	546	1.9
All other causes	9,070	31.9

Note: Number in parentheses shows rank for all Americans if the cause of death is among top 15.
Source: National Center for Health Statistics, Health, United States, 2008, Internet site http://www.cdc.gov/nchs/hus.htm

Table 13.24 Leading Causes of Death for Children Aged 1 to 4, 2005

(number and percent distribution of deaths accounted for by the 10 leading causes of death for children aged 1 to 4, 2005)

	number	percent distribution
All causes	**4,756**	**100.0%**
1. Accidents (unintentional injuries) (5)	1,664	35.0
2. Congenital malformations, deformations, and chromosomal abnormalities	522	11.0
3. Malignant neoplasms (cancer) (2)	377	7.9
4. Homicide (15)	375	7.9
5. Diseases of the heart (1)	151	3.2
6. Influenza and pneumonia (8)	110	2.3
7. Septicemia (10)	85	1.8
8. Cerebrovascular diseases (3)	62	1.3
9. Certain conditions originating in perinatal period	58	1.2
10. Chronic lower respiratory diseases (4)	56	1.2
All other causes	1,296	27.2

Note: Number in parentheses shows rank for all Americans if the cause of death is among top 15.
Source: National Center for Health Statistics, Health, United States, 2008, Internet site http://www.cdc.gov/nchs/hus.htm

Table 13.25 Leading Causes of Death for Children Aged 5 to 14, 2005

(number and percent distribution of deaths accounted for by the 10 leading causes of death for children aged 5 to 14, 2005)

		number	percent distribution
All causes		**6,602**	**100.0%**
1.	Accidents (unintentional injuries) (5)	2,415	36.6
2.	Malignant neoplasms (cancer) (2)	1,000	15.1
3.	Congenital malformations, deformations, and chromosomal abnormalities	396	6.0
4.	Homicide (15)	341	5.2
5.	Suicide (11)	272	4.1
6.	Diseases of the heart (1)	252	3.8
7.	Influenza and pneumonia (8)	106	1.6
8.	Chronic lower respiratory disease (4)	104	1.6
9.	Cerebrovascular diseases (3)	95	1.4
10.	Septicemia (10)	81	1.2
	All other causes	1,540	23.3

Note: Number in parentheses shows rank for all Americans if the cause of death is among top 15.
Source: National Center for Health Statistics, Health, United States, 2008, Internet site http://www.cdc.gov/nchs/hus.htm

14

Housing

■ The homeownership rate of families with children differs by family type. Married couples with children had a homeownership rate of 80 percent in 2007. In contrast, only 44 percent of single-parent families are homeowners.

■ The highest housing costs are borne not by older parents, who can better afford it, but by the youngest parents, who tend to be more recent homebuyers. Families with preschoolers paid a median of $1,443 a month for housing in 2007.

■ Families with three or more preschoolers own the most expensive homes, with a median value of $260,521 in 2007—36 percent higher than the national median. It is likely that their homes are worth less today.

■ Mobility rates are highest for the youngest children as their parents search for bigger and better housing before their children start school. Seventeen percent of children aged 1 to 4 moved between 2007 and 2008.

Most Married Couples with Children Are Homeowners

For single-parent families, the rate is below 50 percent.

The homeownership rate of families with children is almost identical to the overall homeownership rate, at 68 percent in 2007. But the homeownership rate of families with children differs starkly by type of family.

Married couples with children had a homeownership rate of 80 percent in 2007. The rate is lowest for couples with only one preschooler—in other words, the youngest parents, who have just started a family. The rate peaks at 85 percent among couples with school-aged children and no preschoolers—in other words, among older parents.

Only 44 percent of single-parent families are homeowners. The rate nears 50 percent among single-parent families with school-aged children and no preschoolers.

■ Married couples are more likely than single parents to be homeowners because many have two incomes and can better afford the costs of homeownership.

Among households with children, homeownership varies by family type

(homeownership rate of families with children under age 18, by type of family, 2007)

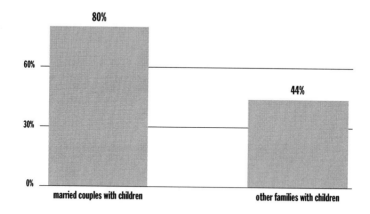

Table 14.1 Families with Children by Homeownership Status, 2007

(number and percent distribution of total households and families with children under age 18 by type of family and number of children, by homeownership status, 2007; numbers in thousands)

	total	owner	renter
TOTAL HOUSEHOLDS	**110,692**	**75,647**	**35,045**
Total families with children	**37,836**	**25,659**	**12,177**
Married-couple families	**25,054**	**20,049**	**5,006**
One child under 6 only	3,283	2,342	941
One under 6, one or more 6 to 17	4,273	3,323	950
Two or more under 6 only	2,350	1,691	659
Two or more under 6, one or more 6 to 17	1,387	1,014	373
One or more 6 to 17 only	13,761	11,679	2,082
Other families with children	**12,781**	**5,611**	**7,172**
One child under 6 only	1,736	569	1,167
One under 6, one or more 6 to 17	1,757	672	1,084
Two or more under 6 only	769	247	521
Two or more under 6, one or more 6 to 17	593	175	417
One or more 6 to 17 only	7,928	3,947	3,981
Percent distribution			
TOTAL HOUSEHOLDS	**100.0%**	**68.3%**	**31.7%**
Total families with children	**100.0**	**67.8**	**32.2**
Married-couple families	**100.0**	**80.0**	**20.0**
One child under 6 only	100.0	71.3	28.7
One under 6, one or more 6 to 17	100.0	77.8	22.2
Two or more under 6 only	100.0	72.0	28.0
Two or more under 6, one or more 6 to 17	100.0	73.1	26.9
One or more 6 to 17 only	100.0	84.9	15.1
Other families with children	**100.0**	**43.9**	**56.1**
One child under 6 only	100.0	32.8	67.2
One under 6, one or more 6 to 17	100.0	38.2	61.7
Two or more under 6 only	100.0	32.1	67.8
Two or more under 6, one or more 6 to 17	100.0	29.5	70.3
One or more 6 to 17 only	100.0	49.8	50.2

Source: Bureau of the Census, American Housing Survey for the United States: 2007, Internet site http://www.census.gov/hhes/www/housing/ahs/ahs07/ahs07.html; calculations by New Strategist

Homeowners with Preschoolers Pay the Most for Housing

Many bought during the housing bubble.

The housing costs of families with children are higher than average. This makes sense since families with children need more space than, say, someone who lives alone or a couple without children. In 2007, the average homeowner paid $927 per month in housing costs, including mortgages, real estate taxes, property insurance, and utilities. The average homeowner family with children faces a higher $1,350 per month in housing costs.

Interestingly, the highest housing costs are borne not by older parents who can better afford it, but by the youngest parents who tend to be more recent homebuyers. Families with preschoolers pay a median of $1,443 a month for housing. Those with two or more preschoolers pay more than $1,500 a month—78 percent more than the average household.

Among renter families with children, housing costs are highest among those with school-aged children and no preschoolers—in other words, among older parents. The median monthly housing cost for all renter families with children was $822 in 2007. It peaks at $962 for renters with three or more school-aged children and no preschoolers.

■ Some of the families that bought houses as prices were peaking are losing their homes in the economic downturn.

Families with children pay more for housing

(median monthly housing costs for total households and families with children, by homeownership status, 2007)

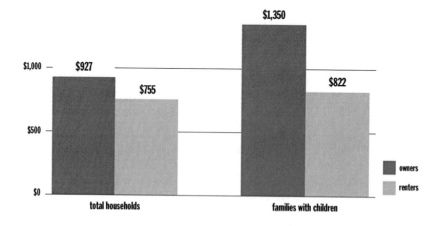

Table 14.2 Median Monthly Housing Costs of Households with Children, 2007

(median monthly housing costs and indexed costs for total homeowners and homeowners with own, never-married children under age 18 by age of child, number of children, and housing tenure, 2007)

	median monthly cost			indexed cost		
	total	owners	renters	total	owners	renters
TOTAL HOUSEHOLDS	$843	$927	$755	100	110	90
Total families with children	1,122	1,350	822	133	160	98
Families with children under age 6 only	1,057	1,443	768	125	171	91
One child	1,012	1,387	768	120	165	91
Two children	1,132	1,500+	770	134	178+	91
Three or more children	1,153	1,500+	733	137	178+	87
Families with children aged 6 to 17 only	1,135	1,305	844	135	155	100
One child	1,034	1,211	796	123	144	94
Two children	1,218	1,380	863	144	164	102
Three or more children	1,234	1,422	962	146	169	114
Families with children in both age groups	1,149	1,402	851	136	166	101
Two children	1,131	1,366	853	134	162	101
Three or more children	1,165	1,434	850	138	170	101

Note: Housing costs include utilities, mortgages, real estate taxes, property insurance, and regime fees. The index is calculated by dividing median monthly housing costs for each household type by the median cost for total households and multiplying by 100.
Source: Bureau of the Census, American Housing Survey for the United States: 2007, Internet site http://www.census.gov/hhes/ www/housing/ahs/ahs07/ahs07.html; calculations by New Strategist

Housing Values Are Highest among Couples with Preschoolers

It is likely that their homes are worth less today.

Families with three or more preschoolers own the most expensive homes, with a median value of $260,521 in 2007—36 percent higher than the national median. It is no surprise that these families have the priciest homes since they are the ones most likely to have bought recently because their families were expanding.

Among all homeowner families with children, housing values are lowest for those with only one preschooler or one school-aged child, at just 8 percent above the national median. These families are least likely to have felt pressure to buy a bigger home in recent years.

■ Housing values have most certainly declined from the 2007 figures shown in the table, since prices were close to their peak in that year.

Families with children own more expensive homes

(median housing value of total homeowners and homeowner families with children under age 18, 2007)

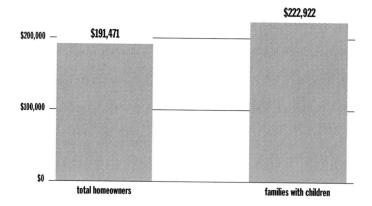

	total homeowners	families with children
	$191,471	$222,922

Table 14.3 Value of Owner-Occupied Homes with Children under Age 18, 2007

(number of total homeowners and homeowners with own, never-married children under age 18 by age of child, number of children, and value of home; median value of housing unit, and indexed median value, 2007)

	number (in 000s)	under $100,000	$100,000– $149,999	$150,000– $199,999	$200,000– $299,999	$300,000– $399,999	$400,000– $499,999	$500,000– $749,999	$750,000 or more	median value of home ($)	indexed median value
TOTAL HOMEOWNERS	75,647	18,779	11,048	9,643	13,132	8,060	4,740	6,234	4,013	191,471	100
Total families with children	23,198	4,566	3,161	2,907	4,211	2,831	1,669	2,296	1,557	222,922	116
Families with children under age 6 only	4,327	728	663	590	845	505	325	406	264	221,573	116
One child	2,563	449	456	346	488	293	186	213	132	206,358	108
Two children	1,546	237	181	218	332	184	118	156	119	241,042	126
Three or more children	218	42	26	27	24	27	21	37	14	260,521	136
Families wiith children aged 6 to 17 only	14,370	2,854	1,915	1,788	2,508	1,762	1,035	1,492	1,017	225,028	118
One child	6,810	1,501	882	930	1,198	845	428	630	396	207,656	108
Two children	5,604	970	786	665	974	692	455	620	443	239,066	125
Three or more children	1,956	383	247	193	336	225	151	242	179	246,238	129
Families with children in both age groups	4,501	983	583	529	859	564	309	398	275	218,102	114
Two children	2,129	478	276	244	410	275	157	174	114	216,040	113
Three or more children	2,372	505	307	285	449	289	152	224	161	219,982	115

Source: Bureau of the Census, American Housing Survey for the United States: 2007, Internet site http://www.census.gov/hhes/www/housing/ahs/ahs07/ahs07.html; calculations by New Strategist

Older Children Are Less Likely to Move

Families try to stay put as children enter middle and high school.

Children under age 18 have a slightly higher mobility rate than the average person. Between 2007 and 2008, 11.9 percent of Americans aged 1 or older moved from one house to another. Among children under age 18, the mobility rate was 12.6 percent.

The mobility rate is highest for the youngest children as their parents search for bigger and better housing before their children start school. Seventeen percent of children aged 1 to 4 moved between 2007 and 2008. The figure falls as children age, bottoming out at 9 percent among 15-to-17-year-olds. The household mobility statistics confirm this pattern, as the mobility rate is highest among families with preschoolers (21 percent) and lowest among families with school-aged children only (9 percent).

Most moves are local, with movers remaining in the same county. Among children under age 16 who moved between 2007 and 2008, nearly half (44 percent) moved for housing reasons. Family reasons ranked second, at 32 percent. Only 18 percent moved because of their parents' employment situation.

■ The percentage of children who move because their parents want cheaper housing may rise in the coming years.

Among children, mobility rates are highest for preschoolers

(percent of people aged 1 to 17 who moved between March 2007 and March 2008, by age)

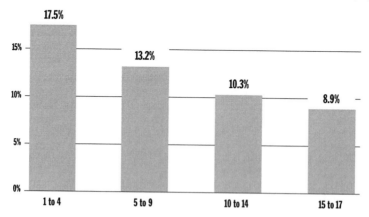

Table 14.4 Geographic Mobility of Children by Age and Type of Move, 2007–08

(total number of people aged 1 or older, and number and percent who moved between March 2007 and March 2008, by age and type of move; numbers in thousands)

	total	total movers	same county	different county, same state	different state total	same region	different region	movers from abroad
Total, 1 or older	**294,851**	**35,166**	**23,013**	**6,282**	**4,727**	**2,248**	**2,479**	**1,145**
Under age 18	70,149	8,809	6,185	1,281	1,091	544	547	247
Aged 1 to 4	16,648	2,908	2,055	429	342	176	166	82
Aged 5 to 9	20,018	2,651	1,863	404	318	147	171	65
Aged 10 to 14	20,038	2,054	1,427	290	283	133	150	52
Aged 15 to 17	13,445	1,196	840	158	148	88	60	48
Aged 18 or older	224,702	26,359	16,829	4,998	3,636	1,706	1,930	896

PERCENT DISTRIBUTION BY MOBILITY STATUS

	total	total movers	same county	different county, same state	different state total	same region	different region	movers from abroad
Total, 1 or older	**100.0%**	**11.9%**	**7.8%**	**2.1%**	**1.6%**	**0.8%**	**0.8%**	**0.4%**
Under age 18	100.0	12.6	8.8	1.8	1.6	0.8	0.8	0.4
Aged 1 to 4	100.0	17.5	12.3	2.6	2.1	1.1	1.0	0.5
Aged 5 to 9	100.0	13.2	9.3	2.0	1.6	0.7	0.9	0.3
Aged 10 to 14	100.0	10.3	7.1	1.4	1.4	0.7	0.7	0.3
Aged 15 to 17	100.0	8.9	6.2	1.2	1.1	0.7	0.4	0.4
Aged 18 or older	100.0	11.7	7.5	2.2	1.6	0.8	0.9	0.4

PERCENT DISTRIBUTION OF MOVERS BY TYPE OF MOVE

	total	total movers	same county	different county, same state	different state total	same region	different region	movers from abroad
Total, 1 or older	–	**100.0%**	**65.4%**	**17.9%**	**13.4%**	**6.4%**	**7.0%**	**3.3%**
Under age 18	–	100.0	70.2	14.5	12.4	6.2	6.2	2.8
Aged 1 to 4	–	100.0	70.7	14.8	11.8	6.1	5.7	2.8
Aged 5 to 9	–	100.0	70.3	15.2	12.0	5.5	6.5	2.5
Aged 10 to 14	–	100.0	69.5	14.1	13.8	6.5	7.3	2.5
Aged 15 to 17	–	100.0	70.2	13.2	12.4	7.4	5.0	4.0
Aged 18 or older	–	100.0	63.8	19.0	13.8	6.5	7.3	3.4

Note: "–" means not applicable.
Source: Bureau of the Census, Geographic Mobility: 2007 to 2008, Detailed Tables, Internet site http://www.census.gov/population/www/socdemo/migrate/cps2008.html; calculations by New Strategist

Table 14.5 Geographic Mobility of Families with Children, 2007–08

(total number and percent distribution of family householders aged 15 to 54 by mobility status and presence of own children under age 18 at home, March 2007 to March 2008; numbers in thousands)

	total	total movers	same county	different county, same state	different state	movers from abroad
Total family householders	**52,162**	**6,422**	**4,360**	**1,037**	**821**	**204**
No children under age 18	18,040	2,013	1,262	382	292	77
With children under age 18	34,122	4,413	3,099	655	532	127
Under age 6 only	8,366	1,769	1,227	284	206	52
Under age 6 and aged 6 to 17	7,156	955	669	146	118	22
Aged 6 to 17 only	18,600	1,689	1,203	225	208	53
PERCENT DISTRIBUTION BY MOBILITY STATUS						
Total family householders	**100.0%**	**12.3%**	**8.4%**	**2.0%**	**1.6%**	**0.4%**
No children under age 18	100.0	11.2	7.0	2.1	1.6	0.4
With children under age 18	100.0	12.9	9.1	1.9	1.6	0.4
Under age 6 only	100.0	21.1	14.7	3.4	2.5	0.6
Under age 6 and aged 6 to 17	100.0	13.3	9.3	2.0	1.6	0.3
Aged 6 to 17 only	100.0	9.1	6.5	1.2	1.1	0.3
PERCENT DISTRIBUTION OF MOVERS BY TYPE OF MOVE						
Total family householders	**–**	**100.0%**	**67.9%**	**16.1%**	**12.8%**	**3.2%**
No children under age 18	–	100.0	62.7	19.0	14.5	3.8
With children under age 18	–	100.0	70.2	14.8	12.1	2.9
Under age 6 only	–	100.0	69.4	16.1	11.6	2.9
Under age 6 and aged 6 to 17	–	100.0	70.1	15.3	12.4	2.3
Aged 6 to 17 only	–	100.0	71.2	13.3	12.3	3.1

Note: "–" means not applicable.
Source: Bureau of the Census, Geographic Mobility: 2007 to 2008, Detailed Tables, Internet site http://www.census.gov/population/www/socdemo/migrate/cps2008.html; calculations by New Strategist

Table 14.6 Reason for Moving among Children under Age 16, 2007–08

(number and percent distribution of movers under age 16 by primary reason household head moved and share of total movers between March 2007 and March 2008; numbers in thousands)

	total movers	movers under age 16		
		number	percent distribution	share of total
TOTAL MOVERS	**35,167**	**8,009**	**100.0%**	**22.8%**
Family reasons	**10,738**	**2,567**	**32.1**	**23.9**
Change in marital status	1,987	418	5.2	21.0
To establish own household	3,682	738	9.2	20.0
Other family reasons	5,069	1,411	17.6	27.8
Employment reasons	**7,352**	**1,435**	**17.9**	**19.5**
New job or job transfer	2,940	602	7.5	20.5
To look for work or lost job	794	130	1.6	16.4
To be closer to work/easier commute	2,183	431	5.4	19.7
Retired	140	0	0.0	0.0
Other job-related reason	1,295	272	3.4	21.0
Housing reasons	**14,098**	**3,535**	**44.1**	**25.1**
Wanted own home, not rent	2,033	462	5.8	22.7
Wanted better home/apartment	4,866	1,289	16.1	26.5
Wanted better neighborhood	1,778	466	5.8	26.2
Wanted cheaper housing	2,872	636	7.9	22.1
Other housing reasons	2,549	682	8.5	26.8
Other reasons	**2,978**	**473**	**5.9**	**15.9**
To attend or leave college	872	39	0.5	4.5
Change of climate	212	57	0.7	26.9
Health reasons	460	45	0.6	9.8
Natural disaster	61	15	0.2	24.6
Other reasons	1,373	317	4.0	23.1

Source: Bureau of the Census, Geographic Mobility: 2007 to 2008, Detailed Tables, Internet site http://www.census.gov/population/www/socdemo/migrate/cps2008.html; calculations by New Strategistt

15

Income

■ The median income of households with children under age 18 at home was $61,027 in 2007. Sharp differences exist, however, by household type.

■ Married couples with children under age 18 at home had a median income of $76,836 in 2007. In contrast, female-headed families with children had a median income of just $28,584.

■ The poverty rate among the iGeneration (people under age 13 in 2007) was an above-average 19.1 percent. The iGeneration accounts for more than one-quarter of the nation's poor.

Children in Married-Couple Families Are Better Off

Among families with children, married couples are far more affluent than single parents.

The financial well-being of children depends greatly on the type of household in which they live. Those living with married parents are far better off than those living in other types of households.

Among households with children under age 18 at home, the median income of married couples stood at $76,836 in 2007. This compares with a median of $45,880 for male-headed families and just $28,584 for female-headed families. Nonfamily households with children (such as cohabiting couples in which the child is not related to the householder), of which there are few, had a relatively high median income of $56,017.

Married couples with children aged 6 to 17 and none younger have the highest incomes, a median of $82,773 in 2007. Thirty-eight percent have incomes of $100,000 or more. The incomes of male- and female-headed families with school-aged children also surpass the incomes of those with preschoolers. Most householders with school-aged children are in their peak earning years, which accounts for their above-average incomes. Female-headed families with preschoolers have the lowest incomes—a median of just $17,630 in 2007.

■ Black children are worse off financially than non-Hispanic white children because they are much less likely to live in married-couple families.

Single-parent families have the lowest incomes

(median income of families with children under age 18 at home, by family type, 2007)

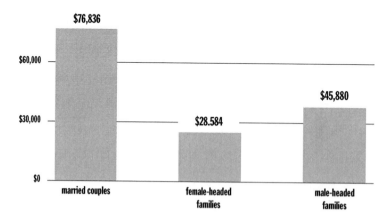

Table 15.1 Income of Households with Children under Age 18 by Household Type, 2007

(number and percent distribution of households with children under age 18 at home, by household income and household type, 2007; households in thousands as of 2008)

		family households			nonfamily households
	total	married couples	female-headed families	male-headed families	
Total households with children	**39,349**	**26,487**	**9,725**	**2,708**	**430**
Under $10,000	2,064	407	1,513	135	8
$10,000 to $19,999	3,115	905	1,884	279	48
$20,000 to $29,999	3,659	1,589	1,653	364	54
$30,000 to $39,999	3,647	1,897	1,335	382	35
$40,000 to $49,999	3,429	2,135	935	313	45
$50,000 to $59,999	3,317	2,296	708	275	37
$60,000 to $69,999	3,007	2,302	422	246	38
$70,000 to $79,999	2,900	2,351	346	163	42
$80,000 to $89,999	2,366	1,983	235	117	31
$90,000 to $99,999	1,898	1,645	164	60	27
$100,000 or more	9,946	8,976	531	376	64
Median income	$61,027	$76,836	$28,584	$45,880	$56,017
Total households with children	**100.0%**	**100.0%**	**100.0%**	**100.0%**	**100.0%**
Under $10,000	5.2	1.5	15.6	5.0	1.9
$10,000 to $19,999	7.9	3.4	19.4	10.3	11.2
$20,000 to $29,999	9.3	6.0	17.0	13.4	12.6
$30,000 to $39,999	9.3	7.2	13.7	14.1	8.1
$40,000 to $49,999	8.7	8.1	9.6	11.6	10.5
$50,000 to $59,999	8.4	8.7	7.3	10.2	8.6
$60,000 to $69,999	7.6	8.7	4.3	9.1	8.8
$70,000 to $79,999	7.4	8.9	3.6	6.0	9.8
$80,000 to $89,999	6.0	7.5	2.4	4.3	7.2
$90,000 to $99,999	4.8	6.2	1.7	2.2	6.3
$100,000 or more	25.3	33.9	5.5	13.9	14.9

Source: Bureau of the Census, 2008 Current Population Survey Annual Social and Economic Supplement, Internet site http://www.census.gov/hhes/www/macro/032008/hhinc/new04_000.htm; calculations by New Strategist

Table 15.2 Household Income of Married-Couple Families with Children under Age 18, 2007

(number and percent distribution of total married-couple households and those with related children under age 18 at home, by household income and age of children, 2007; households in thousands as of 2008)

	total	with one or more children			
		total	all under 6	some under 6, some 6 to 17	all 6 to 17
Total married-couple families	**58,395**	**26,450**	**6,459**	**5,859**	**14,133**
Under $10,000	1,064	412	99	112	202
$10,000 to $19,999	2,673	909	271	267	371
$20,000 to $29,999	4,533	1,597	452	459	689
$30,000 to $39,999	4,800	1,906	508	534	861
$40,000 to $49,999	4,963	2,139	549	585	1,004
$50,000 to $59,999	4,941	2,301	551	577	1,174
$60,000 to $69,999	4,746	2,285	578	509	1,199
$70,000 to $79,999	4,637	2,350	664	483	1,203
$80,000 to $89,999	4,051	1,978	445	392	1,143
$90,000 to $99,999	3,429	1,638	368	311	961
$100,000 or more	18,557	8,933	1,975	1,632	5,326
Median income	$72,589	$76,711	$72,710	$66,937	$82,773
Total married-couple families	**100.0%**	**100.0%**	**100.0%**	**100.0%**	**100.0%**
Under $10,000	1.8	1.6	1.5	1.9	1.4
$10,000 to $19,999	4.6	3.4	4.2	4.6	2.6
$20,000 to $29,999	7.8	6.0	7.0	7.8	4.9
$30,000 to $39,999	8.2	7.2	7.9	9.1	6.1
$40,000 to $49,999	8.5	8.1	8.5	10.0	7.1
$50,000 to $59,999	8.5	8.7	8.5	9.8	8.3
$60,000 to $69,999	8.1	8.6	8.9	8.7	8.5
$70,000 to $79,999	7.9	8.9	10.3	8.2	8.5
$80,000 to $89,999	6.9	7.5	6.9	6.7	8.1
$90,000 to $99,999	5.9	6.2	5.7	5.3	6.8
$100,000 or more	31.8	33.8	30.6	27.9	37.7

Source: Bureau of the Census, 2008 Current Population Survey Annual Social and Economic Supplement, Internet site http:// pubdb3.census.gov/macro/032008/faminc/new03_000.htm; calculations by New Strategist

Table 15.3 Household Income of Female-Headed Families with Children under Age 18, 2007

(number and percent distribution of total female-headed households and those with related children under age 18 at home, by household income and age of children, 2007; households in thousands as of 2008)

	total	with one or more children			
		total	all under 6	some under 6, some 6 to 17	all 6 to 17
Total female-headed families	**14,411**	**9,718**	**2,040**	**1,952**	**5,725**
Under $10,000	2,211	1,920	673	465	781
$10,000 to $19,999	2,588	2,003	413	479	1,110
$20,000 to $29,999	2,338	1,726	313	403	1,011
$30,000 to $39,999	1,905	1,330	223	234	874
$40,000 to $49,999	1,421	839	140	125	574
$50,000 to $59,999	1,078	569	83	79	405
$60,000 to $69,999	757	354	47	48	258
$70,000 to $79,999	562	283	36	32	215
$80,000 to $89,999	426	183	30	23	130
$90,000 to $99,999	251	106	15	13	81
$100,000 or more	877	405	65	52	288
Median income	$30,296	$24,949	$17,630	$20,779	$29,506
Total female-headed families	**100.0%**	**100.0%**	**100.0%**	**100.0%**	**100.0%**
Under $10,000	15.3	19.8	33.0	23.8	13.6
$10,000 to $19,999	18.0	20.6	20.2	24.5	19.4
$20,000 to $29,999	16.2	17.8	15.3	20.6	17.7
$30,000 to $39,999	13.2	13.7	10.9	12.0	15.3
$40,000 to $49,999	9.9	8.6	6.9	6.4	10.0
$50,000 to $59,999	7.5	5.9	4.1	4.0	7.1
$60,000 to $69,999	5.3	3.6	2.3	2.5	4.5
$70,000 to $79,999	3.9	2.9	1.8	1.6	3.8
$80,000 to $89,999	3.0	1.9	1.5	1.2	2.3
$90,000 to $99,999	1.7	1.1	0.7	0.7	1.4
$100,000 or more	6.1	4.2	3.2	2.7	5.0

Source: Bureau of the Census, 2008 Current Population Survey Annual Social and Economic Supplement, Internet site http://pubdb3.census.gov/macro/032008/faminc/new03_000.htm; calculations by New Strategist

Table 15.4 Household Income of Male-Headed Families with Children under Age 18, 2007

(number and percent distribution of total male-headed households and those with related children under age 18 at home, by household income and age of children, 2007; households in thousands as of 2008)

	total	with one or more children total	all under 6	some under 6, some 6 to 17	all 6 to 17
Total male-headed families	**5,103**	**2,700**	**774**	**346**	**1,580**
Under $10,000	332	219	96	29	94
$10,000 to $19,999	578	352	130	60	161
$20,000 to $29,999	658	428	167	54	206
$30,000 to $39,999	721	408	104	57	247
$40,000 to $49,999	581	307	76	39	192
$50,000 to $59,999	507	250	67	22	159
$60,000 to $69,999	390	187	38	21	128
$70,000 to $79,999	254	105	16	10	79
$80,000 to $89,999	226	93	21	12	58
$90,000 to $99,999	177	66	9	12	46
$100,000 or more	678	286	49	28	209
Median income	$44,358	$38,083	$29,651	$35,010	$44,403
Total male-headed families	**100.0%**	**100.0%**	**100.0%**	**100.0%**	**100.0%**
Under $10,000	6.5	8.1	12.4	8.4	5.9
$10,000 to $19,999	11.3	13.0	16.8	17.3	10.2
$20,000 to $29,999	12.9	15.9	21.6	15.6	13.0
$30,000 to $39,999	14.1	15.1	13.4	16.5	15.6
$40,000 to $49,999	11.4	11.4	9.8	11.3	12.2
$50,000 to $59,999	9.9	9.3	8.7	6.4	10.1
$60,000 to $69,999	7.6	6.9	4.9	6.1	8.1
$70,000 to $79,999	5.0	3.9	2.1	2.9	5.0
$80,000 to $89,999	4.4	3.4	2.7	3.5	3.7
$90,000 to $99,999	3.5	2.4	1.2	3.5	2.9
$100,000 or more	13.3	10.6	6.3	8.1	13.2

Source: Bureau of the Census, 2008 Current Population Survey Annual Social and Economic Supplement, Internet site http:// pubdb3.census.gov/macro/032008/faminc/new03_000.htm; calculations by New Strategist

Children Have the Highest Poverty Rate

The iGeneration accounts for more than one-quarter of the nation's poor.

Children and young adults are much more likely to be poor than middle-aged or older adults. While 12.5 percent of Americans were poor in 2007, the poverty rate among the iGeneration (people under age 13 in 2007) was a larger 19.1 percent. Children under age 13 account for 27 percent of the nation's poor. Black and Hispanic members of the iGeneration are much more likely to be poor (35.9 and 29.6 percent, respectively) than non-Hispanic whites or Asians (10.8 and 11.5 percent, respectively). Non-Hispanic whites account for only 31 percent of the iGen poor.

Children under age 18 living in families headed by married couples are much less likely to be poor than those in single-parent families. Only 6.7 percent of children in married-couple families are poor versus 37.0 percent of those in female-headed families. The poverty rate is even higher among black (43.7 percent) and Hispanic children (46.6 percent) living in female-headed single-parent families.

■ The poverty rate for the iGeneration is well above average because many live in female-headed families—the poorest household type.

In the iGeneration, non-Hispanic whites have the lowest poverty rate

(percent of people under age 13 who live below poverty level, by race and Hispanic origin, 2007)

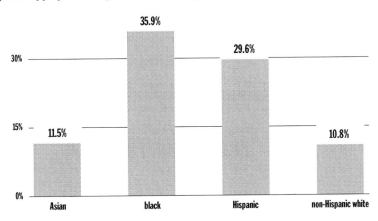

Table 15.5 People below Poverty Level by Age, Race, and Hispanic Origin, 2007

(number, percent, and percent distribution of people below poverty level by age, race, and Hispanic origin, 2007; people in thousands as of 2008)

	total	Asian	black	Hispanic	non-Hispanic white
NUMBER IN POVERTY					
Total people	**37,276**	**1,467**	**9,668**	**9,890**	**16,032**
iGeneration (under 13)	10,008	306	3,137	3,463	3,143
Under age 18	13,325	431	4,178	4,483	4,256
Aged 18 to 64	20,401	891	4,743	5,408	9,597
Aged 65 or older	3,557	145	749	437	2,180
PERCENT IN POVERTY					
Total people	**12.5%**	**10.2%**	**24.4%**	**21.5%**	**8.2%**
iGeneration (under 13)	19.1	11.5	35.9	29.6	10.8
Under age 18	18.0	11.9	33.8	28.7	10.1
Aged 18 to 64	10.9	9.4	19.8	17.9	7.7
Aged 65 or older	9.7	11.2	23.3	17.1	7.4
PERCENT DISTRIBUTION OF POOR BY AGE					
Total people	**100.0%**	**100.0%**	**100.0%**	**100.0%**	**100.0%**
iGeneration (under 13)	26.8	20.9	32.4	35.0	19.6
Under age 18	35.7	29.4	43.2	45.3	26.5
Aged 18 to 64	54.7	60.7	49.1	54.7	59.9
Aged 65 or older	9.5	9.9	7.7	4.4	13.6
PERCENT DISTRIBUTION OF POOR BY RACE AND HISPANIC ORIGIN					
Total people	**100.0%**	**3.9%**	**25.9%**	**26.5%**	**43.0%**
iGeneration (under 13)	100.0	3.1	31.3	34.6	31.4
Under age 18	100.0	3.2	31.4	33.6	31.9
Aged 18 to 64	100.0	4.4	23.2	26.5	47.0
Aged 65 or older	100.0	4.1	21.1	12.3	61.3

Note: Numbers do not add to total because Asians and blacks include those who identify themselves as being of the race alone and those who identify themselves as being of the race in combination with other races, because Hispanics may be of any race, and because not all races are shown. Non-Hispanic whites are those who identify themselves as being white alone and not Hispanic.

Source: Bureau of the Census, 2008 Current Population Survey Annual Social and Economic Supplement, Internet site http://www.census.gov/hhes/www/macro/032008/pov/new34_100.htm; calculations by New Strategist

Table 15.6 Families with Children in Poverty by Family Type, Race, and Hispanic Origin, 2007

(number and percent of families with children under age 18 in poverty, and percent distribution of families with children in poverty, by type of family and race and Hispanic origin of householder, 2007; families in thousands as of 2008)

	total	Asian	black	Hispanic	non-Hispanic white
NUMBER IN POVERTY					
Total families with children in poverty	**5,830**	**178**	**1,706**	**1,759**	**2,176**
Married couples	1,765	109	194	766	678
Female householders, no spouse present	3,593	65	1,385	881	1,283
Male householders, no spouse present	471	4	128	112	215
PERCENT IN POVERTY					
Total families with children	**15.0%**	**9.6%**	**29.0%**	**24.9%**	**9.2%**
Married couples	6.7	7.1	8.5	16.4	3.8
Female householders, no spouse present	37.0	27.8	43.7	46.6	29.2
Male householders, no spouse present	17.5	5.1	29.5	22.0	13.2
PERCENT DISTRIBUTION OF FAMILIES IN POVERTY BY RACE AND HISPANIC ORIGIN					
Total families with children in poverty	**100.0%**	**3.1%**	**29.3%**	**30.2%**	**37.3%**
Married couples	100.0	6.2	11.0	43.4	38.4
Female householders, no spouse present	100.0	1.8	38.5	24.5	35.7
Male householders, no spouse present	100.0	0.8	27.2	23.8	45.6
PERCENT DISTRIBUTION OF FAMILIES IN POVERTY BY FAMILY TYPE					
Total families with children in poverty	**100.0%**	**100.0%**	**100.0%**	**100.0%**	**100.0%**
Married couples	30.3	61.2	11.4	43.5	31.2
Female householders, no spouse present	61.6	36.5	81.2	50.1	59.0
Male householders, no spouse present	8.1	2.2	7.5	6.4	9.9

Note: Numbers do not add to total because Asians and blacks are those who identify themselves as being of the race alone and those who identify themselves as being of the race in combination with other races. Non-Hispanic whites are those who identify themselves as being white alone and not Hispanic. Hispanics may be of any race.
Source: Bureau of the Census, 2008 Current Population Survey, Internet site http://pubdb3.census.gov/macro/032008/pov/new04_100_01.htm

16

Labor Force

■ Working parents are the norm for the iGeneration. Among women with children under age 18, fully 71 percent were in the labor force in 2007.

■ In the 62 percent majority of married couples with children under age 18, both husband and wife are employed. In just 30 percent, the father is the only employed parent.

■ Most children are in day care. Among the nation's preschoolers, only 39 percent are cared for only by their parents. The 61 percent majority are in nonparental care at least some of the time.

■ Children from affluent families and with college-educated mothers are more likely than other children to be in day care, and they are also more likely to be in center-based day care programs.

Most Children Have Working Parents

For the iGeneration, working mothers are by far the norm.

Among women with children under age 18, fully 71 percent were in the labor force in 2007 (the iGeneration was aged 0 to 13 in that year). Fifty-one percent of women with children under age 18 are employed full-time. Even among women with infants, 55 percent are in the labor force, and most of the workers have full-time jobs.

In 62 percent of married couples with children under age 18, both husband and wife are employed. In just 30 percent, the father is the only employed parent. Children in single-parent families also have parents who work. Seventy-three percent of women who head single-parent families have jobs, as do 84 percent of their male counterparts.

■ With working parents being the norm, family life is highly scheduled.

For most children in married-couple families, mom and dad are at work

(percent distribution of married couples with children under age 18 by labor force status of parents, 2007)

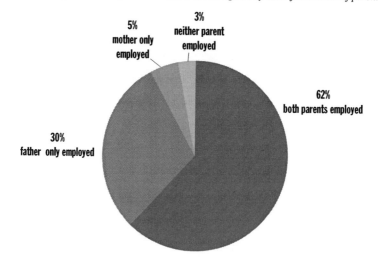

5%
mother only
employed

3%
neither parent
employed

62%
both parents employed

30%
father only employed

Table 16.1 Labor Force Status of Women by Presence of Children, 2007

(number and percent distribution of women aged 16 or older by labor force status and presence and age of own children under age 18 at home, 2007; numbers in thousands)

	civilian population	civilian labor force				not in labor force
		total	employed			
			total	full-time	part-time	
TOTAL WOMEN	**119,694**	**70,988**	**67,792**	**51,056**	**16,736**	**48,706**
No children under age 18	**82,577**	**44,620**	**42,635**	**32,003**	**10,632**	**37,957**
With children under age 18	**37,117**	**26,368**	**25,157**	**19,053**	**6,104**	**10,749**
Children aged 6 to 17, none younger	20,599	15,910	15,310	11,910	3,400	4,689
Children under age 6	16,518	10,458	9,847	7,143	2,704	6,060
Children under age 3	9,659	5,721	5,354	3,783	1,571	3,938
Children under age 1	3,346	1,845	1,721	1,208	513	1,501
TOTAL WOMEN	**100.0%**	**59.3%**	**56.6%**	**42.7%**	**14.0%**	**40.7%**
No children under age 18	**100.0**	**54.0**	**51.6**	**38.8**	**12.9**	**46.0**
With children under age 18	**100.0**	**71.0**	**67.8**	**51.3**	**16.4**	**29.0**
Children aged 6 to 17, none younger	100.0	77.2	74.3	57.8	16.5	22.8
Children under age 6	100.0	63.3	59.6	43.2	16.4	36.7
Children under age 3	100.0	59.2	55.4	39.2	16.3	40.8
Children under age 1	100.0	55.1	51.4	36.1	15.3	44.9

Source: Bureau of Labor Statistics, Employment Characteristics of Families, Internet sites http://www.bls.gov/news.release/famee.t05.htm and http://www.bls.gov/news.release/famee.t06.htm

Table 16.2 Labor Force Status of Families with Children under Age 18, 2007

(number and percent distribution of families by employment status of parent and age of youngest own child under age 18 at home, by family type, 2007; numbers in thousands)

		youngest child	
	total	6 to 17	under 6
NUMBER			
Married couples with children under age 18	**25,125**	**13,823**	**11,302**
One or both parents employed	**24,459**	**13,435**	**11,024**
Mother employed	16,855	10,126	6,729
Both parents employed	15,627	9,341	6,287
Mother employed not father	1,228	785	442
Father employed, not mother	7,614	3,309	4,295
Neither parent employed	**666**	**388**	**278**
Female-headed families with children under age 18	**8,554**	**5,224**	**3,329**
Mother employed	6,224	4,070	2,154
Mother not employed	2,330	1,155	1,175
Male-headed families with children under age 18	**2,043**	**1,250**	**793**
Father employed	1,713	1,043	671
Father not employed	330	207	122
PERCENT DISTRIBUTION			
Married couples with children under age 18	**100.0%**	**100.0%**	**100.0%**
One or both parents employed	**97.3**	**97.2**	**97.5**
Mother employed	67.1	73.3	59.5
Both parents employed	62.2	67.6	55.6
Mother employed, not father	4.9	5.7	3.9
Father employed, not mother	30.3	23.9	38.0
Neither parent employed	**2.7**	**2.8**	**2.5**
Female-headed families with children under age 18	**100.0**	**100.0**	**100.0**
Mother employed	72.8	77.9	64.7
Mother not employed	27.2	22.1	35.3
Male-headed families with children under age 18	**100.0**	**100.0**	**100.0**
Father employed	83.8	83.4	84.6
Father not employed	16.2	16.6	15.4

Source: Bureau of Labor Statistics, Employment Characteristics of Families, Internet site http://www.bls.gov/news.release/famee.t04.htm

Most Preschoolers Are in Day Care

The children of the most affluent and highly educated mothers are most likely to be in day care.

Among the nation's preschoolers, only 39 percent are in parental care only, according to a 2005 study (the latest data available). The 61 percent majority are in nonparental care at least some of the time. More than one in three are in a center-based program, such as a day care center, prekindergarten, nursery school, or Head Start. The children of mothers with a college degree are most likely to use nonparental care (70 percent) and be in a center-based program (46 percent). Similarly, children in families with the highest incomes are most likely to be in nonparental care (68 percent) and be in a center-based program (42 percent).

Among children in kindergarten through 3rd grade, 53 percent are cared for by their parents before and after school and 47 percent are in nonparental care. Among children in 4th through 8th grade, a larger 53 percent are in nonparental care before and after school, but only because 22 percent take care of themselves. Most 4th through 8th graders participate in after-school activities, religious activities and sports being most popular. Non-Hispanic white children are far more likely than black or Hispanic children to take part in after-school activities (63 percent versus 40 and 35 percent, respectively).

■ The differences in participation in after-school activities by race and Hispanic origin have long-term effects on school performance and college admissions.

Non-Hispanic white children are much more likely than others to participate in after-school activities

(percent of children in 4th to 8th grades who participate in after-school activities, by race and Hispanic origin, 2005)

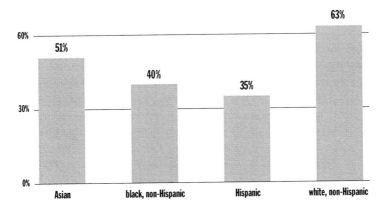

Table 16.3 Day Care Arrangements of Preschoolers, 2005

(percent distribution of children aged 0 to 6 not yet in kindergarten, by type of care, child and family characteristics, 2005)

| | | | nonparental care | | | |
| | | | | care in a home | | |
	total	parental care only	total	by a relative	by a nonrelative	center-based program
TOTAL CHILDREN	100.0%	39.2%	60.8%	22.3%	13.9%	36.1%
Age						
Aged 0 to 2	100.0	49.3	50.7	22.0	15.6	19.6
Aged 3 to 6	100.0	23.6	73.7	22.7	11.7	57.1
Race and Hispanic origin						
Asian	100.0	43.5	56.5	21.3	9.0	37.0
Black, non-Hispanic	100.0	30.1	69.9	27.7	10.2	43.9
Hispanic	100.0	50.5	49.5	21.2	10.4	25.2
White non-Hispanic	100.0	37.2	62.8	21.0	17.0	37.8
Poverty status						
Below poverty level	100.0	49.2	50.8	23.3	8.0	28.3
100 to 199 percent above poverty level	100.0	47.2	52.8	23.5	9.3	29.4
200 percent or more above poverty level	100.0	31.6	68.4	21.4	18.3	42.2
Family type						
Two parents	100.0	42.9	57.1	18.8	14.1	34.4
Two parents, married	100.0	41.8	58.2	18.6	14.2	35.8
Two parents, unmarried	100.0	53.0	47.0	20.4	13.0	21.7
One parent	100.0	24.9	75.1	36.0	13.4	42.3
No parents	100.0	33.1	66.9	28.3	10.0	43.6
Mother's educational attainment						
Less than high school	100.0	63.7	36.3	16.1	5.5	18.9
High school graduate/GED	100.0	44.4	55.6	24.1	9.9	30.7
Vocational/technical/some college	100.0	36.5	63.5	25.8	14.5	35.2
College graduate	100.0	30.5	69.5	19.1	19.2	45.8
Mother's employment status						
Employed 35 or more hours per week	100.0	14.7	85.3	31.8	23.3	47.6
Employed fewer than 35 hours per week	100.0	30.3	69.7	30.5	18.0	37.8
Looking for work	100.0	53.3	46.7	20.7	7.5	23.3
Not in labor force	100.0	66.1	33.9	7.8	3.6	25.8
Region						
Northeast	100.0	38.3	61.7	21.0	15.1	37.9
Midwest	100.0	38.0	62.0	22.3	11.1	38.8
South	100.0	36.7	63.3	23.8	18.8	33.5
West	100.0	43.9	56.1	21.8	12.6	33.1

Note: Numbers may not sum to total because there may be more than one type of nonparental care arrangement. Center-based care includes day care centers, prekindergartens, nursery schools, Head Start programs, and other early childhood education programs.
Source: Federal Interagency Forum on Child and Family Statistics, America's Children in Brief: Key National Indicators of Well-Being, 2008, Internet site http://childstats.gov/americaschildren/tables.asp

Table 16.4 Before- and After-School Activities of Children, 2005

(percent distribution of children in kindergarten through eighth grade, by type of before- and after-school care, poverty status, race, and Hispanic origin, 2005)

	total	poverty status			race and Hispanic origin			
		below poverty	100–199% above poverty level	200% or more above poverty level	Asian	black, non-Hispanic	Hispanic	white, non-Hispanic
Kindergarten to third grade								
TOTAL CHILDREN	100.0%	100.0%	100.0%	100.0%	100.0%	100.0%	100.0%	100.0%
Care arrangements								
Parent care only	53.1	52.0	54.5	53.0	49.9	34.6	55.3	58.3
Nonparental care	46.9	48.0	45.5	47.0	50.1	65.4	44.7	41.7
Home-based care	23.6	25.2	24.5	22.6	26.5	32.2	20.4	22.0
Center-based care	24.4	25.0	21.6	25.2	21.4	39.8	23.4	20.5
Activities used for supervision	5.2	3.1	5.3	6.0	13.4	5.8	3.2	4.8
Self-care	2.6	5.1	3.6	1.3	3.6	4.1	4.2	1.6
Activities*								
Any activity	46.2	24.3	34.0	59.5	45.8	30.4	30.4	56.2
Sports	31.8	12.1	19.5	44.3	29.3	16.8	20.8	40.2
Religious activities	19.4	13.5	14.8	23.4	11.5	14.6	11.9	24.0
Arts	17.2	6.0	10.8	24.1	27.1	8.3	8.2	21.8
Scouts	12.9	5.3	8.0	17.8	11.1	4.9	3.8	18.2
Academic activities	4.7	3.8	3.8	5.3	7.4	4.4	3.5	5.1
Community services	4.2	1.9	3.0	5.5	2.6	3.3	1.7	5.3
Clubs	3.2	1.3	2.4	4.3	4.2	1.1	1.8	4.3
Fourth to eighth grade								
TOTAL CHILDREN	100.0%	100.0%	100.0%	100.0%	100.0%	100.0%	100.0%	100.0%
Care arrangements								
Parent care only	46.9	46.7	45.2	47.6	44.2	34.5	45.0	51.2
Nonparental care	53.1	53.3	54.8	52.4	55.8	65.5	55.0	48.8
Home-based care	18.1	15.0	20.0	18.4	17.5	24.1	18.6	16.4
Center-based care	19.0	21.3	21.3	17.4	21.9	28.9	25.4	14.2
Activities used for supervision	9.0	7.8	6.9	10.2	11.9	10.5	7.5	8.9
Self-care	22.2	23.5	23.8	21.2	21.0	27.1	19.6	21.1
Activities*								
Any activity	53.7	30.4	40.5	65.9	51.2	39.7	35.4	63.3
Sports	39.3	18.6	26.1	50.8	37.2	24.2	26.7	47.8
Religious activities	24.9	12.5	20.0	30.7	18.3	20.9	14.8	29.7
Arts	21.5	9.7	12.5	28.5	25.5	13.3	13.2	25.8
Community services	12.7	5.0	10.6	15.9	13.1	8.2	7.1	15.6
Scouts	10.1	4.8	6.4	13.2	7.7	5.6	5.4	13.3
Academic activities	9.7	6.6	7.1	11.6	13.0	12.0	5.9	10.0
Clubs	8.7	3.7	4.6	11.8	8.9	4.9	4.1	11.0

* "Activities" are organized programs outside of school hours that are not part of a before- or after-school program.
Note: Numbers may not sum to total because there may be more than one type of arrangement or activity.
Source: Federal Interagency Forum on Child and Family Statistics, America's Children in Brief: Key National Indicators of Well-Being, 2008, Internet site http://childstats.gov/americaschildren/tables.asp

17

Living Arrangements

■ Seventy percent of children under age 18 lived with two parents in 2008—down from 85 percent in 1970.

■ The proportion of children who live with two parents (married or unmarried) ranges from a low of 38 percent among black children to a high of 85 percent among Asian children.

■ Non-Hispanic white children are more likely than Asian, black, or Hispanic children to participate in sports, clubs, and lessons.

■ The percentage of teenagers who have dinner with a parent every day ranges from a high of 68 percent for those with the least-educated parents to a low of 42 percent for those with the most-educated parents.

■ Although most children live in a nice neighborhood, a substantial proportion does not. Twenty percent of children are kept inside the house because of danger.

Most Married Couples Do Not Have Children under Age 18 at Home

Among those who do, few have more than one or two.

Among the nation's 78 million families, only 46 percent include children under age 18. When children aged 18 or older are also considered, the 60 percent majority of families include children. Among married couples, only 43 percent have children under age 18 at home and 54 percent have children of any age living with them. Female-headed families are more likely to have children at home—58 percent include children under age 18 and 85 percent include children of any age. A much smaller 42 percent of male-headed families include children under age 18.

Among married couples with children under age 18 in their home, 39 percent have only one and another 39 percent have two. Female-headed families are more likely to have only one child under age 18 at home (49 percent), and male-headed families are most likely to have only one (61 percent).

■ The traditional nuclear family—husband, wife, and children under age 18—accounts for a shrinking share of households as a growing proportion of Baby Boomers become empty-nesters.

Only 20 percent of married couples have preschoolers

(percent of married-couple households with children of selected ages in the home, 2008)

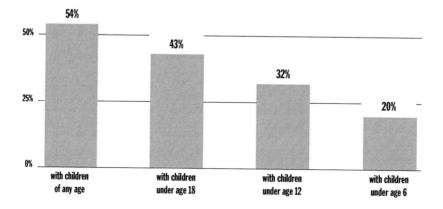

Table 17.1 Total Families by Presence and Age of Children, 2008

(number and percent distribution of family households by presence and age of own children under age 18 and type of family, 2008; numbers in thousands)

	total	married couples	female householder, no spouse present	male householder, no spouse present
TOTAL FAMILY HOUSEHOLDS	**77,873**	**58,370**	**14,404**	**5,100**
With children of any age	**46,995**	**31,696**	**12,206**	**3,093**
With children under age 18	35,709	25,173	8,374	2,162
With children under age 12	26,125	18,722	5,933	1,470
With children under age 6	15,733	11,510	3,312	912
Percent distribution by presence and age of children				
TOTAL FAMILY HOUSEHOLDS	**100.0%**	**100.0%**	**100.0%**	**100.0%**
With children of any age	**60.3**	**54.3**	**84.7**	**60.6**
With children under age 18	45.9	43.1	58.1	42.4
With children under age 12	33.5	32.1	41.2	28.8
With children under age 6	20.2	19.7	23.0	17.9
Percent distribution by family type				
TOTAL FAMILY HOUSEHOLDS	**100.0%**	**75.0%**	**18.5%**	**6.5%**
With children of any age	**100.0**	**67.4**	**26.0**	**6.6**
With children under age 18	100.0	70.5	23.5	6.1
With children under age 12	100.0	71.7	22.7	5.6
With children under age 6	100.0	73.2	21.1	5.8

Source: Bureau of the Census, America's Families and Living Arrangements: 2008, Current Population Survey Annual Social and Economic Supplement, Internet site http://www.census.gov/population/www/socdemo/hh-fam/cps2008.html; calculations by New Strategist

Table 17.2 Families by Number of Children under Age 18, 2008

(number and percent distribution of family households with own children under age 18 by number of children and type of family, 2008; numbers in thousands)

	total	married couples	female householder, no spouse present	male householder, no spouse present
Total families with children under age 18	**35,709**	**25,173**	**8,374**	**2,162**
One child	15,160	9,733	4,104	1,323
Two children	13,158	9,886	2,675	597
Three children	5,234	3,953	1,107	174
Four or more children	2,157	1,602	487	68
PERCENT DISTRIBUTION BY NUMBER OF CHILDREN				
Total families with children under age 18	**100.0%**	**100.0%**	**100.0%**	**100.0%**
One child	42.5	38.7	49.0	61.2
Two children	36.8	39.3	31.9	27.6
Three children	14.7	15.7	13.2	8.0
Four or more children	6.0	6.4	5.8	3.1
PERCENT DISTRIBUTION BY FAMILY TYPE				
Total families with children under age 18	**100.0%**	**70.5%**	**23.5%**	**6.1%**
One child	100.0	64.2	27.1	8.7
Two children	100.0	75.1	20.3	4.5
Three children	100.0	75.5	21.2	3.3
Four or more children	100.0	74.3	22.6	3.2

Source: Bureau of the Census, America's Families and Living Arrangements: 2008, Current Population Survey Annual Social and Economic Supplement, Internet site http://www.census.gov/population/www/socdemo/hh-fam/cps2008.html; calculations by New Strategist

Most Children Have Siblings in the Household

The largest share of children has a parent with a college degree.

Among the nation's 74 million children, about one in five is the only child in the household. Thirty-eight percent are sharing their living quarters with one brother or sister, and a substantial 41 percent have two or more siblings in the home.

The largest share of children lives in a family with a relatively low income. In 2008, fully 44 percent of children under age 18 lived in a family with an annual income below $50,000. Another 32 percent had a family income between $50,000 and $99,999. A fortunate 24 percent of children live in families with incomes of $100,000 or more.

More than one-third of the nation's children under age 18 have a parent with a bachelor's degree or even more education. Another 28 percent have parents with some college experience or an associate's degree. Combining these two categories reveals that the 62 percent majority of children have parents with college experience.

■ Because so many children have parents with college experience, the pressure on children to attend college themselves is intense.

Many children must share a bathroom with brothers and sisters

(percent distribution of children under age 18 by number of siblings in the home, 2008)

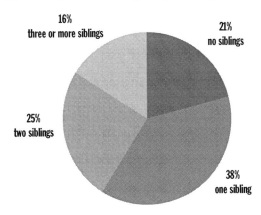

16%
three or more siblings

21%
no siblings

25%
two siblings

38%
one sibling

Table 17.3 Children under Age 18 by Family Characteristics, 2008

(number and percent distribution of children under age 18 by child and family characteristics, 2008; numbers in thousands)

	number	percent distribution
TOTAL CHILDREN UNDER AGE 18	**74,104**	**100.0%**
Sex of child		
Female	36,227	48.9
Male	37,877	51.1
Age of child		
Under age 1	4,254	5.7
Aged 1 to 2	8,396	11.3
Aged 3 to 5	12,286	16.6
Aged 6 to 8	12,040	16.2
Aged 9 to 11	11,774	15.9
Aged 12 to 14	12,192	16.5
Aged 15 to 17	13,162	17.8
Number of siblings in household		
None	15,495	20.9
One	28,477	38.4
Two	18,440	24.9
Three or more	11,693	15.8
Family income		
Under $10,000	5,657	7.6
$10,000 to $19,999	6,506	8.8
$20,000 to $29,999	7,363	9.9
$30,000 to $39,999	6,974	9.4
$40,000 to $49,999	6,306	8.5
$50,000 to $74,999	13,606	18.4
$75,000 to $99,999	9,926	13.4
$100,000 or more	17,766	24.0
Education of parent		
Not a high school graduate	7,949	10.7
High school graduate	17,054	23.0
Some college or associate's degree	20,552	27.7
Bachelor's degree or more	25,732	34.7
No parents present	2,818	3.8
Parents' labor force status		
Two parents, both in labor force	31,986	43.2
Two parents, father only in labor force	16,234	21.9
One parent, mother in labor force	12,757	17.2
One parent, mother not in labor force	4,131	5.6
No parents present	2,818	3.8
One parent, father in labor force	2,244	3.0
Two parents, mother only in labor force	2,126	2.9
Two parents, neither in labor force	1,439	1.9
One parent, father not in labor force	369	0.5

Source: Bureau of the Census, America's Families and Living Arrangements: 2008, Current Population Survey Annual Social and Economic Supplement, Internet site http://www.census.gov/population/www/socdemo/hh-fam/cps2008.html; calculations by New Strategist

Most Moms Are in the Labor Force

Stay-at-home mothers are not the norm, even among couples with preschoolers.

Among married couples with children under age 15, the 70 percent majority has a mother in the labor force. Only 26 percent have a mom who stays home to care for her family. Stay-at-home dads are even less common. Fewer than 1 percent of married couples with children under age 15 have a father who is not in the labor force because he is caring for the family.

Couples with preschoolers are only slightly more likely than average to have a stay-at-home mother, at 32 percent. They are about equally as likely to have a stay-at-home father, at 1 percent.

■ Perhaps no characteristic distinguishes today's children from those in the past more than working parents. With both mother and father in the labor force, family life has become much more complicated.

One-third of couples with preschoolers have a stay-at-home mom

(percent distribution of married-couple family groups with children under age 6 by labor force status of mother during past year, 2008)

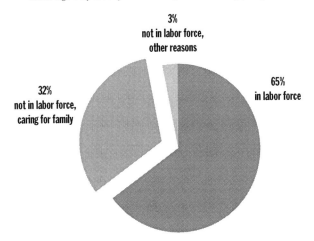

3%
not in labor force,
other reasons

32%
not in labor force,
caring for family

65%
in labor force

Table 17.4 Stay-at-Home Parents among Married Couples, 2008

(number and percent distribution of married-couple family groups with children under age 15 by stay-at-home status of mother and father and age of child, 2008; numbers in thousands)

	with children under age 15		with children under age 6	
	number	percent distribution	number	percent distribution
Total married-couple family groups	**22,445**	**100.0%**	**11,848**	**100.0%**
Mother's labor force status in past year				
In labor force one or more weeks	15,770	70.3	7,715	65.1
Not in labor force, caring for family	5,907	26.3	3,786	32.0
Not in labor force, other reason	767	3.4	347	2.9
Father's labor force status in past year				
In labor force one or more weeks	21,409	95.4	11,416	96.4
Not in labor force, caring for family	197	0.9	116	1.0
Not in labor force, other reason	838	3.7	315	2.7

Note: Married-couple family groups include married-couple householders and married couples living in households headed by others.
Source: Bureau of the Census, America's Families and Living Arrangements: 2008, Current Population Survey Annual Social and Economic Supplement, Internet site http://www.census.gov/population/www/socdemo/hh-fam/cps2008.html; calculations by New Strategist

Seventy Percent of Children Live with Two Parents

Fewer than 4 percent live with their father only.

Among the nation's 74 million children under age 18, the 70 percent majority lived with two parents in 2008—down from 85 percent in 1970. The proportion of children who live with two parents (married or unmarried) ranges from a low of 38 percent among black children to a high of 85 percent among Asian children. A smaller share of children lives with two biological parents, ranging from 29 percent of blacks to 76 percent of Asians.

The proportion of children who live with their mother only ranges from a low of 11 percent among Asians to a high of 50 percent among blacks. Few children live with only their father regardless of race or Hispanic origin.

■ The poverty rate among children is unlikely to decline significantly until fewer children live in single-parent families.

Children's living arrangements vary greatly by race and Hispanic origin

(percent of children who live with two married, biological parents, by race and Hispanic origin, 2008)

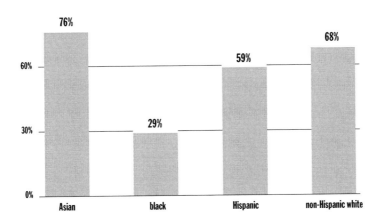

Table 17.5 Living Arrangements of Children, 1970 to 2008

(number and percent distribution of children under age 18 by living arrangement, 1970 to 2008; numbers in thousands)

	total		children living with			
	number	percent	two parents	mother only	father only	neither parent
Total children						
2008	74,104	100.0%	69.9%	22.8%	3.5%	3.8%
2007*	73,746	100.0	70.7	22.6	3.2	3.5
2007*	73,746	100.0	67.8	24.2	4.5	3.5
2006	73,664	100.0	67.4	23.3	4.7	4.6
2005	73,523	100.0	67.4	23.4	4.7	4.5
2000	72,012	100.0	69.1	22.4	4.2	4.2
1995	70,254	100.0	68.7	23.5	3.5	4.3
1990	64,137	100.0	72.5	21.6	3.1	2.8
1985	62,475	100.0	73.9	20.9	2.5	2.7
1980	63,427	100.0	76.7	18.0	1.7	3.7
1975	66,087	100.0	80.3	15.5	1.5	2.7
1970	69,162	100.0	85.2	10.8	1.1	2.9

* Before 2007, the Current Population Survey classified children as living with two parents only if the parents were married. Beginning in 2007, children were counted as living with two parents if there were two parents in the home regardless of marital status. Results for both the original and new methodology in 2007 are shown here for comparative purposes.
Source: Bureau of the Census, Families and Living Arrangements, Historical Time Series, Internet site http://www.census.gov/population/www/socdemo/hh-fam.html; calculations by New Strategist

Table 17.6 Living Arrangements of Children, 2008: Total Children

(number and percent distribution of total children under age 18 by living arrangement, 2008; numbers in thousands)

	number	percent distribution
TOTAL CHILDREN	**74,104**	**100.0%**
Living with two parents	**51,785**	**69.9**
Married parents	49,426	66.7
Unmarried parents	2,360	3.2
Biological mother and father	46,427	62.7
Married parents	44,376	59.9
Biological mother and stepfather	3,183	4.3
Biological father and stepmother	930	1.3
Biological mother and adoptive father	195	0.3
Biological father and adoptive mother	42	0.1
Adoptive mother and father	795	1.1
Other	213	0.3
Living with one parent	**19,501**	**26.3**
Mother only	16,888	22.8
Father only	2,613	3.5
Living with no parents	**2,818**	**3.8**
Grandparents	1,510	2.0
Other	1,308	1.8

Source: Bureau of the Census, Current Population Survey Annual Social and Economic Supplement, America's Families and Living Arrangements: 2008, detailed tables, Internet site http://www.census.gov/population/www/socdemo/hh-fam/cps2008 .html; calculations by New Strategist

Table 17.7 Living Arrangements of Children, 2008: Asian Children

(number and percent distribution of Asian children under age 18 by living arrangement, 2008; numbers in thousands)

	number	percent distribution
ASIAN CHILDREN	**3,608**	**100.0%**
Living with two parents	**3,058**	**84.8**
Married parents	2,979	82.6
Unmarried parents	79	2.2
Biological mother and father	2,826	78.3
Married parents	2,758	76.4
Biological mother and stepfather	88	2.4
Biological father and stepmother	36	1.0
Biological mother and adoptive father	7	0.2
Biological father and adoptive mother	4	0.1
Adoptive mother and father	94	2.6
Other	2	0.1
Living with one parent	**469**	**13.0**
Mother only	384	10.6
Father only	85	2.4
Living with no parents	**81**	**2.2**
Grandparents	18	0.5
Other	63	1.7

Note: Asians are those who identify themselves as being of the race alone and those who identify themselves as being of the race in combination with other races.
Source: Bureau of the Census, Current Population Survey Annual Social and Economic Supplement, America's Families and Living Arrangements: 2008, detailed tables, Internet site http://www.census.gov/population/www/socdemo/hh-fam/cps2008 .html; calculations by New Strategist

Table 17.8 Living Arrangements of Children, 2008: Black Children

(number and percent distribution of black children under age 18 by living arrangement, 2008; numbers in thousands)

	number	percent distribution
BLACK CHILDREN	**12,424**	**100.0%**
Living with two parents	**4,781**	**38.5**
Married parents	4,360	35.1
Unmarried parents	421	3.4
Biological mother and father	3,981	32.0
Married parents	3,611	29.1
Biological mother and stepfather	459	3.7
Biological father and stepmother	107	0.9
Biological mother and adoptive father	25	0.2
Biological father and adoptive mother	0	0.0
Adoptive mother and father	167	1.3
Other	42	0.3
Living with one parent	**6,652**	**53.5**
Mother only	6,247	50.3
Father only	405	3.3
Living with no parents	**991**	**8.0**
Grandparents	616	5.0
Other	375	3.0

Note: Blacks are those who identify themselves as being of the race alone and those who identify themselves as being of the race in combination with other races.
Source: Bureau of the Census, Current Population Survey Annual Social and Economic Supplement, America's Families and Living Arrangements: 2008, detailed tables, Internet site http://www.census.gov/population/www/socdemo/hh-fam/cps2008 .html; calculations by New Strategist

Table 17.9 **Living Arrangements of Children, 2008: Hispanic Children**

(number and percent distribution of Hispanic children under age 18 by living arrangement, 2008; numbers in thousands)

	number	percent distribution
HISPANIC CHILDREN	**15,644**	**100.0%**
Living with two parents	**10,902**	**69.7**
Married parents	10,046	64.2
Unmarried parents	855	5.5
Biological mother and father	9,982	63.8
Married parents	9,195	58.8
Biological mother and stepfather	635	4.1
Biological father and stepmother	139	0.9
Biological mother and adoptive father	28	0.2
Biological father and adoptive mother	8	0.1
Adoptive mother and father	81	0.5
Other	28	0.2
Living with one parent	**4,132**	**26.4**
Mother only	3,764	24.1
Father only	368	2.4
Living with no parents	**610**	**3.9**
Grandparents	235	1.5
Other	375	2.4

Source: Bureau of the Census, Current Population Survey Annual Social and Economic Supplement, America's Families and Living Arrangements: 2008, detailed tables, Internet site http://www.census.gov/population/www/socdemo/hh-fam/cps2008 .html; calculations by New Strategist

Table 17.10 Living Arrangements of Children, 2008: Non-Hispanic White Children

(number and percent distribution of non-Hispanic white children under age 18 by living arrangement, 2008; numbers in thousands)

	number	percent distribution
NON-HISPANIC WHITE CHILDREN	**42,051**	**100.0%**
Living with two parents	**32,712**	**77.8**
Married parents	31,700	75.4
Unmarried parents	1,012	2.4
Biological mother and father	29,365	69.8
Married parents	28,534	67.9
Biological mother and stepfather	1,969	4.7
Biological father and stepmother	641	1.5
Biological mother and adoptive father	133	0.3
Biological father and adoptive mother	31	0.1
Adoptive mother and father	436	1.0
Other	137	0.3
Living with one parent	**8,239**	**19.6**
Mother only	6,522	15.5
Father only	1,717	4.1
Living with no parents	**1,101**	**2.6**
Grandparents	618	1.5
Other	483	1.1

Note: Non-Hispanic whites are those who identify themselves as being white alone and not Hispanic.
Source: Bureau of the Census, Current Population Survey Annual Social and Economic Supplement, America's Families and Living Arrangements: 2008, detailed tables, Internet site http://www.census.gov/population/www/socdemo/hh-fam/cps2008 .html; calculations by New Strategist

Many Children Do Not Participate in Extracurricular Activities

Non-Hispanic whites are most likely to be involved in sports, clubs, and lessons.

When it is time to fill out college applications, non-Hispanic white children have a clear advantage. Many have participated in a long list of extracurricular activities that can be used to impress college admissions officers. Non-Hispanic white children are more likely than Asian, black, or Hispanic children to participate in sports, clubs, and lessons because their parents have the time and money to shuttle them from one activity to another.

According to a Census Bureau survey of family life, 51 percent of non-Hispanic white teens participated in sports, 40 percent participated in clubs, and 35 percent in lessons in 2006. Sixteen percent took part in all three. These figures are well above those for any other racial or ethnic group. Similarly, children from the most affluent families, with the most educated parents, were much more likely than others to be involved in extracurricular activities.

■ The advantages that accrue to the children of highly educated, affluent parents help them get into college, which explains why most college students have college-educated parents.

Minorities are much less likely to participate in sports, clubs, and lessons

(percent of children aged 12 to 17 who participated in extracurricular sports, clubs, and lessons, by race and Hispanic origin, 2006)

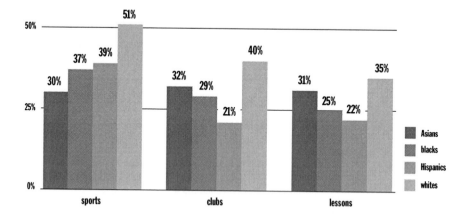

Table 17.11 Extracurricular Activities of Children, 2006

(percent of children aged 6 to 17 who participate in extracurricular sports, clubs, or lessons by characteristics of child and parent, by age of child, 2006)

	sports		clubs		lessons		all three activities	
	6 to 11	12 to 17	6 to 11	12 to 17	6 to 11	12 to 17	6 to 11	12 to 17
TOTAL CHILDREN	**39.1%**	**45.3%**	**31.1%**	**34.0%**	**33.0%**	**30.9%**	**11.5%**	**12.0%**
Race and Hispanic origin of child								
Asian alone	26.5	30.0	21.2	31.7	42.9	31.1	7.9	5.9
Black alone	24.1	36.8	24.9	28.7	24.0	25.1	6.3	8.3
Hispanic	26.0	38.9	18.8	20.9	21.9	22.0	4.5	4.6
Non-Hispanic white	48.3	51.0	37.7	39.5	39.0	35.3	15.5	15.7
Parent's highest level of educational attainment								
Less than high school	17.1	32.1	14.2	17.8	14.7	16.1	2.7	4.4
High school graduate	28.4	38.9	23.0	25.9	21.9	23.2	5.5	7.1
Some college	40.3	44.4	32.9	35.2	31.8	30.7	10.6	11.1
Associate's degree	41.3	46.4	32.2	35.0	33.0	31.9	11.2	11.8
Bachelor's degree	54.8	60.1	43.1	49.9	50.0	47.0	20.4	23.1
Advanced degree	60.5	57.8	46.8	49.7	58.2	46.4	25.7	21.8
Monthly family income								
Under $1,500	22.4	31.6	20.9	23.2	18.1	20.3	4.9	5.8
$1,500 to $2,999	26.5	33.6	25.8	25.3	22.0	21.8	6.7	6.5
$3,000 to $4,499	36.2	42.5	30.7	31.7	31.3	28.2	9.6	9.1
$4,500 to $5,999	41.4	47.4	33.5	33.4	31.4	31.2	11.8	12.8
$6,000 or more	54.1	56.5	38.3	43.0	47.1	40.3	17.8	17.8

Source: Bureau of the Census, A Child's Day: 2006 (Selected Indicators of Child Well-Being), Detailed Tables, Internet site http://www.census.gov/population/www/socdemo/2006_detailedtables.html

Most Parents Have Dinner with Their Children Daily

The most educated and affluent parents are least likely to have dinner with their children every day.

The percentage of parents who eat breakfast and dinner with their children every day during a typical week falls as children age into their teenage years. The 58 percent majority of preschoolers have breakfast with a parent every day during a typical week. Among 12-to-17-year-olds, the figure is just 24 percent.

The percentage of children who have dinner with a parent every day falls from 80 percent among preschoolers to 57 percent among teenagers. Interestingly, the most affluent and educated parents are least likely to have dinner with their children every day. For teenagers, the figure ranges from a high of 68 percent among those whose parent did not graduate from high school to a low of 42 percent for those whose parent has a graduate-level degree.

■ Educated and affluent parents often have demanding careers that take them away from home.

Most teens with educated parents do not have dinner with them daily

(percent of children aged 12 to 17 who have dinner with a parent every day during a typical week, by educational attainment of parent, 2006)

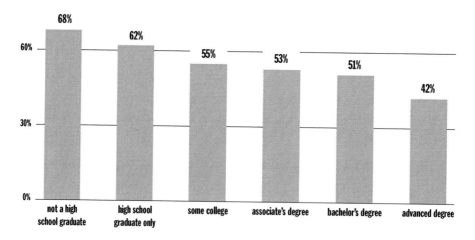

Table 17.12 Meals with Children, 2006

(percent of children under age 18 whose designated parent had selected meals with them every day during a typical week last month by characteristics of child and parent, by age of child, 2006)

	breakfast with parent every day			dinner with parent every day		
	under 6	6 to 11	12 to 17	under 6	6 to 11	12 to 17
TOTAL CHILDREN	**57.5%**	**40.5%**	**24.2%**	**79.7%**	**73.0%**	**56.5%**
Race and Hispanic origin of child						
Asian alone	65.2	48.5	26.3	84.4	78.8	55.7
Black alone	50.6	35.1	21.1	78.0	69.8	57.9
Hispanic	60.5	43.8	29.9	84.7	83.1	69.3
Non-Hispanic white	57.9	40.7	23.1	77.9	70.0	52.0
Parent's highest level of educational attainment						
Less than high school	65.0	42.2	26.3	84.8	79.8	68.5
High school graduate only	57.2	41.4	26.2	80.9	74.9	61.7
Some college	57.1	34.6	21.5	79.1	71.9	54.8
Associate's degree	50.3	39.2	21.4	78.0	72.9	53.3
Bachelor's degree	59.5	43.9	25.6	79.1	68.8	51.3
Advanced degree	57.2	45.3	24.8	75.8	70.5	42.3
Monthly family income						
Under $1,500	61.1	43.6	29.7	83.1	78.5	67.9
$1,500 to $2,999	59.9	38.6	25.3	81.5	74.4	64.5
$3,000 to $4,499	55.3	39.7	23.7	79.4	73.6	59.6
$4,500 to $5,999	55.5	38.2	22.0	78.6	71.8	51.8
$6,000 or more	55.6	41.8	22.9	77.4	70.0	48.7

Source: Bureau of the Census, A Child's Day: 2006 (Selected Indicators of Child Well-Being), Detailed Tables, Internet site http://www.census.gov/population/www/socdemo/2006_detailedtables.html

Most Children Live in Neighborhoods Where People Help Each Other

Nearly half of children live in a neighborhood where there are people who might be a bad influence, however.

In a survey of family life, the Census Bureau queried the parents of children under age 18 about their neighborhood. For the most part, parents reported being in the kind of neighborhood where people help one another and children can play safely outside. Seventy-three percent of children live in a neighborhood where people help each other, 75 percent live where people watch one another's children, and 80 percent live where adults nearby would help children outside if necessary. But nearly half (46 percent) of children live in a neighborhood in which there are people who might be a bad influence.

Although most children live in a nice neighborhood, a substantial proportion does not. Twenty percent of children are kept inside the house because of danger. The proportion rises as high as 35 percent among Hispanic children. Among children from the poorest families, 33 percent are kept inside for safety. In the richest families, only 12 percent must stay inside.

■ Although most children live in friendly, safe neighborhoods, a substantial proportion does not.

Hispanic children are most likely to be kept inside for safety

(percent of children who are kept inside the house because of danger, by race and Hispanic origin, 2006)

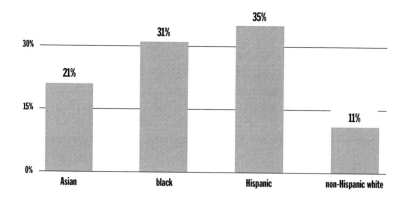

Table 17.13 Neighborhood Characteristics of Children, 2006

(percent of children under age 18 whose parent agrees that the child lives in a neighborhood with the selected characteristics, by characteristic of child and parent, 2006)

	people help each other	people watch each other's children	there are people I can count on	there are people who might be a bad influence	adults nearby would help children outside the house	children are kept inside the house because of danger	there are safe places for children to play
TOTAL CHILDREN	**73.1%**	**75.2%**	**77.6%**	**46.3%**	**80.3%**	**19.5%**	**81.3%**
Race and Hispanic origin of child							
Asian alone	71.7	66.0	71.0	29.7	70.2	21.0	76.2
Black alone	61.6	66.4	66.7	54.2	74.4	30.9	71.3
Hispanic	63.6	67.5	69.5	45.0	71.5	34.8	71.9
Non-Hispanic white	79.7	80.7	83.9	45.3	85.5	11.3	87.4
Parent's highest level of educational attainment							
Less than high school	61.2	69.2	70.3	48.1	73.7	33.7	70.5
High school graduate	70.6	72.8	74.8	48.8	77.8	23.8	77.6
Some college	71.4	73.7	76.2	49.5	80.3	18.2	80.7
Associate's degree	72.5	76.0	77.6	48.9	80.9	18.3	81.6
Bachelor's degree	81.8	80.2	83.9	39.7	84.7	11.4	89.1
Advanced degree	83.4	81.1	86.3	36.4	86.6	10.3	90.8
Monthly family income							
Under $1,500	62.4	69.8	69.9	54.6	75.1	32.8	72.2
$1,500 to $2,999	67.4	69.3	72.0	49.3	74.6	26.5	75.0
$3,000 to $4,499	69.7	73.0	74.9	47.7	78.1	20.4	80.0
$4,500 to $5,999	74.7	76.3	80.5	47.3	79.7	14.1	83.1
$6,000 or more	81.8	81.2	84.2	40.3	86.9	12.0	88.2

Source: Bureau of the Census, A Child's Day: 2006 (Selected Indicators of Child Well-Being), Detailed Tables, Internet site http://www.census.gov/population/www/socdemo/2006_detailedtables.html

18

Population

■ The iGeneration numbers 57 million, a figure that includes everyone born in 1995 or later (under age 14 in 2008). The iGeneration accounts for 19 percent of the total population.

■ America's children are much more diverse than middle-aged or older people. While non-Hispanic whites accounted for 66 percent of all Americans in 2008, their share is a smaller 56 percent among the iGeneration.

■ Among schoolchildren, most of those who do not speak English at home are able to speak English very well. Only 26 percent of the Spanish speakers aged 5 to 17, for example, cannot speak English very well.

■ Among children under age 15, Hispanics outnumber blacks in the West and Northeast. Blacks outnumber Hispanics in the Midwest and South. Children under age 15 account for 26 percent of the population of Utah. They are only 17 percent of the populations of Vermont and Maine.

The iGeneration Is Already Larger than Gen X

Nearly one in five Americans is in the iGeneration.

The iGeneration numbers 57 million, a figure that includes everyone born in 1995 or later (under age 14 in 2008). The iGeneration accounts for 19 percent of the total population, making it larger than Generation X or the generations that precede the Baby Boom.

Depending on the end date for the iGeneration, its size could grow to rival that of Millennials in the years ahead. The iGeneration is certain to outnumber Boomers with time because the Baby-Boom generation is shrinking with age.

■ The iGeneration is the most diverse, making it a difficult market to target.

The iGeneration is already bigger than Gen X

(percent distribution of the population by generation, 2008)

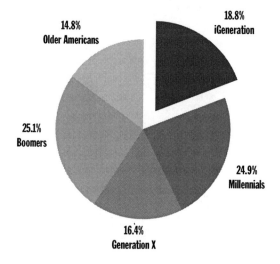

14.8%
Older Americans

18.8%
iGeneration

25.1%
Boomers

24.9%
Millennials

16.4%
Generation X

Table 18.1 Population by Age and Generation, 2008

(number and percent distribution of people by age and generation, 2008; numbers in thousands)

	number	percent distribution
Total people	**304,060**	**100.0%**
Under age 15	61,126	20.1
Under age 5	21,006	6.9
Aged 5 to 9	20,065	6.6
Aged 10 to 14	20,055	6.6
Aged 15 to 19	21,514	7.1
Aged 20 to 24	21,059	6.9
Aged 25 to 29	21,334	7.0
Aged 30 to 34	19,598	6.4
Aged 35 to 39	20,994	6.9
Aged 40 to 44	21,507	7.1
Aged 45 to 49	22,880	7.5
Aged 50 to 54	21,492	7.1
Aged 55 to 59	18,583	6.1
Aged 60 to 64	15,103	5.0
Aged 65 to 69	11,349	3.7
Aged 70 to 74	8,774	2.9
Aged 75 to 79	7,275	2.4
Aged 80 to 84	5,750	1.9
Aged 85 or older	5,722	1.9
Total people	**304,060**	**100.0**
iGeneration (under age 14)	57,115	18.8
Millennial (aged 14 to 31)	75,757	24.9
Generation X (aged 32 to 43)	49,958	16.4
Baby Boom (aged 44 to 62)	76,319	25.1
Older Americans (aged 63 or older)	44,911	14.8

Source: Bureau of the Census, Population Estimates, Internet site http://www.census.gov/popest/national/asrh/ NC-EST2008-sa.html; calculations by New Strategist

Table 18.2 Population by Age and Sex, 2008

(number of people by age and sex, and sex ratio by age, 2008; numbers in thousands)

	total	female	male	sex ratio
Total people	**304,060**	**154,135**	**149,925**	**97**
Under age 15	61,126	29,856	31,269	105
Under age 5	21,006	10,258	10,748	105
Aged 5 to 9	20,065	9,806	10,259	105
Aged 10 to 14	20,055	9,792	10,262	105
Aged 15 to 19	21,514	10,487	11,027	105
Aged 20 to 24	21,059	10,214	10,845	106
Aged 25 to 29	21,334	10,393	10,941	105
Aged 30 to 34	19,598	9,639	9,959	103
Aged 35 to 39	20,994	10,425	10,569	101
Aged 40 to 44	21,507	10,762	10,746	100
Aged 45 to 49	22,880	11,566	11,314	98
Aged 50 to 54	21,492	10,954	10,539	96
Aged 55 to 59	18,583	9,569	9,015	94
Aged 60 to 64	15,103	7,867	7,236	92
Aged 65 to 69	11,349	6,042	5,306	88
Aged 70 to 74	8,774	4,816	3,959	82
Aged 75 to 79	7,275	4,178	3,097	74
Aged 80 to 84	5,750	3,510	2,239	64
Aged 85 or older	5,722	3,858	1,864	48

Note: The sex ratio is the number of males per 100 females.
Source: Bureau of the Census, Population Estimates, Internet site http://www.census.gov/popest/national/asrh/NC-EST2008-sa.html; calculations by New Strategist

The Nation's Children Are Diverse

Hispanics outnumber blacks in the iGeneration.

America's children are much more diverse than middle-aged or older people. While non-Hispanic whites accounted for 66 percent of all Americans in 2008, their share is a smaller 56 percent among the iGeneration—children under age 14.

Among the iGeneration, Hispanics account for a larger share of the population than blacks—22 percent are Hispanic and 17 percent are black. Twenty-five percent of children under age 5 are Hispanic.

■ Racial and ethnic differences between young and old may divide the nation in the years ahead as older non-Hispanic whites attempt to govern young Hispanics, blacks, and Asians.

Minorities account for a large share of children

(minority share of population by generation, 2008)

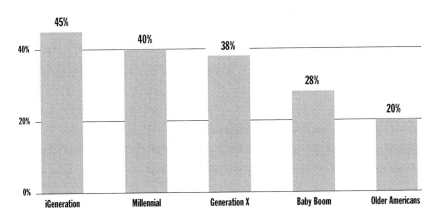

Table 18.3 Population by Age, Race, and Hispanic Origin, 2008

(number and percent distribution of people by age, race, and Hispanic origin, 2008; numbers in thousands)

	total	Asian	black	Hispanic	non-Hispanic white
Total people	**304,060**	**15,480**	**41,127**	**46,944**	**199,491**
Under age 15	61,126	3,381	10,234	13,742	33,947
Under age 5	21,006	1,242	3,573	5,288	11,065
Aged 5 to 9	20,065	1,107	3,298	4,464	11,222
Aged 10 to 14	20,055	1,033	3,363	3,989	11,660
Aged 15 to 19	21,514	1,018	3,667	3,850	12,903
Aged 20 to 24	21,059	1,027	3,307	3,663	12,949
Aged 25 to 29	21,334	1,206	3,166	4,141	12,740
Aged 30 to 34	19,598	1,334	2,724	4,041	11,456
Aged 35 to 39	20,994	1,404	2,823	3,730	12,981
Aged 40 to 44	21,507	1,210	2,847	3,279	14,085
Aged 45 to 49	22,880	1,107	2,882	2,795	15,964
Aged 50 to 54	21,492	986	2,563	2,187	15,615
Aged 55 to 59	18,583	829	2,068	1,650	13,907
Aged 60 to 64	15,103	612	1,471	1,204	11,706
Aged 65 to 69	11,349	443	1,075	853	8,899
Aged 70 to 74	8,774	339	829	653	6,899
Aged 75 to 79	7,275	255	614	496	5,871
Aged 80 to 84	5,750	176	438	346	4,763
Aged 85 or older	5,722	154	419	313	4,807

PERCENT DISTRIBUTION BY RACE AND HISPANIC ORIGIN

Total people	**100.0%**	**5.1%**	**13.5%**	**15.4%**	**65.6%**
Under age 15	100.0	5.5	16.7	22.5	55.5
Under age 5	100.0	5.9	17.0	25.2	52.7
Aged 5 to 9	100.0	5.5	16.4	22.2	55.9
Aged 10 to 14	100.0	5.1	16.8	19.9	58.1
Aged 15 to 19	100.0	4.7	17.0	17.9	60.0
Aged 20 to 24	100.0	4.9	15.7	17.4	61.5
Aged 25 to 29	100.0	5.7	14.8	19.4	59.7
Aged 30 to 34	100.0	6.8	13.9	20.6	58.5
Aged 35 to 39	100.0	6.7	13.4	17.8	61.8
Aged 40 to 44	100.0	5.6	13.2	15.2	65.5
Aged 45 to 49	100.0	4.8	12.6	12.2	69.8
Aged 50 to 54	100.0	4.6	11.9	10.2	72.7
Aged 55 to 59	100.0	4.5	11.1	8.9	74.8
Aged 60 to 64	100.0	4.1	9.7	8.0	77.5
Aged 65 to 69	100.0	3.9	9.5	7.5	78.4
Aged 70 to 74	100.0	3.9	9.5	7.4	78.6
Aged 75 to 79	100.0	3.5	8.4	6.8	80.7
Aged 80 to 84	100.0	3.1	7.6	6.0	82.8
Aged 85 or older	100.0	2.7	7.3	5.5	84.0

Note: Numbers do not add to total because Asians and blacks include those who identified themselves as being of the race alone and those who identified themselves as being of the race in combination with other races, and because Hispanics may be of any race. Non-Hispanic whites include those who identified themselves as being white alone and not Hispanic.
Source: Bureau of the Census, Population Estimates, Internet site http://www.census.gov/popest/national/asrh/ NC-EST2008-sa.html; calculations by New Strategist

Children Account for Few Immigrants

Young adults are the largest share of immigrants admitted in 2008.

In 2008, more than 1 million immigrants were admitted to the United States, and only 166,000 of them were under age 15 (the iGeneration was under age 14 in that year). Young adults in their twenties and thirties account for a much larger number of immigrants.

The under-15 age group accounted for 15 percent of total immigrants admitted to the United States in 2008. By five-year age group, 30-to-34-year-olds account for the largest share of immigrants—13 percent in 2008.

■ Immigrants are adding to the diversity of the population.

Many immigrants are young adults

(percent distribution of immigrants admitted in 2008, by age, 2008)

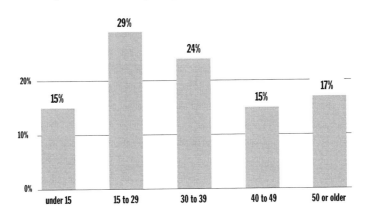

Table 18.4 Newly Arrived Immigrants by Age, 2008

(number and percent distribution of immigrants admitted in 2008, by age)

	number	percent distribution
Total immigrants	**1,107,126**	**100.0%**
Under age 15	165,879	15.0
Under age 1	8,280	0.7
Aged 1 to 4	29,998	2.7
Aged 5 to 9	52,993	4.8
Aged 10 to 14	74,608	6.7
Aged 15 to 19	94,697	8.6
Aged 20 to 24	104,332	9.4
Aged 25 to 29	121,416	11.0
Aged 30 to 34	140,132	12.7
Aged 35 to 39	124,341	11.2
Aged 40 to 44	92,627	8.4
Aged 45 to 49	69,868	6.3
Aged 50 to 54	53,848	4.9
Aged 55 to 59	43,789	4.0
Aged 60 to 64	35,586	3.2
Aged 65 to 74	45,399	4.1
Aged 75 or older	15,205	1.4

Note: Immigrants are those granted legal permanent residence in the United States. They either arrive in the United States with immigrant visas issued abroad or adjust their status in the United States from temporary to permanent residence. Numbers may not sum to total because "age not stated" is not shown.
Source: Department of Homeland Security, 2008 Yearbook of Immigration Statistics, Internet site http://www.uscis.gov/ graphics/shared/statistics/yearbook/index.htm

Many Children Do Not Speak English at Home

Most are Spanish speakers, and most also speak English very well.

Fifty-five million residents of the United States speak a language other than English at home, according to the Census Bureau's 2007 American Community Survey—20 percent of the population aged 5 or older. Among those who do not speak English at home, 62 percent speak Spanish.

One in five children aged 5 to 17 does not speak English at home. Fully 72 percent of them are Spanish speakers. Most children who do not speak English at home are also able to speak English "very well." Only 26 percent of the Spanish speakers aged 5 to 17, for example, cannot speak English very well. Among all U.S. residents who speak Spanish at home, a much larger 47 percent cannot speak English very well.

■ The language barrier is a bigger problem for adults than for children.

Few children who speak Spanish at home cannot speak English very well

(percent of people aged 5 or older and aged 5 to 17 who speak Spanish at home and do not speak English "very well," 2007)

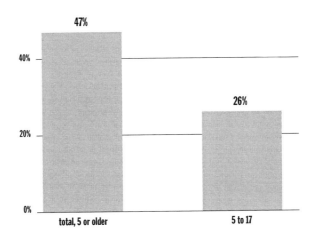

Table 18.5 Language Spoken at Home by People Aged 5 to 17, 2007

(number and percent distribution of people aged 5 or older and aged 5 to 17 who speak a language other than English at home by language spoken at home and ability to speak English very well, by age, 2007; numbers in thousands)

	total		aged 5 to 17	
	number	percent distribution	number	percent distribution
Total, aged 5 or older	**280,950**	**100.0%**	**53,237**	**100.0%**
Speak only English at home	225,506	80.3	42,319	79.5
Speak a language other than English at home	55,444	19.7	10,918	20.5
Speak English less than very well	24,469	8.7	2,748	5.2
Total who speak a language other than English at home	**55,444**	**100.0**	**10,918**	**100.0**
Speak Spanish at home	34,547	62.3	7,872	72.1
Speak other Indo-European language at home	10,321	18.6	1,479	13.5
Speak Asian or Pacific Island language at home	8,316	15.0	1,173	10.7
Speak other language at home	2,260	4.1	394	3.6
Speak Spanish at home	34,547	100.0	7,872	100.0
Speak English less than very well	16,368	47.4	2,068	26.3
Speak other Indo-European language at home	10,321	100.0	1,479	100.0
Speak English less than very well	3,384	32.8	289	19.6
Speak Asian or Pacific Island language at home	8,316	100.0	1,173	100.0
Speak English less than very well	4,042	48.6	320	27.3
Speak other language at home	2,260	100.0	394	100.0
Speak English less than very well	676	29.9	71	17.9

Source: Bureau of the Census, 2007 American Community Survey, Internet site http://factfinder.census.gov/servlet/ DatasetMainPageServlet?_program=ACS&_submenuId=&_lang=en&_ts=; calculations by New Strategist"

The Largest Share of Children Lives in the South

More than one in four residents of Utah is under age 15.

The South is home to the largest share of the population, and consequently to the largest share of the iGeneration. In 2008, 37 percent of children under age 15 lived in the South (the iGeneration was under age 14 in that year), according to Census Bureau estimates. In the South, they account for 20 percent of the population.

Among children under age 15, Hispanics outnumber blacks in the West and Northeast. Blacks outnumber Hispanics in the Midwest and South.

Children under age 15 account for 26 percent of the population of Utah. They are only 17 percent of the populations of Vermont and Maine.

■ The iGeneration will be a growing force in every state and region in the years ahead.

The Northeast is home to just 17 percent of children under age 15

(percent distribution of children under age 15 by region, 2008)

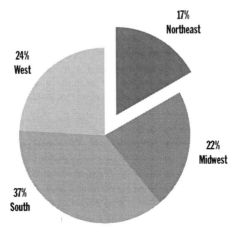

17%
Northeast

24%
West

22%
Midwest

37%
South

Table 18.6 Population by Age and Region, 2008

(number and percent distribution of people by age and region, 2008; numbers in thousands)

	total	Northeast	Midwest	South	West
Total people	**304,060**	**54,925**	**66,561**	**111,719**	**70,855**
Under age 15	61,126	10,116	13,236	22,900	14,874
Under age 5	21,006	3,339	4,463	7,971	5,232
Aged 5 to 9	20,065	3,309	4,343	7,573	4,840
Aged 10 to 14	20,055	3,468	4,429	7,355	4,802
Aged 15 to 19	21,514	3,899	4,769	7,749	5,097
Aged 20 to 24	21,059	3,739	4,619	7,627	5,074
Aged 25 to 29	21,334	3,477	4,573	7,957	5,327
Aged 30 or older	179,027	33,694	39,365	65,485	40,483

PERCENT DISTRIBUTION BY AGE

Total people	**100.0%**	**100.0%**	**100.0%**	**100.0%**	**100.0%**
Under age 15	20.1	18.4	19.9	20.5	21.0
Under age 5	6.9	6.1	6.7	7.1	7.4
Aged 5 to 9	6.6	6.0	6.5	6.8	6.8
Aged 10 to 14	6.6	6.3	6.7	6.6	6.8
Aged 15 to 19	7.1	7.1	7.2	6.9	7.2
Aged 20 to 24	6.9	6.8	6.9	6.8	7.2
Aged 25 to 29	7.0	6.3	6.9	7.1	7.5
Aged 30 or older	58.9	61.3	59.1	58.6	57.1

PERCENT DISTRIBUTION BY REGION

Total people	**100.0%**	**18.1%**	**21.9%**	**36.7%**	**23.3%**
Under age 15	100.0	16.5	21.7	37.5	24.3
Under age 5	100.0	15.9	21.2	37.9	24.9
Aged 5 to 9	100.0	16.5	21.6	37.7	24.1
Aged 10 to 14	100.0	17.3	22.1	36.7	23.9
Aged 15 to 19	100.0	18.1	22.2	36.0	23.7
Aged 20 to 24	100.0	17.8	21.9	36.2	24.1
Aged 25 to 29	100.0	16.3	21.4	37.3	25.0
Aged 30 or older	100.0	18.8	22.0	36.6	22.6

Source: Bureau of the Census, State Population Estimates, Internet site http://www.census.gov/popest/states/asrh/; calculations by New Strategist

Table 18.7 iGeneration by Region, Race, and Hispanic Origin, 2007

(number and percent distribution of people under age 15 by region, race, and Hispanic origin, 2007; numbers in thousands)

	total under 15	Asian	black	Hispanic	non-Hispanic white
United States	**60,897**	**2,433**	**8,832**	**13,081**	**34,138**
Northeast	10,151	521	1,423	1,572	6,372
Midwest	13,289	331	1,661	1,274	9,517
South	22,711	552	4,990	4,505	11,926
West	14,746	1,030	758	5,730	6,323
PERCENT DISTRIBUTION BY RACE AND HISPANIC ORIGIN					
United States	**100.0%**	**4.0%**	**14.5%**	**21.5%**	**56.1%**
Northeast	100.0	5.1	14.0	15.5	62.8
Midwest	100.0	2.5	12.5	9.6	71.6
South	100.0	2.4	22.0	19.8	52.5
West	100.0	7.0	5.1	38.9	42.9
PERCENT DISTRIBUTION BY REGION					
United States	**100.0%**	**100.0%**	**100.0%**	**100.0%**	**100.0%**
Northeast	16.7	21.4	16.1	12.0	18.7
Midwest	21.8	13.6	18.8	9.7	27.9
South	37.3	22.7	56.5	34.4	34.9
West	24.2	42.3	8.6	43.8	18.5

Note: Numbers do not add to total because Asians and blacks are only those who identified themselves as being of the race alone and because Hispanics may be of any race. Non-Hispanic whites are those who identified themselves as being white alone and not Hispanic.
Source: Bureau of the Census, 2007 American Community Survey, Internet site http://factfinder.census.gov/home/saff/main .html?_lang=en; calculations by New Strategist

Table 18.8 State Populations by Age, 2008

(total number of people and number under age 15 by state, 2008; numbers in thousands)

	total population	under age 15			
		total	under 5	5 to 9	10 to 14
United States	**304,060**	**61,126**	**21,006**	**20,065**	**20,055**
Alabama	4,662	926	311	307	308
Alaska	686	148	52	48	48
Arizona	6,500	1,434	516	472	446
Arkansas	2,855	583	202	192	189
California	36,757	7,731	2,705	2,492	2,535
Colorado	4,939	1,009	358	335	315
Connecticut	3,501	664	212	219	233
Delaware	873	170	59	56	55
District of Columbia	592	93	36	29	28
Florida	18,328	3,304	1,141	1,081	1,082
Georgia	9,686	2,128	741	711	676
Hawaii	1,288	237	87	75	74
Idaho	1,524	345	122	114	109
Illinois	12,902	2,632	894	866	872
Indiana	6,377	1,312	443	434	435
Iowa	3,003	587	201	192	194
Kansas	2,802	583	203	192	188
Kentucky	4,269	834	285	275	274
Louisiana	4,411	915	311	305	299
Maine	1,316	222	71	72	78
Maryland	5,634	1,100	372	361	367
Massachusetts	6,498	1,168	384	384	400
Michigan	10,003	1,946	626	641	679
Minnesota	5,220	1,036	358	336	341
Mississippi	2,939	635	221	208	206
Missouri	5,912	1,170	399	382	389
Montana	967	180	61	58	60
Nebraska	1,783	371	132	121	118
Nevada	2,600	561	199	184	178
New Hampshire	1,316	237	75	77	85
New Jersey	8,683	1,686	557	556	573
New Mexico	1,984	417	148	137	132
New York	19,490	3,604	1,208	1,173	1,223
North Carolina	9,222	1,871	653	623	595
North Dakota	641	117	42	37	39
Ohio	11,486	2,240	744	737	760
Oklahoma	3,642	754	267	248	239
Oregon	3,790	716	243	235	237
Pennsylvania	12,448	2,246	737	733	776
Rhode Island	1,051	186	61	60	65
South Carolina	4,480	879	303	290	286

	total population	under age 15			
		total	under 5	5 to 9	10 to 14
South Dakota	804	164	59	53	53
Tennessee	6,215	1,224	416	405	403
Texas	24,327	5,657	2,027	1,880	1,750
Utah	2,736	723	269	241	213
Vermont	621	103	33	34	37
Virginia	7,769	1,511	523	498	490
Washington	6,549	1,269	433	415	421
West Virginia	1,814	317	105	105	107
Wisconsin	5,628	1,078	362	353	362
Wyoming	533	106	38	34	34

Source: Bureau of the Census, State Population Estimates, Internet site http://www.census.gov/popest/states/asrh/; calculations by New Strategist

Table 18.9 Distribution of State Populations by Age, 2008

(percent distribution of people under age 15 by state and age, 2008; numbers in thousands)

	total population	under age 15			
		total	under 5	5 to 9	10 to 14
United States	**100.0%**	**20.1%**	**6.9%**	**6.6%**	**6.6%**
Alabama	100.0	19.9	6.7	6.6	6.6
Alaska	100.0	21.5	7.6	6.9	7.0
Arizona	100.0	22.1	7.9	7.3	6.9
Arkansas	100.0	20.4	7.1	6.7	6.6
California	100.0	21.0	7.4	6.8	6.9
Colorado	100.0	20.4	7.3	6.8	6.4
Connecticut	100.0	19.0	6.0	6.3	6.7
Delaware	100.0	19.5	6.8	6.4	6.3
District of Columbia	100.0	15.7	6.1	4.8	4.7
Florida	100.0	18.0	6.2	5.9	5.9
Georgia	100.0	22.0	7.6	7.3	7.0
Hawaii	100.0	18.4	6.8	5.9	5.8
Idaho	100.0	22.6	8.0	7.5	7.2
Illinois	100.0	20.4	6.9	6.7	6.8
Indiana	100.0	20.6	6.9	6.8	6.8
Iowa	100.0	19.5	6.7	6.4	6.5
Kansas	100.0	20.8	7.2	6.9	6.7
Kentucky	100.0	19.5	6.7	6.4	6.4
Louisiana	100.0	20.7	7.0	6.9	6.8
Maine	100.0	16.8	5.4	5.5	5.9
Maryland	100.0	19.5	6.6	6.4	6.5
Massachusetts	100.0	18.0	5.9	5.9	6.1
Michigan	100.0	19.5	6.3	6.4	6.8
Minnesota	100.0	19.8	6.9	6.4	6.5
Mississippi	100.0	21.6	7.5	7.1	7.0
Missouri	100.0	19.8	6.8	6.5	6.6
Montana	100.0	18.6	6.3	6.0	6.2
Nebraska	100.0	20.8	7.4	6.8	6.6
Nevada	100.0	21.6	7.7	7.1	6.8
New Hampshire	100.0	18.0	5.7	5.9	6.5
New Jersey	100.0	19.4	6.4	6.4	6.6
New Mexico	100.0	21.0	7.5	6.9	6.6
New York	100.0	18.5	6.2	6.0	6.3
North Carolina	100.0	20.3	7.1	6.8	6.4
North Dakota	100.0	18.3	6.5	5.7	6.1
Ohio	100.0	19.5	6.5	6.4	6.6
Oklahoma	100.0	20.7	7.3	6.8	6.6
Oregon	100.0	18.9	6.4	6.2	6.3
Pennsylvania	100.0	18.0	5.9	5.9	6.2
Rhode Island	100.0	17.7	5.8	5.7	6.2
South Carolina	100.0	19.6	6.8	6.5	6.4

	total population	under age 15			
		total	under 5	5 to 9	10 to 14
South Dakota	100.0%	20.4%	7.3%	6.5%	6.6%
Tennessee	100.0	19.7	6.7	6.5	6.5
Texas	100.0	23.3	8.3	7.7	7.2
Utah	100.0	26.4	9.8	8.8	7.8
Vermont	100.0	16.6	5.3	5.4	6.0
Virginia	100.0	19.4	6.7	6.4	6.3
Washington	100.0	19.4	6.6	6.3	6.4
West Virginia	100.0	17.5	5.8	5.8	5.9
Wisconsin	100.0	19.1	6.4	6.3	6.4
Wyoming	100.0	19.9	7.2	6.4	6.3

Source: Bureau of the Census, State Population Estimates, Internet site http://www.census.gov/popest/states/asrh/; calculations by New Strategist

19

Spending

■ The spending of married couples with preschoolers rose by a small 2 percent to $62,403 between 2000 and 2007, after adjusting for inflation. This household type reined in its spending on some products and services as the cost of health insurance and other necessities climbed.

■ Married couples with school-aged children rank among the most affluent households in the nation, but they are cautious spenders. In 2007, they spent $70,766 on average, 8 percent more than in 2000 after adjusting for inflation.

■ Single parents with children under age 18 at home spent 10 percent more in 2007 than in 2000, after adjusting for inflation. This household type spent 20 percent more on food away from home and 17 percent more on health insurance.

The Spending of Married Couples with Children Has Increased

But their spending on some items plunged between 2000 and 2007.

Married couples with children spend much more than average because they have the highest incomes and the largest households. In 2007, couples with children of any age at home spent an average of $69,101, much greater than the $49,638 spent by the average household.

Between 2000 and 2007, couples with children boosted their spending by 7 percent, after adjusting for inflation. This was slightly less than the 8 percent spending increase experienced by the average household. Couples with children have increased their spending on a mix of discretionary and nondiscretionary items. Their spending on food away from home rose by 9 percent during those years, entertainment by 14 percent, mortgage interest by 17 percent, education by 21 percent, cash contributions by 32 percent, and gasoline by 51 percent. They cut their spending on other items as their priorities changed. Couples with children spent 27 percent less in 2007 than in 2000 on new cars and trucks, 10 percent less on furniture, and 18 percent less on apparel.

■ The economic downturn will cause many couples with children to curtail their spending on food away from home and entertainment.

Married couples with children boosted their spending on a number of items

(percent change in spending by married couples with children of any age at home on selected items, 2000 and 2007; in 2007 dollars)

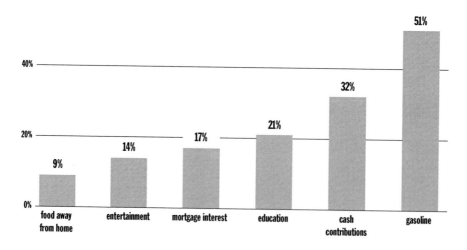

Table 19.1 Average Spending of Total Married Couples with Children, 2000 and 2007

(average annual spending of married-couple consumer units with children of any age at home, 2000 and 2007; percent change, 2000–07; in 2007 dollars)

	2007	2000	percent change 2000–07
Number of consumer units (in 000s)	29,984	28,777	4.2%
Average annual spending	$69,101	$64,522	7.1
FOOD	8,876	8,731	1.7
Food at home	5,080	5,246	–3.2
Cereals and bakery products	693	819	–15.4
Cereals and cereal products	221	289	–23.5
Bakery products	472	530	–10.9
Meats, poultry, fish, and eggs	1,113	1,340	–16.9
Beef	319	403	–20.9
Pork	208	272	–23.6
Other meats	154	178	–13.6
Poultry	213	249	–14.5
Fish and seafood	159	184	–13.7
Eggs	60	53	13.3
Dairy products	581	579	0.3
Fresh milk and cream	239	242	–1.2
Other dairy products	342	337	1.4
Fruits and vegetables	848	855	–0.8
Fresh fruits	287	260	10.4
Fresh vegetables	269	254	5.9
Processed fruits	159	197	–19.5
Processed vegetables	133	143	–7.2
Other food at home	1,845	1,653	11.6
Sugar and other sweets	181	207	–12.6
Fats and oils	128	136	–5.9
Miscellaneous foods	995	815	22.1
Nonalcoholic beverages	480	429	12.0
Food prepared by household on trips	61	65	–6.2
Food away from home	3,796	3,485	8.9
ALCOHOLIC BEVERAGES	470	477	–1.4
HOUSING	23,078	20,628	11.9
Shelter	13,458	11,671	15.3
Owned dwellings	10,819	9,135	18.4
Mortgage interest and charges	6,961	5,948	17.0
Property taxes	2,470	1,948	26.8
Maintenance, repairs, insurance, other expenses	1,387	1,239	11.9
Rented dwellings	1,774	1,809	–1.9
Other lodging	865	727	18.9

	2007	2000	percent change 2000–07
Utilities, fuels, and public services	**$4,518**	**$3,829**	**18.0%**
Natural gas	631	477	32.3
Electricity	1,688	1,398	20.7
Fuel oil and other fuels	177	144	22.5
Telephone services	1,449	1,321	9.7
Water and other public services	573	488	17.5
Household services	**1,786**	**1,470**	**21.5**
Personal services	1,074	903	18.9
Other household services	712	567	25.5
Housekeeping supplies	**789**	**846**	**−6.8**
Laundry and cleaning supplies	191	244	−21.9
Other household products	418	407	2.7
Postage and stationery	180	195	−7.7
Household furnishings and equipment	**2,527**	**2,813**	**−10.2**
Household textiles	186	195	−4.6
Furniture	657	732	−10.3
Floor coverings	75	85	−12.3
Major appliances	300	349	−14.1
Small appliances, miscellaneous housewares	132	147	−10.1
Miscellaneous household equipment	1,177	1,303	−9.7
APPAREL AND SERVICES	**2,723**	**3,310**	**−17.7**
Men and boys	**644**	**822**	**−21.7**
Men, aged 16 or older	451	562	−19.8
Boys, aged 2 to 15	193	260	−25.8
Women and girls	**1,045**	**1,267**	**−17.5**
Women, aged 16 or older	756	937	−19.3
Girls, aged 2 to 15	289	330	−12.4
Children under age 2	**189**	**208**	**−9.3**
Footwear	**494**	**578**	**−14.5**
Other apparel products and services	**350**	**435**	**−19.5**
TRANSPORTATION	**12,609**	**13,351**	**−5.6**
Vehicle purchases	**4,919**	**6,460**	**−23.9**
Cars and trucks, new	2,185	2,984	−26.8
Cars and trucks, used	2,575	3,392	−24.1
Other vehicles	159	84	88.6
Gasoline and motor oil	**3,421**	**2,262**	**51.2**
Other vehicle expenses	**3,639**	**4,036**	**−9.8**
Vehicle finance charges	476	643	−26.0
Maintenance and repairs	1,010	1,025	−1.4
Vehicle insurance	1,391	1,321	5.3
Vehicle rental, leases, licenses, other charges	762	1,049	−27.3
Public transportation	**630**	**591**	**6.6**

	2007	2000	percent change 2000–07
HEALTH CARE	**$3,328**	**$2,777**	**19.9%**
Health insurance	1,765	1,362	29.6
Medical services	940	840	11.8
Drugs	472	435	8.6
Medical supplies	151	140	8.1
ENTERTAINMENT	**3,915**	**3,448**	**13.5**
Fees and admissions	1,100	1,023	7.5
Audio and visual equipment and services	1,334	1,028	29.7
Pets, toys, hobbies, and playground equipment	756	600	26.1
Other entertainment supplies, services	725	797	–9.0
PERSONAL CARE PRODUCTS, SERVICES	**768**	**926**	**–17.1**
READING	**137**	**212**	**–35.4**
EDUCATION	**1,643**	**1,356**	**21.2**
TOBACCO PRODUCTS, SMOKING SUPPLIES	**316**	**431**	**–26.7**
MISCELLANEOUS	**892**	**1,075**	**–17.0**
CASH CONTRIBUTIONS	**1,937**	**1,469**	**31.9**
PERSONAL INSURANCE AND PENSIONS	**8,408**	**6,330**	**32.8**
Life and other personal insurance	489	724	–32.4
Pensions and Social Security	7,918	–	–
PERSONAL TAXES	**2,826**	**5,367**	**–47.3**
Federal income taxes	1,906	4,175	–54.3
State and local income taxes	658	983	–33.0
Other taxes	263	211	24.8
GIFTS FOR PEOPLE IN OTHER HOUSEHOLDS	**1,103**	**1,524**	**–27.6**

Note: The Bureau of Labor Statistics uses consumer unit rather than household as the sampling unit in the Consumer Expenditure Survey. For the definition of consumer unit, see the glossary. Spending on gifts is also included in the preceding product and service categories. Average spending is rounded to the nearest dollar, but the percent change calculation is based on unrounded figures. "–" means comparable data are not available.
Source: Bureau of Labor Statistics, 2000 and 2007 Consumer Expenditure Survey, Internet site http://www.bls.gov/cex/; calculations by New Strategist

Parents of Preschoolers Spend Cautiously

The spending of married couples with preschoolers rose slowly between 2000 and 2007.

The spending of married couples with preschoolers increased by just 2 percent between 2000 and 2007, well below the 8 percent spending increase registered by the average household during those years.

Couples with preschoolers cut their spending on groceries (food at home) by 4 percent between 2000 and 2007, but they spent 11 percent more on food away from home. They spent 24 percent less on furniture, but 30 percent more on audio and visual equipment and services. As the homeownership rate rose, they spent more on owned dwellings, and their spending on mortgage interest rose by 15 percent. They spent 29 percent less on women's clothes, 32 percent less on boys' clothes, and 11 percent less on girls' clothes. Their spending on new cars and trucks plummeted by 39 percent, while spending on used vehicles fell 24 percent. Out-of-pocket spending on health insurance climbed 20 percent.

■ The spending patterns of couples with preschoolers has been mixed, partly because the segment is economically diverse.

Married couples with preschoolers spent more on some things, less on others

(percent change in spending by married couples with oldest child under age 6, 2000 to 2007; in 2007 dollars)

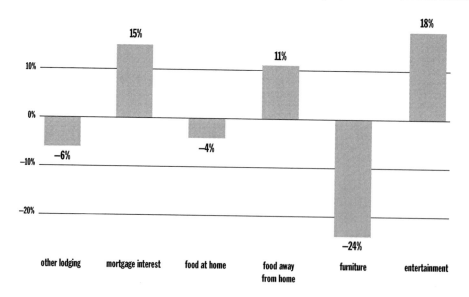

Table 19.2 Average Spending of Married Couples with Preschoolers, 2000 and 2007

(average annual spending of married-couple consumer units with oldest child under age 6, 2000 and 2007; percent change, 2000–07; in 2007 dollars)

	2007	2000	percent change 2000–07
Number of consumer units (in 000s)	5,865	5,291	10.8%
Average annual spending	$62,403	$61,114	2.1
FOOD	7,137	7,004	1.9
Food at home	4,243	4,406	–3.7
Cereals and bakery products	516	653	–20.9
Cereals and cereal products	163	224	–27.2
Bakery products	353	429	–17.6
Meats, poultry, fish, and eggs	784	986	–20.5
Beef	254	295	–13.9
Pork	151	182	–16.9
Other meats	103	130	–20.8
Poultry	138	206	–33.0
Fish and seafood	93	131	–29.1
Eggs	45	40	13.3
Dairy products	514	500	2.9
Fresh milk and cream	229	212	8.1
Other dairy products	285	288	–1.0
Fruits and vegetables	735	745	–1.4
Fresh fruits	264	226	16.6
Fresh vegetables	222	222	0.2
Processed fruits	141	183	–23.0
Processed vegetables	107	113	–5.5
Other food at home	1,694	1,523	11.2
Sugar and other sweets	121	153	–20.9
Fats and oils	92	89	3.3
Miscellaneous foods	1,069	883	21.1
Nonalcoholic beverages	367	344	6.6
Food prepared by household on trips	45	54	–16.9
Food away from home	2,894	2,598	11.4
ALCOHOLIC BEVERAGES	513	452	13.6
HOUSING	24,354	22,519	8.2
Shelter	13,815	12,520	10.3
Owned dwellings	10,757	9,469	13.6
Mortgage interest and charges	7,568	6,604	14.6
Property taxes	2,037	1,811	12.5
Maintenance, repairs, insurance, other expenses	1,152	1,052	9.5
Rented dwellings	2,637	2,603	1.3
Other lodging	421	448	–6.0

	2007	2000	percent change 2000–07
Utilities, fuels, and public services	**$3,828**	**$3,376**	**13.4%**
Natural gas	526	433	21.3
Electricity	1,431	1,151	24.3
Fuel oil and other fuels	169	137	23.1
Telephone services	1,204	1,258	–4.3
Water and other public services	497	396	25.5
Household services	**3,431**	**2,866**	**19.7**
Personal services	2,811	2,396	17.3
Other household services	620	470	32.0
Housekeeping supplies	**750**	**744**	**0.8**
Laundry and cleaning supplies	154	181	–14.7
Other household products	449	364	23.5
Postage and stationery	147	200	–26.5
Household furnishings and equipment	**2,531**	**3,013**	**–16.0**
Household textiles	238	216	10.4
Furniture	657	869	–24.4
Floor coverings	87	55	57.1
Major appliances	296	319	–7.2
Small appliances, miscellaneous housewares	141	151	–6.3
Miscellaneous household equipment	1,112	1,403	–20.7
APPAREL AND SERVICES	**2,400**	**3,119**	**–23.0**
Men and boys	**470**	**648**	**–27.4**
Men, aged 16 or older	348	470	–25.9
Boys, aged 2 to 15	122	178	–31.5
Women and girls	**696**	**936**	**–25.6**
Women, aged 16 or older	531	750	–29.2
Girls, aged 2 to 15	165	185	–11.0
Children under age 2	**545**	**600**	**–9.1**
Footwear	**380**	**541**	**–29.7**
Other apparel products and services	**309**	**395**	**–21.8**
TRANSPORTATION	**10,876**	**12,938**	**–15.9**
Vehicle purchases	**4,529**	**6,736**	**–32.8**
Cars and trucks, new	1,935	3,179	–39.1
Cars and trucks, used	2,565	3,391	–24.4
Other vehicles	29	165	–82.4
Gasoline and motor oil	**2,717**	**1,919**	**41.6**
Other vehicle expenses	**3,112**	**3,793**	**–18.0**
Vehicle finance charges	476	663	–28.3
Maintenance and repairs	760	857	–11.3
Vehicle insurance	1,075	1,152	–6.7
Vehicle rental, leases, licenses, other charges	801	1,119	–28.4
Public transportation	**517**	**490**	**5.5**

	2007	2000	percent change 2000–07
HEALTH CARE	**$2,826**	**$2,284**	**23.7%**
Health insurance	1,480	1,234	19.9
Medical services	919	660	39.3
Drugs	340	290	17.2
Medical supplies	88	101	–13.0
ENTERTAINMENT	**3,102**	**2,638**	**17.6**
Fees and admissions	704	585	20.3
Audio and visual equipment and services	1,118	863	29.5
Pets, toys, hobbies, and playground equipment	703	579	21.4
Other entertainment supplies, services	576	609	–5.5
PERSONAL CARE PRODUCTS, SERVICES	**637**	**781**	**–18.5**
READING	**105**	**210**	**–49.9**
EDUCATION	**431**	**506**	**–14.8**
TOBACCO PRODUCTS, SMOKING SUPPLIES	**257**	**331**	**–22.4**
MISCELLANEOUS	**749**	**827**	**–9.5**
CASH CONTRIBUTIONS	**1,407**	**1,021**	**37.8**
PERSONAL INSURANCE AND PENSIONS	**7,607**	**6,488**	**17.3**
Life and other personal insurance	306	580	–47.3
Pensions and Social Security	7,301	–	–
PERSONAL TAXES	**2,665**	**5,014**	**–46.8**
Federal income taxes	1,806	3,925	–54.0
State and local income taxes	667	910	–26.7
Other taxes	193	177	9.0
GIFTS FOR PEOPLE IN OTHER HOUSEHOLDS	**618**	**1,105**	**–44.1**

Note: The Bureau of Labor Statistics uses consumer unit rather than household as the sampling unit in the Consumer Expenditure Survey. For the definition of consumer unit, see the glossary. Spending on gifts is also included in the preceding product and service categories. Average spending is rounded to the nearest dollar, but the percent change calculation is based on unrounded figures. "–" means comparable data are not available.
Source: Bureau of Labor Statistics, 2000 and 2007 Consumer Expenditure Survey, Internet site http://www.bls.gov/cex/; calculations by New Strategist

Spending of Couples with School-Aged Children Sees Average Rise

They spent less on many categories between 2000 and 2007, however.

Married couples with school-aged children rank among the most affluent households in the nation, and their spending—at $70,766 in 2007—was far above average. Between 2000 and 2007, these households boosted their spending by 8 percent—equal to the spending increase registered by the average household during those years.

Spending trends among couples with school-aged children are a mixed bag, reflecting compromises between budgeting for necessities and outfitting themselves with the accessories of a middle-class lifestyle. Couples with school-aged children cut their spending on food at home (groceries) by 5 percent between 2000 and 2007, after adjusting for inflation. But their spending on food away from home rose 10 percent. They spent 8 percent less on alcoholic beverages, but 12 percent more on entertainment. Their spending on mortgage interest rose 20 percent, while they spent 23 percent less on new and used vehicles.

Couples with school-aged children spent 34 percent more on out-of-pocket health insurance costs in 2007 than in 2000. They spent 26 percent more on education

■ With income growing only slowly, parents with school-aged children have become cautious spenders.

Couples with school-aged children are spending much more for health insurance

(percent change in spending by married couples with children aged 6 to 17 on selected items, 2000 to 2007; in 2007 dollars)

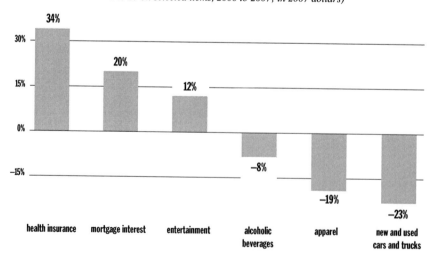

Table 19.3 Average Spending of Married Couples with School-Aged Children, 2000 and 2007

(average annual spending of married-couple consumer units with oldest child aged 6 to 17, 2000 and 2007; percent change, 2000–07; in 2007 dollars)

	2007	2000	percent change 2000–07
Number of consumer units (in 000s)	15,265	15,396	–0.9%
Average annual spending	$70,766	$65,225	8.5
FOOD	**9,151**	**9,040**	**1.2**
Food at home	**5,115**	**5,368**	**–4.7**
Cereals and bakery products	730	845	–13.6
Cereals and cereal products	242	308	–21.5
Bakery products	488	536	–8.9
Meats, poultry, fish, and eggs	1,122	1,391	–19.3
Beef	325	415	–21.8
Pork	209	284	–26.5
Other meats	153	184	–16.9
Poultry	213	253	–15.8
Fish and seafood	159	202	–21.4
Eggs	63	53	18.9
Dairy products	605	598	1.1
Fresh milk and cream	254	252	0.9
Other dairy products	351	347	1.2
Fruits and vegetables	856	863	–0.8
Fresh fruits	290	259	12.0
Fresh vegetables	271	256	5.7
Processed fruits	157	203	–22.8
Processed vegetables	138	144	–4.5
Other food at home	1,802	1,671	7.8
Sugar and other sweets	192	212	–9.4
Fats and oils	127	142	–10.6
Miscellaneous foods	945	816	15.8
Nonalcoholic beverages	465	430	8.2
Food prepared by household on trips	73	71	2.8
Food away from home	**4,036**	**3,672**	**9.9**
ALCOHOLIC BEVERAGES	**405**	**439**	**–7.8**
HOUSING	**24,032**	**20,991**	**14.5**
Shelter	**14,343**	**12,083**	**18.7**
Owned dwellings	11,627	9,557	21.7
Mortgage interest and charges	7,621	6,358	19.9
Property taxes	2,619	1,931	35.6
Maintenance, repairs, insurance, other expenses	1,387	1,268	9.4
Rented dwellings	1,779	1,858	–4.2
Other lodging	937	669	40.0

	2007	2000	percent change 2000–07
Utilities, fuels, and public services	**$4,567**	**$3,845**	**18.8%**
Natural gas	632	478	32.2
Electricity	1,722	1,409	22.2
Fuel oil and other fuels	188	142	32.3
Telephone services	1,442	1,320	9.3
Water and other public services	583	496	17.5
Household services	**1,644**	**1,424**	**15.4**
Personal services	886	796	11.3
Other household services	758	630	20.4
Housekeeping supplies	**767**	**872**	**–12.0**
Laundry and cleaning supplies	197	272	–27.6
Other household products	379	415	–8.8
Postage and stationery	191	184	3.7
Household furnishings and equipment	**2,711**	**2,766**	**–2.0**
Household textiles	181	189	–4.3
Furniture	763	765	–0.2
Floor coverings	88	72	21.8
Major appliances	299	330	–9.4
Small appliances, miscellaneous housewares	121	144	–16.3
Miscellaneous household equipment	1,259	1,267	–0.6
APPAREL AND SERVICES	**2,766**	**3,417**	**–19.1**
Men and boys	**663**	**863**	**–23.2**
Men, aged 16 or older	379	507	–25.2
Boys, aged 2 to 15	284	356	–20.3
Women and girls	**1,169**	**1,317**	**–11.3**
Women, aged 16 or older	736	837	–12.0
Girls, aged 2 to 15	433	482	–10.1
Children under age 2	**121**	**123**	**–1.5**
Footwear	**524**	**647**	**–19.0**
Other apparel products and services	**289**	**467**	**–38.1**
TRANSPORTATION	**12,688**	**12,816**	**–1.0**
Vehicle purchases	**4,912**	**6,143**	**–20.0**
Cars and trucks, new	2,218	2,864	–22.6
Cars and trucks, used	2,475	3,200	–22.7
Other vehicles	218	78	178.5
Gasoline and motor oil	**3,474**	**2,247**	**54.6**
Other vehicle expenses	**3,605**	**3,843**	**–6.2**
Vehicle finance charges	478	623	–23.2
Maintenance and repairs	998	996	0.2
Vehicle insurance	1,393	1,182	17.8
Vehicle rental, leases, licenses, other charges	736	1,043	–29.4
Public transportation	**697**	**584**	**19.4**

	2007	2000	percent change 2000–07
HEALTH CARE	**$3,286**	**$2,710**	**21.2%**
Health insurance	1,742	1,298	34.2
Medical services	957	880	8.7
Drugs	434	394	10.2
Medical supplies	153	138	10.5
ENTERTAINMENT	**4,366**	**3,913**	**11.6**
Fees and admissions	1,386	1,263	9.7
Audio and visual equipment and services	1,398	1,104	26.6
Pets, toys, hobbies, and playground equipment	767	659	16.5
Other entertainment supplies, services	816	886	–7.9
PERSONAL CARE PRODUCTS, SERVICES	**758**	**932**	**–18.7**
READING	**143**	**210**	**–31.7**
EDUCATION	**1,560**	**1,243**	**25.5**
TOBACCO PRODUCTS, SMOKING SUPPLIES	**321**	**405**	**–20.7**
MISCELLANEOUS	**883**	**1,156**	**–23.6**
CASH CONTRIBUTIONS	**1,991**	**1,529**	**30.2**
PERSONAL INSURANCE AND PENSIONS	**8,416**	**6,423**	**31.0**
Life and other personal insurance	504	710	–29.1
Pensions and Social Security	7,912	–	–
PERSONAL TAXES	**2,730**	**5,700**	**–52.1**
Federal income taxes	1,812	4,390	–58.7
State and local income taxes	654	1,091	–40.0
Other taxes	264	219	20.5
GIFTS FOR PEOPLE IN OTHER HOUSEHOLDS	**1,104**	**1,381**	**–20.1**

Note: The Bureau of Labor Statistics uses consumer unit rather than household as the sampling unit in the Consumer Expenditure Survey. For the definition of consumer unit, see the glossary. Spending on gifts is also included in the preceding product and service categories. Average spending is rounded to the nearest dollar, but the percent change calculation is based on unrounded figures. "–" means comparable data are not available.
Source: Bureau of Labor Statistics, 2000 and 2007 Consumer Expenditure Survey, Internet site http://www.bls.gov/cex/; calculations by New Strategist

Single Parents Increased Their Spending

They are spending more on many items, but less on some.

Single parents with children under age 18 at home spent $38,239 in 2007—10 percent more than they spent in 2000, after adjusting for inflation.

Spending trends for single-parent families have experienced both ups and downs in the past few years. Between 2000 and 2007, single parents spent 20 percent more on food away from home but 6 percent less on alcoholic beverages, after adjusting for inflation. They cut their spending on personal care products and services by 24 percent, but boosted their out-of-pocket spending on health insurance by 17 percent. Like most other household types, they spent more on mortgage interest as the homeownership rate—and housing prices—increased. As they outfitted those homes, their spending on furniture rose 10 percent. Single parents spent 31 percent less on used cars and trucks in 2007 than in 2000, but 65 percent more on gasoline. They reduced their spending on apparel by 10 percent.

■ With families being forced to devote more money to out-of-pocket health insurance costs, Americans will have less discretionary income to spend in the years ahead.

Single parents are cutting corners on some things, not on others

(percent change in spending by single-parent families with children under age 18 at home, 2000 to 2007; in 2007 dollars)

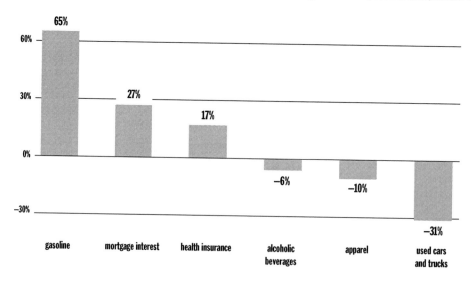

Table 19.4 Average Spending of Single Parents with Children under Age 18, 2000 and 2007

(average annual spending of single parents with children under age 18 at home, 2000 and 2007; percent change, 2000–07; in 2007 dollars)

	2007	2000	percent change 2000–07
Number of consumer units (in 000s)	7,139	6,132	16.4%
Average annual spending	$38,239	$34,826	9.8
FOOD	5,614	5,123	9.6
Food at home	3,295	3,187	3.4
Cereals and bakery products	456	467	–2.4
Cereals and cereal products	149	184	–19.1
Bakery products	307	282	9.0
Meats, poultry, fish, and eggs	793	908	–12.7
Beef	191	269	–28.9
Pork	168	191	–12.2
Other meats	113	110	3.1
Poultry	146	184	–20.7
Fish and seafood	132	112	17.9
Eggs	42	40	5.7
Dairy products	356	336	6.0
Fresh milk and cream	153	141	8.6
Other dairy products	203	195	4.1
Fruits and vegetables	492	491	0.1
Fresh fruits	148	137	7.8
Fresh vegetables	131	141	–7.0
Processed fruits	110	126	–13.0
Processed vegetables	104	87	20.0
Other food at home	1,198	985	21.6
Sugar and other sweets	115	129	–10.7
Fats and oils	82	94	–12.7
Miscellaneous foods	663	432	53.4
Nonalcoholic beverages	317	290	9.2
Food prepared by household on trips	21	39	–45.5
Food away from home	2,319	1,936	19.8
ALCOHOLIC BEVERAGES	212	225	–5.8
HOUSING	14,354	12,922	11.1
Shelter	8,512	7,623	11.7
Owned dwellings	3,931	3,368	16.7
Mortgage interest and charges	2,584	2,040	26.7
Property taxes	902	778	16.0
Maintenance, repairs, insurance, other expenses	445	550	–19.1
Rented dwellings	4,323	3,992	8.3
Other lodging	258	264	–2.2

	2007	2000	percent change 2000–07
Utilities, fuels, and public services	$3,214	$2,812	14.3%
Natural gas	369	368	0.1
Electricity	1,265	1,039	21.7
Fuel oil and other fuels	80	52	54.5
Telephone services	1,121	1,075	4.3
Water and other public services	380	277	37.2
Household services	**1,056**	**946**	**11.6**
Personal services	662	706	–6.2
Other household services	395	241	64.0
Housekeeping supplies	**500**	**443**	**12.8**
Laundry and cleaning supplies	174	182	–4.3
Other household products	237	169	40.6
Postage and stationery	90	93	–2.9
Household furnishings and equipment	**1,071**	**1,098**	**–2.5**
Household textiles	77	72	6.6
Furniture	359	328	9.6
Floor coverings	26	26	–1.8
Major appliances	153	125	22.2
Small appliances, miscellaneous housewares	62	43	43.0
Miscellaneous household equipment	394	502	–21.5
APPAREL AND SERVICES	**2,077**	**2,313**	**–10.2**
Men and boys	**361**	**489**	**–26.2**
Men, aged 16 or older	149	178	–16.4
Boys, aged 2 to 15	212	312	–32.0
Women and girls	**977**	**978**	**–0.1**
Women, aged 16 or older	679	641	6.0
Girls, aged 2 to 15	299	336	–11.0
Children under age 2	**118**	**134**	**–11.7**
Footwear	**435**	**495**	**–12.1**
Other apparel products and services	**186**	**217**	**–14.2**
TRANSPORTATION	**6,359**	**6,041**	**5.3**
Vehicle purchases	**2,139**	**2,815**	**–24.0**
Cars and trucks, new	635	631	0.6
Cars and trucks, used	1,498	2,179	–31.3
Other vehicles	5	5	3.8
Gasoline and motor oil	**1,771**	**1,076**	**64.5**
Other vehicle expenses	**2,085**	**1,828**	**14.1**
Vehicle finance charges	217	261	–16.9
Maintenance and repairs	504	566	–10.9
Vehicle insurance	1,069	667	60.3
Vehicle rental, leases, licenses, other charges	295	332	–11.2
Public transportation	**364**	**321**	**13.2**

	2007	2000	percent change 2000–07
HEALTH CARE	**$1,282**	**$1,221**	**5.0%**
Health insurance	640	545	17.3
Medical services	383	437	−12.4
Drugs	202	175	15.7
Medical supplies	57	65	−12.3
ENTERTAINMENT	**2,062**	**1,725**	**19.5**
Fees and admissions	468	486	−3.8
Audio and visual equipment and services	831	712	16.8
Pets, toys, hobbies, and playground equipment	487	307	58.6
Other entertainment supplies, services	275	219	25.5
PERSONAL CARE PRODUCTS, SERVICES	**522**	**685**	**−23.8**
READING	**61**	**92**	**−33.3**
EDUCATION	**768**	**476**	**61.5**
TOBACCO PRODUCTS, SMOKING SUPPLIES	**256**	**360**	**−28.9**
MISCELLANEOUS	**746**	**944**	**−21.0**
CASH CONTRIBUTIONS	**729**	**490**	**48.8**
PERSONAL INSURANCE AND PENSIONS	**3,197**	**2,208**	**44.8**
Life and other personal insurance	145	181	−19.7
Pensions and Social Security	3,052	–	–
PERSONAL TAXES	**445**	**719**	**−38.1**
Federal income taxes	143	425	−66.4
State and local income taxes	179	244	−26.8
Other taxes	122	49	147.1
GIFTS FOR PEOPLE IN OTHER HOUSEHOLDS	**695**	**822**	**−15.5**

Note: The Bureau of Labor Statistics uses consumer unit rather than household as the sampling unit in the Consumer Expenditure Survey. For the definition of consumer unit, see the glossary. Spending on gifts is also included in the preceding product and service categories. Average spending is rounded to the nearest dollar, but the percent change calculation is based on unrounded figures. "–" means comparable data are not available.
Source: Bureau of Labor Statistics, 2000 and 2007 Consumer Expenditure Survey, Internet site http://www.bls.gov/cex/; calculations by New Strategist

Married Couples with Children Spend More than Average

Single parents spend much less than average on most products and services.

Because married couples with children under age 18 have higher-than-average incomes and larger-than-average households, their spending is also above average. Overall, couples with preschoolers spend 26 percent more than the average household, and couples with school-aged children spend 43 percent more than average. Single-parent families, in contrast, spend 23 percent less than average. Married couples with preschoolers account for 6 percent of total household spending, while those with school-aged children account for a much larger 18 percent. Single parents control just 5 percent of household spending.

Couples with preschoolers spend much more than average on items needed by young children. They spend nearly seven times the average on household personal services (mostly day care) and nearly six times the average on clothes for infants.

Couples with school-aged children at home spend much more than average on most products and services. Rent, drugs, tobacco, and gifts for people in other households are the only exceptions.

Single parents spend less than average in all but a few categories. They are above average spenders on rent, household personal services (mostly day care), and children's clothes.

■ Many married couples with children under age 18 are recent homebuyers who bought during the housing bubble. This explains why their mortgage interest payments are 95 to 96 percent above average.

Married couples with school-aged children spend the most

(indexed average annual spending of households with children by type of household, 2007)

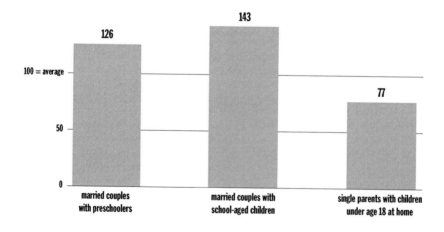

Table 19.5 Indexed Spending of Households with Children, 2007

(indexed spending of total consumer units and consumer units with children under age 18 at home, by type of consumer unit, 2007)

	total consumer units	married couples, oldest child under age 6	married couples, oldest child aged 6 to 17	single parents with children under age 18
Number of consumer units (in 000s)	120,171	5,865	15,265	7,139
Indexed average annual spending	100	126	143	77
FOOD	100	116	149	92
Food at home	100	122	148	95
Cereals and bakery products	100	112	159	99
Cereals and cereal products	100	114	169	104
Bakery products	100	111	154	97
Meats, poultry, fish, and eggs	100	101	144	102
Beef	100	118	150	88
Pork	100	101	139	112
Other meats	100	99	147	109
Poultry	100	97	150	103
Fish and seafood	100	76	130	108
Eggs	100	105	147	98
Dairy products	100	133	156	92
Fresh milk and cream	100	149	165	99
Other dairy products	100	122	150	87
Fruits and vegetables	100	123	143	82
Fresh fruits	100	131	144	73
Fresh vegetables	100	117	143	69
Processed fruits	100	126	140	98
Processed vegetables	100	111	144	108
Other food at home	100	137	145	97
Sugar and other sweets	100	98	155	93
Fats and oils	100	101	140	90
Miscellaneous foods	100	164	145	102
Nonalcoholic beverages	100	110	140	95
Food prepared by household on trips	100	105	170	49
Food away from home	100	108	151	87
ALCOHOLIC BEVERAGES	100	112	89	46
HOUSING	100	144	142	85
Shelter	100	138	143	85
Owned dwellings	100	160	173	58
Mortgage interest and charges	100	195	196	66
Property taxes	100	119	153	53
Maintenance, repairs, insurance, other expenses	100	102	123	39
Rented dwellings	100	101	68	166
Other lodging	100	61	136	37

	total consumer units	married couples, oldest child under age 6	married couples, oldest child aged 6 to 17	single parents with children under age 18
Utilities, fuels, and public services	**100**	**110**	**131**	**92**
Natural gas	100	110	132	77
Electricity	100	110	132	97
Fuel oil and other fuels	100	112	125	53
Telephone services	100	108	130	101
Water and other public services	100	115	134	88
Household services	**100**	**349**	**167**	**107**
Personal services	100	677	213	160
Other household services	100	109	133	69
Housekeeping supplies	**100**	**117**	**120**	**78**
Laundry and cleaning supplies	100	110	141	124
Other household products	100	129	109	68
Postage and stationery	100	97	126	59
Household furnishings and equipment	**100**	**141**	**151**	**60**
Household textiles	100	179	136	58
Furniture	100	147	171	80
Floor coverings	100	189	191	57
Major appliances	100	128	129	66
Small appliances, miscellaneous housewares	100	140	120	61
Miscellaneous household equipment	100	132	150	47
APPAREL AND SERVICES	**100**	**128**	**147**	**110**
Men and boys	**100**	**108**	**152**	**83**
Men, aged 16 or older	100	99	108	42
Boys, aged 2 to 15	100	145	338	252
Women and girls	**100**	**93**	**156**	**130**
Women, aged 16 or older	100	85	117	108
Girls, aged 2 to 15	100	135	355	245
Children under age 2	**100**	**586**	**130**	**127**
Footwear	**100**	**116**	**160**	**133**
Other apparel products and services	**100**	**112**	**105**	**67**
TRANSPORTATION	**100**	**124**	**145**	**73**
Vehicle purchases	**100**	**140**	**151**	**66**
Cars and trucks, new	100	123	141	40
Cars and trucks, used	100	164	158	96
Other vehicles	100	28	208	5
Gasoline and motor oil	**100**	**114**	**146**	**74**
Other vehicle expenses	**100**	**120**	**139**	**80**
Vehicle finance charges	100	156	157	71
Maintenance and repairs	100	103	135	68
Vehicle insurance	100	100	130	100
Vehicle rental, leases, licenses, other charges	100	168	154	62
Public transportation	**100**	**96**	**130**	**68**

	total consumer units	married couples, oldest child under age 6	married couples, oldest child aged 6 to 17	single parents with children under age 18
HEALTH CARE	100	99	115	45
Health insurance	100	96	113	41
Medical services	100	130	135	54
Drugs	100	71	90	42
Medical supplies	100	75	130	48
ENTERTAINMENT	100	115	162	76
Fees and admissions	100	107	211	71
Audio and visual equipment and services	100	113	142	84
Pets, toys, hobbies, and playground equipment	100	126	137	87
Other entertainment supplies, services	100	117	166	56
PERSONAL CARE PRODUCTS, SERVICES	100	108	129	89
READING	100	89	121	52
EDUCATION	100	46	165	81
TOBACCO PRODUCTS, SMOKING SUPPLIES	100	80	99	79
MISCELLANEOUS	100	93	109	92
CASH CONTRIBUTIONS	100	77	109	40
PERSONAL INSURANCE AND PENSIONS	100	143	158	60
Life and other personal insurance	100	99	163	47
Pensions and Social Security	100	145	157	61
PERSONAL TAXES	100	119	122	20
Federal income taxes	100	115	115	9
State and local income taxes	100	143	140	38
Other taxes	100	98	135	62
GIFTS FOR PEOPLE IN OTHER HOUSEHOLDS	100	52	92	58

Note: The index compares the spending of consumer units with children with the spending of the average consumer unit by dividing the spending of consumer units with children by average spending in each category and multiplying by 100. An index of 100 means the spending of consumer units with children equals average spending. An index of 130 means the spending of consumer units with children is 30 percent above average, while an index of 70 means the spending of consumer units with children is 30 percent below average. The Bureau of Labor Statistics uses consumer unit rather than household as the sampling unit in the Consumer Expenditure Survey. For the definition of consumer unit, see the glossary.
Source: Bureau of Labor Statistics, 2007 Consumer Expenditure Survey, Internet site http://www.bls.gov/cex/; calculations by New Strategist

Table 19.6 Market Share of Spending Controlled by Households with Children, 2007

(percent of total household spending accounted for by consumer units with children under age 18 at home, 2007)

| | total consumer units | consumer units with children under age 18 | | |
		total	married couples, oldest child under age 6	married couples, oldest child aged 6 to 17	single parents with children under age 18
Number of consumer units (in 000s)	120,171	28,269	5,865	15,265	7,139
Share of consumer units	100.0%	23.5%	4.9%	12.7%	5.9%
Share of total annual spending	100.0	28.8	6.1	18.1	4.6
FOOD	100.0	30.1	5.7	19.0	5.4
Food at home	100.0	30.4	6.0	18.8	5.6
Cereals and bakery products	100.0	31.5	5.5	20.2	5.9
Cereals and cereal products	100.0	33.3	5.6	21.5	6.2
Bakery products	100.0	30.7	5.4	19.6	5.8
Meats, poultry, fish, and eggs	100.0	29.3	4.9	18.3	6.1
Beef	100.0	30.1	5.7	19.1	5.3
Pork	100.0	29.3	4.9	17.7	6.7
Other meats	100.0	30.0	4.8	18.7	6.5
Poultry	100.0	29.9	4.7	19.1	6.1
Fish and seafood	100.0	26.7	3.7	16.6	6.4
Eggs	100.0	29.5	5.1	18.6	5.8
Dairy products	100.0	31.8	6.5	19.9	5.5
Fresh milk and cream	100.0	34.1	7.3	21.0	5.9
Other dairy products	100.0	30.2	5.9	19.1	5.2
Fruits and vegetables	100.0	29.0	6.0	18.1	4.9
Fresh fruits	100.0	29.0	6.4	18.2	4.4
Fresh vegetables	100.0	27.9	5.7	18.1	4.1
Processed fruits	100.0	29.8	6.1	17.8	5.8
Processed vegetables	100.0	30.1	5.4	18.3	6.4
Other food at home	100.0	30.8	6.7	18.4	5.7
Sugar and other sweets	100.0	29.9	4.8	19.7	5.5
Fats and oils	100.0	28.0	4.9	17.7	5.4
Miscellaneous foods	100.0	32.6	8.0	18.5	6.1
Nonalcoholic beverages	100.0	28.8	5.4	17.7	5.7
Food prepared by household on trips	100.0	29.6	5.1	21.6	2.9
Food away from home	100.0	29.7	5.3	19.2	5.2
ALCOHOLIC BEVERAGES	100.0	19.5	5.5	11.3	2.8
HOUSING	100.0	30.1	7.0	18.0	5.0
Shelter	100.0	29.9	6.7	18.2	5.0
Owned dwellings	100.0	33.2	7.8	21.9	3.5
Mortgage interest and charges	100.0	38.3	9.5	24.9	3.9
Property taxes	100.0	28.4	5.8	19.5	3.1
Maintenance, repairs, insurance, other expenses	100.0	22.9	5.0	15.6	2.3
Rented dwellings	100.0	23.5	4.9	8.7	9.9
Other lodging	100.0	22.4	3.0	17.2	2.2

	total consumer units	consumer units with children under age 18		
		total	married couples, oldest child under age 6	married couples, oldest child aged 6 to 17	single parents with children under age 18
Utilities, fuels, and public services	**100.0%**	**27.5%**	**5.4%**	**16.7%**	**5.5%**
Natural gas	100.0	26.6	5.3	16.7	4.6
Electricity	100.0	27.9	5.4	16.8	5.8
Fuel oil and other fuels	100.0	24.4	5.5	15.8	3.1
Telephone services	100.0	27.8	5.3	16.5	6.0
Water and other public services	100.0	27.9	5.6	17.1	5.2
Household services	**100.0**	**44.6**	**17.0**	**21.2**	**6.4**
Personal services	100.0	69.7	33.1	27.1	9.5
Other household services	100.0	26.4	5.3	16.9	4.1
Housekeeping supplies	**100.0**	**25.6**	**5.7**	**15.2**	**4.6**
Laundry and cleaning supplies	100.0	30.6	5.4	17.9	7.4
Other household products	100.0	24.2	6.3	13.9	4.1
Postage and stationery	100.0	24.2	4.7	16.0	3.5
Household furnishings and equipment	**100.0**	**29.6**	**6.9**	**19.2**	**3.5**
Household textiles	100.0	29.5	8.7	17.3	3.4
Furniture	100.0	33.7	7.2	21.7	4.8
Floor coverings	100.0	36.9	9.2	24.3	3.4
Major appliances	100.0	26.6	6.3	16.4	3.9
Small appliances, misc. housewares	100.0	25.7	6.8	15.2	3.6
Miscellaneous household equipment	100.0	28.3	6.5	19.0	2.8
APPAREL AND SERVICES	**100.0**	**31.5**	**6.2**	**18.7**	**6.6**
Men and boys	**100.0**	**29.6**	**5.3**	**19.4**	**4.9**
Men, aged 16 or older	100.0	21.1	4.8	13.7	2.5
Boys, aged 2 to 15	100.0	65.0	7.1	42.9	15.0
Women and girls	**100.0**	**32.1**	**4.5**	**19.8**	**7.7**
Women, aged 16 or older	100.0	25.5	4.1	14.9	6.4
Girls, aged 2 to 15	100.0	66.2	6.6	45.1	14.6
Children under age 2	**100.0**	**52.7**	**28.6**	**16.5**	**7.5**
Footwear	**100.0**	**33.9**	**5.7**	**20.4**	**7.9**
Other apparel products and services	**100.0**	**22.8**	**5.5**	**13.3**	**4.0**
TRANSPORTATION	**100.0**	**28.8**	**6.1**	**18.4**	**4.3**
Vehicle purchases	**100.0**	**30.0**	**6.8**	**19.2**	**3.9**
Cars and trucks, new	100.0	26.3	6.0	17.9	2.4
Cars and trucks, used	100.0	33.7	8.0	20.1	5.7
Other vehicles	100.0	28.0	1.3	26.4	0.3
Gasoline and motor oil	**100.0**	**28.5**	**5.6**	**18.5**	**4.4**
Other vehicle expenses	**100.0**	**28.3**	**5.9**	**17.7**	**4.8**
Vehicle finance charges	100.0	31.8	7.6	19.9	4.2
Maintenance and repairs	100.0	26.3	5.0	17.2	4.1
Vehicle insurance	100.0	27.4	4.9	16.5	5.9
Vehicle rental, leases, licenses, other charges	100.0	31.4	8.2	19.6	3.7
Public transportation	**100.0**	**25.2**	**4.7**	**16.5**	**4.0**

	total consumer units	consumer units with children under age 18		
		total	married couples, oldest child under age 6	married couples, oldest child aged 6 to 17	single parents with children under age 18
HEALTH CARE	100.0%	22.1%	4.8%	14.6%	2.7%
Health insurance	100.0	21.5	4.7	14.3	2.5
Medical services	100.0	26.7	6.3	17.1	3.2
Drugs	100.0	17.4	3.4	11.5	2.5
Medical supplies	100.0	23.0	3.6	16.5	2.9
ENTERTAINMENT	100.0	30.7	5.6	20.6	4.5
Fees and admissions	100.0	36.2	5.2	26.8	4.2
Audio and visual equipment and services	100.0	28.5	5.5	18.0	5.0
Pets, toys, hobbies, playground equipment	100.0	28.7	6.1	17.4	5.2
Other entertainment supplies, services	100.0	30.0	5.7	21.0	3.3
PERSONAL CARE PRODUCTS AND SERVICES	100.0	26.9	5.3	16.4	5.3
READING	100.0	22.8	4.3	15.4	3.1
EDUCATION	100.0	28.0	2.2	21.0	4.8
TOBACCO PRODUCTS AND SMOKING SUPPLIES	100.0	21.2	3.9	12.6	4.7
MISCELLANEOUS	100.0	23.9	4.5	13.9	5.5
CASH CONTRIBUTIONS	100.0	20.0	3.8	13.9	2.4
PERSONAL INSURANCE AND PENSIONS	100.0	30.6	7.0	20.0	3.6
Life and other personal insurance	100.0	28.3	4.8	20.7	2.8
Pensions and Social Security	100.0	30.7	7.1	20.0	3.6
PERSONAL TAXES	100.0	22.5	5.8	15.5	1.2
Federal income taxes	100.0	20.8	5.6	14.7	0.5
State and local income taxes	100.0	27.0	7.0	17.8	2.3
Other taxes	100.0	25.6	4.8	17.1	3.7
GIFTS FOR PEOPLE IN OTHER HOUSEHOLDS	100.0	17.7	2.5	11.7	3.4

Note: Market shares are calculated by first multiplying average spending by the total number of households. Using those aggregate figures, the total spending of each segment is then divided by the total for all households to determine each segment's share of the total. The Bureau of Labor Statistics uses consumer unit rather than household as the sampling unit in the Consumer Expenditure Survey. For the definition of consumer unit, see the glossary.
Source: Bureau of Labor Statistics, 2007 Consumer Expenditure Survey, Internet site http://www.bls.gov/cex/; calculations by New Strategist

Time Use

■ Most, but not all, of today's young children have working mothers. Among those mothers, there are substantial differences in time use depending on their employment status.

■ Employed mothers spend less time caring for children than mothers who are not employed, in part because they are more likely to have older children who require less care.

■ Among dual-income couples with children, mothers have less leisure time than fathers—2.92 hours per day for mothers and 3.73 hours per day for fathers.

Among Mothers, Time Use Varies Sharply by Employment Status

For fathers, time use varies depending on the employment status of their wives.

Most, but not all, of today's young children have working mothers. Among those mothers, there are substantial differences in time use depending on their employment status. Mothers who are employed full-time spend less time sleeping, doing housework, and shopping than mothers who do not work. Employed mothers also spend less time caring for children than mothers who are not employed, in part because they are more likely to have older children who require less care.

Among couples, fathers with wives who work full-time spend more time in household activities each day (1.39 hours) than fathers whose wives are not employed (1.05 hours). But they spend less time caring for household children —0.79 hours per day for fathers with employed wives versus 0.83 hours per day for fathers whose wives are not employed. Behind this difference is the fact that fathers with wives who do not work are more likely to have younger children at home who require more care.

■ Among dual-income couples with children, mothers have less leisure time than fathers.

Working mothers have less leisure time

(average number of hours per day of leisure time for married couples with children under age 18 in which both spouses work full-time, by sex, 2003–06)

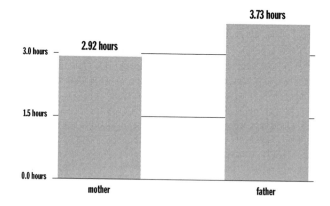

Table 20.1 Time Use of Married Mothers with Children under Age 18 by Employment Status, 2003–06

(average hours per day married mothers with own children under age 18 spend in primary activities, percent participating in primary activities, and index of not employed mothers to mothers employed full-time, by employment status, 2003–06)

	average hours			percent participating		
	employed full-time	not employed	index, not employed to employed full-time	employed full-time	not employed	index, not employed to employed full-time
Married mothers with children under age 18						
TOTAL, ALL ACTIVITIES	**24.00**	**24.00**	**100**	**100.0%**	**100.0%**	**100**
Personal care activities	**9.00**	**9.42**	**105**	**100.0**	**100.0**	**100**
Sleeping	8.18	8.77	107	99.9	100.0	100
Household activities	**2.05**	**3.64**	**178**	**88.6**	**95.8**	**108**
Housework	0.89	1.69	190	55.5	77.4	139
Food preparation and cleanup	0.78	1.44	185	73.9	88.6	120
Lawn and garden care	0.10	0.14	140	6.4	9.8	153
Purchasing goods and services	**0.60**	**0.82**	**137**	**53.1**	**57.5**	**108**
Grocery shopping	0.14	0.23	164	19.1	26.3	138
Consumer goods purchases, except grocery shopping	0.37	0.47	127	38.9	39.4	101
Caring for and helping household members	**1.22**	**2.48**	**203**	**72.1**	**86.0**	**119**
Caring for and helping household children	1.19	2.45	206	70.7	85.0	120
Physical care	0.52	1.07	206	50.6	72.3	143
Education-related activities	0.10	0.23	230	11.0	20.0	182
Reading to/with children	0.04	0.09	225	9.0	15.3	170
Playing/doing hobbies with children	0.19	0.52	274	14.1	27.9	198
Working and work-related activities	**5.18**	**0.10**	**2**	**69.1**	**3.3**	**5**
Working	5.14	0.02	0	68.7	0.8	1
Leisure and sports	**2.93**	**4.19**	**143**	**93.1**	**96.4**	**104**
Socializing and communicating	0.66	0.92	139	41.1	48.5	118
Watching television	1.46	2.22	152	71.4	80.0	112
Participating in sports, exercise, and recreation	0.16	0.23	144	13.3	16.2	122
Travel	**1.39**	**1.17**	**84**	**94.5**	**85.0**	**90**
Travel related to caring for and helping household children	0.23	0.28	122	39.6	41.9	106
Other activities	**1.63**	**2.19**	**134**	**97.6**	**98.2**	**101**

Note: Primary activities are those respondents identified as their main activity. Other activities done simultaneously are not included. The index is calculated by dividing time use or participation rate of mothers who are not employed by time use or participation rate of mothers who are employed and multiplying by 100.
Source: Bureau of Labor Statistics, Married Parents' Use of Time, 2003–06 American Time Use Survey, Internet site http://www .bls.gov/news.release/atus2.toc.htm; calculations by New Strategist

Table 20.2 Time Use of Married Mothers with Children Aged 6 to 17 by Employment Status, 2003–06

(average hours per day married mothers with youngest own child aged 6 to 17 spend in primary activities, percent participating in primary activities, and index of not employed mothers to mothers employed full-time, by employment status, 2003–06)

	average hours			percent participating		
Married mothers with youngest child aged 6 to 17	employed full-time	not employed	index, not employed to employed full-time	employed full-time	not employed	index, not employed to employed full-time
TOTAL, ALL ACTIVITIES	**24.00**	**24.00**	**100**	**100.0%**	**100.0%**	**100**
Personal care activities	**8.96**	**9.33**	**104**	**100.0**	**100.0**	**100**
Sleeping	8.09	8.61	106	99.9	100.0	100
Household activities	**2.13**	**3.96**	**186**	**88.9**	**96.2**	**108**
Housework	0.92	1.80	196	57.3	76.6	134
Food preparation and cleanup	0.78	1.47	188	73.1	88.8	121
Lawn and garden care	0.12	0.17	142	7.4	12.5	169
Purchasing goods and services	**0.60**	**0.90**	**150**	**53.3**	**61.8**	**116**
Grocery shopping	0.13	0.27	208	19.2	31.7	165
Consumer goods purchases, except grocery shopping	0.37	0.50	135	39.3	41.0	104
Caring for and helping household members	**0.74**	**1.39**	**188**	**61.3**	**75.5**	**123**
Caring for and helping household children	0.71	1.34	189	59.1	73.3	124
Physical care	0.20	0.38	190	31.8	49.1	154
Education-related activities	0.12	0.32	267	12.8	25.7	201
Reading to/with children	0.02	0.04	200	3.1	6.7	216
Playing/doing hobbies with children	0.04	0.08	200	3.4	6.0	176
Working and work-related activities	**5.39**	**0.15**	**3**	**71.3**	**4.5**	**6**
Working	5.35	0.03	1	70.8	0.9	1
Leisure and sports	**3.08**	**4.64**	**151**	**93.6**	**97.1**	**104**
Socializing and communicating	0.65	0.96	148	41.5	49.4	119
Watching television	1.51	2.39	158	72.1	81.6	113
Participating in sports, exercise, and recreation	0.17	0.29	171	13.8	18.7	136
Travel	**1.39**	**1.32**	**95**	**94.9**	**87.2**	**92**
Travel related to caring for and helping household children	0.20	0.33	165	36.1	44.0	122
Other activities	**1.71**	**2.32**	**136**	**97.8**	**97.5**	**100**

Note: Primary activities are those respondents identified as their main activity. Other activities done simultaneously are not included. The index is calculated by dividing time use or participation rate of mothers who are not employed by time use or participation rate of mothers who are employed and multiplying by 100.
Source: Bureau of Labor Statistics, Married Parents' Use of Time, 2003–06 American Time Use Survey, Internet site http://www.bls.gov/news.release/atus2.toc.htm; calculations by New Strategist

Table 20.3 Time Use of Married Mothers with Children under Age 6 by Employment Status, 2003–06

(average hours per day married mothers with own children under age 6 spend in primary activities, percent participating in primary activities, and index of not employed mothers to mothers employed full-time, by employment status, 2003–06)

	average hours			percent participating		
	employed full-time	not employed	index, not employed to employed full-time	employed full-time	not employed	index, not employed to employed full-time
Married mothers with youngest child under age 6						
TOTAL, ALL ACTIVITIES	24.00	24.00	100	100.0%	100.0%	100
Personal care activities	9.06	9.48	105	100.0	100.0	100
Sleeping	8.31	8.89	107	100.0	100.0	100
Household activities	1.92	3.42	178	88.1	95.5	108
Housework	0.84	1.61	192	52.5	78.0	149
Food preparation and cleanup	0.77	1.41	183	75.3	88.5	118
Lawn and garden care	0.08	0.11	138	4.7	7.9	168
Purchasing goods and services	0.61	0.76	125	52.7	54.6	104
Grocery shopping	0.15	0.20	133	18.9	22.5	119
Consumer goods purchases, except grocery shopping	0.36	0.45	125	38.2	38.2	100
Caring for and helping household members	1.99	3.24	163	89.4	93.2	104
Caring for and helping household children	1.97	3.21	163	89.1	93.1	104
Physical care	1.04	1.54	148	80.5	88.2	110
Education-related activities	0.07	0.17	243	8.2	16.1	196
Reading to/with children	0.08	0.12	150	18.4	21.3	116
Playing/doing hobbies with children	0.42	0.82	195	31.1	43.0	138
Working and work-related activities	4.84	0.07	1	65.6	2.5	4
Working	4.81	0.02	0	65.3	0.7	1
Leisure and sports	2.70	3.89	144	92.3	96.0	104
Socializing and communicating	0.66	0.89	135	40.4	47.8	118
Watching television	1.38	2.10	152	70.2	78.9	112
Participating in sports, exercise, and recreation	0.14	0.18	129	12.5	14.4	115
Travel	1.39	1.06	76	93.9	83.5	89
Travel related to caring for and helping household children	0.28	0.25	89	45.4	40.5	89
Other activities	1.50	2.09	139	97.3	98.7	101

Note: Primary activities are those respondents identified as their main activity. Other activities done simultaneously are not included. The index is calculated by dividing time use or participation rate of mothers who are not employed by time use or participation rate of mothers who are employed and multiplying by 100.
Source: Bureau of Labor Statistics, Married Parents' Use of Time, 2003–06 American Time Use Survey, Internet site http://www .bls.gov/news.release/atus2.toc.htm; calculations by New Strategist

Table 20.4 Time Use of Dual- and Single-Earner Married Couples with Children under Age 18, 2003–06

(average hours per day married couples with children under age 18 spend in primary activities by employment status, and index of mother's time to father's, 2003–06)

	both spouses work full-time		index of mother's time to father's	mother not employed, father employed full-time		index of mother's time to father's
	mother	father		mother	father	
TOTAL, ALL ACTIVITIES	**24.00**	**24.00**	**100**	**24.00**	**24.00**	**100**
Personal care activities	**8.97**	**8.63**	**104**	**9.38**	**8.72**	**108**
Sleeping	8.15	8.04	101	8.73	8.10	108
Household activities	**2.08**	**1.39**	**150**	**3.69**	**1.05**	**351**
Housework	0.91	0.28	325	1.71	0.16	1,069
Food preparation and cleanup	0.79	0.32	247	1.45	0.22	659
Lawn and garden care	0.10	0.25	40	0.14	0.21	67
Purchasing goods and services	**0.62**	**0.39**	**159**	**0.81**	**0.40**	**203**
Grocery shopping	0.14	0.07	200	0.24	0.08	300
Consumer goods purchases, except grocery shopping	0.38	0.25	152	0.46	0.26	177
Caring for and helping household members	**1.23**	**0.81**	**152**	**2.57**	**0.86**	**299**
Caring for and helping household children	1.20	0.79	152	2.54	0.83	306
Physical care	0.52	0.25	208	1.10	0.26	423
Education-related activities	0.10	0.07	143	0.25	0.06	417
Reading to/with children	0.04	0.02	200	0.09	0.03	300
Playing/doing hobbies with children	0.19	0.23	83	0.54	0.30	180
Working and work-related activities	**5.14**	**5.98**	**86**	**0.11**	**6.26**	**2**
Working	5.12	5.94	86	0.03	6.23	0
Leisure and sports	**2.92**	**3.73**	**78**	**4.09**	**3.60**	**114**
Socializing and communicating	0.65	0.61	107	0.90	0.68	132
Watching television	1.44	2.05	70	2.15	1.90	113
Participating in sports, exercise, and recreation	0.16	0.29	55	0.24	0.30	80
Travel	**1.41**	**1.47**	**96**	**1.17**	**1.46**	**80**
Travel related to caring for and helping household children	0.24	0.14	171	0.29	0.09	322
Other activities	**1.63**	**1.61**	**101**	**2.17**	**1.66**	**131**

Note: Primary activities are those respondents identified as their main activity. Other activities done simultaneously are not included. The index is calculated by dividing mother's time by father's time and multiplying by 100.
Source: Bureau of Labor Statistics, Married Parents' Use of Time, 2003–06 American Time Use Survey, Internet site http://www .bls.gov/news.release/atus2.toc.htm; calculations by New Strategist

Glossary

adjusted for inflation Income or a change in income that has been adjusted for the rise in the cost of living, or the consumer price index (CPI-U-RS).

age Classification by age is based on the age of the person at his/her last birthday.

American Housing Survey The AHS collects national and metropolitan-level data on the nation's housing, including apartments, single-family homes, and mobile homes. The nationally representative survey, with a sample of 55,000 homes, is conducted by the Census Bureau for the Department of Housing and Urban Development every other year.

American Indians In this book, American Indians include Alaska Natives (Eskimos and Aleuts) unless those groups are shown separately.

American Time Use Survey Under contract with the Bureau of Labor Statistics, the Census Bureau collects ATUS information, which reveals how people spend their time. The ATUS sample is drawn from U.S. households that have completed their final month of interviews for the Current Population Survey. One individual from each selected household is chosen to participate in the ATUS. Respondents are interviewed by telephone only once about their time use on the previous day.

Asian Includes Native Hawaiians and other Pacific Islanders unless those groups are shown separately.

Baby Boom Americans born between 1946 and 1964.

Baby Bust Americans born between 1965 and 1976, also known as Generation X.

Behavioral Risk Factor Surveillance System A collaborative project of the Centers for Disease Control and Prevention and U.S. states and territories. It is an ongoing data collection program designed to measure behavioral risk factors in the adult population aged 18 or older. All 50 states, three territories, and the District of Columbia take part in the survey, making the BRFSS the primary source of information on the health-related behaviors of Americans.

black A racial category that includes those who identified themselves as "black" or "African American."

central cities The largest city in a metropolitan area. The balance of the metropolitan area outside the central city is regarded as the "suburbs."

Consumer Expenditure Survey An ongoing study of the day-to-day spending of American households administered by the Bureau of Labor Statistics. The CEX includes an interview survey and a diary survey. The average spending figures shown in this book are the integrated data from both the diary and interview components of the survey. Two separate, nationally representative samples are used for the interview and diary surveys. For the interview survey, about 7,500 consumer units are interviewed on a rotating panel basis each quarter for five consecutive quarters. For the diary survey, 7,500 consumer units keep weekly diaries of spending for two consecutive weeks.

consumer unit *(on spending tables only)* For convenience, the term consumer unit and households are used interchangeably in the spending section of this book, although consumer units are somewhat different from the Census Bureau's households. Consumer units are all related members of a household, or financially independent members of a household. A household may include more than one consumer unit.

Current Population Survey A nationally representative survey of the civilian noninstitutional population aged 15 or older. It is taken monthly by the Census Bureau for the Bureau of Labor Statistics, collecting information from more than 50,000 households on employment and unemployment. In March of each year, the survey includes the Annual Social and Economic Supplement (formerly called the Annual Demographic Survey), which is the source of most national data on the characteristics of Americans, such as educational attainment, living arrangements, and incomes.

disability As defined by the National Health Interview Survey, respondents aged 18 or older are asked whether they have difficulty in physical functioning, probing whether respondents can perform nine activities by themselves without using special equipment. The categories are walking a quarter mile; standing for two hours; sitting for two hours; walking up 10 steps without resting; stooping, bending, kneeling; reaching over one's head; grasping or handling small objects; carrying a 10-pound object; and pushing/pulling a large object. Adults who report that any of these activities is very difficult or they cannot do it at all are defined as having physical difficulties.

dual-earner couple A married couple in which both the householder and the householder's spouse are in the labor force.

earnings The amount of money a person receives from his or her job. *See also* Income.

employed All civilians who did any work as a paid employee or farmer/self-employed worker, or who worked 15 hours or more as an unpaid farm worker or in a family-owned business, during the reference period. All those who have jobs but who are temporarily absent from their jobs due to illness, bad weather, vacation, labor management dispute, or personal reasons are considered employed.

expenditure The transaction cost including excise and sales taxes of goods and services acquired during the survey period. The full cost of each purchase is recorded even though full payment may not have been made at the date of purchase. Average expenditure figures may be artificially low for infrequently purchased items such as cars because figures are calculated using all consumer units within a demographic segment rather than just purchasers. Expenditure estimates include money spent on gifts for others.

family A group of two or more people (one of whom is the householder) related by birth, marriage, or adoption and living in the same household.

family household A household maintained by a householder who lives with one or more people related to him or her by blood, marriage, or adoption.

female/male householder A woman or man who maintains a household without a spouse present. May head family or nonfamily households.

foreign-born population People who are not U.S. citizens at birth.

full-time employment Thirty-five or more hours of work per week during a majority of the weeks worked.

full-time, year-round Fifty or more weeks of full-time employment during the previous calendar year.

Generation X Americans born between 1965 and 1976, also known as the baby-bust generation.

Hispanic Because Hispanic is an ethnic origin rather than a race, Hispanics may be of any race. While most Hispanics are white, there are black, Asian, and American Indian Hispanics.

household All the persons who occupy a housing unit. A household includes the related family members and all the unrelated persons, if any, such as lodgers, foster children, wards, or employees who share the housing unit. A person living alone is counted as a household. A group of unrelated people who share a housing unit as roommates or unmarried partners is also counted as a household. Households do not include group quarters such as college dormitories, prisons, or nursing homes.

household, race/ethnicity of Households are categorized according to the race or ethnicity of the householder only.

householder The person (or one of the persons) in whose name the housing unit is owned or rented or, if there is no such person, any adult member. With married couples, the householder may be either the husband or wife. The householder is the reference person for the household.

householder, age of The age of the householder is used to categorize households into age groups such as those used in this book. Married couples, for example, are classified according to the age of either the husband or wife, depending on which one identified him or herself as the householder.

housing unit A house, an apartment, a group of rooms, or a single room occupied or intended for occupancy as separate living quarters. Separate living quarters are those in which the occupants do not live and eat with any other persons in the structure and that have direct access from the outside of the building or through a common hall that is used or intended for use by the occupants of another unit or by the general public. The occupants may be a single family, one person living alone, two or more families living together, or any other group of related or unrelated persons who share living arrangements.

Housing Vacancy Survey A supplement to the Current Population Survey, which provides quarterly and annual data on rental and homeowner vacancy rates, characteristics of units available for occupancy, and homeownership rates by age, household type, region, state, and metropolitan area. The Current Population Survey sample includes 51,000 occupied housing units and 9,000 vacant units.

housing value The respondent's estimate of how much his or her house and lot would sell for if it were for sale.

iGeneration Americans born from 1995 to the present.

immigration The relatively permanent movement (change of residence) of people into the country of reference.

income Money received in the preceding calendar year by each person aged 15 or older from each of the following sources: (1) earnings from longest job (or self-employment), (2) earnings from jobs other than longest job, (3) unemployment compensation, (4) workers' compensation, (5) Social Security, (6) Supplemental Security income, (7) public assistance, (8) veterans' payments, (9) survivor benefits, (10) disability benefits, (11) retirement pensions, (12) interest, (13) dividends, (14) rents and royalties or estates and trusts, (15) educational assistance, (16) alimony, (17) child support, (18) financial assistance from outside the household, and other periodic income. Income is reported in several ways in this book. Household income is the combined income of all household members. Income of persons is all income accruing to a person from all sources. Earnings are the money a person receives from his or her job.

industry The industry in which a person worked longest in the preceding calendar year.

job tenure The length of time a person has been employed continuously by the same employer.

labor force The labor force tables in this book show the civilian labor force only. The labor force includes both the employed and the unemployed (people who are looking for work). People are counted as in the labor force if they were working or looking for work during the reference week in which the Census Bureau fields the Current Population Survey.

labor force participation rate The percent of the civilian noninstitutional population that is in the civilian labor force, which includes both the employed and the unemployed.

married couples with or without children under age 18 Refers to married couples with or without own children under age 18 living in the same household. Couples without children under age 18 may be parents of grown children who live elsewhere, or they could be childless couples.

median The amount that divides the population or households into two equal portions: one below and one above the median. Medians can be calculated for income, age, and many other characteristics.

median income The amount that divides the income distribution into two equal groups, half having incomes above the median, half having incomes below the median. The medians for households or families are based on all households or families. The median for persons are based on all persons aged 15 or older with income.

Medical Expenditure Panel Survey A nationally representative survey that collects detailed information on the health status, access to care, health care use and expenses and health insurance coverage of the civilian noninstitutionalized population of the U.S. and nursing home residents. MEPS comprises four component surveys: the Household Component, the Medical Provider Component, the Insurance Component, and the Nursing Home Component. The Household Component is the core survey, is conducted each year, and includes 15,000 households and 37,000 people.

metropolitan statistical area A city with 50,000 or more inhabitants, or a Census Bureau-defined urbanized area of at least 50,000 inhabitants and a total metropolitan population of at least 100,000 (75,000 in New England). The county (or counties) that contains the largest city becomes the "central county" (counties), along with any adjacent counties that have at least 50 percent of their population in the urbanized area surrounding the largest city. Additional "outlying counties" are included in the MSA if they meet specified requirements of commuting to the central counties and other selected requirements of metropolitan character (such as population density and percent urban). In New England, MSAs are defined in terms of cities and towns rather than counties. For this reason, the concept of NECMA is used to define metropolitan areas in the New England division.

Millennial generation Americans born between 1977 and 1994.

mobility status People are classified according to their mobility status on the basis of a comparison between their place of residence at the time of the March Current Population Survey and their place of residence in March of the previous year. Nonmovers are people living in the same house at the end of the period as at the beginning of the period. Movers are people living in a different house at the end of the period than at the beginning of the period. Movers from abroad are either citizens or aliens whose place of residence is outside the United States at the beginning of the period, that is, in an outlying area under the jurisdiction of the United States or in a foreign country. The mobility status for children is fully allocated from the mother if she is in the household; otherwise it is allocated from the householder.

National Ambulatory Medical Care Survey An annual survey of visits to nonfederally employed office-based physicians who are primarily engaged in direct patient care. Data are collected from physicians rather than patients, with each physician assigned a one-week reporting period. During that week, a systematic random sample of visit characteristics are recorded by the physician or office staff.

National Health and Nutrition Examination Survey A continuous survey of a representative sample of the U.S. civilian noninstitutionalized population. Respondents are interviewed at home about their health and nutrition, and the interview is followed up by a physical examination that measures such things as height and weight in mobile examination centers.

National Health Interview Survey A continuing nationwide sample survey of the civilian noninstitutional population of the U.S. conducted by the Census

Bureau for the National Center for Health Statistics. Each year, data are collected from more than 100,000 people about their illnesses, injuries, impairments, chronic and acute conditions, activity limitations, and the use of health services.

National Hospital Ambulatory Medical Care Survey The NHAMCS, sponsored by the National Center for Health Statistics, is an annual national probability sample survey of visits to emergency departments and outpatient departments at non-Federal, short stay and general hospitals. Data are collected by hospital staff from patient records.

National Hospital Discharge Survey This survey has been conducted annually since 1965, sponsored by the National Center for Health Statistics, to collect nationally representative information on the characteristics of inpatients discharged from nonfederal, short-stay hospitals in the U.S. The survey collects data from a sample of approximately 270,000 inpatient records acquired from a national sample of about 500 hospitals.

National Household Education Survey The NHES, sponsored by the National Center for Education Statistics, provides descriptive data on the educational activities of the U.S. population, including after-school care and adult education. The NHES is a system of telephone surveys of a representative sample of 45,000 to 60,000 households in the U.S.

National Nursing Home Survey This is a series of national sample surveys of nursing homes, their residents, and staff conducted at various intervals since 1973-74 and sponsored by the National Center for Health Statistics. Data for the survey are obtained through personal interviews with administrators and staff, and occasionally with self-administered questionnaires, in a sample of about 1,500 facilities.

National Survey of Family Growth The 2002 NSFG, sponsored by the National Center for Health Statistics, is a nationally representative survey of the civilian noninstitutional population aged 15 to 44. In-person interviews were completed with 12,571 men and women, collecting data on marriage, divorce, contraception, and infertility. The 2002 survey updates previous NSFG surveys taken in 1973, 1976, 1988, and 1995.

National Survey on Drug Use and Health Formerly called the National Household Survey on Drug Abuse, this survey, sponsored by the Substance Abuse and Mental Health Services Administration, has been conducted since 1971. It is the primary source of information on the use of illegal drugs by the U.S. population. Each year, a nationally representative sample of about 70,000 individuals aged 12 or older are surveyed in the 50 states and the District of Columbia.

net worth The amount of money left over after a household's debts are subtracted from its assets.

nonfamily household A household maintained by a householder who lives alone or who lives with people to whom he or she is not related.

nonfamily householder A householder who lives alone or with nonrelatives.

non-Hispanic People who do not identify themselves as Hispanic are classified as non-Hispanic. Non-Hispanics may be of any race.

non-Hispanic white People who identify their race as white and who do not indicate a Hispanic origin.

nonmetropolitan area Counties that are not classified as metropolitan areas.

occupation Occupational classification is based on the kind of work a person did at his or her job during the previous calendar year. If a person changed jobs during the year, the data refer to the occupation of the job held the longest during that year.

occupied housing units A housing unit is classified as occupied if a person or group of people is living in it or if the occupants are only temporarily absent—on vacation, example. By definition, the count of occupied housing units is the same as the count of households.

outside central city The portion of a metropolitan county or counties that falls outside of the central city or cities; generally regarded as the suburbs.

own children Sons and daughters, including stepchildren and adopted children, of the householder. The totals include never-married children living away from home in college dormitories.

owner occupied A housing unit is "owner occupied" if the owner lives in the unit, even if it is mortgaged or not fully paid for. A cooperative or condominium unit is "owner occupied" only if the owner lives in it. All other occupied units are classified as "renter occupied."

part-time employment Less than 35 hours of work per week in a majority of the weeks worked during the year.

percent change The change (either positive or negative) in a measure that is expressed as a proportion of the starting measure. When median income changes from $20,000 to $25,000, for example, this is a 25 percent increase.

percentage point change The change (either positive or negative) in a value which is already expressed as a percentage. When a labor force participation rate changes from 70 percent of 75 percent, for example, this is a 5 percentage point increase.

poverty level The official income threshold below which families and people are classified as living in poverty. The threshold rises each year with inflation and varies depending on family size and age of householder.

primary activity In the time use tables, those activities that respondents identify as their main activity. Other activities done simultaneously are not included.

proportion or share The value of a part expressed as a percentage of the whole. If there are 4 million people aged 25 and 3 million of them are white, then the white proportion is 75 percent.

race Race is self-reported and can be defined in three ways. The "race alone" population comprises people who identify themselves as only one race. The "race in combination" population comprises people who identify themselves as more than one race, such as white and black. The "race, alone or in combination" population includes both those who identify themselves as one race and those who identify themselves as more than one race.

regions The four major regions and nine census divisions of the United States are the state groupings as shown below:

Northeast:
—New England: Connecticut, Maine, Massachusetts, New Hampshire, Rhode Island, and Vermont
—Middle Atlantic: New Jersey, New York, and Pennsylvania

Midwest:
—East North Central: Illinois, Indiana, Michigan, Ohio, and Wisconsin
—West North Central: Iowa, Kansas, Minnesota, Missouri, Nebraska, North Dakota, and South Dakota

South:
—South Atlantic: Delaware, District of Columbia, Florida, Georgia, Maryland, North Carolina, South Carolina, Virginia, and West Virginia
—East South Central: Alabama, Kentucky, Mississippi, and Tennessee
—West South Central: Arkansas, Louisiana, Oklahoma, and Texas

West:
—Mountain: Arizona, Colorado, Idaho, Montana, Nevada, New Mexico, Utah, and Wyoming
—Pacific: Alaska, California, Hawaii, Oregon, and Washington

renter occupied *See* Owner Occupied.

Retirement Confidence Survey An annual survey, sponsored by the Employee Benefit Research Institute, the American Savings Education Council, and Mathew Greenwald & Associates, of a nationally representative sample of 1,000 people aged 25 or older. Respondents are asked a core set of questions that have been asked since 1996, measuring attitudes and behavior towards retirement.

rounding Percentages are rounded to the nearest tenth of a percent; therefore, the percentages in a distribution do not always add exactly to 100.0 percent. The totals, however, are always shown as 100.0. Moreover, individual figures are rounded to the nearest thousand without being adjusted to group totals, which are independently rounded; percentages are based on the unrounded numbers.

self-employment A person is categorized as self-employed if he or she was self-employed in the job held longest during the reference period. Persons who report self-employment from a second job are excluded, but those who report wage-and-salary income from a second job are included. Unpaid workers in family businesses are excluded. Self-employment statistics include only nonagricultural workers and exclude people who work for themselves in incorporated business.

sex ratio The number of men per 100 women.

suburbs *See* Outside Central City.

Survey of Consumer Finances A triennial survey taken by the Federal Reserve Board. It collects data on the assets, debts, and net worth of American households. For the 2007 survey, the Federal Reserve Board interviewed more than 4,000 households.

unemployed Those who, during the survey period, had no employment but were available and looking for work. Those who were laid off from their jobs and were waiting to be recalled are also classified as unemployed.

white A racial category that includes many Hispanics (who may be of any race) unless the term "non-Hispanic white" is used.

Youth Risk Behavior Surveillance System Created by the Centers for Disease Control to monitor health risks being taken by young people at the national, state, and local level. The national survey is taken every two years based on a nationally representative sample of 16,000 students in 9th through 12th grade in public and private schools.

Bibliography

Agency for Healthcare Research and Quality
    Internet site http://www.ahrq.gov/
    —Medical Expenditure Panel Survey, Internet site http://www.meps.ahrq.gov/mepsweb/ survey_comp/household.jsp

Bureau of Labor Statistics
    Internet site http://www.bls.gov
    —2000 and 2007 Consumer Expenditure Surveys, Internet site http://www.bls.gov/cex/
    —2007 American Time Use Survey, Internet site http://www.bls.gov/tus/home.htm
    —2007 American Time Use Survey, Summary Table 2. Number of persons and average hours per day by detailed activity classification (travel reported separately), 2007 annual averages, unpublished tables received upon special request
    —Characteristics of Minimum Wage Workers, 2008, Internet site http://www.bls.gov/cps/ minwage2008tbls.htm
    —College Enrollment and Work Activity of 2008 High School Graduates, Internet site http://www.bls.gov/news.release/hsgec.toc.htm
    —Contingent and Alternative Employment Arrangements, Internet site http://www.bls .gov/news.release/conemp.toc.htm
    —Economic and Employment Projections, Internet site http://www.bls.gov/news.release/ ecopro.toc.htm
    —Employee Benefits Survey, Internet site http://www.bls.gov/ncs/ebs/benefits/2008/ ownership_civilian.htm
    —Employee Tenure, Internet site http://www.bls.gov/news.release/tenure.toc.htm
    —Employment Characteristics of Families, Internet site http://www.bls.gov/news.release/ famee.toc.htm
    —Labor Force Statistics from the Current Population Survey, Internet site http://www.bls .gov/cps/tables.htm#empstat
    —*Monthly Labor Review*, "Labor Force Projections to 2016: More Workers in Their Golden Years," November 2007, Internet site http://www.bls.gov/opub/mlr/2007/11/contents.htm
    —*Monthly Labor Review*, "Youth enrollment and employment during the school year," February 2008, Internet site http://www.bls.gov/opub/mlr/2008/02/contents.htm
    —Table 15. Employed persons by detailed occupation, sex, and age, Annual Average 2008 (Source: Current Population Survey), unpublished table received upon special request

Bureau of the Census
    Internet site http://www.census.gov
    —2007 American Community Survey, Internet site http://factfinder.census.gov/servlet/ DatasetMainPageServlet?_program=ACS&_submenuId=&_lang=en&_ts=1
    —2008 Current Population Survey Annual Social and Economic Supplement, Internet site http://www.census.gov/hhes/www/income/dinctabs.html

—2008 National Population Projections, Internet site http://www.census.gov/population/www/projections/2008projections.html

—A Child's Day: 2006 (Selected Indicators of Child Well-Being), Detailed Tables, Internet site http://www.census.gov/population/www/socdemo/2006_detailedtables.html

—American Housing Survey for the United States in 2007, Internet site http://www.census.gov/hhes/www/housing/ahs/ahs07/ahs07.html

—America's Families and Living Arrangements, 2008 Current Population Survey Annual Social and Economic Supplement, Internet site http://www.census.gov/population/www/socdemo/hh-fam/cps2008.html

—Educational Attainment, Historical Tables, Internet site http://www.census.gov/population/www/socdemo/educ-attn.html

—Educational Attainment in the United States: 2008, Detailed Tables, Current Population Survey Annual Social and Economic Supplement, Internet site http://www.census.gov/population/www/socdemo/education/cps2008.html

—Families and Living Arrangements, Historical Time Series, Current Population Survey Annual Social and Economic Supplements, Internet site http://www.census.gov/population/www/socdemo/hh-fam.html

—Fertility of American Women, Current Population Survey—June 2006, Detailed Tables, Internet site http://www.census.gov/population/www/socdemo/fertility/cps2006.html

—Geographic Mobility: 2007 to 2008, Detailed Tables, Current Population Survey Annual Social and Economic Supplement, Internet site http://www.census.gov/population/www/socdemo/migrate/cps2008.html

—Geographical Mobility/Migration, Current Population Survey Annual Social and Economic Supplements, Internet site http://www.census.gov/population/www/socdemo/migrate.html

—Health Insurance, Internet site http://pubdb3.census.gov/macro/032008/health/toc.htm

—Historical Health Insurance Tables, Internet site http://www.census.gov/hhes/www/hlthins/historic/index.html

—Historical Income Tables, Current Population Survey Annual Social and Economic Supplements, Internet site http://www.census.gov/hhes/www/income/histinc/histinctb.html

—Housing Vacancy Surveys, Internet site http://www.census.gov/hhes/www/housing/hvs/hvs.html

—National Population Estimates, Internet site http://www.census.gov/popest/national/asrh/NC-EST2008-sa.html

—Number, Timing, and Duration of Marriages and Divorces: 2004, Detailed Tables, Internet site http://www.census.gov/population/www/socdemo/marr-div/2004detailed_tables.html

—School Enrollment, Historical Tables, Internet site http://www.census.gov/population/www/socdemo/school.html

—School Enrollment—Social and Economic Characteristics of Students: October 2007, detailed tables, Internet site http://www.census.gov/population/www/socdemo/school/cps2007.html

—State Population Estimates, Internet site http://www.census.gov/popest/states/asrh/

Centers for Disease Control and Prevention

Internet site http://www.cdc.gov

—Behavioral Risk Factor Surveillance System, Prevalence Data, Internet site http://apps
.nccd.cdc.gov/brfss/

—Cases of HIV/AIDS and AIDS, Internet site http://www.cdc.gov/hiv/topics/surveillance/
resources/reports/2006report/table3.htm

—"Youth Risk Behavior Surveillance–United States, 2007," *Mortality and Morbidity Weekly
Report*, Vol. 57/SS-4, June 6, 2008; Internet site http://www.cdc.gov/HealthyYouth/yrbs/
index.htm

Department of Homeland Security

Internet site http://www.dhs.gov/index.shtm

—Immigration, 2008 Yearbook of Immigration Statistics, Internet site http://www.uscis
.gov/graphics/shared/statistics/yearbook/index.htm

Employee Benefit Research Institute

Internet site http://www.ebri.org/

—Retirement Confidence Surveys, Internet site http://www.ebri.org/surveys/rcs/

—"Employment-Based Retirement Plan Participation: Geographic Differences and Trends,
2007," *Issue Brief* 322, October 2008, Internet site http://www.ebri.org/publications/ib/
index.cfm?fa=ibDisp&content_id=3989

—"Ownership of Individual Accounts (IRAs) and 401(k)-Type Plans," by Craig Copeland,
Notes, Vol. 29, No. 5, May 2008; Internet site http://www.ebri.org/publications/notes/index
.cfm?fa=main&doc_type=2

Federal Interagency Forum on Child and Family Statistics

Internet site http://childstats.gov

—America's Children in Brief: Key National Indicators of Well-Being, 2008, Internet site
http://childstats.gov/americaschildren/tables.asp

Federal Reserve Board

Internet site http://www.federalreserve.gov/pubs/oss/oss2/scfindex.html

—"Changes in U.S. Family Finance from 2004 to 2007: Evidence from the Survey of Consumer Finances," *Federal Reserve Bulletin*, February 2009, Internet site http://www
.federalreserve.gov/pubs/oss/oss2/2007/scf2007home.html

National Center for Education Statistics

Internet site http://nces.ed.gov

—The Condition of Education, Internet site http://nces.ed.gov/programs/coe/

—Digest of Education Statistics: 2008, Internet site http://nces.ed.gov/programs/digest/

— National Household Education Surveys Program, Parent and Family Involvement in Education, 2006–07 School Year, Internet site http://nces.ed.gov/pubsearch/pubsinfo
.asp?pubid=2008050

National Center for Health Statistics

Internet site http://www.cdc.gov/nchs

—*2006 National Hospital Discharge Survey,* National Health Statistics Report, No. 5, 2008, Internet site http://www.cdc.gov/nchs/about/major/hdasd/listpubs.htm

—*Ambulatory Medical Care Utilization Estimates for 2006*, National Health Statistics Reports, No. 8, 2008, Internet site http://www.cdc.gov/nchs/about/major/ahcd/adata .htm#CombinedReports

—*Anthropometric Reference Data for Children and Adults: United States, 2003–2006*, National Health Statistics Reports, Number 10, 2008, Internet site http://www.cdc.gov/nchs/ products/pubs/pubd/nhsr/nhsr.htm

—*Births: Final Data for 2006*, National Vital Statistics Reports, Vol. 57, No. 7, 2009, Internet site http://www.cdc.gov/nchs/products/nvsr.htm#57_12

—*Births: Preliminary Data for 2007*, National Vital Statistics Reports, Vol. 57, No. 12, 2009, Internet site http://www.cdc.gov/nchs/products/nvsr.htm#57_12

—*Complementary and Alternative Medicine Use Among Adults and Children: United States, 2007*, National Health Statistics Report, No. 12, 2008, Internet site http://nccam.nih.gov/ news/camstats/2007/index.htm

—*Deaths: Final Data for 2006*, National Vital Statistics Reports, Vol. 57, No. 14, 2009, Internet site http://www.cdc.gov/nchs/products/nvsr.htm#vol57

—*Fertility, Contraception, and Fatherhood: Data on Men and Women from Cycle 6 of the 2002 National Survey of Family Growth*, Vital and Health Statistics, Series 23, No. 26, 2006; Internet site http://www.cdc.gov/nchs/nsfg.htm

—*Fertility, Family Planning, and Reproductive Health of U.S. Women: Data from the 2002 National Survey of Family Growth*, Vital and Health Statistics, Series 23, No. 25, 2005; Internet site http://www.cdc.gov/nchs/nsfg.htm

—*Health Characteristics of Adults 55 Years of Age and Over: United States, 2000-2003, Advance Data, No. 370,* 2006, Internet site http://www.cdc.gov/nchs/nhis.htm

—*National Ambulatory Medical Care Survey: 2006 Summary,* National Health Statistics Report, No. 3, 2008, Internet site http://www.cdc.gov/nchs/about/major/ahcd/adata.htm

—National Center for Chronic Disease Prevention and Health Promotion, Prevalence Data, Internet site http://apps.nccd.cdc.gov/HRQOL/

—*National Hospital Ambulatory Medical Care Survey: 2006 Emergency Department Summary,* National Health Statistics Report, No. 4, 2007, Internet site http://www.cdc.gov/nchs/ about/major/ahcd/adata.htm

—*National Hospital Ambulatory Medical Care Survey: 2006 Outpatient Department Summary,* National Health Statistics Report, No. 4, 2008, Internet site http://www.cdc.gov/nchs/ about/major/ahcd/adata.htm

—*Health United States 2008,* Internet site http://www.cdc.gov/nchs/hus.htm

—*Sexual Behavior and Selected Health Measures: Men and Women 15-44 Years of Age, United States, 2002*, Advance Data, No. 362, 2005; Internet site http://www.cdc.gov/nchs/ nsfg.htm

—*Summary Health Statistics for U.S. Adults: National Health Interview Survey, 2007*, Series 10, No. 240, 2008, Internet site http://www.cdc.gov/nchs/nhis.htm

—*Summary Health Statistics for U.S. Children: National Health Interview Survey, 2007*, Series 10, No. 239, 2008, Internet site http://www.cdc.gov/nchs/nhis.htm

—*Summary Health Statistics for the U.S. Population: National Health Interview Survey, 2007*, Series 10, No. 238, 2008, Internet site http://www.cdc.gov/nchs/nhis.htm

National Sporting Goods Association

Internet site http://www.nsga.org

—Sports Participation, Internet site http://www.nsga.org

Substance Abuse and Mental Health Services Administration

Internet site http://www.samhsa.gov

—National Survey on Drug Use and Health, 2007, Internet site http://www.oas.samhsa.gov/nsduh.htm

Survey Documentation and Analysis, Computer-assisted Survey Methods Program, University of California, Berkeley

Internet site http://sda.berkeley.edu/

—General Social Surveys, 1972-2008 Cumulative Data Files, Internet site http://sda.berkeley.edu/cgi-bin32/hsda?harcsda+gss08

Index